THE CHURCH AND THE JEWS

The Biblical Relationship

Why use A word Church vs Christianity?
Why ignore all New Testament
writings?

by

Dan Gruber

The Church and the Jews: The Biblical Relationship

Copyright © 1991, 1997, 2001 by Dan Gruber

Elijah Publishing
P.O. Box 776
Hanover, NH 03755

ISBN 0-9669253-3-5

Contents

ILLUSTRATIONS

INTRODUCTION

When it comes to the relationship of Jew and Gentile, the major thrust of all traditional church theology is separation. (It is also the thrust of all traditional rabbinic theology.) God's major thrust, on the other hand, is reconciliation—to take two and form them into one new creation. As in the marriage of a man and a woman, so in the biblical joining of Jew and Gentile, God's purpose is neither subjugation nor the annihilation of the individual, but rather mutual strengthening, service, and fruitfulness.

Theology that sets "the Church" in opposition to "the Jews" is "anti-Judaic" theology. Anti-Judaic theology arose as a response to the "chosenness" of the Jewish people.

There was an anti-Judaic tendency that began very early. Paul addresses it in his letter to the Romans. We will examine his comments in detail later.

The Council of Nicea, in 325 A.D., was a distinct turning point in the history of the church. **Since that time, all accepted church theology has been built upon an anti-Judaic foundation.** The theological changes embraced at Nicea made it impossible for the church to be faithful to its God-given mission.

These institutional changes were fundamental and monumental. They were sevenfold:

1. The rejection of the literal meaning of Scripture in its context.

2. The subjugation of Scripture to the authority of a Church hierarchy.

3. The determination that Church doctrine and practice would be in opposition to the Jews.

4. The establishment of compulsory conformity in practice.

5. The acceptance of the State and the sword as the means of maintaining purity in the Church. (The cross was transformed from a means of victory over sin for the individual to a means of victory over sinners for the society.)

6. The acceptance of the sword of the State—instead of the Sword of the Spirit, the blood of the Lamb and the blood of the believers—as the means of triumph in the world.

7. The acceptance of State support of the Church in exchange for Church support of the State. (The Church surrendered its own prophetic message toward the State.)

These are not insignificant alterations. They are major adulterations. The Church became the Church of Constantine. In this book, we will not fully discuss each of these changes and its consequences, but we will examine the historical evidence and the pivotal theological shift that made all the rest possible and justifiable. We will examine these in the light of the actual Biblical teaching.

The theological shift that took place was basically this: The Church became identified as the "new Israel," replacing the Jews. As the "new Israel," the Church itself was equated with the kingdom of God, since it was the kingdom of Israel that God had promised to restore. Because God had entrusted the sword to the kingdom/nation of Israel, the "new Israel" also picked up the sword.

Though we do not have available all the documents of the Church in the first four centuries of its existence, we have enough to be able to follow the general development of the type of theology which triumphed at Nicea. We have enough to understand the basic issue which resulted in these changes.

Uncovering this anti-Judaic foundation will do two things. First, it will make it easier to discern and understand what has been built upon it and why. Second, it will make it evident why contemporary theologies differ from the Biblical teaching in the ways that they do.

Documenting the historical and contemporary theological errors of most of the Church is obviously a controversial endeavor. The Church, however, was birthed in the midst of controversy. It grew in the midst of controversy. The controversy itself was not an evil. It was necessary for the establishment of correct doctrine.

In the first century, the most heated, controversial, doctrinal issue of all that the Church faced was: "How do the Gentiles fit into all this?" It was a very important issue. Identity, purpose, and destiny depended upon it. It nearly split the early Church. We are nearly two thousand years removed from that time, that culture, and the life of the early Church. So it is very difficult for us to fully appreciate the reasons for the controversy and its intensity, but it is very important that we do so.

Today, the most heated, controversial, doctrinal issue that the Church faces is: "How do the Jews fit into all this?" The Biblical answer is crucial to a proper understanding of the entire Bible. Almost all the rest of our theology and manner of Biblical interpretation flows from our understanding of the relationship of the Church and the Jews. And our behavior is to follow our faith. Our behavior shows our faith.

Through whatever understanding of this relationship we have, we view the past, present, and future of the world, as well as the nature of the age to come. It affects our personal relationship with God, our prayers, our evangelism, our worship, our view of modern Israel, the nations, and the Church. It determines our socio-political perspective and involvement.

The Church as a whole cannot understand its own identity, fulfill its own calling, or reach its own destiny without properly understanding this relationship. It must understand this relationship in accordance with the teaching of the Bible rather than according to the teaching of tradition.

The Bible does not condemn tradition. Nor does it to teach us to reject the wisdom of past ages. It does, however, make it clear that God is not pleased with the traditions and teachings of men that are contrary to His Word.

The Lord told Isaiah, "Because this people draw near with their mouth and honor Me with their lips, but they remove their hearts far from Me, and their fear of Me is tradition learned by rote, therefore behold, I will once again deal marvelously with this people, wondrously marvelous; and the wisdom of their wise men shall perish, and the discernment of their discerning men shall be concealed." (Is.29:13-14)

Jesus quoted the prophecy of Isaiah, saying, " '...in vain do they worship Me, teaching as their doctrines the precepts of men.' Neglecting the commandment of God, you hold to the tradition of men." He was also saying to them, "You nicely set aside the commandment of God in order to keep your tradition...thus invalidating the word of God by your tradition which you have handed down..." (Mk.7:7-9,13)

The natural condition of man, even religious man, has not changed since the days of Isaiah or since the first century. The Word of God remains eternally true. What was done in the synagogue has also been done in the Church.

The Word of God is the standard by which all things, and all people, will be judged. Paul told Timothy, "Be diligent to present yourself approved to God as a workman who does not need to be ashamed, handling accurately the word of truth." (2Tim.2:15)

It is the Biblical text itself that deserves diligent study and accurate handling. When the text itself is studied, it becomes readily apparent that some traditional teachings do not come from the text. They are simply the traditions of men, standing in opposition to God and His purposes.

Tradition has value, but there are historical reasons why tradition strays from Biblical truth. For those who accept the Bible at face value, believing it to be the Word of God, what it teaches is the core of our existence. It is our life, not simply material for proving our points, supporting our prejudices, or confirming our traditions. We want to know what it teaches, because that is what determines how we choose to live our lives.

It is necessary at the outset of this examination to reject certain accepted, but incorrect, usages. They communicate something which is not true, and lead to incorrect doctrine. The Biblical usage must be adopted instead.

1) The terms "Old Testament" and "New Testament" are traditionally used to refer to the two major parts of the Bible. The "Old Testament" is taken to be that part of the Bible which was written before the life of Jesus on the earth. The "New Testament" is taken to be what was written afterwards.

This usage of these terms is very old and well-established. From the historical evidence that we have, it seems that "Irenaeus was the first to apply the term N.T. [New Testament] to sacred scriptures and that after his times the description of them as the "New Testament" '...came into vogue." [1] It seems that Melito of Sardis is to be credited "for the first use of the term Old Covenant or Old Testament to refer to the Bible..." [2] Irenaeus and Melito wrote between 160-190 A.D., eighteen hundred years ago, but more than a century removed from the gospel events.

Though the traditional use of these terms is very old, it is still very incorrect. "Old Testament" and "New Testament" actually refer to the two major covenants which the Lord made with Israel—the "old" covenant of the Law and the "new" covenant in the blood of Jesus. The proper Biblical terms are "Old Covenant" and "New Covenant." These covenants are particular agreements, not designations for the two major parts of the Bible.

When Paul, for example, speaks of the Old Covenant as having faded away (2Co.3), he is speaking of the Covenant of the Law, not of the Scriptures themselves. The Scriptures, and the Law of God which they contain, are eternal. It is only the covenant that has faded away.

The traditional labeling leads to the erroneous belief that the "Old Testament" was for the Jews, and the "New Testament" is for the Church. The traditional labeling leads to the erroneous belief that the "New Testament" is to be interpreted differently than the "Old Testament."

The traditional labeling also leads to the erroneous belief that "the God of the Old Testament" is a God of wrath, and "the God of the New Testament" is a God of mercy. This error is compounded by ignoring both God's love for Israel and God's promises of judgment in the Church, and of wrath and judgment in the world. These are fundamental errors.

God is One. He and His purpose are unchanging. He presents the gospel as the fulfillment of what He planned and promised from the beginning. The plan, the promise, and the fulfillment are inseparable.

Jesus referred to "the Law of Moses [Torah תורה] and the Prophets [Nevi'im נביאים] and the Psalms [Ketuvim כתובים]." (Lk.24:44) The acronym for these parts of the Bible is TaNaKh [תנך]. In our discussion, the term "Tanakh" will be used. Inasmuch as there is no current acronym for the Gospels [Ευαγγελιον], Acts [ΠραΞεις], Epistles [Επιστολες], and Revelation [Αποκαλυψις], the term "New Covenant Scriptures" will be used to encompass them.

2) The meaning of the Hebrew word "goyim" [גוים] is somewhat obscured by its alternate translations as "heathen," "nations," and "Gentiles." This is also true of the equivalent Greek term "ethne" [εθνη] and its variations.

Today, "heathen" means something like "unchurched, primitive pagans." "Nations" now carries the governmental sense of the nation-state, a modern phenomenon. "Gentiles" means those who are not Jewish.

In combination, these different connotations come close to portraying what "goyim" actually means. But there are goyim in the world today who do not have their own state or government. This statist sense is not essential to the meaning of the original words. There are other goyim who are neither unchurched, primitive, nor pagan.

English translations of the Bible and of early Church writings tend to use "heathen(s)" or "nations" for "goyim." This is unfortunate, because it makes it very difficult for readers to understand the nature and intensity of the conflict in the early Church (cf. Acts 15) over the manner in which goyim, i.e. Gentiles, could be saved. It makes it difficult to appreciate what a radically new thing God was doing. It makes it difficult to appreciate both the nature of the Great Commission and the full measure of God's grace.

Some who deal with the Church in different cultures use "people-groups" to more accurately convey the Biblical meaning of "goyim" and "ethne." This is much better, but it still does not convey the radical difference between Israel and the goyim.

Though God promises to make Israel a holy nation [גוי קדוש, cf. Ex.19:6], He makes it clear that Israel is a unique people, not to be "reckoned among the goyim [ובגוים לא יתחשב, Num.23:9]." For our purposes, "Gentile(s)" or "goyim" will be primarily used to denote the Hebrew [גוים] or Greek [εθνη] and their variations.

3) Another error worth avoiding from the outset concerns the names of different individuals and books of the Bible. Most English translations incorrectly substitute "James" for "Jacob" in referring to the brother of John and to the brother of Jesus. The Greek Ιακωβου clearly indicates that they were named "Jacob" [יעקב]. Likewise, the English translations have incorrectly substituted Jude for Judah [Ιουδας יהודה], another brother of Jesus.

In this discussion, they and the letters they wrote will be properly designated by the names "Jacob" and "Judah." In the same way, "Mary" will be correctly referred to as "Miriam" [Μαριαμ מרים]. That was her name.

The difference is not simply one of language, but one of proper identification. It is important to properly understand who these people actually were. They were not Greeks, they were Hebrews. Making them something they were not only leads to other incorrect assumptions and teachings. Recognizing them for who they were makes it easier to understand what the Bible actually does teach.

People naturally see the world around them—other people, cultures, times, and even God Himself—in terms of their own sense of identity and understanding. This is natural enough, but it produces a distorted view of reality. In order to form a proper theology, we must begin differently.

The Bible begins, "In the beginning, God..." That is where we also must begin in order to properly understand the world that God has created. He is the only one who was there in the beginning. It is His desires and purposes which will prevail in the end.

The starting point for examining the Biblical relationship of the Church and the Jews needs to be God Himself. Traditional Church theology begins with the Church. That is why most of the Church, throughout most of its history, has improperly understood the Biblical relationship between the Church and the Jews. God did not begin with the Church.

"There are assumptions peculiar to a time in history which are accepted as true and require no proof. To question them appears almost blasphemous. It is easy to proclaim those ideas at those times, however absurd they may seem to those who live at other times and under a different spirit. Such is the power of prejudice and of the spirit of the age. Tradition indeed makes the word of God of no effect." [3]

The first part of this book traces the history of where, when, and how the Church went wrong. It also establishes how serious the errors and their consequences are.

Then we will start at the proper beginning. The second part of the book presents the relationship of the Church and the Jews as given in the Bible.

The third part presents the views of this relationship as given in traditional and contemporary Church theologies. It examines and clarifies their fundamental errors.

The book is written to the Church, but is also important for anyone interested in the historical or contemporary Jewish-Christian dialogue, or in an understanding of the Middle East that goes beyond one-dimensional geo-politics. Some will not like it, but the question here is not what men like or dislike, but rather what the Bible actually teaches.

Throughout the book, comments in [brackets] are occasionally added to quotations for explanatory reasons. All **bold** emphasis is added.

FOOTNOTES

1. W.C. van Unnik, "Η καινη διαθηκη—A Problem in the Early History of the Canon," *Studia Patristica*, Vol.IV, Berlin, 1961, P.214, citing J.N.D. Kelly, *Early Christian Doctrines*, London, 1958, P.56
2. *Melito of Sardis, On Pascha and Fragments,* edited by Stuart George Hall, Oxford Clarendon Press, 1979, P.xxx
3. Bob Mears, Personal correspondence, 6/15/91

PART ONE:

THE HISTORICAL DEVELOPMENT OF ANTI-JUDAIC THEOLOGY

EUSEBIUS' *ECCLESIASTICAL HISTORY*

The *Ecclesiastical History* of Eusebius Pamphilus is the acknowledged history of the Church from the end of the Book of Acts to the Council of Nicea. "A unique work, it remains the most important single source for the history of the Church in those centuries." [1] Unfortunately, it is a source that is recognized to contain some serious "untruths."

Eusebius' *Ecclesiastical History* was written during the reign of the Emperor Constantine. Constantine is known as the first Christian emperor.

The Church had endured centuries of persecution. Constantine decreed an end to it, although it briefly reappeared later, and began to exalt the Church. It was he who convened the Council of Nicea.

With this dramatic political shift came an equally dramatic theological shift. Eusebius himself played an important role in bringing about that theological shift. "Eusebius' outlook was conditioned by the new political settlement between the Empire and the Church as well as by his theological upbringing and allegiance to certain views which he inherited from Origen.

"In his political philosophy, clearly articulated in *Vita Constantini* [Life of Constantine] and in *Oratio de Laudibus Constantini* [Oration in Praise of Constantine], the Emperor was the image of God and the representative of the Almighty. The Emperor acted as the interpreter of the Logos. He imitated the philanthropy of the Son of God. In the gathering of all the bishops with the Emperor Constantine on the day of his tricennalia [30th anniversary of his reign], Eusebius saw the image of the Messianic banquet.

"For Eusebius, there was no longer a precise and definite distinction between the Church and the Empire. They appeared to merge into each other. The structure of the Emperor's earthly government, declares Eusebius, is according to the pattern of the divine original." [2]

What is the divine original that the Emperor and his empire were to reflect? The pivotal issue theologically was the nature of the fulfilled kingdom of God. If the kingdom was to be fulfilled through a personal earthly reign of Jesus the Messiah from Jerusalem, then the Jews were inescapably part of that kingdom, which would follow the repentance of Israel. In that case, God's faithfulness to the Jews had not expired. The kingdom was still future.

On the other hand, if Constantine, the emerging Holy Roman Empire, and the State-exalted Church were the kingdom, then there was no need for the Jews. The fulness of the kingdom was in the present.

Moreover, if the Jews had no special significance for the fulfilled kingdom of God, then God had no need or plan for them. In that case, the rejection and replacement of the Jews was the means of fulfilling the kingdom. Instead of being natural citizens of the kingdom, whether loyal or disloyal, the Jews became the enemies of the kingdom. If that were the case, then the Church needed to recognize and proclaim it.

Eusebius firmly believed, in the fourth century, that the Church was the "new Israel," replacing the Jews. He firmly believed that there was no distinct future for the Jews in the plan of God. [3] Whenever he discusses the issue of a physical millennium, he treats it as an heretical view. ("Millennium" comes from the Latin *mille annum*, a thousand years.) Following Origen, Eusebius rejected the normal meaning of the Scriptures that promise restoration to the Jewish people. Or he ignored these Scriptures altogether. (We will examine this in greater detail later.)

The belief in the restoration of the Jewish people and the establishment in Israel of a millennial kingdom was not an heretical view, as we shall see. It had been the prevailing view. In fact, it had been the established orthodoxy. In the first and second centuries, it was the view that Eusebius chose to champion that the early Church had considered to be heresy.

In writing any book, an author chooses what to include and what to leave out. In writing history, a faithful historian will make those choices so as to present an accurate picture of the past. Eusebius was intentionally inaccurate. He had his own agenda.

"No source might [be] used that contradicted or conflicted with the apostolic tradition as Eusebius conceived it." [4] Eusebius ignored the sources that showed the apostolic tradition to be different from what he thought it should be. He was intent on creating an apostolic tradition that was different from what the apostles had actually believed and taught.

"...Eusebius was the product of the Alexandrine school of theology [that of Origen]. To him orthodox tradition was primarily just the tradition preserved at Alexandria, in its entirety and without any contradictions." [5]

"The point of these examples, only two of many, is that they show Eusebius as advocate; it was not his intention, in writing about Constantine or about the Church in general, to provide an impartial account." [6] "As scholarship became more critical, however, historians began to look at the VC [*De Vita Constantini*, Eusebius' *Life of Constantine*] more and more warily, until ultimately the great nineteenth-century rationalist Jakob Burckhardt angrily dismissed its author as '**the first thoroughly dishonest historian of antiquity**,' 'the most disgusting of all eulogists.' " [7]

But Eusebius had a reason for what he did. The image that Eusebius wanted to present, the Church that he wanted to help create, was more important to him than the historical reality. Before he wrote his *Ecclesiastical History*, he had already completed a six volume defense of Origen. He wanted to convince the Church that Origen was correct. Eusebius maintained that purpose in his *Ecclesiastical History*.

FOOTNOTES

1. H.A. Drake, *In Praise of Constantine, A Historical Study and New Translation of Eusebius' Tricennial Orations*, Univ. of California Press, Berkeley, 1976, P.7
2. V. Kesich, "Empire-Church Relations and the Third Temptation," *Studia Patristica*, Vol. IV, Berlin, 1961, Pp.468-469
3. *The Ecclesiastical History of Eusebius Pamphilus*, translated by Christian Frederick Cruse, Baker Book House, Grand Rapids, MI, 1989, E.g. Bk. of Martyrs, Ch.11, P.369
4. B. Gustafson, "Eusebius' Principles in handling his Sources, as found in his Church History, Books I-VII," *Studia Patristica*, op.cit., P.437
5. ibid., P.441
6. H.A. Drake, *In Praise of Constantine, A Historical Study and New Translation of Eusebius' Tricennial Orations*, op. cit., P.10
7. ibid., P.8

ORIGEN'S SYSTEM OF INTERPRETATION

Origen's work is dated around the beginning of the third century. There were others before Origen who interpreted the Scriptures in an allegorical way, but Origen is credited with being the father of the allegorical method of interpretation. The reason for that is that Origen, in a comprehensive system, made allegory the only way to truly understand the Scriptures.

In Origen's system of interpretation, he often denied the ordinary sense of the text, and replaced it with allegories which he made up. These allegories then became the real meaning of the text. There was no way to challenge the allegories on the basis of the text, since what the text actually said was no longer what it meant.

In this allegorical system, when the text said, "Israel," it meant "the Church" and not the Jews, so long as the promise or comment was good. If the promise or comment was not good, then "Israel" still meant "the Jews," and not "the Church."

Philip Schaff, the noted 19th century church historian said that, "Origen was the greatest scholar of his age, and the most gifted, most industrious, and most cultivated of all the ante-Nicene fathers. Even heathens and heretics admired or feared his brilliant talent and vast learning. His knowledge embraced all departments of the philology, philosophy, and theology of his day. With this he united profound and fertile thought, keen penetration, and glowing imagination." [1]

Though he was very sympathetic towards Origen, Schaff noted that, "he can by no means be called orthodox, either in the Catholic or in the Protestant sense. His leaning to idealism, his predilection for Plato, and his noble effort to reconcile Christianity with reason, and to commend it even to educated heathens and Gnostics, led him into many grand and fascinating errors. Among these are his extremely ascetic and almost docetistic conception of corporeity, his denial of a material resurrection, his doctrine of the pre-existence of the pre-temporal fall of souls (including the pre-existence of the human soul of Christ); of eternal creation, of the extension of the work of redemption to the inhabitants of the stars and to all rational creatures, and of the final restoration of all men and fallen angels...." [2]

Yet, in Schaff's opinion, "Origen's greatest service was in exegesis. He is father of the critical investigation of Scripture, and his commentaries are still useful to scholars for their suggestiveness....His great defect is the neglect of the grammatical and historical sense and his constant desire to find a hidden mystic meaning. He even goes further in this direction than the Gnostics, who everywhere saw transcendental, unfathomable mysteries. His hermeneutical principle assumes a threefold sense — somatic, psychic, and pneumatic; or literal, moral, and spiritual. His allegorical interpretation is ingenious, but often runs far away from the text and degenerates into the merest caprice; while at times it gives way to the opposite extreme of a carnal literalism, by which he justifies his ascetic extravagance." [3]

His system of interpretation produced great errors. For some of the doctrines which he believed and taught, Origen was considered by many to be an heretic. During his lifetime, he was excommunicated by two church councils held in Alexandria in 231 and 232 A.D. After his death as well, his views were officially condemned by some in the Church as heretical. Today there is no question that some of his teachings would be considered heretical enough to place him outside the believing Church.

Nevertheless, "Most of the Greek fathers of the third and fourth centuries stood more or less under the influence of the spirit and the works of Origen, without adopting all his peculiar speculative views. The most distinguished among his disciples are Gregory Thaumaturgus, Dionysius of Alexandria, surnamed the Great, Heraclas, Hieracas, Pamphilus; in a wider sense also Eusebius, Gregory of Nyssa and other eminent divines of the Nicene age." [4]

Though these men of the third- and fourth-century Church did not accept all the teachings which Origen's system of interpretation generated, they did accept the system itself. With only the sparse historical information that we have available, we are still able to trace the transmission of that system. It is Origen's system of interpretation that produces the anti-Judaic "New Israel" theology where the Church replaces the Jews in the plan and purpose of God.

"...[I]n his youthful zeal for ascetic holiness, he [Origen] even committed the act of self-emasculation, partly to fulfil literally the mysterious words of Christ, in Matt. 19:12, for the sake of the kingdom of God, partly to secure himself against all temptation and calumny which might arise from his intercourse with many female catechumens. By this inconsiderate and misdirected heroism, which he himself repented in his riper years, he incapacitated himself, according to the canons of the church, for the clerical office. Nevertheless, a long time afterwards, in 228, he was ordained presbyter by two friendly bishops, Alexander of Jerusalem, and Theoctistus of Caesarea in Palestine, who had, even before this, on a former visit of his, invited him while a layman, to teach publicly in their churches, and to expound the Scriptures to their people." [5]

Origen and his writings were well received in the Roman province of "Palestine," especially in Caesarea. Though it was a violation of the existing canons of the Church, Origen was ordained a presbyter there. The churches there did not accept his ex-communication.

This attitude of the churches in the Roman province of "Palestine" is understandable in an historical sense. Almost all the Jews in Judea and Samaria had either died in the Bar Kokhba Rebellion of 132-135 A.D., or had been carried off into slavery by the victorious Romans. Before the gospel was preached to Gentiles, there were Jewish churches "throughout all Judea and Galilee and Samaria." (Acts 9:31)

From the end of the Bar Kokhba Rebellion on, all Jews were forbidden to even enter the precincts of Jerusalem. The city itself had been destroyed and renamed Aelia, in honor of the divine nature of Aelia Hadrianus, i.e. the Emperor Hadrian (who destroyed Jerusalem) as the Roman god Jupiter. Up until that time, the bishops of Jerusalem had all been Jewish. If there were bishops in Caesarea before that time, they also would have almost certainly been Jewish.

The Roman Empire had destroyed or removed the Jewish bishops and churches. They were replaced by Gentile ones. The Gentile bishops and churches naturally began to think of themselves as having replaced the Jews.

In his *Dialogue with Trypho the Jew,* Justin, who was from Samaria, had expressed the belief that the destruction of Jerusalem and all the suffering that attended the unsuccessful Bar Kokhba Rebellion was a judgment of God for the failure to believe in Jesus. A large theological step was then taken from that view to the teaching that God had cast off the Jews, and had replaced them with the Gentile Church. There are obvious natural reasons why such a teaching would appeal to the Gentile bishops and churches in "Palestine."

Origen's system of interpretation provided a way for overcoming the scriptural obstacles to such teaching. Origen taught that some scriptures are to be understood only allegorically, some are to be understood only literally, and some are to be understood both allegorically and literally. While that appears on the surface to be an acceptable approach to the Scriptures, there are several serious problems that it causes. One example from Origen's work will make them evident.

The children of Israel were in the wilderness shortly after God had redeemed them out of Egypt. The Bible says that, "Then Amalek came and fought against Israel at Rephidim. And Joshua did as Moses told him, and fought against Amalek; and Moses, Aaron, and Hur went up to the top of the hill. So it came about when Moses held his hand up, that Israel prevailed, and when he let his hand down, Amalek prevailed. But Moses' hands were heavy. Then they took a stone and put it under him, and he sat on it; and Aaron and Hur supported his hands, one on one side and one on the other. Thus his hands were steady until the sun set. So Joshua overwhelmed Amalek and his people with the edge of the sword." (Ex.17:9-13)

It is obvious that there is no natural, causal relationship between the height of the hands of Moses and the military success of Israel. So it is logical to conclude that the supernatural intervention of God on behalf of Israel is meant to teach a lesson. The text invites the reader to find and learn that lesson which goes beyond the primary meaning of the text.

The Talmud says, "[It is written] and it came to pass, when Moses held up his hand that Israel prevailed, etc. Now did the hands of Moses wage war or crush the enemy? Not so; only the text signifies that so long as Israel turns their thoughts above and subjected their hearts to their Father in heaven they prevailed, but otherwise they fell. The same lesson may be taught thus. [It is written], Make thee a fiery serpent and set it up on a pole, and it shall come to pass that everyone that is bitten, when he seeth it, shall live. Now did the serpent kill or did the serpent keep alive? No; [what it indicates is that] when Israel turned their thoughts above and subjected their hearts to their Father in heaven, they were healed, but otherwise they pined away." [6] Different first- and second-century rabbis gave slightly different non-literal interpretations to this same text, referring the raised arms of Moses to Israel's doing the will of God and keeping the Law.

There is much evidence that Origen was familiar with the rabbinic writings, and even these particular interpretations. Eusebius says, "so great was the research which Origen applied in the investigation of the holy Scriptures, that he also studied the Hebrew language; and those original works written in the Hebrew and in the hands of the Jews, he procured as his own. He also investigated the editions [translations/Targums] of others, who, besides the seventy [the Septuagint], had published translations of the Scriptures, and some different from the well-known translations of Aquila, Symmachus and Theodotion..." [7]

"A clear illustration of the way in which Origen seizes on a Jewish interpretation of a biblical passage and adapts it to suit the new dispensation is his handling of Moses' upraised arms during the battle with Amalek....The usual Christian interpretation of Moses' arms is to see in them a symbol of the Cross. Origen is attracted by the Jewish interpretation, but he cannot resist twisting it slightly so as to read as a condemnation of the Synagogue....

Origen comments, " 'If our actions are elevated and do not rest on the ground, Amalek is defeated...Thus if the people keeps the law, it raises up Moses' arms and the adversary is defeated; if it does not keep the law; Amalek is strengthened....I think that by this figure Moses also represents the two peoples, showing that one is the people of the Gentiles, which raises Moses' arms and extends them, that is to say elevates what Moses wrote and establishes its understanding on a high level and thereby conquers, while the other is the people which, because it does not raise Moses' arms or lift them off the ground, and does not consider that there is anything deep or subtle in him, is conquered by its enemies and laid low.'

"It is no exaggeration to say that, for Origen, the whole of the debate between the Church and the Synagogue can be reduced to the one question of the interpretation of scripture....The difference between Judaism and Christianity is that Christians perceive the mysteries which are only hinted at in the Bible, whereas Jews are only capable of a strictly literal reading of the text. (It may be thought remarkable that Origen, of all people, who was well acquainted with Jewish exegesis in all its aspects, should have perpetuated this myth of 'Jewish literalism', but perpetuate it he certainly does.)" [8]

The Bible itself makes it clear that it contains signs and symbols, types and foreshadows, metaphors and parables, visions, dreams, and mysteries, as well as spiritual lessons that transcend the description of a particular incident. Paul speaks of some of the events that happened to Israel in the Exodus and after it. He tells New Covenant believers, "Now these things happened to them as an example, and they were written for our instruction, upon whom the ends of the ages have come." (1Co.10:11)

He reminds Timothy that "All Scripture is inspired by God [lit. 'God-breathed'] and profitable for teaching, for reproof, for correction, for training in righteousness; that the man of God may be adequate, equipped for every good work." (2Tim.3:16-17) In order for what happened to someone else to have meaning for us, there must be a transcendent lesson. The lesson, however, can only be learned from understanding what actually happened, not by ignoring or altering the reality to fit what we already have chosen to believe.

Unfortunately, Origen chose to ignore or alter reality to make it fit with his beliefs. In his theological battle against those in the Church who held to the plain meaning of the text, Origen decided to portray them as disgraceful "Jews" who were rejecting the Lord.

Though Origen knew that God had given the New Covenant Scriptures to the world through Jewish men, he wrote that it is "the people of the Gentiles, which raises Moses' arms and extends them, that is to say elevates what Moses wrote and establishes its understanding on a high level..." He was referring to the New Covenant Scriptures as that elevation of the writings of Moses, but the reality that it was all written or dictated by Jews did not fit with the point that he wanted to make. So he distorted the reality.

Anyone who did not accept his allegorical system of interpretation was nothing more than "a Jew," and really did not belong in the Church. Origen maintained, "If anyone wishes to hear and understand these words literally he ought to gather with the Jews rather than with the Christians. But if he wishes to be a Christian and a disciple of Paul, let him hear Paul saying that 'the Law is spiritual' [and] declaring that these words are 'allegorical' when the Law speaks of Abraham and his wife and sons." [9]

The rabbis did not hold to a strictly literal method of understanding Scripture, far from it. Origen knew that. But the reality did not support his beliefs, so he distorted the reality rather than change his beliefs.

This is a major problem with allegorical and mystical interpretation. How can anyone test the truth of a particular allegorical or mystical interpretation? What makes it true?

Is there any way to delineate what is acceptable and what is not? Whose allegorical or mystical interpretation is right or authoritative? Does it even matter if the facts are actually quite different than the interpreter claims?

The Scriptures present themselves as the standard of Truth by which all else, including interpretation, is to be judged. Yet the very manner of an allegorical and mystical system of interpretation, by denying the plain sense and meaning of the text, makes that standard useless. The "real" meaning of the Scriptures is no longer in what they actually say. "For Origen, the standard itself became invisible to all but 'the perfect man' (*ho teleios*, perhaps 'the initiate') [who] can attain to an understanding of the spiritual law." [10]

How does one know which scriptures are to be understood which way? If, for example, the basic prophecies concerning the first coming of the Messiah were literally fulfilled, then why should we expect the prophecies concerning His second coming to have only mystical fulfillment? The literal fulfillment of prophecy is of tremendous significance to the gospel. Without the literal fulfillment of prophecy, there is no gospel.

Even the genealogies in Matthew and Luke are essential to the gospel. To the allegorist, what could be more "carnal" than a literal understanding of Jewish genealogies? But those genealogies establish the legal right of Jesus to the throne of David. His physical descent from David was essential to God's plan of redemption for the world.

Origen's teachings arise from, and demand, an anti-Judaic outlook. He disinherited the Jews and set the Church in their place. Those scriptures that promised judgment on Israel (or the Jews, or Jacob, etc.) were still to be understood in their literal sense. But those scriptures that promised blessing on Israel (or the Jews, or Jacob, etc.) were henceforth only to be understood as referring to the Church.

That made the churches in "Palestine" the sole geographical heirs of the gospel, worthy of special reverence. Origen was invited to teach there, despite the dissension which his teachings aroused elsewhere. He was made a presbyter there, despite the canons of the Church. His teachings were carefully recorded and kept there.

From there, his teachings spread to other parts of the Church. "Gregory, surnamed Thaumaturgus, 'the wonder-worker,' was converted from heathenism in his youth by Origen at Caesarea, in Palestine, spent eight years in his society, and then, after a season of contemplative retreat, labored as bishop of Neo-Caesarea in Pontus from 244 to 270 with extraordinary success."[11]

"Pamphilus, a great admirer of Origen, a presbyter and theological teacher at Caesarea in Palestine, and a martyr of the persecution of Maximinus (309), was not an author himself, but one of the most liberal and efficient promoters of Christian learning. He did invaluable service to future generations by founding a theological school and collecting a large library, from which his pupil and friend Eusebius (hence called 'Eusebius Pampili'), Jerome, and many others, drew or increased their useful information. Without that library the church history of Eusebius would be far less instructive than it is now. Pamphilus transcribed with his own hand useful books, among others the Septuagint from the Hexapla of Origen. He aided poor students and distributed the Scriptures. While in prison, he wrote a defense of Origen, which was completed by Eusebius in six books, but only the first remains in the Latin version of Rufinus, whom Jerome charges with wilful alterations. It is addressed to the confessors who were condemned to the mines of Palestine, to assure them of the orthodoxy of Origen from his own writings, especially on the trinity and the person of Christ." [12]

The views of Origen had been declared to be heretical, but, led by Pamphilus, the churches in "Palestine" established a theological school and library dedicated to establishing Origen's views as the true orthodoxy throughout the entire Church. Pamphilus taught Eusebius, and Eusebius wholeheartedly gave himself to the task of defending the views of Origen.

Eusebius did that explicitly in the six volume defense of Origen which he completed, but he also did it in his *Ecclesiastical History*. Origen's heresy was to triumph in the fourth century at the Council of Nicea through Eusebius, Constantine, and those who followed them.

"The letters from the emperor cited in the *Vita Constantini*, one of which must date even before Nicea, show both the closeness of the relationship that had grown up between the two men and also Constantine's acceptance of the role which Eusebius had cast for him." [13] Before we take a look at that Council and its decisions, we need to first examine the pivotal theological issue — the nature of the fulfilled Kingdom of God.

FOOTNOTES

1. Philip Schaff, *History of the Christian Church, Vol.II, Ante-Nicene Christianity, A.D. 100-325*, Charles Scribner's Sons, NY, 1883, P.790
2. ibid., P.791
3. P.792
4. P.797
5. P.788
6. Maurice Simon, translator, "Rosh Hashanah III.5," in *The Babylonian Talmud*, ed. Isadore Epstein, The Soncino Press, London, 1938, Pp.133-134
7. *The Ecclesiastical History of Eusebius Pamphilus*, Bk.6, Ch.16, Pp.235-236
8. N.R.M. De Lange, *Origen and the Jews*, Cambridge Univ. Press, Cambridge, 1976, P.82, n.59
9. Ronald E. Heine, translator, *Origen, Homilies on Genesis and Exodus*, in *The Fathers of the Church*, Vol.71, Catholic University Press, Washington, D.C., 1982, Homily VI, Pp.121-122
10. De Lange, op. cit., P.83, n.65
11. Schaff, op. cit., P.797
12. ibid., P.807
13. W.H.C. Frend, "Church and State: Perspective and Problems in the Patristic Era," *Studia Patristica, Vol.XVII, Part One*, Pergamon Press, Oxford, 1982, P.40

EUSEBIUS' *HISTORY* AND THE MILLENNIUM

Eusebius was the friend of Constantine, and he wrote, in part, to affirm the new Church-State relationship that Constantine had established. That new Church-State relationship was antagonistic to the expected kingdom of God that had been proclaimed by the apostles. In the new relationship, the Church would establish the kingdom of God through the State. Once this new relationship was accepted, it became necessary to change the expectation of what the kingdom of God would be.

"The overwhelming usage of 'kingdom' in the second-century Christian literature is eschatological," [1] that is, the second-century Christians expected the establishment of the kingdom of God to come with the return of Jesus at the end of the age. They understood that there was a sense and a reality in which the kingdom of God was already present, but its fulfillment would only come with the destruction of the kingdoms of this world.

"With Origen in the early third century there arose a thinker who was able to incorporate the 'Gnostic' dimension of the kingdom, the inward rule of God in the soul, into orthodox thought...Origen thus marks the turning point." [2] In this Gnostic view, the fulness of the kingdom of God was to come with the individual believer's spiritual growth, and with the spiritual growth of the Church as a whole. The return of Jesus to judge the nations and to redeem Israel became unnecessary for the establishment of the kingdom throughout the earth.

With the introduction of Origen's allegorical method of interpretation in the third century, the faith of the Church concerning the kingdom began to change. As the anti-Judaic posture spread in the Church, what was once considered heresy was put forward as the new orthodoxy. The Millennial restoration of Israel began to be considered a carnal, Jewish doctrine which no orthodox Christian could believe.

On different issues in his *Ecclesiastical History*, Eusebius often quotes from earlier writers in the Church who embraced views similar to his own. That is natural and acceptable for any writer who seeks to support and establish his own views. On the issue of a literal, Millennial restoration of the kingdom to Israel — THE theological issue on which the new Church-State relationship would stand or fall — Eusebius does not quote from any in the early Church who embraced his own view. He does not because he cannot. There were none who supported his view.

Eusebius shows that he had early Church writings on this issue. But these writings expressed a faith in a literal, Millennial restoration of the kingdom to Israel. Since Eusebius rejected that view, and because he wanted to brand it as heresy, he chose not to quote from any of the early Church writers at all.

So it is understandable that those who accept the writings of Eusebius as an accurate representation of the theology of the early Church tend to believe as he did. Unfortunately, Eusebius is not faithful in this regard.

Eusebius happens to reveal, albeit quite reluctantly, that the "new Israel" view which he embraced was not held by the apostles or by those who were instructed by them. One such student of the apostles was Papias who was taught by the Apostle John, by Philip the evangelist (Acts 21:8), and by others. He was an associate of Polycarp. In one section, Eusebius says, "At this time, also, Papias was well known as bishop of the church at Hierapolis, a man well skilled in all manner of learning, and well acquainted with the Scriptures." [3] Throughout the *Ecclesiastical History*, with one exception, and in the writings of all others who spoke of him, Papias is characterized as a very godly man of exceptional learning, faithful to the teachings of the apostles.

The one exception occurs when Eusebius mentions that "he [Papias] says there would be a certain millennium after the resurrection, and that there would be a corporeal reign of Christ on this very earth; which things he appears to have imagined, as if they were authorized by the apostolic narrations, not understanding correctly those matters which they propounded mystically in their representations. For he was very limited in his comprehension, as is evident from his discourses; yet he was the cause why most of the ecclesiastical writers, urging the antiquity of the man, were carried away by a similar opinion; as, for instance, Irenaeus, or any other that adopted such sentiments." [4]

Several things should be noted about Eusebius' comments. **First**, Papias presented the teaching of "a certain millennium after the resurrection, and that there would be a corporeal reign of Christ on this very earth...as if they were authorized by the apostolic narrations..." That is to say that Papias affirmed that the apostles taught that this was so.

Papias spent many years learning from John and others of the earliest leaders of the Church. Eusebius gives no support for his assertion that Papias, who was universally acknowledged and praised as faithful to the apostolic teaching, "imagined" such substantial departures from the teaching of the apostles.

Second, although Eusebius elsewhere praises Papias for his virtue and learning, here he demeans him as deceived and dull. The only "evidence" that Eusebius has for this derogatory characterization is that Papias believed in a millennial reign of Messiah on the earth. In contradiction to his praises elsewhere, Eusebius demeans Papias here because he wants to undermine such belief.

There is ample evidence in support of the great spiritual understanding of Papias. Among other faithful endeavors which he performed, Papias is credited with having written the Gospel of John at the dictation of the Apostle. The Gospel of John is certainly not an un-spiritual document.

Third, Eusebius admits that "most of the ecclesiastical writers, urging the antiquity of the man, were carried away by a similar opinion." Therefore, according to Eusebius, most of the ecclesiastical writers believed "that there would be a corporeal reign of Christ on this very earth." Eusebius asserts, without any supporting evidence, that the only reason they believed it was "the antiquity" of Papias.

During the time of Papias, and before, there were some who held to a variety of different doctrinal errors. "Most of the ecclesiastical writers" were not lead astray by the "antiquity" of these false teachers. Nor were they lead astray by the antiquity of Papias.

It was not in Papias' antiquity alone that these believers trusted. Papias lived a consistent life of proven service to the Lord, His apostles, and His Church. That is why most of the ecclesiastical writers trusted his transmission of the apostolic teaching. Eusebius did also, except in this one instance.

Eusebius' opposition to this apostolic teaching was so great, that he certainly would have, if he could have, presented the teaching of anyone contemporary with the apostles or their disciples who believed in the "mystical," spiritual interpretation which he himself adopted. However, he is not able to present the writings of anyone - not one — from that earlier age who believed as he did. He had the documents. He had the full support of the Emperor Constantine. But he still could not produce any evidence in support of his position.

That being the case, Eusebius chose not to present the millennial teaching of "most of the ecclesiastical writers," because it contradicted his own beliefs. In fact, he does not quote from any of them on this matter. Their writings were known and still in circulation in the early fourth century when Eusebius wrote his *Ecclesiastical History*.

Jerome, who wrote at about the end of the fourth century, said, "This (Papias) is said to have promulgated the Jewish tradition of a Millennium, and he is followed by Irenaeus, Apollinarius and the others who say that after the resurrection the Lord will reign in the flesh with the saints." [5] Irenaeus and Apollinarius are also described by Eusebius as learned, virtuous, faithful witnesses of the apostolic faith.

Eusebius says, "About this time also, the beloved disciple of Jesus, John the apostle and evangelist, still surviving, governed the churches in Asia, after his return from exile on the island, and the death of Domitian. But that he was still living until this time, it may suffice to prove, by the testimony of two witnesses. These, as maintaining sound doctrine in the church, may surely be regarded as worthy of all credit: and such were

Irenaeus and Clement of Alexandria. Of these, the former, in the second book against heresies..."[6]

According to Eusebius, Irenaeus maintained sound doctrine in the church. He wrote against heresies. He was a faithful and true witness. Irenaeus believed that the Lord would reign in the flesh on earth with the saints.

Jerome, since he also rejected "the Jewish tradition of a Millennium," did not quote from "the others." He rejected the writings of the "most," or all, of the early Church that believed in it. Their writings were still available when he wrote. As with Eusebius, Jerome was also unable to offer evidence to the contrary from other early Church writers.

Eusebius, Jerome, and others had these writings available to them, but they did not want to make them known. These writings of "most of the ecclesiastical writers" who promulgated "the Jewish tradition of a Millennium" are not available to us today. That is not, however, evidence that the Church never believed as they did. It is only evidence that some later in the Church did not care to preserve these writings.

Part of one of those early writings that has survived, "The Revelation of Peter," clearly speaks of a restoration of Israel. In a portion parallel to Matthew 24, Mark 13, and Luke 21, Jesus is seated on the Mount of Olives, and the disciples come to him asking, "Make known unto us what are the signs of thy Parousia [appearing] and of the end of the world..."[7] As Jesus tells them the signs, He admonishes them, "And ye, receive ye the parable of the fig-tree thereon: as soon as its shoots have gone forth and its boughs have sprouted, the end of the world will come."[8]

Peter then asks Jesus to explain the parable of the fig tree that signals the end of the age and the coming of the Lord. (cf. Mt.24:32-36; Mk.13:28-32; Lk.21:29-33) Jesus replies, "Do you not understand that the fig tree is the house of Israel? Truly, I tell you, when its branches have sprouted at the end of the world, false Christs shall arise. They will arouse expectation and say, 'I am the Christ who once came into the world.' But this liar is not the Christ. When they reject him, he will murder with the sword. Then shall the branches of the fig tree, which is the house of Israel, shoot forth. There shall be many martyrs by his hand...."[9]

"The Revelation of Peter," a short work which does not speak of much more than the restoration of Israel, was not considered an heretical document, far from it. The "Muratorian Canon," written about 180 A.D., lists the writings which the Church (or part of it) then acknowledged as canonical. It mentions, "...We also accept a Revelation by John and one by Peter, although some of us do not want the latter to be read aloud in the Church."[10]

"The Revelation of Peter" was considered part of the canon. It was accepted as the Word of God. Yet some in the Church did not want it to be read to the people. Certainly that is unusual. (Eusebius was familiar with "The Revelation of Peter," but he did not quote from it.)

Those in the Church who did not want "The Revelation of Peter" to be publicly read were not arguing that it was not the Word of God. It simply contained material that they did not like. Even if they thought it was the Word of God, they did not want it to be read to the Church. Though today we do not consider it canonical, it still is firm documentary evidence of what the early Church believed.

Justin's *Dialogue with Trypho the Jew*, dated about 160 A.D., also offers evidence of what the early Church believed. It is interesting as a seemingly transitional work. The dialogue apparently took place shortly after the Bar Kokhba Rebellion of 132-135 A.D., but was not written down for at least twenty years.

Justin points to the desolation of Israel and says to Trypho, "And therefore all this has happened to you rightly and well. For ye slew the Just One and His prophets before Him, and now ye reject, and, as far as in you lies, dishonour those that set their hope on Him, and God Almighty and Maker of the universe who sent Him, cursing in your synagogues them that believe on Christ. For you have not authority to raise your own hands against us, because of them who are now supreme. But as often as you could, this also ye did." [11]

Justin believed that the Church was the true Israel, but not in the replacement sense later adopted. "For we are the true and spiritual Israelitish nation, and the race of Judah and of Jacob and Isaac and Abraham, who when he was still uncircumcised received witness from God for his faith, and was blessed, and was called father of many nations — we, I say, are all this, who were brought nigh to God by Him who was crucified, even Christ..." [12]

"As therefore from that one Jacob, who was also surnamed Israel, your whole nation was addressed as Jacob and Israel, so **also** we who keep the commmandments of Christ, are, by virtue of Christ who begat us unto God, both called and in fact are, Jacob and Israel and Judah and Joseph and David, and true children of God."[13]

Justin maintains that Gentiles "who keep the commandments of Christ, are, by virtue of Christ" **also** full members of Israel. He does not seem to believe that the Church has replaced the Jews, but rather that Gentile Christians have been grafted into Israel through Jesus. "When therefore God blesses, and calls this people Israel, and cries aloud that it is His inheritance, how is it that you do not repent, both for deceiving yourselves as though you alone were Israel, and for cursing the people that is blessed of God?" [14]

"Trypho said: Do you indeed intend to say that none of us shall inherit anything in the holy mountain of God?

"And I replied: I do not mean that. But they who persecuted Christ, and still persecute Him, and do not repent, shall not inherit anything in the holy mountain. While the nations [Gentiles] that have believed on Him, and have repented for all the sins they have committed — **they shall inherit, with all the patriarchs and the prophets and the righteous men that have been born of Israel.**" [15]

According to Justin, it is not Jews **only** who are now Israel, but **also** Gentiles who believe in Jesus. For Justin, because the Gentiles who believe in Jesus are now part of Israel, they also, along with the righteous Jews, will inherit what God has promised Israel.

As for the nature of that inheritance, Trypho pointedly asks, " 'do you acknowledge of a truth that this place Jerusalem will be rebuilt, and expect that your people will be gathered together and rejoice with Christ, together with the patriarchs and the prophets, and the saints of our race, or even of them who became proselytes, before your Christ came...?'

[Justin replies,] 'I have acknowledged to you earlier that I and many others do hold this opinion, even as you also know well that this is to take place. But I also informed you that even many Christians of pure and godly mind do not accept it. For I made it clear to you that those who are Christians in name, but in reality are godless and impious heretics, teach in all respects what is blasphemous and godless and foolish....For it is not men, or the doctrines of men, that I choose to follow, but God and the doctrines that come from Him.

"For even if you yourselves have ever met with some so-called Christians, who yet do not acknowledge this, but even dare to blaspheme the God of Abraham, and the God of Isaac, and the God of Jacob... But I, and all other entirely orthodox Christians, know that there will be a resurrection of the flesh, and also a thousand years in a Jerusalem built up and adorned and enlarged, as the prophets Ezekiel and Isaiah, and all the rest, acknowledge."[16]

"And, further, a man among us named John, one of the apostles of Christ, prophesied in a Revelation made to him that they who have believed our Christ will spend a thousand years in Jerusalem, and that afterwards the universal, and, in one word, eternal resurrection of all at once, will take place, and also the judgment." [17]

For Justin, "all entirely orthodox Christians" believed that Jesus would reign on the earth for a thousand years in a glorified Jerusalem. Those "so-called Christians who yet do not acknowledge this...in reality are godless and impious heretics" who "dare to blaspheme the God of Abraham, and the God of Isaac, and the God of Jacob."

Eusebius knew Justin's *Dialogue with Trypho*. He quotes from it, praising Justin as "a true lover of sound philosophy." He characterizes Justin as courageous, a man "of cool deliberation and judgment." [18]

But when it comes to Justin's declaration that those who do not acknowledge the future coming and reign of the Lord on the earth from Jerusalem are "godless and impious heretics," Eusebius ignores Justin. He neither quotes, nor mentions, nor comments. He cannot pretend that Justin was lead astray by Papias, so he simply pretends that Justin never said what he said. For Eusebius, it is not part of the history of the Church, because it is not what he wants the Church to believe.

THE PASSOVER CONTROVERSY

One issue that stands out in the reversal of the apostolic teaching is the Passover controversy that was finally settled at the Council of Nicea. To this day, almost all the Church follows the clearly erroneous decree which came forth from that council.

There were two main issues for the Council of Nicea. The first concerned the heretical writings of Arius and his followers.

"But there was another subject which occasioned considerable uneasiness in the Church, viz. the difference which arose among the orientals [those of the East, i.e. those who were not part of the western Roman Empire] with respect to the proper day of keeping Easter, some celebrating that festival in the manner of the Jews, and others following the custom of Christians throughout the rest of the world...The emperor, therefore, finding that the quiet of the Church was not a little disturbed by these two evils [the Passover controversy and the Arian heresy], assembled (by the advice of some of the prelates, according to Rufinus,) a general council, inviting, by letter, all the bishops to meet at Nice, in Bithynia, and furnishing them with a means of conveyance. In consequence, a great number of them, not less than three hundred and eighteen, arrived from various cities and territories, attended by a vast concourse of the inferior clergy. Daily and ample provision was made by Constantine for the support and accommodation of this numerous body." [19]

When they assembled, Constantine greeted them with an admonition against disunity: "It was, my dear friends, my most cherished wish, that I might one day enjoy the sight of this convention. Having been indulged in this desire, I return thanks to God, the ruler of all, who, in addition to innumerable other favors, has granted me this greatest of all blessings, to see you assembled together, and united in your minds. May no malignant foe disturb in future our public happiness. After the complete subversion, by the help of God our preserver, of the tyranny of those, who warred against the Most High, let no malevolent demon again expose the divine law, in any other manner, to slander and detraction. An internal sedition in the Church is, in my apprehension, more dangerous and formidable than any war, in which I can be engaged; nor do foreign concerns, however

Apparently Victor withdrew his decree, but the controversy was not resolved. It was merely muted for a time. The church at Rome continued to press for its own supremacy. Jerusalem had already been physically destroyed, but it still had to be destroyed as a spiritual competitor. The issue, in a slightly altered form, was finally settled by the Council of Nicea in 325 A.D.

There it was decided that all the churches should celebrate the Passover, or actually Easter, on the ecclesiastically chosen Sunday rather than the Biblical date. All the churches were thus informed. The Emperor Constantine sent his personal exhortation to all the churches concerning the decision of the Council.

What the Emperor said had great weight. After all, Constantine was the one who had ended the persecution of the churches. He was the founder of the holy Roman Empire. He openly, personally professed the Christian faith. He had convened the council. The churches, therefore, were more than willing to hear whatever he had to say to them.

What he had to say to them is a clear presentation of the sentiment and theology that ruled in the Council of Nicea. It expresses what then became the nearly universal sentiment and theology of the Church. So, though the letter is long, it is well worthwhile to look at the complete text of the Emperor's personal exhortation to all the churches. It was a major force in changing the nature of the Church and of subsequent Western and world history. There are some very significant elements in it.

"Constantine, august, to the Churches.

"Having experienced, in the flourishing state of public affairs, the greatness of the divine goodness I thought it especially incumbent on me to endeavor that the happy multitudes of the Catholic [i.e. universal] Church should preserve one faith, be united in unfeigned love, and harmoniously join in their devotions to Almighty God. But this could not otherwise be effected in a firm and solid manner, than by an examination, for this purpose, of whatever pertains to our most holy religion, by all the bishops, or the greater part of them at least, assembled together. Having therefore convened as many as possible, I myself being present, and, as it were, one of you, (nor do I deny that I exceedingly rejoice in being your fellow-servant,) every thing was examined, until a unanimous sentiment, pleasing to God, who sees all things, was brought to light; so that no pretence was left for dissension or controversy respecting the faith.

"When the question arose concerning the most holy day of Easter, it was decreed by common consent to be expedient, that this festival should be celebrated on the same day by all, in every place. For what can be more beautiful, what more venerable and becoming, than that this festival, from which we receive the hope of immortality, should be suitably observed by all in one and the same order, and by a certain rule. And truly, in the first place, it seemed to every one a most unworthy thing that we should follow the custom of the Jews in the celebration of this most holy solemnity, who, polluted wretches! having stained their hands with a nefarious crime, are justly blinded in their minds.

"It is fit, therefore, that, rejecting the practice of this people, we should perpetuate to all future ages the celebration of this rite, in a more legitimate order, which we have kept from the first day of our Lord's passion even to the present times. Let us then have nothing in common with the most hostile rabble of the Jews. We have received another method from the Saviour. A more lawful and proper course is open to our most holy religion. In pursuing this course with a unanimous consent, let us withdraw ourselves, my much honored brethren, from that most odious fellowship.

"It is indeed in the highest degree preposterous, that they should superciliously vaunt themselves, that truly without their instruction, we cannot properly observe this rite. For what can they rightly understand, who, after the tragical death of our Lord, being deluded and darkened in their minds, are carried away by an unrestrained impulse wherever their inborn madness may impel them. Hence therefore it is, that, even in this particular, they do not perceive the truth, so that continually wandering in the grossest error, instead of duly reforming their calculation, they commemorate the passover twice in the same [Roman] year. Why then should we follow those who are acknowledged to labor under a grievous error? for we will never tolerate the keeping of a double passover in one year.

"But if what I have said should not be thought sufficient, it belongs to your ready discernment, both by diligence and prayer, to use every means, that the purity of your minds may not be affected by a conformity in any thing with the customs of the vilest of mankind. Besides, it should be considered that any dissension in a business of such importance, and in a religious institution of so great solemnity, would be highly criminal. For the Saviour has bequeathed us one festal day of our liberation, that is, the day of his most holy passion; and it was his pleasure that his Church should be one; the members of which, although dispersed in many and various places, are yet nourished by the same spirit, that is by the will of God.

"Let the sagacity of your holiness only consider, how painful and indecorous it must be, for some to be experiencing the rigors of abstinence, and others to be unbending their minds in convivial enjoyment on the same day; and after Easter, for some to be indulging in feasting and relaxation, while others are occupied in the observance of the prescribed fasts. Wherefore, that a suitable reformation should take place in this respect, and that one rule should be followed, is the will of divine providence, as all, I think, must perceive.

"As it is necessary that this fault should be so amended that we may have nothing in common with the usage of these parricides and murderers of our Lord; and as that order is most convenient which is observed by all the churches of the West, as well as those of the southern and northern parts of the world, and also by some in the East, it was judged therefore to be most equitable and proper, and I pledged myself that this arrangement should meet your approbation, viz. that the custom which prevails with one consent in the city of Rome, and throughout all Italy, Africa and Egypt, in Spain, Gaul, Britain, Lybia, the whole of Greece, the diocese of Asia, Pontus and Cilicia, would be gladly embraced by your prudence, considering that not only the greatest number of churches exist in the places which have been already mentioned, but also that it is most religious and equitable that all should wish what the strictest reason seems to require, and to have no fellowship with the perjury of the Jews.

"And, to sum up the whole in a few words, it was agreeable to the common judgment of all, that the most holy feast of Easter should be celebrated on one and the same day. Nor is it becoming, that in so sacred an observance there should be any diversity; and it is better to follow that decision, in which all participation in the sin and error of others is avoided.

"This being the case, receive with cheerfulness the heavenly and truly divine command. For whatever is transacted in the holy councils of the bishops, is to be referred to the divine will. Wherefore, having announced to our beloved brethren what has been already written, it is your duty to receive and establish the arguments already stated, and the observance of the most holy day; that when I shall come into your beloved presence, so long desired by me, I may be able to celebrate, with you, on one and the same day, the holy festival, and that in all things I may rejoice with you; seeing that the cruelty of the devil is taken away by divine power, through my instrumentality, and that your faith, your peace and concord is everywhere flourishing.

"May God preserve you, my beloved brethren." [26]

In this letter, Constantine officially establishes an anti-Judaic foundation for the doctrine and practice of the Church, and declares that contempt for the Jews, and separation from them, is the only proper Christian attitude.

"...it seemed to every one a most unworthy thing that we should follow the custom of the Jews in the celebration of this most holy solemnity, who, polluted wretches! having stained their hands with a nefarious crime, are justly blinded in their minds. It is fit, therefore, that, **rejecting the practice of this people, we should perpetuate to all future ages the celebration of this rite, in a more legitimate order....Let us then have nothing in common with the most hostile rabble of the Jews...**

"In pursuing this course with a unanimous consent, let us withdraw ourselves...from that most odious fellowship.

"Why then should we follow those who are acknowledged to labor under a grievous error? ...But if what I have said should not be thought sufficient, it belongs to your ready discernment, both by diligence and prayer, that the purity of your minds may not be affected by a conformity in any thing with **the customs of the vilest of mankin**d...

"As it is necessary that this fault should be so amended that **we may have nothing in common with the usage of these parricides and murderers of our Lord**...

"it is most religious and equitable that all should wish what the strictest reason seems to require, and to have no fellowship with the perjury of the Jews... ."

Constantine attributed this anti-Judaic foundation to Jesus —"We have received another method from the Saviour. A more lawful and proper course is open to our most holy religion." — **and commands, with all the authority of the Emperor, that the entire Church accept and promote such attitudes, doctrine, and practice, since whatever the bishops decide in council is the will of God. He threatens that any dissent from these views must be considered highly criminal.**

"...every thing was examined, until a unanimous sentiment, pleasing to God, who sees all things, was brought to light; so that no pretence was left for dissension or controversy respecting the faith... .

"...Besides, it should be considered that **any dissension in a business of such importance, and in a religious institution of so great solemnity, would be highly criminal.**

"...and as that order is most convenient which is observed by all the churches of the West...**receive with cheerfulness the heavenly and truly divine command. For whatever is transacted in the holy councils of the bishops, is to be referred to the divine will.**

"Wherefore, having announced to our beloved brethren what has been already written, **it is your duty to receive and establish the arguments already stated**, and the observance of the most holy day; that when I shall come into your beloved presence, so long desired by me, I may be able to celebrate, with you, on one and the same day, the holy festival, and that in all things I may rejoice with you; seeing that the cruelty of the devil is taken away by divine power, through my instrumentality..."

All of this was written so that no Christian would celebrate Passover on the Biblically ordained day of the 14th of Nisan. (Eusebius apparently provided the new calendar for determining the day to be celebrated.) This is not an insignificant letter.

The most revealing question to ask is, "When did God give such authority over the Church to Constantine?" It is a question that was not really articulated at that time nor in most of the sixteen and a half centuries since.

The relationship of Church and State which began under Constantine was seen as the greatest blessing of God. There was an end to what had seemed like endless persecution. But with that end of persecution and the beginning of a new alliance came great compromises which have distorted the nature of the Church to this day.

At the conclusion of the Council of Nicea, Constantine held a banquet which vividly demonstrated what had happened to the Church of the One despised and rejected of men. At the banquet, Eusebius greatly praised the Emperor before the assembled leaders of the Church.

Eusebius himself describes the proceedings: "...No one of the bishops was absent from the imperial banquet, which was more admirably conducted than can possibly be described. The guards and soldiers, disposed in a circle, were stationed at the entrance of the palace with drawn swords. The men of God passed through the midst of them without fear, and went into the most private apartments of the royal edifice. Some of them were then admitted to the table of the emperor, and others took the places assigned to them on either side. It was a lively image of the kingdom of Christ, and appeared more like a dream than a reality." [27]

Eusebius is somewhat misleading. It is true that some of the Church leaders were brought into close relationship to the emperor, his private apartments, and his table — in time, such privileges became a measure of religious success — but it is highly doubtful that all the men of God walked through the circle of guards and soldiers without fear. The emperor intended the drawn swords to teach a lesson.

On the Passover controversy, the Council of Nicea had chosen an anti-Biblical course and demanded conformity to it. The swords were a way of indicating the necessity of conforming to the official decree.

"St. Athanasius remarks a difference of language, in pronouncing on this subject [the Passover], from that which was used in reference to the faith [the Arian controversy]. With respect to the latter it is said, 'this is the catholic faith, we believe,' &c., in order to show that it was no new determination, but an apostolic tradition. Accordingly, no date is given to this decision, neither the day nor the year being mentioned. But with regard to Easter, it is said, 'we have resolved as follows,' in order to show that all were expected to obey....But not withstanding the decision of the council there were some quartodecimans [from the Latin for 14th], as they were termed, who remained pertinaciously attached to the celebration of Easter on the fourteenth of the moon, and among others the Audeans, schismatics of Mesopotamia. They found fault with the council, reproachfully remarking, that this was the first time that the ancient tradition, through complaisance for Constantine, had been departed from." [28]

In convening the council, Constantine had already declared that whoever would disturb the unity of the Church was a "malignant foe" motivated by a "malevolent demon," exposing God's law to "slander and detraction." He had already declared that, "an internal sedition in the Church is, in my apprehension, more dangerous and formidable than any war, in which I can be engaged...and hoping that by my interference, a remedy might be applied to the evil, I sent for you all, without delay."

Constantine had achieved political victory, in the name of the Lord, by the sword. He was not about to trade in his weapons. He intended to use what had brought him victory in the Empire to achieve victory in the Church.

"He [Constantine] published also another letter, or more properly an edict, directed to the bishops and people, condemning Arius and his writings...that if any book written by Arius shall be found, it shall be committed to the flames, that no monument of his corrupt doctrine may descend to future ages. He declares that whoever shall be convicted of having concealed any book composed by Arius, instead of burning it, shall suffer death immediately after his apprehension...At the same time, Arius and the two prelates who adhered the most obstinately to his party, Secundus and Theonas, were banished by the emperor." [29]

From that point on, Church doctrine was to be enforced by the sword of the State. Those who would not conform were to be exiled or put to death. The books of heretics —those who taught what was contrary to the accepted teaching — were to be burned and exterminated from the earth. After all, as Constantine had written, "no pretence was left for dissension or controversy respecting the faith."

The Church ceased to be the Church of Jesus, and became the Church of Constantine. It was no longer the bride of Messiah. It had become the bride of Caesar.

The light within turned to darkness. The Church changed from a means of salvation into a means of destruction. It poisoned the waters of eternal life, turning them into an everflowing fountain of death. Through the centuries, the Constantinian Church has sought and brought the death of millions and millions of people throughout the world. Many of them have been Jewish.

Jesus had warned His followers, "The kings of the Gentiles lord it over them; and those who have authority over them are called 'Benefactors.' But not so with you, but let him who is the greatest among you become as the youngest, and the leader as the servant." (Lk.22:25-26) Constantine presented himself as the Benefactor of the Church, having ended the persecution, and therefore expected the Church to conform to his will. The prophetic voice of the Church vis a vis the State was silenced, and a hierarchical structure was imposed upon it.

That Constantine should reign over the earth for God was seen as a high spiritual truth. That Jesus, the King of kings, should reign over all the earth from Jerusalem was derided as carnal and unspiritual.

Under Constantine, Eusebius wrote a history of the Church that pointedly eliminated any positive reference to the restoration of Israel and the earthly reign of Jesus. The only place that remained for the Jews in the plan and purpose of God was to serve as the earthly, temporal representation of the eternal misery and condemnation that awaited all who were outside the Church.

The Church was now officially *Contra Judaeos* and *Adversus Judaeos* — set against and set in opposition to the Jews. Thus was established the anti-Judaic foundation on which both doctrine and practice were then built. The historical and theological eradication of the Jews prepared the way for the "lawful" attempts to physically eradicate them.

The "holy councils" to which Constantine referred produced a new "divine will." The Church itself replaced the power of God with the might of the Roman Empire. The Church became its own kingdom. The Church, which had been persecuted for so long by "the cruelty of the devil," was soon to become the persecutor.

At that time, it seems that there was no one to contest such a decision in the Holy Roman Empire. Gone were the days of the prophets and apostles. Gone were men like Polycarp and Polycrates, who were willing to tell the religious authorities in the Church, as Peter and John had told the religious authorities in the Sanhedrin, "We must obey God, rather than men."

The Church made a significant official change both in doctrine and in the way doctrine was to be established. As Constantine wrote "to the Catholic Church of Alexandria," "For what was approved by 300 bishops can only be considered as the pleasure of God, especially as the Holy Spirit, dwelling in the minds of so many and such worthy men, has clearly shown the divine will." [30] God's Truth was to be determined by Church councils, and not by the Word of God. Consequently, the teaching which was a blasphemous heresy to Justin Martyr became the new, unchallengeable orthodoxy.

It is remarkable that this change was made over such a clear, but seemingly insignificant issue as when the Church should celebrate the Passover. The Bible sets the date for Passover as the fourteenth of Nisan. That is when Jesus celebrated the Passover. The apostles did the same.

The Apostle Paul, whose ministry was to the Gentiles, observed the Biblical dates. The book of Acts records, simply in passing, that Passover (Acts 20:7), Shavuos/Pentecost (Acts 20:16), and Yom Kippur/the Day of Atonement (Acts 27:9) were fixed, significant dates for Paul. The Church built by the Apostles knew when Passover was, but from the Council of

Nicea on, the Church over which Constantine presided would no longer observe the Biblical date, because it was too Jewish.

The Bible itself was too Jewish. The doctrines of men, on the other hand, could be whatever men wanted them to be.

As a final note on the Council of Nicea, Canon VII speaks of the Bishop of Aelia. "Aelia" is the name that the Roman Emperor Hadrian had given to Jerusalem after the end of the Bar Kokhba rebellion.

"Canon VII: Since custom and ancient tradition require that the bishop of Aelia be held in veneration, let him have the next degree of honor to the metropolitan [the bishop of Caesarea], without prejudice to the appropriate authority of the latter." [31] Jerusalem had her name taken away, and she was placed in subjection to the church that had embraced Origen.

Constantine and Eusebius institutionalized many serious errors. They made changes that were to plunge the Church and the world into a literal thousand years of darkness. They laid a different foundation than Jesus and His apostles had laid. A new era in the history of the Church had begun. In actuality, a new Church began.

"Eusebius tells the story in *The Last Days of Constantine*. 'All these edifices the emperor consecrated with the desire of perpetuating the memory of the Apostles of our Saviour before all men. He had, however, another object in erecting this building (i.e., the Church of the Apostles at Constantinople): an object at first unknown, but which afterwards became evident to all. He had, in fact, made a choice of this spot in the prospect of his own death, anticipating with extraordinary fervour of faith that his body would share their title with the Apostles themselves, and that he should thus even after death become the subject, with them, of the devotions which should be performed to their honour in this place, and for this reason he bade men assemble for worship there at the altar which he placed in the midst. He accordingly caused twelve coffins to be set up in this church, like sacred pillars in honour and memory of the apostolic band, in the centre of which his own was placed, having six of theirs on either side of it. Thus, as I said, he had provided with prudent foresight an honourable resting-place for his body after death, and, having long before secretly formed this resolution, he now consecrated this church to the Apostles, believing that this tribute to their memory would be of no small advantage to his own soul. Nor did God disappoint him of that which he so ardently expected and desired.' " [32]

"Planning the Church of the Apostles, Constantine had dreamed of resting there forever in the midst of the Twelve, not merely one of them, but a symbol of, if not a substitute for, their Leader. During the months of the church's construction, his agents had been busy in Palestine collecting alleged relics [i.e. bones] of the apostles and their companions, to be laid up in the church with his body, awaiting the general resurrection." [33]

"The project was started but not completed. However, an official search was made for the locations of the bodies of the Apostles, and this official search was possibly the precipitating cause for the inventory which was made for the Apostolic remains or relics. After this time there arose the practice of the veneration of relics." [34]

Constantine sought bones and buildings as the focus of worship. Worship that focused on a building naturally "neglected the weightier provisions of the law: justice and mercy and faithfulness." Those are indispensable parts of the worship that God seeks. In the new order, worship gained a form, an appearance, without life, light, or service.

Jesus had said, "those who worship God must worship in spirit and truth." It was not the building, but the people. It was not the city, but the Spirit.

Constantine built buildings which were called churches, and people who were not the Church began to fill them. They "went to church," but they did not seek to "be the Church."

Rome was to become the new "holy city," geographically defining and confining worship. In many ways, Constantine laid a new foundation for the Church. To this day, the Church bears his image. That is what he intended.

Paul had warned the Gentile believers in Rome, "Don't be arrogant towards the natural branches. Don't be ignorant of God's faithfulness to the Jewish people." There were three things that especially characterize the theology and practice of the Constantinian church, the church built on an anti-Judaic foundation: 1. Arrogance towards the Jews; 2. Ignorance of God's plan for Israel and the transformation of the world; and 3. A leadership that has acted as lord and not as servant.

FOOTNOTES

1. E. Ferguson, "The Terminology of Kingdom in the Second Century," in *Studia Patristica, Vol.XVII*, P.670, edited by Elizabeth A. Livingstone, Pergamon Press, Oxford, 1982
2. ibid., P.673
3. *The Ecclesiastical History of Eusebius Pamphilus*, translated by Christian Frederick Cruse, op. cit., Bk.3, Ch.36, P.120
4. ibid., Bk.3, Ch.39, P.126
5. J.B. Lightfoot and J.R. Harmer, editors, *The Apostolic Fathers*, Baker Book House, Grand Rapids, MI, 1988, P.532 (de vir. illust. 18)
6. *The Ecclesiastical History of Eusebius Pamphilus*, Bk.3, Ch.23, P.104-105
7. Edgar Hennecke, *The New Testament Apocrypha*, Vol. 2, edited by Wilhelm Schneemelcher, translated by R. McL. Wilson, The Westminster Press, Phila., 1965, P.668 For the full text of this section, chapter 2, in the Ethiopic text, see Pp.668-669
8. ibid., P.668
9. Eberhard Arnold, *The Early Christians after the Death of the Apostles*, Plough Press, Farmington, PA., 1972, P.295
10. ibid., P.167
11. *Justin Martyr, The Dialogue with Trypho*, translated by A. Lukyn Williams, S.P.C.K.,

London, 1930, Pp.33-34, Sec. 16.4

12. ibid., P.24, Sec. 11.5
13. ibid., Pp.256-257, Sec. 123.7-9
14. ibid., P.255, Sec. 123.6
15. ibid., P.52, Sec. 25.6-26.1
16. ibid., P.169, Sec. 80.1-5
17. ibid., P.172, Sec. 81.4
18. *The Ecclesiastical History of Eusebius Pamphilus*, Bk.4, Ch.8, Pp.135-136
19. "A Historical View of the Council of Nice," Isaac Boyle, *The Ecclesiastical History of Eusebius Pamphilus*, translated by Christian Frederick Cruse, Baker Book House, Grand Rapids, 1989, Pp.9-10 of section following the ecclesiastical history.
20. ibid., P.16, quoting Theodoret, I.7
21. Les Juifs dan l'empire romain I, Paris 1914, P.308ff, quoted in "A Note on the Quartodecimans," C.W. Dugmore, *Studia Patristica*, Vol.IV, Berlin, 1961, P.412
22. *The Ecclesiastical History of Eusebius Pamphilus*, op. cit., Bk. 5, Ch. 23, P.207
23. ibid., Bk.5, Ch.24, Pp.208-209
24. ibid., Bk. 5, Ch. 24, Pp.210-211
25. ibid., Bk.4 , Ch.14, P.141
26. ibid., Pp.51-54, following the ecclesiastical history.
27. ibid., "A Historical View of the Council of Nice," Isaac Boyle, P.27
28. ibid., Pp.22-23
29. ibid., P.26
30. ibid., P.51, following the ecclesiastical history.
31. ibid., P.56
32. J. Stevenson, *A New Eusebius*, P.395, quoted in *The Search for the Twelve Apostles*, William Steuart McBirnie, Tyndale House, Wheaton, IL., 1977, P.19
33. John Holland Smith, *Constantine the Great*, Pp.301-302, quoted in *The Search for the Twelve Apostles*, William Steuart McBirnie, Pp.19-20
34. *The Search for the Twelve Apostles*, P.20

PART TWO:

THE BIBLICAL RELATIONSHIP

SECTION A:
ESTABLISHING THE CONTEXT

4

IN THE BEGINNING

Why did God create heaven and earth? Why did He create man? Gentiles? Jews? What did He want?

The answer is expressed in different, complementary ways throughout the Bible. Jesus, in speaking to the Samaritan woman at Jacob's well, expressed it this way: "An hour is coming, and now is, when the true worshipers shall worship the Father in Spirit and in Truth; for the Father also seeks such people to worship Him." (Jn.4:23) God created heaven and earth that they might declare His glory. He intends to fill them with a people who will worship Him in Spirit and in Truth.

The Greek word for "worship" used here, προσκυνεω, has the sense of bowing down before God—an act of adoration in recognition of His sovereignty. Loyalty and obedience demonstrate the recognition of His sovereignty. During His temptation in the wilderness, Jesus rebuked the devil, saying, "It is written, 'You shall worship the Lord your God, and serve Him only.' " (Mt.4:10, citing Dt.6:13) Worship and service are inseparable.

The parallel Hebrew word, תשׁתחוה, has the same meaning. It is used, for example, in Ex.20:3,5: "You shall not have any gods beside Me...you shall not worship them or serve them."

Genuine worship and love of God includes the recognition that He alone is Lord, the One to be obeyed. Genuine worship and love of God entails a life of service. As Paul expressed it, "[Jesus the Messiah] gave Himself for us, that He might redeem us from every lawless deed and purify for Himself a people for His own possession, zealous for good deeds." (Titus 2:14)

Neither mental assent nor the verbal repetition of correct formulas are acceptable substitutes. The verbal expression of faith without the life of faith is unacceptable to God. As Jacob, the brother of the Lord, reminded us, "Even so, faith, if it has no works, is dead, being by itself." (Jacob 2:17)

Jesus clearly taught that God's commandment to Israel remains today "the first and the greatest commandment": "And you shall love the Lord your God with all your heart and with all your soul and with all your might." (Dt.6:5) You must love God with all your heart. That means that you cannot merely perform the outward tasks, but reserve your desires for someone or something else. That also is unacceptable to God. Your heart must belong to Him. From that complete love, trust, and surrender comes a willing obedience to Him.

God is actively seeking such a people — a people who will worship Him in Spirit and in Truth — and has been from the beginning. He is seeking "a people," i.e. "one people," not two or more.

He desires a people who will not exalt their desires or imaginations above His Word; a people who will not forsake Him, "the fountain of living waters, to hew for themselves cisterns, broken cisterns, that can hold no water." (Jer.2:13) God created this world according to His own desire. He will assuredly have for Himself that people for which He created it.

"Worthy art Thou, our Lord and our God, to receive glory and honor and power; for Thou didst create all things, and because of Thy will they existed and were created." (Rev.4:11)

5

THE BEGINNING OF MAN

"Then God said, 'Let us make man [Adam, אדם] in our image, according to our likeness; and let them rule over the fish of the sea and over the birds of the sky and over the cattle and over all the earth, and over every creeping thing that creeps on the earth' And God created the Man [ha-Adam, האדם] in His own image, in the image of God He created him; male and female He created them." (Gen.1:27)

From the beginning, man was created to rule over all the earth. From the beginning, God looked upon man as more than one: "Let us make man...let them rule...He created him...He created them." He created one man, but that man contained more than himself alone.

"So the Lord God caused a deep sleep to fall upon the man [ha-Adam, האדם], and he slept; then He took one of his ribs, and closed up the flesh at that place. And the Lord God built the rib which He had taken from the man [ha-Adam, האדם] into a woman, and brought her to the man [ha-Adam, האדם]." (Gen.2:21-22) "He created them male and female, and He blessed them and named them Man [Adam/ אדם] in the day when they were created." (Gen.5:2)

In the Garden, Adam and Eve turned away from their Creator. They chose instead something that was good to eat, pleasing to look at, and desirable to make them wise. They chose the things of the flesh rather than the things of the Spirit. They believed a lie rather than holding fast to the Truth. They chose not to worship God in Spirit and in Truth.

For generation after generation, the children of Man also lusted after physical things rather than the things of the Spirit. They were envious and when they could not get what they wanted, they fought and quarrelled. (cf. Jacob 4:1-5) When they could not get what they wanted, they committed murder.

They filled the earth with violence, rather than with the glory of the Lord. So God cleansed the earth of them. He sent a flood to destroy and remove the children of Man from the earth.

Noah alone, with his family, found grace in the eyes of the Lord. Noah was not sinless, but he was righteous, walking with God. (Gen.6:8,9) Everyone is called to walk with God, but most people choose not to.

"He has told you, O man, what is good; and what does the Lord require of you, but to do justice, to love mercy, and to walk humbly with your God?" (Mic.6:8) In Noah's obedience, his humility can be seen. He sought to serve God and not himself.

Noah's humility enabled him to receive God's grace. For, "God is opposed to the proud, but gives grace to the humble." (Jacob 4:6;Prov. 3:34) It was only the grace of God that stood between Noah and destruction. So it is for everyone who walks with God.

"And God blessed Noah and his sons and said to them, 'Be fruitful and multiply, and fill the earth.' " (Gen.9:1) God still had a blessing for the children of Adam. He still intended to make it possible for them to fulfill His initial purpose in creating Man.

Noah had three sons — Shem, Ham, and Japheth. God identified Himself by name with Shem. Noah said, "Blessed be the Lord, the God of Shem..." (Gen.9:26)

"And also to Shem, the father of all the children of Eber...children were born." (Gen.10:21) Eber was a great grandson of Shem. He and his children are singled out as the heirs of Shem. God was choosing a particular human lineage, yet to be created, to further His plan of redemption.

There were exceptions, but as a whole, the descendants of Noah rebelled against the Lord. Instead of spreading abroad to fill the earth, they chose to stay in one place to make a name for themselves. They chose to build their tower and their kingdom at Babel. This rebellion at the Tower of Babel is the mother of all future rebellions against God.

"And the Lord came down to see the city and the tower which the sons of the Man [האדם] had built. And the Lord said, 'Behold, they are one people, and they all have the same language. And this is what they began to do, and now nothing which they purpose to do will be impossible for them. Come, let Us go down and there confuse their language, that they may not understand one another's speech.' So the Lord scattered them abroad from there over the face of the whole earth; and they stopped building the city. Therefore its name was called Babel, because there the Lord confused the language of the whole earth; and from there the Lord scattered them abroad over the face of the earth." (Gen.11:5-9)

Up until that point in time, all people were of one kind, simply "generic" children of Adam, the Man. The children of Adam were united in their rebellion against their Creator. There was great power in their unity — "nothing which they purpose to do will be impossible for them." So God divided them. That division and dispersion marks the beginning of the nations, i.e. the Gentiles, the heathen, the goyim [גוים].

6

THE BEGINNING OF THE GENTILES

In dividing the children of Adam into smaller groups of people, the Lord limited the effects of their rebellion. He indelibly marked the history of man without God as one of division, but He created the framework that He would later use to demonstrate the true nature of unity. They wanted to make a name for themselves, so God gave them many names, the names of all the nations.

Initially, the goyim were simply all those people descended from those who sought to build the Tower of Babel. Later, the descendants of Abraham, Isaac, and Jacob are separated out from the goyim. The goyim are then all those people descended from those who sought to build the Tower of Babel, but not descended from Abraham, Isaac, and Jacob. I.e., the goyim are all those who are not Jewish. The comparable Greek term in the New Covenant Scriptures for goyim is ethne [εθνη, εθνεσιν, εθνων, εθνος].

From the Tower of Babel on, each and every nation—all the Gentiles [goyim]—failed to be a people worshipping God in Spirit and in Truth. In Tanakh, the Gentiles are generally portrayed as proud, immoral and brutal, earning for themselves the wrath of God. (There were exceptions, which we shall look at later.)

When God redeemed Israel out of Egypt, He warned them against being like the Gentiles. "For My angel will go before you and bring you in to the land of the Amorites, the Hittites, the Perizzites, the Canaanites, the Hivites and the Jebusites; and I will completely destroy them. You shall not worship their gods, nor serve them, nor do according to their deeds; but you shall utterly overthrow them, and break their sacred pillars in pieces....They shall not live in your land, lest they make you sin against Me; for if you serve their gods, it will surely be a snare to you." (Ex.23:23-24,33)

"Watch yourself that you make no covenant with the inhabitants of the land into which you are going, lest it become a snare in your midst...lest you make a covenant with the inhabitants of the land and they play the harlot with their gods, and sacrifice to their gods, and someone invite you to eat of his sacrifice; and you take some of his daughters for your sons, and his daughters play the harlot with their gods, and cause your sons also to play the harlot with their gods." (Ex.34:12,15-16)

The Lord called Israel to be holy, which necessitated separation from the Gentiles. He told Israel, "You shall not do what is done in the land of Egypt where you lived, nor are you to do what is done in the land of Canaan where I am bringing you; you shall not walk in their statutes." (Lev.18:3) Then the Lord explains what the practices of the Gentiles are that Israel is not to imitate—incest, sexual impurity, homosexuality, bestiality, etc. He concludes, "Do not defile yourselves by any of these thing; for by all these the nations which I am casting out before you have become defiled." (Lev.18:24)

Before the people of Israel were to enter the land of Israel, the God of Israel again warned them about the Gentiles and their idolatry. "Then the Lord spoke to Moses in the plains of Moab by the Jordan opposite Jericho, saying, 'Speak to the sons of Israel and say to them, When you cross over the Jordan into the land of Canaan, then you shall drive out all the inhabitants of the land from before you, and destroy all their figured stones, and destroy all their molten images and demolish all their high places.

"...But if you do not drive out the inhabitants of the land from before you, then it shall come about that those whom you let remain of them will become as pricks in your eyes and as thorns in your sides, and they shall trouble you in the land in which you live. And it shall come about that as I plan to do to them, so I will do to you.' " (Num.33:51-52,55-56) God promised terrible judgments if the Jewish people allowed the Gentiles to remain in their midst.

"And when the Lord your God shall deliver them before you, and you shall smite them, then you shall utterly destroy them. You shall make no covenant with them and show no favor to them. Furthermore, you shall not intermarry with them; you shall not give your daughters to their sons, nor shall you take their daughters for your sons. For they will turn your sons away from following Me to serve other gods; then the anger of the Lord will be kindled against you, and He will quickly destroy you.

"But thus you shall do to them: you shall tear down their altars, and smash their sacred pillars, and hew down their Asherim, and burn their graven images with fire. For you are a holy people to the Lord your God; the Lord your God has chosen you to be a people for His own possession out of all the peoples who are on the face of the earth." (Dt.7:1-6)

God's purpose was to keep Israel holy, to have a people to worship Him, and Him alone, in Spirit and in Truth. "When you enter the land which the Lord your God gives you, you shall not learn to do according to the detestable things of those Gentiles. There shall not be found among you anyone who makes his son or his daughter pass through the fire, one who uses divination, one who practices witchcraft, or one who interprets omens, or a sorcerer, or one who casts a spell, or a medium, or a spiritist, or one who calls up the dead.

"For whoever does these things is detestable to the Lord; and because of these detestable things the Lord your God will drive them out before you. You shall be blameless before the Lord your God. For those Gentiles which you shall dispossess listen to those who practice witchcraft and to diviners, but as for you, the Lord your God has not allowed you to do so." (Dt.18:9-14)

These were the deeds not only of the Gentiles in the land of Canaan, but throughout all the earth. In each book of the Law of Moses, God taught Israel to be separate from the Gentiles, and not to live like them.

That is why the Lord warned of the terrible judgments that would come upon Israel if she committed the abominations of the Gentiles. The ultimate judgment would be exile among the Gentiles. If the Jewish people would not be separate, if they would not be different, then God would banish them to live among the Gentiles.

The Gentiles established their reputations and made names for themselves. History records, however, and the Bible declares, their utter failure in terms of God's redemptive purpose in the earth.

So God took one man, a Gentile—for that's all there were at the time—and promised to make a new people from him.

7

THE BEGINNING OF THE JEWS

Diagram 1 is the first of a series that portrays the relationship of Jews, Gentiles, and the Church. None of the diagrams are intended to be to scale. They simply portray the nature of the relationship.

Out of all the Gentiles, God set one man apart for Himself. From this man He made a new people, physically and covenantally distinguished from all the others. The circle in the diagram surrounds those people and indicates their distinctness from all the Gentiles.

"Now the Lord said to Abram, 'Go forth from your country, and from your relatives and from your father's house, to the land which I will show you; and I will make a great nation, and I will bless you, and make your

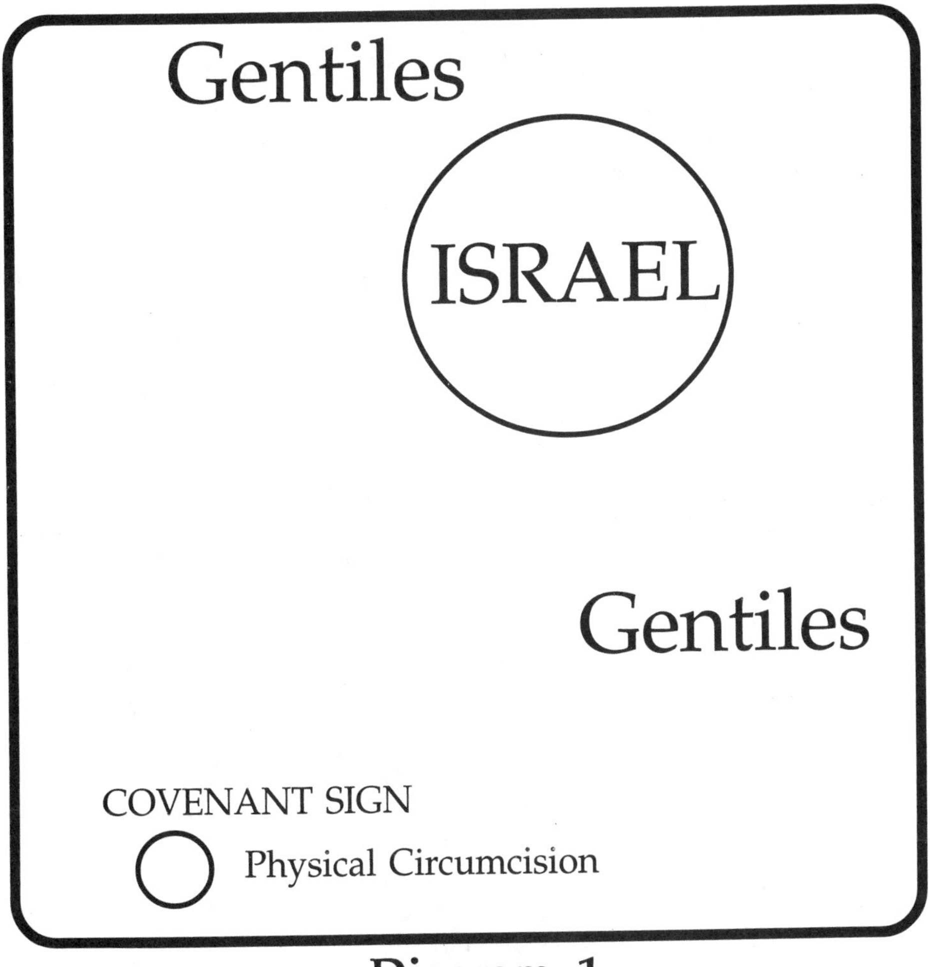

Gentiles

ISRAEL

Gentiles

COVENANT SIGN
Physical Circumcision

Diagram 1

name great; and so you shall be a blessing; and I will bless those who bless you, and the one who curses you I will curse. And in you all the families of the earth shall be blessed.' " (Gen.12:1-3)

The new people created from Abram was to be different and set apart from the Gentiles. " Behold, a people who dwells apart, and shall not be reckoned among the Gentiles." (Num.23:9) God instituted the covenant of circumcision with Abram to set apart this new people. "This is My covenant, which you shall keep, between Me and you and your seed after you: every male among you shall be circumcised. And you shall be circumcised in the flesh of your foreskin; and it shall be the sign of the covenant between Me and you." (Gen.17:10,11)

Yet strangely enough, in instituting the covenant, God said, "No longer shall your name be called Abram [exalted father], but your name shall be Abraham [father of a multitude]; for I will make you the father of a multitude of goyim." (Gen.17:5) In setting Abraham apart to be the father of the Jews, God also declared His intention to make him the father of a multitude of Gentiles.

The change of Abraham's name had great significance. Nevertheless, for clarity, the Bible later refers to "Abraham" whether speaking of him before his name was changed or after. This is true both in Tanakh (cf. Is.51:2), and in the New Covenant Scriptures. (cf. Gal.3:6,8,9,16,18; Rom.4:3,9,12,13)

When Abraham initially responded to the call of God, he "took Sarai his wife and Lot his nephew, and all their possessions which they had accumulated, and the persons which they had acquired in Haran, and they set out for the land of Canaan..." (Gen.12:5) "The persons which they had acquired" is literally "the souls that they had made." Therefore the rabbis say that these were people (Gentiles) who became proselytes to the faith of Abraham.[1]

Abraham trained his household well. His nephew Lot had separated from him, moved into Sodom, and had been taken captive when Sodom was attacked. "And when Abram heard that his relative had been taken captive, he led out his trained men [literally, "his dedicated ones"], born in his house, three hundred and eighteen, and went in pursuit as far as Dan." (Gen.14:14) Because Abraham had trained these "sons of his house," they were dedicated, faithful, and obedient.

King Solomon also spoke of his "homeborn slaves," literally the "sons of the house," but there is no mention of his following the example of Abraham in training them. (Eccl. 2:7) Solomon was searching for the purpose of life in wisdom and pleasure, but Abraham was looking for the son who would make the promises of God a reality to him.

"And Abram said, 'O Lord God, what wilt Thou give me, since I go childless, and the heir of my house is Eliezer of Damascus?' And Abram said, 'Behold Thou hast given no seed to me, and behold a son of my house [literally] is my heir.' Then behold, the word of the Lord came to him saying, 'This man will not be your heir; but one who shall come forth from your own body [literally "inward parts"], he shall be your heir.' " (Gen.15:2-4)

Apparently, Eliezer of Damascus was a faithful servant, trained by his master. Eliezer had the faith of Abraham but was not physically descended from him. We are told that, "A servant who acts wisely will rule over a son who acts shamefully, and will share in the inheritance among brothers." (Prov.17:2) Nevertheless, God had promised Abraham that he would physically father a son who would be his heir. The physical descent was necessary.

Since Sarah could not conceive, Abraham prayed that his son Ishmael, born of Sarah's handmaiden Hagar, would be his heir. Ishmael was physically circumcised and the son of Abraham, but God told Abraham that his descendants would not be named, and his inheritance from God would not go, through Ishmael. His name and his inheritance would go to Isaac, his child who would be born of Sarah. (Gen.21:12)

Ishmael was Abraham's descendant, literally his "seed" (Gen.21:13), but in the sight of God, he was not truly Abraham's son. For when God called Abraham to offer up Isaac, He said, "Take now your son, your **only** son, whom you love, Isaac, and go to the land of Moriah; and offer him there as a burnt offering on one of the mountains of which I will tell you." (Gen.22:2) From God's perspective, the only true son of Abraham was Isaac. He was physically descended from Abraham, and he had Abraham's faith. The physical descent was not sufficient.

Ishmael was also circumcised. That also was not sufficient. Though he was physically descended from Abraham and had been physically circumcised according to the covenant that God made with Abraham, he still was not considered a true son.

Abraham died, but the faithfulness and promise of God continued to and through Isaac. God continued to select out a particular lineage for His plan of redemption. He continued to call Himself by the name of His people. He now became "the God of Isaac."

"And Isaac prayed to the Lord on behalf of his wife because she was barren; and the Lord answered him and Rebekah his wife conceived." (Gen.25:21) Rebekah gave birth to twins, Esau and Jacob. Esau was the first born. They had the same mother and the same father, but they were to be two peoples, and not one. (Gen.25:23)

Contrary to custom and law, the younger son, Jacob, inherited the promise, the blessing, and the name of Abraham. He was Jewish, but his twin brother Esau, was not. God made that choice, according to his purpose, before either of them was born. God became "the God of Jacob."

Jacob married two sisters, Leah and Rachel, and had children by them and their two maidservants. God said to Jacob, "I am God Almighty; Be fruitful and multiply; a nation and a company of nations [goyim] shall come from you, and kings shall come forth from you. And the land which I gave to Abraham and Isaac, I will give to you, and I will give the land to your descendants after you." (Gen.35:11-12)

Jacob, whom God named "Israel," had twelve sons, who gave their names to the twelve tribes of Israel. His fourth son was Judah [Yehudah, יהודה], from the root word that means "praise." The name "Jews" [Yehudim, יהודים] is also derived from this root. Jews were created to be a praise to God.

The word "Jew," in its different forms, appears about two hundred times throughout the Bible. There is a question, in the minds of some, as to whom is properly designated by the term. What is the proper Biblical understanding of the term "Jew"? Is there a difference between "Jew," "Hebrew," and "Israelite"? The only way to know is by looking at how the terms are used in the Bible.

"Hebrew" [עברי] is the oldest term. It is derived from the name of Eber [עבר]. Eber was the great, great, great, great-grandfather of Abraham.

The word is first applied in the Bible to Abraham: "Then a fugitive came and told Abram the Hebrew." (Gen.14:13) Joseph is described as a "Hebrew slave." (Gen.39:17).

Later, the children of Israel all became slaves in Egypt. "...And the sons of Israel sighed because of the bondage, and they cried out; and their cry for help because of their bondage rose up to God. So God heard their groaning; and God remembered His covenant with Abraham, Isaac, and Jacob. And God saw the sons of Israel, and God took notice of them." (Ex.2:23-25)

God chose Moses to redeem His people out of Egypt. He appeared to Moses in a burning bush, and told him, "I am the God of your father, the God of Abraham, the God of Isaac, and the God of Jacob. ...and you...will come to the king of Egypt, and you will say to him, 'The Lord, the God of the Hebrews, has met with us. So now, please, let us go a three days journey into the wilderness, that we may sacrifice to the Lord our God.' " (Ex.3:6,18)

"The God of Abraham, the God of Isaac, and the God of Jacob" calls Himself "the Lord, the God of the Hebrews." He calls all of Jacob's descendants in Egyptian bondage "Hebrews." God identified Himself with the people He created.

The Hebrews are also called "the sons of Israel," i.e. Israelites. These are equivalent terms. Moses told all Israel, "If your kinsman, a Hebrew man or woman, is sold to you, then he shall serve you six years, but in the seventh year you shall set him free." (Dt.15:12)

Jonah said, "I am a Hebrew, and I fear the Lord God of heaven who made the sea and the dry land." (Jon.1:9) So the word "Hebrew" is applied in the Bible to describe Abraham, Joseph, Jonah, all of Jacob's descendants in Egyptian bondage, and all Israel.

"Judah" was used to designate the southern kingdom from the time when

Israel was divided in the days of Rehoboam, since, "None but the tribe of Judah followed the house of David." (1K.12:20) Even then, however, the term "Judah" also included the tribe of Benjamin, the Levites, and priests. Also, there were those from other tribes of Israel who chose to be part of Judah. (2Ch.10:17; 11:14,16; 15:9; 31:6)

The kingdom of Judah was not limited to the descendants of Judah, and the term "Jews" was not used to exclusively designate the descendants of Judah, as opposed to the descendants of his eleven brothers who also lived in the same southern kingdom. In fact, it is not until less than twenty years before the exile of the ten tribes, the northern kingdom of Israel, that the term "Jew" is actually used in the Bible. (cf. 2Kings 16:6)

Mordecai and Esther, from the tribe of Benjamin, are called "Jews" (Esth.2:5-7), as are all the exiles from all the tribes of Israel in all the provinces of Persia (Esth.3:13). The remnant who returned from captivity are called "Jews" (e.g. Ez.4:23), though they were from different tribes. That remnant plus those who had been left in the land were not only from Judah, Benjamin, and Levi, but the rest of Israel as well. (Neh.11:20, cf. v.3)

Some say that Abraham was not Jewish, because the term "Jew" does not appear until later in history, referring to the descendants of Judah. They then make a theological separation between "the Jews" and their fathers. But by that reasoning, neither Isaac, Jacob, Judah, Moses, Aaron, Gideon, Samuel, Jonah, Paul, etc. — would be Jewish either. Nor would any of the descendants of Judah who lived more than twenty years before the exile of the northern kingdom. That is not the way that the term is used in the Bible.

The word is used in the New Covenant Scriptures to designate those who lived in Judea (e.g. Jn.11:54), the religious leaders (e.g. Jn.7:13), the children of Israel in the land as opposed to those from the Diaspora (Acts 10:39), and the children of Israel as opposed to the Gentiles (e.g. Acts 14:5). Paul was from the tribe of Benjamin and called himself a Jew (e.g. Acts 21:39), as well as an Israelite (e.g. 2Co.11:22), and a Hebrew (Phil.3:5). The New Covenant Scriptures also uses the word "Greek" to designate Hellenistic Jews (Acts 6:1; 14:1), the Gentile inhabitants of the territory once encompassed by Alexander's empire (Rom.1:14), and all Gentiles (Rom.2:9,10).

There are some familiar historical and Biblical parallels to this kind of word usage. The name "Yankee" was originally a designation for New Englanders, but during the Civil War, it meant those from the Union side. Today, for people in other countries, it has come to mean a citizen of the United States, whether from Boston, Atlanta, or Los Angeles. The particular meaning of the word is made clear by its context.

In like manner, the term "Jews" has been given to all those who are the descendants of Abraham, Isaac, and Jacob. In the Bible it is generally used synonymously with the term "Israel." By the time of Jesus the term "Jew" had become a universal designation for Abraham, Isaac, Jacob, and their descendants, regardless of their particular tribe or place of residence in Israel or the world.

In retrospect, we call the earlier descendants of Abraham, Isaac, and Jacob by the same term, "Jews," even though that particular word was not used then or there to describe all of them. They were what the New Covenant Scriptures, and we today, indicate by the word.

It is simply the usage of the term that developed later and became universal. The meaning is correctly and understandably applied to other individuals of the same lineage, who lived before the term was universally applied.

Likewise, referring to "Hebrews" as "Jews" is similar to calling Samuel, or any of his predecessors, a "prophet" instead of a "seer." "Formerly in Israel, when a man went to inquire of God, he used to say, 'Come, and let us go to the seer'; for he who is called a prophet now was formerly called a seer." (1Sam.9:9) "When David arose in the morning, the word of the Lord came to the prophet Gad, David's seer, saying..." (2Sam.24:11) Gad is called both a seer and a prophet.

Peter called Samuel a prophet, rather than a seer. (Acts 3:24) There was no reason to use the earlier term. The two terms mean the same thing, but one appeared in common usage chronologically later than the other. The terms became interchangeable.

In an act of repentance, King Zedekiah and those remaining in Jerusalem made a covenant, "that each man should set free his male servant and each man his female servant, a Hebrew man or a Hebrew woman; so that no one should keep them, a Jew his brother, in bondage." (Jer.34:9) "A Jew" and "a Hebrew" are used as equivalent terms. If a man, or woman, is a Hebrew, then he, or she, is a Jew. A Jew is a Hebrew is an Israelite.

FOOTNOTE

1. cf. Sanh.99b, The Babylonian Talmud, Ed. by Isadore Epstein, The Soncino Press, London, 1935, P.675

8

ABRAHAM THE STRANGER

God promised Abraham, "And I will establish My covenant between Me and you and your seed after you throughout their generations for an everlasting covenant, to be God to you and to your seed after you. And I will give to you and to your seed after you, the land of your sojournings, all the land of Canaan, for an everlasting possession; and I will be their God." (Gen.17:8)

This covenant promise was later given by God to Isaac (Gen.17:19,21). It was repeated to Jacob (Gen.28:4,13-15), and to all Israel (Dt.7:3). It serves as a reminder of the faithfulness of God. The God of Israel has given the land of Israel to the people of Israel.

"O seed of Abraham, His servant, O sons of Jacob, His chosen ones! He is the Lord our God; His judgments are in all the earth. He has remembered His covenant forever, the word which He commanded to a thousand generations, the covenant which He made with Abraham, and His oath to Isaac. Then He confirmed it to Jacob for a statute, to Israel as an everlasting covenant, saying, 'To you I will give the land of Canaan as the portion [literally, "measuring line"] of your inheritance.'

"When they were only a few men in number, very few, and strangers in it. And they wandered about from nation to nation, from one kingdom to another people. He permitted no man to oppress them, and He reproved kings for their sakes: 'Do not touch My anointed ones, and do My prophets no harm.' " (Ps.105:6-15)

For two different reasons, all the children of Israel did not enjoy the land promised to them. Some failed to enjoy it because of their unfaithfulness to God. God told Moses, "None of the men who came up from Egypt, from twenty years old and upward, shall see the land which I swore to Abraham, to Isaac and to Jacob; for they did not follow Me fully, except Caleb the son of Jephunneh the Kenizzite and Joshua the son of Nun, for they have followed the Lord fully." (Num.32:11-12)

After the children of Israel had initially entered the land, they were not generally faithful to God. Prolonged infidelity over centuries caused God to exile the people from the land.

Some did not enjoy the land for another reason. Like Abraham, they were strangers and sojourners. We are told about Abraham that when "Sarah died in Kiriath-arba (that is, Hebron) in the land of Canaan; and Abraham went in to mourn for Sarah and to weep for her. Then Abraham rose from before his dead, and spoke to the sons of Heth, saying, 'I am a stranger and a sojourner among you; give me a possession of a grave among you, that I may bury my dead out of my sight.' " (Gen.23:2-4)

God had promised the land of Canaan to Abraham. Abraham was living in the promised land, but he was living in it as a stranger and a sojourner. It was not yet the time for him to possess his inheritance. He even had to purchase a small portion of the land of his inheritance in order to bury his wife.

Stephen reminded the Sanhedrin, "And He [God] gave him [Abraham] no inheritance in it, not even a foot of ground; and yet, even when he had no child, He promised that He would give it to him as a possession, and to his offspring after him." (Acts 7:5)

The Lord admonishes us, "Listen to me, you who pursue righteousness, who seek the Lord: Look to the rock from which you were hewn, and to the quarry from which you were dug. Look to Abraham your father..." (Is.51:1-2) For that reason, it is important to understand what the Bible says to the children of Abraham about "the stranger," the one who doesn't belong. All his days, Abraham was a stranger in the land.

"By faith Abraham, when he was called, obeyed by going out to a place which he was to receive for an inheritance; and he went out, not knowing where he was going. By faith he lived as an alien in the land of promise, as in a foreign land, dwelling in tents with Isaac and Jacob, fellow-heirs of the same promise...All these died in faith, without receiving the promises, but having seen them and having welcomed them from a distance, and having confessed that they were strangers and exiles on the earth." (Heb.11:8-9,13)

Jacob was leaving Canaan to go to his uncle Laban to find a wife. Isaac blessed him, saying, "And may God Almighty bless you and make you fruitful and multiply you, that you may become a company of peoples. May He also give you the blessing of Abraham, to you and to your seed with you; that you may possess the land of your sojournings, which God gave to Abraham." (Gen.28:4)

About ninety years later in the land of Egypt, "Joseph brought his father Jacob and presented him to Pharaoh; and Jacob blessed Pharaoh. And Pharaoh said to Jacob, 'How many years have you lived?' So Jacob said to Pharaoh, 'The years of my sojourning are one hundred and thirty; few and unpleasant have been the years of my life, nor have they attained the years that my fathers lived during the days of their sojourning.' " (Gen.47:7-9)

Abraham, Isaac, and Jacob did not, in their lifetimes, inherit what God promised to them. One day they will, because God is faithful and true. Even David, while he was king over all Israel, said, "Hear my prayer, O Lord, and give ear to my cry; do not be silent at my tears; for I am a stranger with Thee, a sojourner like all my fathers." (Ps.39:12) He knew that the kingdom he then had was still not the home that God had for him.

When David was turning the kingdom over to Solomon, he and the people provided an abundance of silver, gold, and other materials for the building of the Temple. David prayed, "But who am I and who are my people that we should be able to offer as generously as this? For all things come from Thee, and from Thy hand we have given Thee. For we are sojourners before Thee, and tenants, as all our fathers were..." (1 Chr.29:14-15)

Before all Israel entered the land of Canaan, God had told them, "The land, moreover, shall not be sold permanently, for the land is Mine; for you are aliens and sojourners with Me." (Lev.25:23) The writer of Psalm 119 prayed, "I am a stranger in the earth; Do not hide Thy commandments from me....Thy statutes are my songs in the house of my pilgrimage." (Ps.119:19,54)

In this age, the children of Abraham are pilgrims and strangers. They will not find here what they seek. Peter wrote, "Beloved, I urge you as aliens and strangers to abstain from fleshly lusts, which wage war against the soul." (1 Pet.2:11)

Therefore the children of Abraham are to make certain that they do not abuse any strangers in their midst. "And you shall not wrong a stranger or oppress him, for you were strangers in the land of Egypt." (Ex.22:21) "There is to be one law and one ordinance for you and for the alien who sojourns with you." (Num.15:16)

"When a stranger resides with you in your land, you shall not do him wrong. The stranger who resides with you shall be to you as the native among you, and you shall love him as yourself; for you were aliens in the land of Egypt: I am the Lord your God." (Lev.19:33-34)

The letter to the Hebrews reminds the children of Abraham, "Do not neglect to show hospitality to strangers, for by this some have entertained angels without knowing it." (Heb.13:2) All the children of Abraham are to show kindness to strangers, because they know what it is to be a stranger, even in the land of their inheritance.

9

ISRAEL'S SIN AND GOD'S FAITHFULNESS

From its beginning, the history of the Jewish people, the children of Israel, is one of failure. They failed to fulfill God's purpose, just as the Gentiles before them did. The Gentiles failed just as the children of Adam did before them.

During her history, Israel rejected God's Redeemer (Moses, Ex.5:21; 16:3, etc.), His provision (manna, Num.11:5,6), His land (Canaan, Num.13:31-14:10), His King (the Lord Himself, 1Sam.8:7,8), His Covenant (e.g. Neh.9:34-35), and His messengers (e.g.Dan.9:6). Yet despite all this, the Lord remained faithful.

The children of Israel wanted leeks and onions rather than the Promised Land. They turned away from the Lord to live for their own purposes. In reviewing their history, God said through Jeremiah, "Since the day that your fathers came out of the land of Egypt until this day, I have sent you all My servants the prophets, daily rising early and sending them. Yet they did not listen to Me or incline their ear, but stiffened their neck; they did evil more than their fathers." (Jer.7:25,26)

In the wilderness, Aaron yielded to the people and made them a golden calf. "And the Lord said to Moses, 'I have seen this people, and behold, they are a stiff-necked people. Now then let Me alone, that My anger may burn against them, and I will make of you a great nation.' " (Ex.32:9,10)

God would still have been faithful to His promise to Abraham, Isaac, and Jacob, if He had destroyed all their descendants except Moses, and then created a new people from Moses. Most people would have accepted God's offer, but Moses did not. Moses, like God, loved Israel.

So Moses pleaded, 'Why should the Egyptians boast that You could bring them out, but then had to destroy them? Remember your promise to Abraham, Isaac, and Jacob to multiply their descendants as the stars of the heavens, and to give them the land You prepared for them.' (cf. Ex.32:11-13; Num.14:13-19) He was not seeking or willing to have a name and inheritance for himself at Israel's expense.

After rebuking Israel for the sin of rejecting the Lord as King, Samuel told them, "For the Lord will not abandon His people on account of His great name, because the Lord has been pleased to make you a people for Himself. Moreover, as for me, far be it from me that I should sin against the Lord by ceasing to pray for you; but I will instruct you in the good and right way." (1Sam. 12:19-20, 22-23) Samuel did not gloss over Israel's sin— he publicly rebuked it—but because Samuel was a servant of the Lord, he shared the Lord's faithfulness to Israel.

God had sent the northern kingdom of Israel into captivity for the infidelity of the people. "And I saw that for all the adulteries of faithless Israel, I had sent her away and given her a writ of divorce, yet her treacherous sister Judah did not fear; but she went and was a harlot also." (Jer.3:8)

God said that He "divorced" Israel, but continued on to say, "'If you will return, O Israel,' declares the Lord, 'Return to Me. And if you will remove your detested things from My presence, and will not waver, and you will swear, "*As the Lord lives*," in truth, in justice, and in righteousness; then the Gentiles will bless themselves in Him, and in Him they will glory.' " (Jer.4:1-2)

Throughout the book of Hosea the Lord compares Israel to an unfaithful wife who must be judged and sent away. But, "How can I give you up, O Ephraim? How can I surrender you, O Israel? How can I make you like Admah? How can I treat you like Zeboiim? [cf. Dt.29:23] My heart is turned over within Me, all my compassions are kindled...I will heal their apostasy, I will love them freely, for My anger has turned away from them. I will be like the dew to Israel; He will blossom like the lily, and he will take root like Lebanon." (Hos.11:8; 14:4-5)

God declared that there would be distress and exile because of the infidelity of Jacob's children, but went on to promise restoration. "'And fear not, O Jacob My Servant,' declares the Lord, 'And do not be dismayed, O Israel; for behold, I will save you from afar, and your seed from the land of their captivity. And Jacob shall return, and shall be quiet and at ease, and no one shall make him afraid. For I am with you,' declares the Lord, 'to save you. For I will destroy completely all the nations where I have scattered you, only I will not destroy you completely. But I will chasten you justly, and will by no means leave you unpunished.' " (Jer.30:10-11) The judgment is what God's people deserved, the redemption and restoration are the fruit of His love and grace.

It is even as Paul wrote to Timothy, "If we are faithless, He remains faithful; for He cannot deny Himself." (2 Tim.2:13) God was the same in the days of Moses, Samuel, and Ezekiel as He was in the days of Paul. He never changes. This is Israel's security. "For I, the Lord, do not change; therefore you, O sons of Jacob, are not consumed." (Mal.3:6) For as long as God does not change, the sons of Jacob will endure.

"For neither Israel nor Judah has been widowed [literal] by his God, the Lord of hosts, although their land is full of guilt before the Holy One of Israel." (Jer.51:5) The comfort of the New Covenant Scriptures that was written to the Hebrews—"He Himself has said, 'I will never desert you, nor will I ever forsake you,' " (Heb.13:5)—is simply a reminder of God's promise to Israel before they entered the Promised Land. (Dt.31:6,8) The promise is given in the midst of Moses' prophecy of Israel's unfaithfulness, God's judgment upon it, and then her eventual restoration. (Dt.28-32)

Psalm 106 reviews Israel's history of sin and unfaithfulness. It describes the anger of the Lord toward His people, and His judgments upon them. But then it concludes: "Nevertheless He looked upon their distress, when He heard their cry; and He remembered His covenant for their sake, and relented according to the greatness of His lovingkindness. He also made them objects of compassion in the presence of all their captives.

"Save us, O Lord our God, and gather us from among the Gentiles, to give thanks to Thy holy name, and glory in Thy holy name, and glory in Thy praise. Blessed be the Lord, the God of Israel, from everlasting even to everlasting. And let all the people say, 'Amen.' Praise the Lord." (Ps.106:44-48)

The sin of Adam was great, *nevertheless*... The sin of Adam's children was great, *nevertheless*... The sin of the Gentiles was great, *nevertheless*... The sin of Israel was great, *nevertheless*... Man sins, but *nevertheless* God, in judgment, remembers mercy.

10

THE REMNANT

The Bible says of the time of Noah, "...and only Noah was left [יִשָּׁאֶר], and the ones who were with him in the ark." (Gen.7:23) Though the children of Adam as a whole rebelled against the Lord, God kept, by His grace, a small remnant [שְׁאָר] for Himself. If the Lord had not kept that small remnant for Himself, all the children of Adam would have perished.

The same is true of the Jewish people. As Isaiah prophesied, "Unless the Lord of hosts had left us a few survivors, we would be like Sodom, we would be like Gomorrah." (Is.1:9) God completely destroyed the cities of Sodom and Gomorrah.

Abraham's nephew Lot had gone to live in Sodom. He didn't belong there, but he chose to live there. When the two angels came to Sodom and stayed with Lot, the men of the city surrounded the house. When Lot would not deliver his angelic guests up to their degrading passion, "...they said, 'This one came in to sojourn, and already he is acting like a judge; now we will treat you worse than them.' So they pressed hard against Lot and came near to break the door." (Gen.19:9)

God saved Lot, his wife, and his daughters out of Sodom, but then He completely destroyed Sodom and Gomorrah. Isaiah knew that if it had not been for God's grace in keeping a remnant for Himself, all Israel would have been as completely destroyed as Sodom and Gomorrah were. But even as "Noah found grace in the eyes of the Lord," so God poured out His grace upon a remnant in Israel.

There were always some, a few, who chose to be faithful to God. Sometimes it was a very small number. Joshua and Caleb were faithful to God. They believed He could bring them into Canaan, while the other ten spies and the rest of the people were unfaithful and unbelieving. They were part of a faithful remnant.

Even so, Joshua and Caleb had to spend forty years in the wilderness before they could go into the Promised Land with the new generation of Israel. They were part of a people, and the promise was made to a people. So, apart from that people, they could not have their full inheritance.

Isaiah prophesied of the time of Messiah, saying, "Then it will come about in that day that the Gentiles will resort to the root of Jesse, who will stand as a signal for the peoples; and His resting place will be glorious. Then it will happen on that day that the Lord will again recover the second time with His hand the **remnant** of His people, who will remain, from Assyria, Egypt, Pathros, Cush, Elam, Shinar, Hamath, and from the islands of the sea. And He will lift up a standard for the Gentiles and will assemble the banished ones of Israel, and will gather the dispersed of Judah from the four corners of the earth." (Is.11:10-12)

Gentiles will come to Messiah. So will the remnant of Israel. "The banished ones of Israel" and "the dispersed of Judah" will be gathered back "from the four corners of the earth."

That is why the Holy One of Israel says, "Now it will come about in that day that the **remnant** of Israel, and those of the house of Jacob who have escaped, will never again rely on the one who struck them, but will truly rely on the Lord, the Holy One of Israel. A **remnant** will return, the **remnant** of Jacob, to the mighty God. For though your people, O Israel, may be like the sand of the sea, only a **remnant** within them will return; a destruction is determined, overflowing with righteousness." (Is.10:20-22)

For those who return in repentance, there will be restoration. For those who do not, there will be destruction. "To return to the Lord" means "to repent."

In Isaiah, the Lord calls to those who desire restoration: "Listen to Me, you who pursue righteousness, who seek the Lord: Look to the rock from which you were hewn, and to the quarry from which you were dug. Look to Abraham your father, and to Sarah who gave birth to you in pain; when he was one I called him, then I blessed him and multiplied him." (Is.51:1-2)

The children of Abraham are characterized as those who pursue righteousness and seek the Lord. Those who do not, even if they are physically descended from Abraham, as Ishmael was, are not fully his children. Physical descent alone is not sufficient

Isaiah prophesied so extensively about Messiah and about His kingdom that some people speak of "the gospel of Isaiah." Inasmuch as God caused Isaiah to prophesy so extensively about Messiah and His kingdom, He also caused him to prophesy extensively about the remnant of Israel and its return to the land and to the Lord. The two are related.

Isaiah said, "Bind up the testimony, seal the law among my disciples. And I will wait for the Lord who is hiding His face from the house of Jacob; I will even look eagerly for Him. Behold, I and the children whom the Lord has given me are for signs and wonders in Israel from the Lord of hosts, who dwells on Mount Zion." (Is.8:16-18)

Isaiah's children were signs from the Lord to Israel. That is why the Lord named one of Isaiah's sons "She'ar-yashuv" [שאר ישוב]. (Is.7:3) "Isaiah" [ישעיהו] means "the Lord is salvation." "She'ar-yashuv" means "a remnant will return" — a sign of God's grace and faithfulness towards Israel.

Other prophets also spoke about the remnant. The Lord told Jeremiah about their return after exile. "Then I myself shall gather the **remnant** of My flock out of all the countries where I have driven them and shall bring them back to their pasture; and they will be fruitful and multiply." (Jer.23:3)

"For thus says the Lord, 'Sing aloud with gladness for Jacob, and shout among the chiefs of the Gentiles; Proclaim, give praise, and say, *O Lord, save Thy people, the* **remnant** *of Israel*. Behold, I am bringing them from the north country, and I will gather them from the remote parts of the earth, among them the blind and the lame, the woman with child and she who is in labor with child, together; a great company, they shall return here. With weeping they shall come, and by supplication I will lead them; I will make them walk by streams of waters, on a straight path in which they shall not stumble; for I am a father to Israel, and Ephraim is My first-born.' " (Jer.31:7-9)

Ezekiel said, "And the word of the Lord came to me saying, 'Son of Adam, set your face toward the mountains of Israel, and prophesy against them... And the slain will fall among you, and you will know that I am the Lord. However, I shall leave a **remnant**, for you will have those who escaped the sword among the Gentiles when you are scattered among the countries.' " (Ezek.6:1-2,8)

The Lord told Joel, "And it will come about that whoever calls on the name of the Lord will be delivered; For on Mount Zion and in Jerusalem there will be those who escape, as the Lord has said, even among the survivors whom the Lord calls." (Joel 2:32)

In unfaithfulness, Israel refused to be separate from the Gentiles [goyim], so God drove them into exile among the Gentiles [goyim]. Because of God's faithfulness, He promised to bring them back to their own land. As He told Micah, "I will surely assemble all of you, Jacob, I will surely gather the **remnant** of Israel. I will put them together like sheep in the fold; like a flock in the midst of its pasture they will be noisy with men. The breaker goes up before them; They break out, pass through the gate, and go out by it. So their king goes on before them, and the Lord at their head." (Mic.2:12-13)

God promised to "assemble all of Jacob," though they were unfaithful. He promised to gather "the remnant of Israel." He promised to make them into a flock that will be led by their shepherd and king, the Lord Himself.

Diagram 2 shows the faithful remnant within Israel, who are differentiated from their unfaithful brethren by the circumcision of the heart.

Gentiles   Gentiles

Gentiles

Gentiles

COVENANT SIGN

 Physical Circumcision

 Circumcision of the Heart

Diagram 2

STRANGERS IN THE CAMP

With the battle of Jericho, another part of the story begins to come into focus. Rahab knew that the purposes of God for and through Israel could not be defeated. So she hid the two spies and, after the destruction of the city, she and her household were joined to the people of Israel. From the perspective of her countrymen, had they survived, she would have been a traitor and a betrayer. But ultimately, life is only judged by God's standard. We are told in the New Covenant Scriptures that she married Salmon, and became an ancestress of the Messianic line. (Mt.1:5)

In the same way, under very different circumstances, Ruth joined herself to Naomi, a barren, hopeless, Jewish widow. Ruth made the decision to give her life to the people and the God of Israel. "Your people shall be my people, and your God, my God." (Ruth 1:16) She chose the unknown of a new people and a new land, and a walk with God. She was physically and spiritually joined to Israel. She later married Boaz, and also became an ancestress of the Messianic line.

God called Abraham out of the Gentiles [goyim]. He called Israel to be separate from them; not to make any covenant with them, nor to intermarry with them. Ruth and Rahab, though born Gentiles, chose, like Abraham, to leave their people and everything else behind to follow God. Because they made that choice, they were grafted into Israel.

Throughout the history of the Jewish people, there have been numerous Gentiles who have also chosen to be joined to them. There were the souls that Abraham and Sarah made. (Gen.12:5) There were the dedicated ones whom Abraham led out to rescue Lot. (Gen.14:14)

Moses led the Jewish people out of Egypt, "And a mixed multitude also went up with them..." (Ex.12:38) This mixed multitude was occasionally a source of murmuring, complaining, and trouble (Num.11:4), but then so were the sons of Israel with whom they went up. Neither had much to recommend them to God.

Before the people entered into Canaan, "the Lord commanded Moses to make [a covenant] with the sons of Israel in the land of Moab, besides the covenant which He had made with them at Horeb." (Dt.29:1) Moses told the people, "You stand today, all of you, before the Lord your God: your chiefs, your tribes, your elders and your officers, even all the men of Israel, your little ones, your wives, and the alien who is within your camps, from the one who chops your wood to the one who draws your water, that you may enter into the covenant with the Lord your God, and into His oath which the Lord your God is making with you today, in order that He may establish you today as His people and that He may be your God, just as He spoke to you and as He swore to your fathers, to Abraham, Isaac, and Jacob. Now not with you alone am I making this covenant and this oath, but both with those who stand here with us today in the presence of the Lord our God and with those who are not with us here today." (Dt.29:10-15)

Notice two things: 1) the covenant is also made with "the alien who is within your camps," i.e. the Gentiles who have joined themselves to Israel; and 2) the covenant is also made with "those who are not with us here today." Some individuals who did not belong to that time, that place, or that people, were included in the covenant.

The Gibeonites deceived Joshua and the leaders of Israel into thinking that they lived far away. "So the men of Israel took some of their provisions, and did not ask for the counsel of the Lord. And Joshua made peace with them and made a covenant with them, to let them live: and the leaders of the congregation swore an oath to them." (Josh.9:14-15)

When the deception was discovered, Joshua, the leaders, and the people were very angry with the Gibeonites, but chose to honor the covenant and the oath. "And the leaders said to them, 'Let them live.' So they became hewers of wood and drawers of water for the whole congregation, just as the leaders had spoken to them....Joshua made them that day hewers of wood and drawers of water for the congregation and for the altar of the Lord, to this day, in the place which He would choose." (Josh.9:21,27)

Inasmuch as the Lord commanded Moses to tell Israel that the covenant was with them and with "the alien who is within your camps, from the one who chops your wood to the one who draws your water," even "those who are not with us here today," we must conclude that the Gibeonites were included by the Lord God of Israel in the covenant. They had faith in Him. As they initially told Joshua, "Your servants have come from a very far country because of the fame of the Lord your God; for we have heard the report of Him and all that He did in Egypt, and all that He did to the two kings of the Amorites who were beyond the Jordan, to Sihon king of Heshbon and to the king of Bashan who was at Ashtaroth." (Josh.9:9-10)

Earlier, of course, Rahab and her family had joined Israel. "Rahab the harlot and her father's household and all she had, Joshua spared; and she has lived in the midst of Israel to this day, for she hid the messengers whom Joshua sent to spy out Jericho." (Josh.6:25) She chose the Jewish people and their God. "By faith Rahab the harlot did not perish along with those who were disobedient, after she had welcomed the spies in peace." (Heb.11:31)

Ruth made that same choice despite all reason and appearance. It is worth noting that she, like Rahab, was simply grafted into Israel, and glorified in Israel. She was still, however, "Ruth the Moabitess." (Ruth 4:5,10)

During the exile, in the time of Esther and Mordecai, the Jewish people were about to be annihilated by the hatred of Haman. God turned things around, preserved and prospered His people. Though there were great, numerous, and powerful enemies arrayed against them, many joined with the Jewish people for their defense. "The Jews established and made a custom for themselves, and for their descendants, and for all those who allied themselves with them, so that they should not fail to celebrate these two days according to their regulation, and according to their appointed time annually." (Est.9:27)

Many actually became proselytes. "And in each and every province, and in each and every city, wherever the king's commandment and his decree arrived there was gladness and joy for the Jews, a feast and a holiday. And many among the peoples of the land became Jews, for the dread of the Jews had fallen on them." (Est.8:17)

During the time of Nehemiah, many Gentiles also joined themselves to the Jewish people. They, however, did not join themselves to the Lord. They were a means of drawing Israel away from her God. God had forbidden that. "So it came about, that when they heard the law, they excluded all foreigners from Israel." (Neh.13:3)

What then is the position of the strangers who truthfully joined themselves to the Lord and to His people? Can they only be servants as the Gibeonites were? or can they expect to be honored as Ruth and Rahab were?

"Let not the foreigner who has joined himself to the Lord say, 'The Lord will surely separate me from His people.' Neither let the eunuch say, 'Behold, I am a dry tree.' For thus says the Lord, 'To the eunuchs who keep My sabbaths, and choose what pleases Me, and hold fast My covenant, to them I will give in My house and within My walls a memorial, and a name better than that of sons and daughters; I will give them an everlasting name which will not be cut off.

" 'Also the foreigners who join themselves to the Lord, to minister to Him, and to love the name of the Lord, to be His servants, every one who keeps from profaning the sabbath, and holds fast My covenant; even those I will bring to My holy mountain, and make them joyful in My house of prayer. Their burnt offerings and their sacrifices will be acceptable on My altar; for My house will be called a house of prayer for all the peoples.' The Lord God, who gathers the dispersed of Israel, declares, 'Yet others I will gather to them, to those already gathered.' " (Is.56:3-8)

Will the Gentiles who have joined themselves to the Lord be separate from His people? The God of Israel says, 'No. They will be part of My household, My family.' Will the Gentiles who join themselves to the Lord be excluded from the holy place and service of the Lord? God says, 'No. They will worship Me in My house, along with those of the dispersed of Israel whom I have gathered. They will be gathered to the remnant of Israel.'

"In the last days, the mountain of the house of the Lord will be established as the chief of the mountains, and will be raised above the hills: and all the goyim will stream to it. And many peoples will come and say, 'Come, let us go up to the mountain of the Lord, to the house of the God of Jacob; that He may teach us concerning His ways, and that we may walk in His paths, for the law [Torah, תרה, teaching] will go forth from Zion, and the word of the Lord from Jerusalem.' And He will judge between the goyim, and will render decisions for many peoples; and they will hammer their swords into plowshares, nation will not lift up sword against nation, and never again will they learn war." (Is.2:2-3; Mic.4:1-3)

God gave Ezekiel visions of a time to come when living water would flow out of Jerusalem. As this living water goes out of Israel, it brings healing. (Ezek.47:1-12) "And by the river on its bank, on one side and on the other, will grow all kinds of trees for food. Their leaves will not wither, and their fruit will not fail. They will bear every month because their water flows from the sanctuary, and their fruit will be for food and their leaves for healing." (v.12) God later revealed to the Apostle John the same vision. (Rev.22:1-5)

The Lord then instructed Ezekiel, "'So you shall divide this land among yourselves according to the tribes of Israel. And it will come about that you shall divide it by lot for an inheritance among yourselves and among the aliens who stay in your midst, who bring forth sons in your midst. And they shall be to you as the native-born among the sons of Israel; they shall be allotted an inheritance with you among the tribes of Israel. And it will come about that in the tribe with which the alien stays, there you shall give him his inheritance,' declares the Lord." (Ezek.47:21-23)

So, there are these two contrasting images of the Gentiles. The predominant image that is presented in Tanakh is epitomized in Psalm 2:1-2: "Why are the Gentiles in an uproar, and the peoples devising a vain thing? The kings of the earth take their stand, and the rulers take counsel together against the Lord and against His Anointed."

Yet there are numerous scriptures that indicate that God will bring the Gentiles unto Himself. In Romans 15:8-12, Paul cites four such scriptures. "For I say that Messiah has become a servant to the circumcision on behalf of the truth of God to confirm the promises given to the fathers, and for the Gentiles [goyim] to glorify God for His mercy; as it is written, 'Therefore I will give praise to Thee among the Gentiles [goyim], and I will sing to Thy Name.' And again he says, 'Rejoice, O Gentiles [goyim], with His people.' And again, 'Praise the Lord all you Gentiles [goyim], and let all the peoples praise Him.' And again Isaiah says, 'There shall come the root of Jesse, and He who arises to rule over the Gentiles [goyim]; in Him shall the Gentiles [goyim] hope.' " (Ps.18:49; Dt.32:43; Ps.117:1; Is.11:10)

In the beginning, God created Man male and female, but He purposed for them to become one. God created Gentile and Jew, but He also purposed for them to become one. Now we will begin to look at how He has worked out that purpose for Gentile and Jew.

SECTION B:
FULFILLING THE PROMISE

12

THE KING OF THE JEWS

There are hundreds of prophecies in the Law, the Writings, and the Prophets that speak of Messiah. These prophecies tell of who He is, what He will do, where He is to be born, how He will die, etc. A major focus of these prophecies is the role of Messiah as the King of the Jews. It is, in fact, the primary way in which the prophets speak of Messiah.

Let's look briefly at three well-known prophecies—Is.9:6,7; Jer.23:5,6; Mic.5:2—which are quoted in part or in whole in the New Covenant scriptures. Then we will see that there is no marked difference as we go through the rest of the New Covenant Scriptures from beginning to end. These scriptures were recognized by the ancient rabbis as referring to Messiah. The Talmud remarks that, "All the prophets prophesied not but of the days of the Messiah."[1]

Isaiah voiced the prophetic hope of Israel: "For a child will be born to us, a son will be given to us; and the government will rest on His shoulders; and His name will be called Wonderful Counselor, Mighty God, Eternal Father, Prince of Peace. There will be no end to the increase of His government or of peace, on the throne of David and over his kingdom, to establish it and to uphold it with justice and righteousness from then on and forevermore. The zeal of the Lord of hosts will accomplish this." (Is.9:6-7)

It is "to us," i.e. to Israel, that a child will be born and a son will be given. Obviously, the God of Israel is the One who will give this son to His people. This child will be a ruler in Israel. It is on David's throne, that of the King of Israel, that he will sit. It is over David's kingdom that Messiah reigns. It is David's kingdom that Messiah establishes and upholds. Messiah, whom God will give to Israel, is David's son. (Isaiah began to prophesy in the reign of Uzziah, a tenth generation descendant of David.)

This child will be a unique individual, not simply a normal man. His names tell us that. He is characterized by these names —"Wonderful Counselor, Mighty God, Eternal Father, Prince of Peace."

His reign will not be short —"There will be no end to the increase of His government." His reign will never end, not in time, not in space. His eternal reign will be characterized by peace, justice, and righteousness.

That is how the reign of God Himself is characterized. In fact, that is the foundation of His kingdom. "Righteousness and justice are the foundation of Thy throne; lovingkindness and truth go before Thee. How blessed are the people who know the joyful sound! O Lord, they walk in the light of Thy countenance." (Ps.89:14-15)

Jeremiah prophesied, "'Behold, the days are coming,' declares the Lord, 'when I shall raise up for David a righteous Branch; and He will reign as king and act wisely and do justice and righteousness in the land. In His days Judah will be saved, and Israel will dwell securely; and this is His name by which He will be called, *"The Lord our righteousness."* '" (Jer.23:5,6)

Jeremiah was prophesying just before the Babylonians destroyed Jerusalem and put an end to the Davidic kings. The Lord was promising that He would yet raise up a Branch, i.e. a descendant, of David, the root, to be king. He will rule, as David did, over a united kingdom — "Judah will be saved, and Israel will dwell securely." This Son of David is the salvation and security of the Jewish people.

Messiah will act wisely — more wisely than Solomon did — and will do justice and righteousness in the land of Israel. He will be a unique individual, not simply a normal man, for His people will know him as *"The Lord our righteousness."* Under His reign, they will not trust in their own righteousness. They will be made righteous in the Lord.

Micah prophesied, "But as for you, Bethlehem Ephratah, too little to be among the clans of Judah, from you One will go forth for Me to be ruler in Israel. His goings forth are from long ago, from the days of eternity." (Mic.5:2)

God sends the Messiah to rule for Him in Israel. Messiah comes from the kingly tribe of Judah, and from Bethlehem, King David's home town. Bethlehem is the town to which Naomi returned with Ruth at the time of the harvest.

He will be a unique individual, not simply a normal man, for "His goings forth are from long ago, from the days of eternity." Though there will be a time when Messiah goes forth from Bethlehem, He has always been. He comes from eternity to Bethlehem.

The first verse of the New Covenant Scriptures is "The book of the genealogy [γενεσεως] of Jesus the Messiah, the son of David, the son of Abraham." (Mt.1:1) David is not, immediately, the son of Abraham, nor is Jesus, immediately the son of David. This is God's way of stressing not only the physical descent, but also the progression of His work in the earth.

The verse could be restated: 'The family lineage of Jesus the Messiah, heir of David, King of Israel, who came forth from Abraham, the father of the Jewish people.' The New Covenant Scriptures begin with this genealogy because it is indispensable. It is not out of place. Without this Jewish genealogy, there is no Messiah, there is no gospel. That is why the Lord put it first.

The Ethiopian eunuch was reading a Messianic prophecy of Isaiah when Philip came to his chariot. "Now the passage of Scripture which he was reading was this: 'He was led as a sheep to slaughter; and as a lamb before its shearer is silent, so He does not open His mouth. In humiliation His judgment was taken away; who shall relate His generation [γενεαν]? For His life is removed from the earth.' " (Acts 8:32-33, quoting the Septuagint)

The question of the prophecy is essentially: Who will declare His genealogy, γενεα–λογια, the word of His family lineage? The question is asked because the answer has significance. God created the Jewish people for His redemptive purposes, which are not yet finished in the earth. What He promised, He either has done or will do. "...For the spirit of prophecy is the testimony of Jesus." (Rev.19:10) The Jewish genealogy is indispensable to the gospel.

God sent the angel Gabriel "to a virgin engaged to a man whose name was Joseph, of the descendents of David; and the virgin's name was Miriam....And the angel said to her, 'Do not be afraid, Miriam; for you have found favor with God. And behold, you will conceive in your womb, and bear a son, and you shall name Him Jesus. He will be great, and will be called the Son of the Most High; and the Lord God will give Him the throne of His father David; and He will reign over the house of Jacob forever; and His kingdom will have no end.' " (Lk.1:27,30-33)

(The Hebrew name is actually ישוע/Yeshua, short for יהושע/Yehoshua, i.e. Joshua. The Greek, which Gabriel was not speaking, is Ιησουν/Iesous.)

The parallel to Isaiah 9:6-7 is apparent — "There will be no end to the increase of His government or of peace, on the throne of David and over his kingdom." Jesus comes to receive the throne of His father David, King of Israel, and to reign over the house of Jacob, i.e. the Jewish people, forever.

When John, the forerunner of the Lord was born, "his father Zachariah was filled with the Holy Spirit, and prophesied, saying; 'Blessed be the Lord God of Israel, for He has visited us and accomplished redemption for His people, and has raised up a horn of salvation for us in the house of David his servant, as He spoke by the mouth of His holy prophets from of old, salvation from our enemies, and from the hand of all who hate us; to show mercy toward our fathers, and to remember His holy covenant, the oath which He swore to Abraham our father, to grant us that we being delivered from the hand of our enemies might serve Him without fear in holiness and righteousness before Him all our days.' " (Lk.1:67-75)

What the Holy Spirit said through Zachariah parallels what He said through Jeremiah. Messiah is the king descended from David who will bring salvation, security, and righteousness to Israel. God was about to do what He had promised to David and to Abraham.

The Gentile wise men came to Jerusalem looking for the Messiah, but not knowing His Name. Their question was in accord with all that they did know about Him. "Where is He who has been born King of the Jews? For we saw His star in the East, and have come to worship Him." (Mt.2:2) They came to worship the King of the Jews.

Their question and their purpose made Herod very nervous. "And gathering together all the chief priests and scribes of the people, he began to inquire of them where the Messiah was to be born. And they said to him, 'In Bethlehem of Judea; for so it has been written by the prophet, *And you Bethlehem, land of Judah; are by no means least among the leaders of Judah; for out of you shall come forth a ruler, who will shepherd My people Israel.'* " (Mt.2:4-6)

Herod's inquiry as to where the Messiah was to be born showed that he understood who this King of the Jews was. The chief priests and scribes responded by quoting Micah 5:2. Jesus is the shepherd of Israel, who comes forth from Bethlehem to be a ruler over Israel.

On numerous occasions, the gospels record that Jesus openly responded to and accepted worship as "the Son of David," i.e. Messiah the King. For example, Bartimaeus, a blind beggar, "began to cry out and say, 'Jesus, Son of David, have mercy on me!'...and Jesus said to him, 'Go your way; your faith has saved you.' " (Mk.10:47-52)

Matthew records that the entry of Jesus into Jerusalem on a donkey was in fulfillment of the prophecy in Zechariah: "Say to the daughter of Zion, 'Behold your king is coming to you gentle, and mounted on a donkey even on a colt, the foal of a beast of burden.' " (Mt.21:4,5)

The Rabbinic identification of this verse with the Messianic King of Israel was so strong that it was said in the Talmud, "If anyone sees a donkey in his dreams, he will see salvation." [2] Clearly, Matthew intended to identify Jesus as Israel's King. Clearly, that was the purpose of God.

"And the multitudes going before Him, and those who followed after were crying out, 'Hosanna to the Son of David!' " "Blessed is he who comes in the name of the Lord; Blessed is the coming kingdom of our father David; Hosanna in the highest!" (Mt.21:9; Mk.11:9-10)

The multitudes were rejoicing in, and receiving, Messiah, David's Son. They knew that the kingdom of David would come with him. Their understanding was correct.

Jesus did not rebuke them or refuse to receive their worship. "And some of the Pharisees in the multitude said to Him, 'Teacher, rebuke Your disciples.' And He answered and said, 'I tell you, if these become silent, the stones will cry out!' " (Lk.19:39-40)

When Jesus was arrested and brought before Pilate, "Pilate asked Him saying, 'Are you the King of the Jews?' and He answered him and said, 'It is as you say.' " (Lk.23:3) Pilate went out and asked the mob, "Shall I release for you the King of the Jews?" (Jn.18:39)

"Then Pilate therefore took Jesus, and scourged Him. And the soldiers wove a crown of thorns and put it on His head, and arrayed Him in a purple robe; and they began to come up to him, and say, 'Hail, King of the Jews!' and to give Him blows in the face." (Jn.19:1-3) The mockery of the Roman soldiers showed how they despised the Jews and their king. It was political more than religious.

Pilate brought out a scourged, bleeding man, "And he said to the Jews, 'Behold your King!' They therefore cried out, 'Away with Him, away with Him, crucify Him!' Pilate said to them, 'Shall I crucify your King?' The chief priests answered, 'We have no king but Caesar.' " (Jn.19:14-15)

Like every other criminal, Jesus was crucified with His name and His crime on His cross, so that everyone could be warned by who He was and what He had done. It was written in Hebrew, in Latin, and in Greek. All four of the gospels record it: "Jesus King of the Jews." (Mt.27:37; Mk.15:26; Lk.23:38; Jn.19:19) There are not many things that are recorded in all four of the gospels.

"And so the chief priests of the Jews were saying to Pilate, 'Do not write, *"The King of the Jews"*; but that *He said, I am King of the Jews.*' " (Jn.19:21) The chief priests were not willing to recognize Jesus as the King of the Jews. They did not want a public proclamation of their own guilt in putting Israel's Hope to death.

They also did not want the crucifixion of Jesus to arouse popular sympathy. Everyone recognized the title, "King of the Jews," as promising Messianic deliverance from all oppression. Given the hostility of the people toward Roman occupation, the "crime" and the judgment upon it might cause trouble.

Throughout the gospels, Jesus is identified by the Messianic prophecies and titles that designate the King of the Jews. That designation is inseparable from the gospel itself. Thousands of years of anticipation, a life lived in fulfillment of those prophecies, the perfectly prepared plan of salvation — "This was done that it might be fulfilled" — all of this is an integral part of the gospel. The King of the Jews was crucified for the sins of the world.

FOOTNOTES

1. *The Babylonian Talmud*, edited by Isadore Epstein, The Soncino Press, London, 1938, Sanhedrin 99a
2. ibid, Berakhot 56b

13

THE NEW COVENANT

" 'Behold, days are coming,' declares the Lord, 'when I will make a new covenant with the house of Israel and with the house of Judah, not like the covenant which I made with their fathers in the day I took them by the hand to bring them out of the land of Egypt, My covenant which they broke, although I was a husband to them,' declares the Lord.

" 'But this is the covenant which I will make with the house of Israel after those days,' declares the Lord, 'I will put My law within them, and on their heart I will write it; and I will be their God, and they shall be My people. And they shall not teach again, each man his neighbor, saying, "*Know the Lord*," for they shall all know Me, from the least of them to the greatest of them,' declares the Lord, 'for I will forgive their iniquity, and their sin I will remember no more.'

"Thus says the Lord, who gives the sun for light by day, and the fixed order of the moon and the stars for light by night, who stirs up the sea so that its waves roar; the Lord of Hosts is His name: 'If this fixed order departs from before Me,' declares the Lord, 'then the offspring of Israel also shall cease from being a nation before Me for ever.' Thus says the Lord, 'If the heavens above can be measured, and the foundations of the earth searched out below, then I will also cast off all the offspring of Israel for all that they have done,' declares the Lord." (Jer.31:31-37)

Eight times in this brief passage of seven verses, the text of the New Covenant is confirmed as the direct, explicit word of the Lord. Six times we are told that these words are trustworthy because so "declares the Lord." Twice we are admonished, "Thus says the Lord." God wants us to know that every word is important, and that every word will be fulfilled.

The text — God's Words — makes it very clear that a new covenant is promised to the Jewish people. The text also makes it clear that nothing will prevent God from establishing this new covenant which He has promised to the Jewish people. The words themselves cannot be understood in any other way.

God gave the promise of the New Covenant during some very dark days in the history of the Jewish people. Destruction, captivity, and exile had already overtaken those living in the northern kingdom of Israel. The same judgment had now come to those living in the southern kingdom of Judah.

The unfaithfulness of the people of Israel had brought judgment from the God of Israel. In their own land, they had chosen to follow the idolatrous ways of the Gentiles. So God had removed them from their land to go and live among the Gentiles. God had warned His people before they even entered the land that He would do that. (cf. Lev.26 & Dt.28)

Through the destruction of Jerusalem and the Temple, and through the exile among the Gentiles, God was bringing the ultimate judgment upon the Jewish people as a whole for breaking the Covenant of the Law. As Daniel prayed in exile: "Indeed all Israel has transgressed Thy law and turned aside, not obeying Thy voice; so the curse has been poured out on us, along with the oath which is written in the law of Moses the servant of God, for we have sinned against Him.

"Thus He has confirmed His words which He had spoken against us and against our rulers who ruled us, to bring on us great calamity; for under the whole heaven there has not been done anything like what was done to Jerusalem. As it is written in the law of Moses, all this calamity has come on us..." (Dan.9:11-13)

While that calamity, that ultimate judgment, was falling upon the whole house of Israel, God promised that He would yet establish a new covenant. This new covenant would bring the Jewish people into right relationship with their God. Since God makes it clear that He will fulfill this promise, its terms are very important.

To begin with, the New Covenant is made by God with "the house of Israel" and the "house of Judah." The promise is given in the midst of judgment on those "houses." It promises restoration. " 'For, behold, days are coming,' declares the Lord, 'when I will restore the fortunes of My people Israel and Judah.' The Lord says, 'I will also bring them back to the land that I gave to their forefathers, and they shall possess it.' " (Jer.30:3)

God made a covenant "with their fathers in the day I took them by the hand to bring them out of the land of Egypt." The people that God brought out of Egypt are the "fathers" of those with whom God makes the New Covenant. They are the children of Israel, the Jewish people.

It is necessary here to ask some simple questions, because of the pivotal theological importance of understanding this text, and because of the traditional ways in which the text has been ignored. To what is God referring when He says, "the covenant which I made"? He is referring to the Covenant of the Law which He made with all Israel at Sinai.

Did the fathers of the Jewish people keep the Covenant of the Law? No, that is why God speaks of "My covenant which they broke." Was God unfaithful to Israel? No, He says, "I was a husband to them."

God did not forsake His people. He promised to make the New Covenant with the same people whose fathers broke the Old Covenant. Who is that? There is only one possible answer. The Jewish people.

The Lord told Jeremiah, "...the house of Israel and the house of Judah have broken My covenant which I made with their fathers." (Jer.11:10) Nevertheless, God promises them a future restoration: "At that time they shall call Jerusalem 'The Throne of the Lord,' and all the Gentiles will be gathered to it, to Jerusalem, for the name of the Lord; nor shall they walk anymore after the stubbornness of their evil heart. In those days the house of Judah will walk with the house of Israel, and they will come together from the land of the north to the land that I gave to your fathers as an inheritance." (Jer.3:17,18)

The New Covenant is a declaration of God's faithfulness despite Israel's unfaithfulness. It brings restoration — restoration to the land and to the Lord. It creates a holy people for a holy God.

" 'I will put My law within them, and on their heart I will write it; and I will be their God, and they shall be My people. And they shall not teach again, each man his neighbor, saying, *Know the Lord,*" for they shall all know Me, from the least of them to the greatest of them,' declares the Lord, 'for I will forgive their iniquity, and their sin I will remember no more.' "

It is a covenant that is for the benefit and well-being of individual Jews, but the covenant itself is not made with individuals. It is a corporate covenant. It is made with the house of Israel and the house of Judah.

How sure is God's promise to the Jewish people? The Lord directly challenges any who think that He might "cast off all the offspring of Israel for all that they have done." First, He identifies Himself as the Creator and Controller of all things — "Thus says the Lord, who gives the sun for light by day, and the statutes of the moon and the stars for light by night, who stirs up the sea so that its waves roar."

Then He declares that His faithfulness to Israel is as sure as the "statutes" of Creation and the covenant that He made with Noah — "While the earth remains, seedtime and harvest, and cold and heat, and summer and winter, and day and night shall not cease." (Gen.8:22) It is even surer than that. Those who want to see God "cast off all the offspring of Israel for all that they have done" must measure the heavens and search out the foundations of the earth. Not an easy task, to be sure. God is declaring His eternal faithfulness to Israel —"the offspring of Israel" will not "cease from being a nation before Me forever."

The Lord follows this declaration with specific promises concerning physical Jerusalem. (cf. verses 38-40) Through the fulfillment of the New Covenant, God will restore the Jewish people to the land of Israel and to Himself. The promise is as sure as God Himself.

Indeed, more than any other designation, the Lord refers to Himself as "the God of Israel." He calls Himself that hundreds of times throughout the Bible. Nor should we forget that He also calls Himself, "Shepherd of Israel," "Rock of Israel," "Father to Israel," "Stone of Israel," "King of Israel," "Mighty One of Israel," "Holy One of Israel," "God in Israel," "God over Israel," "God to Israel," "God for Israel," etc. He also tells the world that He is "God of Jacob," "Holy One of Jacob," "Mighty One of Jacob," "Portion of Jacob," et alia, et cetera.

This is the way that God wants to be known. That is why those who know Him can say, "The Lord of hosts is with us; the God of Jacob is our stronghold." (Ps.46:7 & 11) That is why He Himself says to Zion, "For your husband is your Maker, whose name is the Lord of hosts; And your Redeemer is the Holy One of Israel, who is called the God of all the earth." (Is.54:5)

God's identity and integrity are bound up in His relationship with Israel. King David prayed, "And what one nation on the earth is like Thy people Israel, whom God went to redeem for Himself as a people and to make a name for Himself, and to do a great thing for Thee and awesome things for Thy land, before **Thy people whom Thou hast redeemed for Thyself from Egypt**, from nations and their gods? For **Thou hast established for Thyself Thy people Israel as Thine own people forever**, and Thou, O Lord, hast become their God." (2Sam.7:23,24)

"AFTER THOSE DAYS"

" 'But this is the covenant which I will make with the house of Israel **after those days**,' declares the Lord."

God often used the lives of the prophets to reinforce their proclamations. In Jesus, the living Word, the life and the proclamation are inseparable. In celebrating the Passover with His disciples, Jesus simply pointed to Himself as the fulfillment of what God had preordained.

Jesus announced the New Covenant when He sat down with His disciples, who were all Jewish, to eat the Passover. Since the days of Jeremiah, Israel had been awaiting the New Covenant which God had promised. At that special Passover with His disciples, Jesus told them that the time had come. Six centuries later, God had not forgotten. He was still faithful.

In commanding the memorial of the Passover and the deliverance from Egypt, God had purposefully established the context for understanding the New Covenant. In his epistles, Paul often refers to this context — in terms of baptism (1Co.10:1-2), communion (1Co.11:23-26), separation (Col.1:13), etc.

"And in the same way He took the cup after they had eaten saying, 'This cup which is poured out for you is the New Covenant in My blood.' " (Luke 22:20) As Passover is celebrated today, the cup after supper is "HaGeulah" [הגאלה], the cup of redemption. Whether it was so then or not, we do not know, but the whole context of Passover is one of redemption through the blood of Lamb. Passover is the feast of redemption. The cup of redemption is the epitome of the feast.

Every covenant of God is literally "cut" rather than "made." Blood must be shed to ratify it. The promised New Covenant is ratified through the blood of Jesus, the Lamb of God. (cf. Heb.7-10) It was only the blood of the lamb on the doorposts and lintel that protected the Jewish people in Egypt.

God prescribed in detail what the people were to do. (Ex.12:1-28) Though there were tens of thousands of lambs that were put to death then, God always speaks of the lamb in the singular. For example, "...Your *lamb* shall be an unblemished male a year old; you may take *it*...then the whole assembly of the congregation of Israel is to kill *it* at twilight..." (vv.5,6)

God was pointing Israel to the Lamb to come. When the Lamb came, He pointed Israel to Himself. He brought the New Covenant in His blood.

The prophecy of Jeremiah concerning the New Covenant is cited in both Hebrews 8:8-12 and Hebrews 10:16,17. "Hebrews" is a letter written to the Jewish believers. The purpose of the quotation is to compare the first covenant, the Covenant of the Law with the second covenant, the New Covenant which Jesus brought. The New Covenant which Jesus brought is explicitly presented as the New Covenant which God promised to the house of Israel and the house of Judah.

"For if that first covenant had been faultless, there would have been no occasion sought for a second. For finding fault with them, He says, 'Behold, days are coming,' declares the Lord, 'when I will effect a new covenant with the house of Israel and with the house of Judah, not like the covenant which I made with their fathers on the day when I took them by the hand to lead them out of the land of Egypt; for they did not continue in My covenant, and I did not care for them,' says the Lord. 'For this is the covenant that I will make with the house of Israel after those days,' says the Lord, 'I will put My laws into their minds, and I will write them upon their hearts; and I will be their God, and they shall be My people. And they shall not teach every one his fellow-citizen, and every one his brother, saying *"Know the Lord,"* for all shall know Me, from the least to the greatest of them. For I will be merciful to their iniquities and I will remember their sin no more.'

"When He said, 'A new covenant,' He has made the first obsolete. But whatever is becoming obsolete and growing old is ready to disappear." (Heb.8:7-13)

The comparison continues: "Now even the first covenant..." (9:1) "And for this reason He is the mediator of a new covenant, in order that since a death has taken place for the redemption of the transgressions that were committed under the first covenant, those who have been called may receive the promise of the eternal inheritance. (9:15) "Therefore even the first covenant was not inaugurated without blood." (9:18)

The first covenant is the "old" covenant, the Covenant of the Law. The second covenant is the "new" covenant, prophesied by Jeremiah, brought by Jesus. This is made clear throughout the New Covenant Scriptures.

The Jewish believers understood the New Covenant in Jesus to be what the God of Israel had promised and was fulfilling to the Jewish people. This is what the Lord revealed to them. This is what the Holy Spirit said through them. This is what the New Covenant Scriptures record.

14

THE REMNANT AND THE NEW COVENANT

The New Covenant is made with "the house of Israel and with the house of Judah," but neither all of Israel nor all of Judah (the two kingdoms) believed. Only a remnant of the whole house of Israel believed. The Lord had told the prophets that would be the case. Since all Israel did not believe, God did not yet have His people to worship Him in Spirit and in Truth.

Those Jews who believed were physically the same as those who did not. They were all circumcised. The difference was in their hearts. That is where the difference had always been between the faithful remnant [שְׁאָר, שְׁאֵרִית] and their unfaithful brethren. Those Jews who believed had circumcised hearts, consecrated to God.

Moses had commanded those who were to enter the Promised Land, "Circumcise then the foreskin of your heart, and stiffen your neck no more." (Dt.10:16) The commandment was the same before the Babylonian invasion and exile, "Circumcise yourselves to the Lord and remove the foreskins of your heart, men of Judah and inhabitants of Jerusalem, lest My wrath go forth like fire and burn with none to quench it, because of the evil of your deeds." (Jer.4:4)

God told Abraham, "You shall be circumcised in the flesh of your foreskin; and it shall be the sign of the covenant between Me and you." (Gen.17:11) Circumcision of the flesh was the "sign" of the covenant; it signified the covenant. It signified the consecration of Abraham and his seed to the Lord. The flesh is circumcised by a knife; the heart is circumcised by "the Word of God which is sharper than any two-edged sword." (Heb.4:12)

God warned Abraham and his descendants that, "an uncircumcised male who is not circumcised in the flesh of his foreskin, that person shall be cut off from his people; he has broken My covenant." (Gen.17:14) That is true for those who are not physically circumcised; and it is also true for those who are not circumcised in their hearts.

And so, "'Behold, the days are coming,' declares the Lord, 'that I will punish all who are circumcised and yet uncircumcised... for all the Gentiles are uncircumcised, and all the house of Israel are uncircumcised of heart.'" (Jer.9:25-26)

This is the distinction that Jesus makes between Abraham's seed and Abraham's children. Both are physically descended from Abraham, but those who are truly Abraham's children have circumcised hearts. That is what physical circumcision was to signify.

Jesus told those around Him, "I know that you are Abraham's offspring [σπερμα, seed]; yet you seek to kill Me, because My word has no entrance in you...If you are Abraham's children [τεκνα], do the deeds of Abraham." (Jn.8:37,39) Where the word of Jesus finds entrance, as a two-edged sword, it circumcises the heart.

The human mind does not like contradictions, but in the sight of God, it is possible to be circumcised and yet uncircumcised. It is possible to be Abraham's seed and not his child. It is possible to be of Israel and not of Israel.

Most Jews did not believe in Jesus, "But it is not as though the word of God has failed. For they are not all Israel who are descended from Israel; neither are they all children because they are Abraham's seed, but: 'through Isaac your seed will be named.' That is, it is not the children of the flesh who are children of God, but the children of the promise are regarded as seed." (Rom.9:6-8, quoting Gen.21:12)

Paul is not saying here that none of those descended from Israel are Israel. Nor is he saying that some who are not descended from Israel are actually Israel. He is simply saying, "they are not all Israel who are descended from Israel." Some descended from Israel are truly Israel. Some are not. It is only the remnant, like Nathaniel (Jn.1:47), who are fully Israel before God.

Paul wrote to the churches in Galatia because there were some Jews who had come to them teaching the Gentile believers that "Unless you are circumcised according to the custom of Moses, you cannot be saved." (Acts 15:1) Here, as with all of Paul's writings, it is necessary to know and keep in mind three things: 1) the audience to whom he is writing, 2) the issue that he is addressing, and 3) the point that he is making.

Some of the Gentiles had believed these false teachers and had submitted to physical circumcision. But the Holy Spirit had already settled the issue. (We shall look at it soon.) So Paul warned the Gentile believers against this false gospel. "For those who are [physically] circumcised do not even keep the Law themselves, but they desire to have you [physically] circumcised, that they may boast in your flesh." (Gal.6:13)

Paul warned those Gentile believers who would not listen, "You have been severed from Messiah, you who are seeking to be justified by law; you have fallen from grace." (Gal.5:4) He called those Jews who were teaching the Gentile believers that they had to be circumcised a "false circumcision." (cf. Phil.3:2; Gal.5:12)

"And those who will walk by this rule, peace and mercy be upon them, and upon the Israel of God." (Gal.6:16) May peace and mercy be upon those Gentiles who will walk according to the true gospel. May peace and mercy be upon those Jews who trust not in their physical circumcision, but in the circumcision of the heart. They will not seek to impose physical circumcision upon the Gentiles. Here Paul calls those Jews with circumcised hearts, that faithful remnant, "the Israel of God."

"For he is not a Jew who is one outwardly; neither is circumcision that which is outward in the flesh. But he is a Jew who is one inwardly; and circumcision is that which is of the heart, by the Spirit, not by the letter; and his praise is not from men, but from God." (Rom.2:28-29) Inasmuch as the Hebrew word for praise is the root word of "Jew," Paul is saying that the true Jew has "his Jewishness" from God, rather than from men. "For we are the true circumcision, who worship in the Spirit of God and glory in Messiah Jesus and put no confidence in the flesh." (Phil.3:3)

In Romans 2:17-29, Paul is specifically addressing those who "bear the name 'Jew,' and rely upon the Law, and boast in God..." (v.17) The "Law" on which they are relying is the Law of Moses, the covenant that God made with Israel after delivering them from Egypt. Paul specifically mentions some of its well-known commandments: "one should not steal...one should not commit adultery...[one should] abhor idols..." (vv.21-22)

He is talking to Jews who appear to themselves and to others to be living according to the Law of God. In fact, they "boast in the Law" (v.23). Paul challenges them, 'Are you really keeping the Law? If you are, then why is the name of God blasphemed among the Gentiles because of you?'

Paul maintains that, whatever their conception of themselves or their outward appearance, the Law is not engraved on their hearts. Inwardly they do not keep its requirements. And it is "not the hearers of the Law [who] are just before God, but the doers of the Law will be justified." (v.13)

If they did keep the requirements of the Law, then their physical circumcision would have great value in signifying the circumcision of their hearts. But Paul, who considered himself blameless "as to the righteousness which is in the Law" (Phil.3:6), knew very well personally that no mere human being could keep the requirements of God's holy Law. [He discusses this more in chapter 7 of Romans.] The physical circumcision of a Jew who transgresses the Law becomes as uncircumcision before God. (v.2:25)

Conversely then, "If therefore the uncircumcised man keep the requirements of the Law, will not his uncircumcision be regarded as circumcision? And will not he who is physically uncircumcised, if he keeps the Law, will he not judge you who though having the letter of the Law and circumcision are a transgressor of the Law?" (vv.26-27)

If a Gentile were to be a doer of the Law, i.e. to keep all its requirements, wouldn't God count that as circumcision? No Gentile could ever do that, but Paul has established a logical, hypothetical case to demonstrate to the Jews to whom he is speaking that physical circumcision alone does not make a man right before God. Nor is it the purpose for which God created the Jewish people. After all, God had told Abraham that physical circumcision was a "sign" of the covenant.

Calvin commented, "It should be added furthermore that one ought not to be overanxious to understand who are the observers of the law of whom

Paul speaks here, since no such can be found. Paul's intention was simply to propose the hypothesis that if any Gentile could be found who kept the law, his righteousness would be of more value without circumcision than the circumcision of the Jews without righteousness." [1]

To be truly Jewish, a Jew needs to have a circumcised heart, an inward surrender to God. Paul himself well understood the distance between loving God's Law and keeping it. As he tells those in Rome to whom he writes, "For the good that I wish, I do not do; but I practice the very evil that I do not wish.... For I joyfully concur with the law of God in the inner man but I see a different law in the members of my body, waging war against the law of my mind, and making me a prisoner of the law of sin which is in my members." (Rom.7:19,22-23)

By God's grace, the believing remnant have found the way to be free from this dilemma. God's Law is holy, righteous, and good, but it demands the death of the one who transgresses it. In Jesus, the righteous demand of the Law is fulfilled, because He died in the place of the transgressors. He rose from the dead so that those who believe in Him may be justified in the New Covenant.

There is now a faithful Jewish remnant, as there has been since God created Israel. Elijah thought he was the only one in Israel who was still faithful to God. Elijah was a man of God. He was a mighty prophet. But he was wrong.

In demonstrating God's continuing faithfulness to Israel, Paul speaks of himself as part of that faithful remnant. Then he affirms, "God has not rejected His people whom He foreknew. Or do you not know what the Scripture says in the passage about Elijah, how he pleads with God against Israel? 'Lord, they have killed Thy prophets, they have torn down Thine altars, and I alone am left, and they are seeking my life.'

"But what is the divine response to him? 'I have kept for Myself seven thousand men who have not bowed the knee to Baal.' In the same way then, there has also come to be at the present time a remnant according to God's gracious choice." (Rom.11:2-5)

Israel's unfaithfulness continued, but God's faithfulness continued too. By God's grace and by God's choice, there is a Jewish remnant that has believed Him. There is a Jewish remnant that has entered into the New Covenant.

FOOTNOTE

1. *Calvin's Commentaries, The Epistles of Paul the Apostle to the Romans and to the Thessalonians*, translated by Ross Mackenzie, edited by David W. Torrance & Thomas F. Torrance, Oliver and Boyd, Edinburgh, 1961, P.56

BEGINNING FROM MOSES

After the resurrection, Jesus appeared to two of the disciples. "And beginning from Moses and from all the prophets, He explained to them the things concerning Himself in all the Scriptures." (Lk.24:27)

Jesus later appeared to the apostles and those with them, and, "He said to them, 'These are My words which I spoke to you while I was still with you, that all things which are written about Me in the Law of Moses and the Prophets and the Psalms (i.e. the Writings) must be fulfilled.' Then He opened their minds to understand the Scriptures." (Lk.24:44)

Jesus gave them understanding of ALL the Messianic prophecies. On that basis, therefore, just before His ascension into heaven, they asked Him a question. They asked Him the one question which, given the nature of those prophecies, was the most logical and pressing.

"And so when they had come together, they were asking Him, saying, 'Lord, is it at this time You are restoring the kingdom to Israel?' He said to them, 'It is not for you to know times or epochs which the Father has fixed by His own authority; but you shall receive power when the Holy Spirit has come upon you; and you shall be My witnesses both in Jerusalem, and in all Judea and Samaria, and even to the remotest part of the earth.' " (Acts 1:7-8)

Jesus did not disavow the restoration of the kingdom to Israel. He confirmed it. He said that God the Father has, by His own authority, fixed a date for it. (We will look at this more later.) It will be. Until that day comes, the disciples need to receive power from the Holy Spirit and be witnesses for Jesus.

Jesus, the Lamb of God, was put to death on Passover. God had created the Passover in Egypt as a representation of what would happen some 1500 years later. The sacrifice of the lamb in Egypt points to, and explains, the sacrifice of the Lamb of God.

Passover culminates in the giving of the Covenant of the Law at Sinai. Tradition says that occurred on Shavuos/Pentecost, although the Bible does not indicate this. Pentecost receives its Greek name from the fifty days that were counted after the Feast of Unleavened Bread. It was not a separate holy day per se, but the conclusion of what began at Passover—the feast which actually fixed the date of Pentecost.

"And when the day of Pentecost was being fulfilled, they [the 120 disciples] were all together in one place...." (Acts 2) Many people think of Pentecost as "the birthday of the Church." For those who understand it that way, it is important to remember that all of the apostles and disciples were Jewish; as were all the three thousand who repented and believed on that day.

On Pentecost, Peter spoke to the "**Men of Judea**" (Acts 2:14), entreating them, "**Men of Israel**, listen to these words:...Let **all the house of Israel** know for certain that God has made Him both Lord and Messiah —this Jesus whom you crucified...For **the promise is for you and your children**, and for all who are far off, as many as the Lord our God shall call to Himself." (Acts 2:22,36,39) This emphasis continues throughout the Book of Acts.

When the lame man was healed at the Beautiful Gate of the Temple, many Jews ran to see what had happened. Peter preached the gospel to them, calling them to repentance. Then he told them that Moses, "And likewise, all the prophets who have spoken, from Samuel and his successors onward, also announced these days. It is **you who are the sons of the prophets, and of the covenant** which God covenanted with your fathers, saying to Abraham, 'And in your seed all the families of the earth shall be blessed.'...For you first God raised up His Servant, and sent Him **to bless you by turning everyone from your wicked ways**." (Acts 3:24-26)

The promise to Abraham is included in "the covenant which God made with your fathers." Paul refers to this same promise as being a proclamation of the gospel: "And the Scripture, foreseeing that God would justify the Gentiles by faith, preached the gospel beforehand to Abraham, saying, 'All the nations shall be blessed in you.' " (Gal.3:8) The gospel is included in the covenant which God made with the fathers of the Jewish people. The Jews are, naturally, the sons of that covenant. The New Covenant, after all, is made with the house of Judah and the house of Israel.

Peter makes it clear that the fulfillment of God's promise to Abraham, Isaac, Jacob, and all Israel is to be found in the New Covenant in Jesus, saying: "He is the one whom God exalted to His right hand as a Prince and a Savior, **to grant repentance to Israel**, and forgiveness of sins, and we are witnesses of these things." (Acts 5:31,32) (Also, see Acts 10:36; 13:26,32,33; the context of Chapter 15; 21:15-26; and 24:10-21.)

As a Jew, Peter was calling other Jews to repentance and faith. That is what the prophets, as faithful Jews, had done before. Peter preached that the crucifixion and resurrection were part of God's ongoing relationship with Israel.

The early Church viewed the New Covenant and the gospel as integral parts of that relationship. They preached it that way. They recorded the New Covenant Scriptures that way.

As Paul, the apostle to the Gentiles, wrote, "Now I make known to you, brethren, the gospel which I preached to you, which also you received, in which also you stand, by which also you are saved, if you hold fast the word which I preached to you, unless you believed in vain. For I delivered to you as of first importance what I also received, that Messiah died for our sins **according to the Scriptures**, and that He was buried, and that He was raised on the third day **according to the Scriptures**...." (1Co.15:1-4)

Paul, like the other apostles and like Jesus Himself, preached the gospel "according to the Scriptures." What Scriptures? The Law, the Prophets and the Writings, i.e. Tanakh.

Paul affirmed that this was the way he always preached: "And so, having obtained help from God, I stand to this day testifying both to small and great, stating nothing but what the Prophets and Moses said was going to take place; that the Messiah was to suffer, and that by reason of His resurrection from the dead He should be the first to proclaim light both to the Jewish people and to the Gentiles." (Acts 26:22-33)

Jesus had chosen to identify Himself and to accept worship as "the Son of David," i.e. Messiah the King of the Jews. He had taught the apostles to know Him in that way. He was crucified as "Jesus of Nazareth, King of the Jews." (Mt.27:37; Mk.15:26; Lk.23:38; Jn.19:19) They never thought of Him or the gospel separate from the Jewish people. They had no other context.

The reason most Jews then did not believe in Jesus was that they did not believe the Law of Moses. That is the way it has always been. "For if you believed Moses, you would believe Me; for he wrote of Me. But if you do not believe his writings, how will you believe My words?" (Jn.5:46-47) "Therefore the Law has become our tutor to lead us to Messiah, that we may be justified by faith." (Gal.3:24) Faith in Moses leads to faith in Jesus.

Jesus told a pair of parables about those who are entrusted with riches in this life. The first was about a steward who had squandered his master's possessions. His master "called him and said to him, 'What is this I hear about you? Give an account of your stewardship, for you can no longer be steward.' " (Lk.16:2)

Before the steward was dismissed from his position, he used the authority he had over his master's goods to forgive others part of what they rightfully owed. He was looking out for his own future, expecting that when his stewardship was ended, his master's debtors would help provide for him.

"And his master praised the unrighteous steward because he had acted shrewdly; for the sons of this age are more shrewd in relation to their own generation than the sons of light....If therefore you have not been faithful in the use of unrighteous Mammon, who will entrust the true riches to you? If you have not been faithful in the use of that which is another's, who will give you that which is your own?" (Lk.16:8,11-12)

There are different kinds of riches in this life. Material possessions are one kind. The things of God are another. They all are to be used faithfully in service to the Master.

Before Jesus began the second parable, He told the Pharisees around Him, "The Law and the Prophets were proclaimed until John; since then the gospel of the kingdom of God is preached, and every one is forcing his way into it, but it is easier for heaven and earth to pass away than for one stroke of a letter of the Law to fail." (16:16-17)

Then He told the second parable. "Now there was a certain rich man, and he habitually dressed in purple and fine linen, gaily living in splendor every day. And a certain poor man named Lazarus was laid at his gate, covered with sores, and longing to be fed with the crumbs which were falling from the rich man's table; besides, even the dogs were coming and licking his sores." (vv.19-20)

Both the rich man and the poor man died, as both rich men and poor men do. "And in Hades he [the rich man] lifted up his eyes, being in torment, and saw Abraham far away, and Lazarus in his bosom. And he cried out and said, 'Father Abraham, have mercy on me, and send Lazarus, that he may dip the tip of his finger in water and cool off my tongue; for I am in agony in this flame.' But Abraham said, 'Child, remember that during your life you received your good things, and likewise Lazarus bad things; but now he is being comforted here, and you are in agony.' " (vv.23-25)

"And he [the rich man] said, 'Then I beg you, Father, that you send him to my father's house — for I have five brothers — that he may warn them, lest they also come to this place of torment.' But Abraham said, 'They have Moses and the Prophets; let them hear them.' But he [the rich man] said, 'No, Father Abraham, but if someone goes to them from the dead, they will repent!' But he [Abraham] said to him, 'If they do not listen to Moses and the Prophets, neither will they be persuaded if someone rises from the dead.' " (Lk.16:31)

Likewise it can be said, 'If they do listen to Moses and the Prophets, then they will be persuaded when Someone rises from the dead.' Jesus was saying to His Jewish audience, 'Believe Moses and the Prophets, and you will believe the gospel. Whatever riches God has entrusted to you, whether material or spiritual, make sure that you do not squander them. There are others who need what you have, and one day you will give account for your stewardship.'

God entrusted to Israel the words of life — all of them. That is both great riches and a great responsibility. What God desires to give to all men, He entrusted to the Jews. Some proved faithful. Some did not.

Many Jews believed. There were the one hundred twenty. There were the three thousand on the day of Pentecost. (Acts 2:41) There were those that the Lord added every day. (Acts 2:47) There were the thousands more who believed when Peter preached at the Temple gate. (Acts 4:4) There were "a great many of the priests [who] were becoming obedient to the faith." (Acts 6:7)

It was one of the greatest revivals in all Jewish history, if not THE GREATEST. When Paul later came to Jerusalem to report on his ministry among the Gentiles, there were many tens of thousands of Jewish believers in Jerusalem alone. (Acts 21:20)

SECTION C:
THE GENTILES TOO

THE SAMARITANS

Jesus had told the disciples, "you shall be My witnesses both in Jerusalem, and in all Judea **and Samaria**..." Being a witness for Him in Jerusalem and in all Judea was not easy, but it was understandable. After all, their message was Jewish. Being a witness for Him in Samaria was harder to understand.

In the first century, Jews and Samaritans did not think highly of each other. There were Biblical reasons why the Jews looked down on the Samaritans. There was the history of the Samaritans.

"In the ninth year of Hoshea, the king of Assyria captured Samaria and carried Israel [the northern kingdom] away into exile to Assyria...And the king of Assyria brought men from Babylon and from Cuthah and from Avva and from Hamath and Sephar-vaim, and settled them in the cities of Samaria in place of the sons of Israel. So they possessed Samaria and lived in its cities.

"And it came about at the beginning of their living there, that they did not fear the Lord; therefore the Lord sent lions among them which killed some of them....Then the king of Assyria commanded, saying, 'Take there one of the priests whom you carried away into exile, and let him go and live there; and let him teach them the custom of the god of the land.'

"So one of the priests whom they had carried away into exile from Samaria came and lived at Bethel, and taught them how they should fear the Lord. But every nation still made gods of its own and put them in the houses of the high places which the people of Samaria had made, every nation in their cities in which they lived." (2Kings 17:6,24-25,27-29)

The priests of the northern kingdom of Israel had led Israel in the idolatry that had resulted in the exile. The new inhabitants of Samaria retained all their idolatrous ways, but added a veneer of worship of the God of Israel, which they were taught by an apostate priest.

The writer of Kings records: "To this day they do according to the earlier customs: they do not fear the Lord, nor do they follow their statutes or their ordinances or the law, or the commandments which the Lord commanded the sons of Jacob, whom He named Israel....So while these Gentiles feared the Lord, they also served their idols; their children likewise and their grandchildren, as their fathers did, so they do to this day." (2Kings 17:34,41)

After Israel's return from exile, God made it clear that they were to have nothing to do with the peoples who were living in the land. Nehemiah said to them, "The God of heaven will give us success; therefore we His servants will arise and build, but you have no portion, right, or memorial in Jerusalem." (Neh.2:20)

Nehemiah found out that some of the returned Jews had married women of the peoples living in the land. "As for their children, half spoke in the language of Ashdod, and none of them was able to speak the language of Judah, but the language of his own people. So I contended with them and cursed them and struck some of them and pulled out their hair, and made them swear by God, 'You shall not give your daughters to their sons, nor take of their daughters for your sons or for yourselves.' " (Neh.13:24-25)

There were good Biblical reasons why the Jews did not have any dealings with the Samaritans. But there were no good reasons for despising them. That is why Jesus told a Jewish audience the uncomplimentary parable of the good Samaritan.

What is the point of the parable? Jesus told it in response to a particular question. "And behold, a certain lawyer stood up and put Him to the test, saying, 'Teacher, what shall I do to inherit eternal life?' " (Lk.10:25) That was the issue, "what shall I do to inherit eternal life?"

"And He said to him, 'What is written in the Law? How does it read to you?' And he answered and said, 'You shall love the Lord your God with all your heart, and with all your soul, and with all your strength, and with all your mind; and your neighbor as yourself.' And He said to him, 'You have answered correctly; do this, and you will live.' " (Lk.10:26-28)

Whoever loves God completely and loves his neighbor as himself will have eternal life. Unfortunately, this is beyondwhat human nature can do.

"But wishing to justify himself, he [the lawyer] said to Jesus, 'And who is my neighbor?' " (Lk.10:29) The man was an expert in the law of Moses. He knew what it said. He could not live by it. He knew that he was not fulfilling that commandment.

He wanted to find a way to escape that hardest of commandments — "you shall love your neighbor as yourself; I am the Lord." (Lev.19:18) He sought to justify his failure to keep the law by defining away his responsibility. If he were allowed to define "neighbor" however he might choose, then he could preserve his self-righteousness.

That is when Jesus told the parable of the good Samaritan. The initial question was still, "what shall I do to inherit eternal life?" Jesus explained that love of one's neighbor — which is essential for eternal life — is active and self-sacrificing. It is that love, not simply being Jewish, that brings eternal life.

At Jacob's well, Jesus encountered a Samaritan woman. Jesus first presented Himself as the source of living water, necessary for eternal life. (vv.10-14) Then He confronted the woman with a particular sin in her life that would keep her from obtaining eternal life. (vv.15-18) She responded by recognizing Him as a prophet, and then raising one of the issues of theological conflict between Samaritans and Jews: "'Our fathers worshiped in this mountain; and you [plural, therefore "Jews"] say that in Jerusalem is the place where men ought to worship.'

"Jesus said to her, 'Woman, believe Me, an hour is coming when neither in this mountain, nor in Jerusalem, shall you worship the Father. You [plural, therefore "Samaritans"] worship that which you [plural] do not know; we worship that which we know; for salvation is from the Jews. But an hour is coming, and now is, when the true worshipers shall worship the Father in spirit and truth; for such people the Father seeks to be His worshipers. God is spirit; and those who worship Him must worship in spirit and truth.' " (Jn.4:20-24)

God is spirit. He is omnipresent. He can be worshipped wherever He is, which is everywhere.

A.W. Tozer has expressed it well: "Wherever we are, God is here. There is no place, there can be no place, where He is not. Ten million intelligences standing at as many points in space and separated by incomprehensible distances can each one say with equal truth, God is here. No point is nearer to God than any other point. It is exactly as near to God from any place as it is from any other place. No one is in mere distance any further from or any nearer to God than any other person is." [1]

The Samaritan woman did not need to go to any particular mountain to worship God. Why was it then necessary for Jesus to mention the Jewishness of the gospel? After all, He knew what a stumbling-block that would place in front of the Samaritans.

Possibly there was no greater obstacle that He could have placed before them. Didn't He want them to believe in Him? Didn't He want them to be saved?

Of course He did. He loved the Samaritans. He loved them then, even as today He loves Muslims, Marxists, and all people. He wants them to repent and believe that they might live.

But God must be known and worshipped in truth. Repentance and faith are not ethereal substances. They have both content and context. To worship God in Spirit and in Truth, people need to know both that content and that context.

On another occasion, Jesus "resolutely set His face to go to Jerusalem; and He sent messengers on ahead of Him. And they went, and entered a village of the Samaritans, to make arrangements for Him. And they did not receive Him, because He was journeying with His face toward Jerusalem. And when His disciples Jacob and John saw this, they said, 'Lord, do you want us to command fire to come down from heaven and consume them?' But He turned and rebuked them. And they went on to another village." (Lk.9:51-56)

In the plan and purpose of God, Jesus was going to Jerusalem. The

Samaritans in the village didn't like that, because they didn't like the Jews. If Jesus was going to Jerusalem, then they were not going to receive Him.

Jacob and John responded in the same antagonistic manner by getting ready "to command fire to come down from heaven and consume them." Jesus rebuked Jacob and John because He came to bring forgiveness, not condemnation. Jesus did not comment on the anti-Jewish hostility of those Samaritans, He simply honored their choice and passed them by.

That is why He told the Samaritan woman at Jacob's well, "You [Samaritans] worship that which you do not know; we [Jews] worship that which we know; for salvation is from the Jews." In effect, Jesus was telling her that God has prepared a way of salvation for all peoples, but He has prepared it in a very narrow way. That may be offensive to some, but it is an integral part of God's eternal plan of redemption. It may be offensive to some, but it is a necessary component of Messiah's identity.

Jesus did not hide His Jewishness, or the Jewishness of the gospel, in order to appeal to Samaritans. His very appearance told to what people He belonged.

Could He have tried to hide His Jewishness, or the Jewishness of the gospel, without being dishonest and deceptive? Could He have tried to hide His Jewishness, or the Jewishness of the gospel, without distorting and denying the gospel and His own identity? Could He have tried to hide His Jewishness or the Jewishness of the gospel without distorting and denying God's initial and unchanging plan of salvation for the world?

Jesus chose to make His Jewishness and the Jewishness of the gospel a central issue. He knew that it was necessary for this Samaritan woman, and for all readers of the New Covenant Scriptures, to be confronted with it.

Throughout their conversation, Jesus was showing the Samaritan woman some hard-to-accept truths that she needed to recognize in order to worship God in Spirit and Truth. 1. Jesus is the source of eternal life. 2. God requires holiness. 3. God is not simply a tribal god whose rule is limited to a particular piece of geography. Instead, He is God of all the earth, and will be worshipped throughout the earth. 4. God has presented Himself and His way of salvation to all the earth through the Jews. (This is not a cultural prescription for the manner of worship, but rather an identification chosen by God, which all must recognize in order to know Whom they are worshipping.)

The Samaritans knew, albeit imperfectly, Tanakh and its Messianic prophecies. Their version of the Pentateuch was sacred to them. They were not pleased to be reminded of God's relationship with the Jews and His promises to them. Since they occupied part of the land of the Jews, they arrogantly claimed to occupy the position of the Jews before God.

The Samaritans were not pleased to be reminded of the false nature of their own religious system. Still, they recognized the authority of the

Messianic prophecies. They knew that the Messiah of the Jews was the savior of the world.

When we recall the general animosity between Samaritans and Jews, and vice versa, we would expect a very negative response on the part of the woman. We would expect that she, and all others then and now who regard the Jews as enemies, would be greatly offended by such a statement. We would expect such a declaration to have a very negative effect on the possibility of successful evangelism.

In the wisdom of God, and by His power, these truths, which would naturally be unpalatable to the Samaritans, had the opposite impact of what the human mind might expect. "And from that city many of the Samaritans believed in Him because of the word of the woman... And many more believed because of His word." (Jn.4:39,41)

After the resurrection of Jesus, the believers proclaimed the gospel in Jerusalem and in Judea. After the death of Stephen, "...a great persecution arose against the church in Jerusalem; and they were all scattered throughout the regions of Judea and Samaria...And Philip went down to the city of Samaria and began proclaiming Messiah to them. And the multitudes with one accord were giving attention to what was said by Philip, as they heard and saw the signs which he was performing.

"...when they believed Philip preaching the good news about the kingdom of God and the name of Jesus the Messiah, they were being baptized, men and women alike....Now when the apostles in Jerusalem heard that Samaria had received the word of God, they sent them Peter and John, who came down and prayed for them, that they might receive the Holy Spirit." (Acts 8:1,5-6,12,14-15)

Philip, Peter, John, and the other disciples who were scattered throughout Samaria did not formulate a new gospel for the Samaritans. They preached the only gospel they had. The same one that Jesus had taught them, the same one that Jesus had previously communicated to the Samaritan woman and her fellow-townsmen. Jesus was their precedent. The Samaritans received that message.

FOOTNOTE

1. A.W. Tozer, *The Pursuit of God*, Christian Publications, Inc. Harrisburg, PA., P.62

17

THE ETHIOPIAN EUNUCH

The first non-Samaritan Gentile to hear and receive the gospel after the resurrection was an Ethiopian eunuch. Philip had been preaching the gospel to the Samaritans. Peter and John had joined him.

"And so, when they had solemnly testified and spoken the word of the Lord, they started back to Jerusalem, and were preaching the gospel to many villages of the Samaritans. But an angel of the Lord spoke to Philip saying, 'Arise and go south to the road that descends from Jerusalem to Gaza.' (This is a desert road.)

"And he arose and went; and behold, there was an Ethiopian eunuch, a court official of Candace, queen of the Ethiopians, who was in charge of all her treasure; and he had come to Jerusalem to worship. And he was returning and sitting in his chariot, and was reading the prophet Isaiah. And the Spirit said to Philip, 'Go up and join this chariot.' " (Acts 8:25-29)

The Ethiopian eunuch had "come to Jerusalem to worship...and was reading the prophet Isaiah." He wanted to worship God in Spirit and in Truth. That's why he had come to Jerusalem. That's why he was reading the prophet Isaiah. So God met him on that road through His servant Philip.

When Philip "preached Jesus to him" (v.35), he believed and asked to be baptized. Philip baptized him, "And when they came up out of the water, the Spirit of the Lord snatched Philip away; and the eunuch saw him no more, but went on his way rejoicing. But Philip found himself at Azotus; and as he passed through he kept preaching the gospel to all the cities, until he came to Caesarea." (vv.39-40)

It all happened quickly and very supernaturally. The Spirit spoke to Philip and he obeyed. The Ethiopian eunuch believed the prophetic testimony about Jesus. Philip was snatched away by the Spirit of the Lord, and the eunuch returned to Ethiopia.

There was no time or way to consider the implications of this new, non-Jewish disciple. Different historical precedents also made it possible to accept him and his worship of the Lord without great dismay. Jesus said, "The Queen of the South shall rise up with the men of this generation at the judgment and condemn them, because she came from the ends of the earth to hear the wisdom of Solomon; and behold, something greater than Solomon is here." (Lk.11:31)

Almost a thousand years earlier, this Ethiopian queen had come to Jerusalem. "Now when the queen of Sheba heard of the fame of Solomon, she came to Jerusalem to test Solomon with difficult questions. She had a very large retinue, with camels carrying spices, and a large amount of gold and precious stones; and when she came to Solomon, she spoke with him about all that was on her heart. And Solomon answered all her questions; nothing was hidden from Solomon which he did not explain to her." (2Chr.9:1,2)

In a remarkable statement, she told Solomon, "Blessed be the Lord your God who delighted in you, setting you on His throne as king for the Lord your God; because your God loved Israel establishing them forever, therefore He made you king over them, to do justice and righteousness." (2Chr.9:8) First, she declared that the Lord delighted in Solomon so much that He set Solomon on His own throne to rule as king for Him.

Second, she declared that God loves Israel and has established Israel forever. Third, she declared that the king of Israel is to do justice and righteousness. That, as we have previously seen, is the primary characteristic of the reign of Messiah, THE Son of David. (e.g., Is.9:6-7; Ps.89:14-15; Jer.23:5,6) God had given great wisdom to her as well.

Before the destruction of Jerusalem, during the reign of Zedekiah, there were men of the royal household who were angered by Jeremiah's gloomy prophesying. "Then they took Jeremiah and cast him into the cistern of Malchijah the king's son, which was in the court of the guardhouse; and they let Jeremiah down with ropes. Now in the cistern there was no water but only mud, and Jeremiah sank into the mud.

"But Ebed-melech the Ethiopian, a eunuch, while he was in the king's palace, heard that they had put Jeremiah into the cistern....and Ebed-melech...spoke to the king saying, 'My lord the king, these men have acted wickedly in all that they have done to Jeremiah the prophet whom they have cast into the cistern; and he will die where he is because of the famine, for there is no more bread in the city.'

"Then the king commanded Ebed-melech the Ethiopian, saying, 'Take thirty men from here under your authority, and bring up Jeremiah the prophet from the cistern before he dies.'...Then Ebed-melech, the Ethiopian said to Jeremiah, 'Now put these worn out clothes and rags under your armpits under the ropes'; and Jeremiah did so. So they pulled Jeremiah up with the ropes and lifted him out of the cistern, and Jeremiah stayed in the court of the guardhouse." (Jer.38:6-13)

"Now the word of the Lord had come to Jeremiah while he was confined in the court of the guardhouse, saying, 'Go and speak to Ebed-melech the Ethiopian, saying, *"Thus says the Lord of hosts, the God of Israel, 'Behold, I am about to bring My words on this city for disaster and not for prosperity; and they will take place before you on that day. But I will deliver you on that day,' declares the Lord, 'and you shall not be given in the hand of the men whom you dread. For I will certainly rescue you, and you will not fall by the sword; but you will have your own life as booty, because you have trusted in Me,' "* 'declares the Lord." (Jer.39:15-18)

Here was another Ethiopian eunuch who had trusted in the Lord God of Israel. Here was another Ethiopian eunuch who had recognized the voice of the prophet. Here was another Ethiopian eunuch who had helped preserve the Jewish people. God remembers such things.

He also remembers everything He has promised. "Let not the foreigner who has joined himself to the Lord say, 'The Lord will surely separate me from His people.' Neither let the eunuch say, 'Behold, I am a dry tree.' For thus says the Lord, 'To the eunuchs who keep My sabbaths, and choose what pleases Me, and hold fast My covenant, to them I will give in My house and within My walls a memorial, and a name better than that of sons and daughters; I will give them an everlasting name which will not be cut off.' " (Is.56:3-5)

It was unusual for an Ethiopian eunuch to be joined to Israel by trusting in Jesus the Messiah, the King of the Jews. It was unusual, but it was not incomprehensible. There was already a way to understand it.

It was quite different for an uncircumcised Roman centurion to do the same. To appreciate how different it was, we will look first at some of what the New Covenant Scriptures say about Gentiles.

18

GENTILES IN THE NEW COVENANT SCRIPTURES

As the Son of David, Jesus had come to raise up, "to establish and to uphold," the kingdom of David. He came to restore the Jewish people to the God of Israel. Jesus Himself did not have a ministry to the Gentiles.

A Canaanite woman cried out to him, "'Have mercy on me, O Lord, Son of David; my daughter is cruelly demon possessed.' But Jesus did not answer her a word. And His disciples came to Him and kept asking Him, saying, 'Send her away, for she is shouting out after us.'

"But He answered and said, 'I was sent only to the lost sheep of the house of Israel.' But she came and began to bow down before Him, saying, 'Lord, help me!' And He answered and said, 'It is not good to take the children's bread and throw it to the dogs.'" (Mt.15:22-26)

Was Jesus intentionally tormenting her? No. He loved her as He loves everyone.

What then did He want from her? She came to Him asking for mercy. She knew that He had the power to set her demon-possessed daughter free. She recognized Him as the Son of David. She was fervent and persevering.

How did Jesus respond? He said, 'Gentiles are not my ministry.' He said, 'The Jews are children of God. The Gentiles are dogs.' What kind of loving Savior is that?

He knew the woman. He knew her better than she knew Him. He was not seeking to torment the woman, but rather to enlighten her. Though she believed in Him, He wanted to make the point that who He was and what He brought belonged to Israel. To Him, that was an important point.

"But she said, 'Yes, Lord; but even the dogs feed on the crumbs which fall from their master's table.' Then Jesus answered and said to her, 'O woman, your faith is great; be it done for you as you wish.' And her daughter was healed at once." (Mt.15:27-28)

She did not dispute His characterization. She accepted it. She did not exalt herself against Israel. She did not want to take anything away from the Jewish people. Surely, she believed, God had something even for those who were not Jewish. That is the faith that Jesus honored.

The portrayal of the Gentiles in the New Covenant is not different from that in Tanakh. It is simply not very well-known. Paul sums up the natural condition of the Gentiles as being "separate from Messiah, excluded from the commonwealth of Israel, and strangers to the covenants of promise, having no hope and without God in the world." (Eph.2:12)

Paul goes on to admonish the Ephesians, "This I say therefore, and affirm together with the Lord, that you walk no longer just as the Gentiles also walk, in the futility of their mind, being darkened in their understanding, excluded from the life of God, because of the ignorance that is in them, because of the hardness of their heart; and they, having become callous, have given themselves over to sensuality, for the practice of every kind of impurity with greediness." (Eph.4:17-19)

He tells the Thessalonians, "For this is the will of God, your sanctification; that is, that you abstain from sexual immorality; that each of you know how to possess his own vessel in sanctification and honor, not in lustful passion, like the Gentiles who do not know God." (1Thes.4:3-5)

Peter reminds believers, "For the time already past is sufficient for you to have carried out the desire of the Gentiles, having pursued a course of sensuality, lusts, drunkenness, carousals, drinking parties and abominable idolatries. And in all this, they are surprised that you do not run with them into the same excess of dissipation, and they malign you; but they shall give account to Him who is ready to judge the living and the dead." (1Pet.4:3-5)

Jesus told the disciples how they should treat an unrepentant brother. For one who "refuses to listen even to the church, let him be to you as the Gentile and the tax-gatherer." (Mt.18:15-17) He said, "Don't be like the hypocrites,"(e.g. Mt.6:5) and "Don't be like the Gentiles." (e.g. Mt.6:7)

There are other New Covenant Scriptures that point to some exceptions among the Gentiles. "And a certain centurion's slave, who was highly regarded by him, was sick and about to die. And when he heard about Jesus, he sent some Jewish elders asking Him to come and save the life of his slave. And when they had come to Jesus, they earnestly entreated Him, saying, 'He is worthy for You to grant this to him; for he loves our nation, and it was he who built us our synagogue.'

"Now Jesus started on His way with them; and when He was already not far from the house, the centurion sent friends saying to Him, 'Lord, do not trouble Yourself further, for I am not fit for You to come under my roof; for this reason I did not even consider myself worthy to come to You, but just say the word, and my servant will be healed. For indeed, I am a man under authority, with soldiers under me; and I say to this one, "*Go!*" and he goes; and to another, "*Come!*" and he comes; and to my slave, "*Do this!*" and he does it.'

"And when Jesus heard this, He marvelled at him, and turned and said to the multitude that was following Him, 'I say to you, not even in Israel have I found such great faith.' And when those who had been sent returned to the house, they found the slave in good health." (Lk.7:2-10)

This was an unusual encounter in several respects. This Roman centurion loved the Jewish people. He loved them so much that he gave the money to build a synagogue for them.

The Jewish elders knew the centurion's love was genuine. It had works.

Because of what he had done for them, they were willing to do something for him. At his request, they went to Jesus and asked Jesus to come and heal the centurion's slave. The centurion obviously cared about his slave, or he would not have made the request.

The Jewish elders believed that Jesus could heal the slave. They believed that Jesus **should** heal the slave because of the centurion's love for Israel. They told Him that. "He is **worthy** for You to grant this to him; for he loves our nation, and it was he who built us our synagogue."

Jesus did not, in any way, disagree. He followed them to grant their request, because He, too, believed that the centurion was worthy. Many years before, a God who does not change had promised Israel, "I will bless those that bless you." He meant what He said. That is why Jesus went and healed the slave of the Roman centurion.

19

THE ROMAN CENTURION

Jesus told His disciples, "You shall be My witnesses both in Jerusalem, and in all Judea and Samaria, **and even to the remotest part of the earth**." Though it was dangerous to do, they had preached the gospel in Jerusalem and in all Judea. Many Jews had believed.

Though it was strange, they had preached the gospel in Samaria. Many Samaritans had believed. What did Jesus have in mind for "the remotest part of the earth"?

We are not told the name of the Roman centurion who sent some Jewish elders to Jesus. Perhaps it was Cornelius, perhaps not. It is difficult to imagine that there were two God-fearing, Israel-loving (to the depths of their purse) centurions in the occupying force that the Roman government stationed in Israel. That is not what the Roman legions were noted for.

Whatever the case may have been, "there was a certain man at Caesarea named Cornelius, a centurion of what was called the Italian cohort, a devout man, and one who feared God with all his household, and gave many alms to the Jewish people, and prayed to God continually. About the ninth hour of the day he clearly saw in a vision an angel of God who had just come in to him, and said to him, 'Cornelius!'

"And fixing his gaze upon him and being much alarmed, he said, 'What is it, Lord!' And he said to him, 'Your prayers and alms have ascended as a memorial before God. And now dispatch some men to Joppa, and send for a man named Simon, who is also called Peter; he is staying with a certain tanner named Simon, whose house is by the sea.' " (Acts 10:1-6)

"Cornelius...feared God with all his household, and gave many alms to the Jewish people, and prayed to God continually." He had a living faith. It was visible in his life, in his actions. That was not unrelated to God's choosing him. As the angel said, "Your prayers and alms have ascended as a memorial before God."

In Joppa, Peter was praying on a housetop. "And he beheld the sky opened up, and a certain object like a great sheet coming down, lowered by four corners to the ground, and there were in it all kinds of four-footed animals and crawling creatures of the earth and birds of the air. And a voice came to him, 'Arise, Peter, kill and eat!' But Peter said, 'By no means, Lord, for I have never eaten anything unholy and unclean.'

"And again a voice came to him a second time, 'What God has cleansed, no longer consider unholy.' And this happened three times; and immediately the object was taken up into the sky.

"Now while Peter was greatly perplexed in mind as to what the vision which he had seen might be, behold, the men who had been sent by Cornelius, having asked directions for Simon's house, appeared at the gate; and calling out, they were asking whether Simon, who was also called Peter, was staying there.

"And while Peter was reflecting on the vision, the Spirit said to him, 'Behold, three men are looking for you. But arise, go downstairs, and accompany them without misgivings; for I have sent them Myself.' " (Acts 10:11-20)

"And Peter went down to the men and said, 'Behold, I am the one you are looking for; what is the reason for which you have come?' And they said, 'Cornelius a centurion, a righteous and God-fearing man well spoken of by the entire nation of the Jews, was divinely directed by a holy angel to send for you to come to his house and hear a message from you.'

"And so he invited them in and gave them lodging. And on the next day he arose and went away with them, and some of the brethren from Joppa accompanied him. And on the following day he entered Caesarea. Now Cornelius was waiting for them, and had called together his relatives and close friends....

"And he said to them, 'You yourselves know how unlawful it is for a man who is a Jew to associate with a foreigner or to visit him; and yet God has shown me that I should not call any man unholy or unclean. That is why I came without even raising any objection when I was sent for. And so I ask for what reason you have sent for me.' " (Acts 10:28-29)

Cornelius explained why he had sent for Peter. "And opening his mouth, Peter said: 'I most certainly understand now that God is not one to show partiality, but in every nation the man who fears Him and does what is right, is welcome to Him. The word which He sent to the sons of Israel, preaching peace through Messiah Jesus (He is Lord of all.)...' " (Acts 10:34-36)

The deeds of Cornelius were righteous. The angel said that was why God had chosen him. Peter reiterated that in saying, "the man who fears Him and works righteousness [literal], is welcome to Him." Jesus had told Nicodemus, "He who practices the truth comes to the light, that his deeds may be manifested as having been wrought in God." (Jn.3:21)

Peter preached the gospel to Cornelius and his household, concluding, " 'And He ordered us to preach to the people, and solemnly to testify that this is the One who has been appointed by God as Judge of the living and the dead. Of Him all the prophets bear witness that through His name every one who believes in Him has received forgiveness of sins.'

"While Peter was still speaking these words, the Holy Spirit fell upon all those who were listening to the message. And all the circumcised believers who had come with Peter were amazed, because the gift of the Holy Spirit had been poured out upon the Gentiles also. For they were hearing them speaking with tongues and exalting God.

"Then Peter answered, 'Surely no one can refuse the water for these to be baptized who have received the Holy Spirit just as we did, can he?' And he ordered them to be baptized in the name of Jesus the Messiah. Then they asked him to stay on for a few days." (Acts 10:42-48)

Peter had gained some understanding of the vision. He knew that the "unholy and unclean" animals represented the Gentiles. He knew that God was somehow accepting and cleansing them.

In the Covenant of the Law, Israel was commanded, "I am the Lord your God, who has separated you from the peoples. You are therefore to make a distinction between the clean animal and the unclean, and between the unclean bird and the clean; and you shall not make yourselves detestable by animal or by bird or by anything that creeps on the ground, which I have separated for you as unclean. Thus you are to be holy to Me, for I the Lord am holy; and **I have set you apart from the peoples** to be Mine." (Lev.20:24b-26)

In the New Covenant, God was doing something new. As Peter later described the incident, "a voice from heaven answered a second time, 'What God has cleansed, no longer consider unholy.' " (Acts 11:9) Those Gentiles who were cleansed by God were no longer to be considered unholy. The faithful Jewish remnant was no longer to stay set apart from the Gentiles whom God had cleansed. That was the beginning of the revelation of the astounding mystery of Messiah, i.e. the Church.

20

THE DEBATE IN JERUSALEM

Peter and the other Jewish believers were amazed that God had poured out His Holy Spirit on uncircumcised Gentiles. They could not comprehend it. The gift of the Holy Spirit was part of God's New Covenant with the house of Israel and the house of Judah. (cf. Ezek.36:22-27-32) The fact that the Gentiles had received the Holy Spirit indicated that they were being brought into the New Covenant relationship with the God of Israel. How could Gentiles receive the Holy Spirit unless they first became proselytes?

Gentile proselytes could receive the Holy Spirit, because they had already become part of Israel. Proselytes had entered into the Covenant of the Law. They had been circumcised. Didn't all Gentiles who wanted to be joined to Israel have to be circumcised as God had commanded Abraham?

Didn't God make that clear throughout Tanakh? Israel was severely punished for embracing uncircumcised Gentiles and their ways. God also made it clear that He would one day gather the Gentiles to Himself, but that had to be in holiness, i.e. in circumcision.

The Lord told Ezekiel in exile, "And you shall say to the rebellious ones, to the house of Israel, 'Thus says the Lord God, *Enough of all your abominations, O house of Israel, when you brought in foreigners, uncircumcised in heart and uncircumcised in flesh, to be in My sanctuary to profane it, even My house, when you offered My food, the fat and the blood; for they made My covenant void... Thus says the Lord God, No foreigner, uncircumcised in heart and uncircumcised in flesh, of all the foreigners who are among the sons of Israel, shall enter My sanctuary.*" (Ezek.44:6-9)

Jesus had said, "Woe to you, scribes and Pharisees, hypocrites, because you travel about on sea and land to make one proselyte; and when he becomes one, you make him twice as much a son of hell as yourselves." (cf. Mt.23:15) Jesus was not speaking against their zeal in making proselytes, but against what it was that they were making proselytes to. The scribes and Pharisees gave the public appearance of making disciples of the Lord, but in actuality they were turning men into hell.

When the Holy Spirit was first poured out on the day of Pentecost, there were proselytes among the watching multitude. (cf. Acts 2:10) Nicolas, "a proselyte from Antioch," was one of the "seven men of good reputation, full of the Spirit and of wisdom" who were put in charge of the daily distribution of food among the believers in Jerusalem. (Acts 6:3,5) There was no other known way for Gentiles who sought righteousness to be joined to Israel.

"Now the apostles and the brethren who were throughout Judea heard that the Gentiles also had received the word of God. And when Peter came up to Jerusalem, those who were circumcised took issue with him, saying, 'You went to uncircumcised men and ate with them.' " (Acts 11:1-3) Hadn't Peter learned anything? Was it necessary for Nehemiah to come back and contend with him, curse him and strike him and pull out his hair, and make him swear by God that he would stay separate from the Gentiles? (cf.Neh.13)

"But Peter began speaking and proceeded to explain to them in orderly sequence, saying, 'I was in the city of Joppa praying...and I heard a voice saying to me...And the Spirit told me to go with them without misgivings.... And as I began to speak, the Holy Spirit fell upon them, just as He did upon us at the beginning. And I remembered the word of the Lord, how He used to say, *"John baptized with water, but you shall be baptized with the Holy Spirit."*

" 'If God therefore gave to them the same gift as He gave to us also after believing in the Lord Jesus the Messiah, who was I that I could stand in God's way?' And when they heard this, they quieted down, and glorified God, saying, 'Well then, God has granted to the Gentiles also the repentance that leads to life.' " (Acts 11:4-18)

What it was that God was doing was still a mystery, but at least it was clear that God was doing something new. God has granted to the Gentiles also, as Gentiles, the repentance that leads to life. Their hearts were being circumcised, but not their flesh. What that meant was not yet understood. Numerous years passed, and still the issue was not settled.

In the meantime, God transformed a young Pharisee into the Apostle to the Gentiles. Saul of Tarsus had guarded the robes of the witnesses as they threw the first stones at Stephen. "And Saul was in hearty agreement with putting him to death. And on that day a great persecution arose against the church in Jerusalem; and they were all scattered throughout the regions of Judea and Samaria, except the apostles.

"And some devout men buried Stephen, and made loud lamentation over him. But Saul began ravaging the church, entering house after house; and dragging off men and women, he would put them in prison." (Acts 8:1-3)

If ever there was a man zealous for God, but not according to knowledge, it was Saul of Tarsus. If ever a man in a rage blindly trampled that which he claimed to desire, it was Saul of Tarsus. If ever there was a man whom God could not reach, it was Saul of Tarsus. Wasn't he a Jew whom not even the grace of God could restore?

As "the army of the king of Babylon was besieging Jerusalem, Jeremiah the prophet was shut up in the court of the guard, which was in the house of the king of Judah." Jeremiah's cousin came to him, saying: "Buy my field, please, that is at Anathoth, which is in the land of Benjamin; for you have the right of possession and the redemption is yours; buy it for yourself." (Jer.32:2,8)

At the word of the Lord, Jeremiah bought the field. "For thus says the Lord of hosts, the God of Israel, 'Houses and vineyards shall again be bought in this land.' " (Jer.32:15) With imminent, promised destruction and exile at the city gates, the restoration of Israel seemed impossible.

So Jeremiah prayed, " 'Ah Lord God! Behold, Thou hast made the heavens and the earth by Thy great power and by Thine outstretched arm! Nothing is too difficult for Thee...Behold, the siege mounds have reached the city to take it; and the city is given into the hand of the Chaldeans who fight against it, because of the sword, the famine, and the pestilence; and what Thou hast spoken has come to pass; and, behold, Thou seest it.

" 'And Thou hast said to me, O Lord God, *Buy for yourself the field with money, and call in witnesses* —although the city is given into the hand of the Chaldeans.'

"Then the word of the Lord came to Jeremiah, saying, 'Behold, I am the Lord, the God of all flesh; is anything too difficult for Me?' " (Jer.32:17,24-27)

The same God, the God of Israel, the One who promised and brought the destruction and exile upon Israel, promised to again bring life and restoration to Israel. How could it be? Nothing is too difficult for Him.

"Now Saul, still breathing threats and murder against the disciples of the Lord, went to the high priest, and asked for letters from him to the synagogues at Damascus, so that if he found any belonging to the Way, both men and women, he might bring them bound to Jerusalem." (Acts 9:1-2)

In Damascus, there was "a certain Ananias, a man who was devout by the standard of the Law, and well spoken of by all the Jews who lived there." (Acts 22:12) Just the thought of a man like Ananias believing in Jesus was probably enough to drive Saul into a rage. The thought of Saul in a rage was enough to drive Ananias to prayer.

Ananias knew that Saul was on his way to Damascus, "still breathing threats and murder against the disciples of the Lord." As Saul later testified, "I persecuted this Way to the death, binding and putting both men and women into prisons...also when they were being put to death I cast my vote against them....and [I] started off for Damascus in order to bring even those who were there to Jerusalem as prisoners to be punished." (Acts 22:4; 26:10; 22:5) Ananias was among "those who were there."

The Lord spoke to Ananias in a vision: " 'Arise and go to the street called Straight, and inquire at the house of Judas for a man from Tarsus named Saul, for behold, he is praying, and he has seen in a vision a man named Ananias come in and lay his hands on him, so that he might regain his sight.'

"But Ananias answered, 'Lord, I have heard from many about this man, how much harm he did to Thy saints in Jerusalem; and here he has authority from the chief priests to bind all who call upon Thy name.'

"But the Lord said to him, 'Go, for he is a chosen instrument of Mine, to bear My name before the Gentiles and kings and the sons of Israel; for I will show him how much he must suffer for My name's sake.' " (Acts 9:11-16)

Ananias was a man of faith, a faithful man, and so he went in obedience to the Lord. The impossible happened. The eyes of Saul of Tarsus were opened, and he was filled with the Holy Spirit. He became a disciple of Jesus of Nazareth, but more than a disciple.

The impossible happened. A Pharisee of Pharisees was sent to call uncircumcised Gentiles to faith in the King of the Jews. "Now there were at Antioch, in the church that was there, prophets and teachers...And while they were ministering to the Lord and fasting, the Holy Spirit said, 'Set apart for Me Barnabas and Saul for the work to which I have called them.' Then, when they had fasted and prayed and laid their hands on them, they sent them away." (Acts 13:1-3)

"And when they reached Salamis, they began to proclaim the word of God in the synagogues of the Jews..." (v.5) The Apostle to the Gentiles began his ministry in the synagogue. He always began it in the synagogue. It was an order of evangelism from which he never departed.

"They arrived at Pisidian Antioch, and on the sabbath day they went into the synagogue and sat down. And after the reading of the Law and the Prophets the synagogue officials sent to them, saying, 'Brethren, if you have any word of exhortation for the people, say it.'

"And Paul [another name of Saul] stood up, and motioning with his hand, he said, 'Men of Israel, and you who fear God [i.e. proselytes], listen: The God of this people Israel chose our fathers, and made the people great during their stay in the land of Egypt...He distributed their land as an inheritance...He raised up David to be their king...From the offspring of this man according to promise God has brought to Israel a Savior, Jesus, after John had proclaimed before His coming a baptism of repentance to all the people of Israel.

" '...Brethren, sons of Abraham's family, and those among you who fear God, to us the word of this salvation is sent out...we preach to you the good news of the promise made to the fathers, that God has fulfilled this promise to our children in that He raised up Jesus...

" 'Therefore let it be known to you, brethren, that through Him forgiveness of sins is proclaimed to you, and through Him everyone who believes is freed from all things, from which you could not be freed through the Law of Moses....' " (vv.14-39)

When Peter preached, or when Philip preached, some believed and some did not. That's how it was when Paul preached. "Now when the meeting of the synagogue had broken up, many of the Jews and of the God-fearing proselytes followed Paul and Barnabas, who, speaking to them, were urging them to continue in the grace of God." (v.43)

Then the unusual began to happen. "And the next Sabbath nearly the whole city assembled to hear the word of God. But when the Jews saw the crowds, they were filled with jealousy, and began contradicting the things spoken by Paul, and were blaspheming." (vv.44-45)

Paul probably heard curses he had once uttered himself — perhaps even ones he had uttered in shutting his ears to the preaching of Stephen. In seeking the destruction of all the Jews who believed in Jesus, Paul had not been content simply to blaspheme on his own. "And as I punished them often in all the synagogues, I tried to force them to blaspheme; and being furiously enraged at them, I kept pursuing them even to the foreign cities." (Acts 26:11)

In Antioch, "Paul and Barnabas spoke out boldly and said, 'It was necessary that the word of God should be spoken to you first; since you repudiate it, and judge yourselves unworthy of eternal life, behold, we are turning to the Gentiles. For thus the Lord has commanded us, I have placed you as a light for the Gentiles, that you should bring salvation to the end of the earth.' " (Acts 13:46-47)

Paul recognized that God's calling for Israel is to be "a light for the Gentiles ...[to] bring salvation to the end of the earth." In his darkened rage, Paul had previously sought to destroy that light. Now that his eyes were opened, nothing would stop him from spreading that light and fulfilling that calling.

In Antioch it was necessary that Paul preach the gospel to the Jews first. Their response was up to them. No matter what they chose, Paul would continue to fulfill his calling as a Jew by bringing the gospel to the Gentiles.

"And when the Gentiles heard this, they began rejoicing and glorifying the word of the Lord; and as many as had been appointed to eternal life believed." (v.48) The most impossible of all impossibilities happened. Gentiles, who had rejected the Lord and had been rejected by Him for two thousand years, began crowding into the kingdom of God. God received them, not as proselytes, but as physically uncircumcised Gentiles.

Paul and Barnabas went from Antioch to Iconium. "And it came about that in Iconium they entered the synagogue of the Jews together, and spoke in such a manner that a great multitude believed, both of Jews and of Greeks." (Acts 14:1) Jews and Greeks alike received salvation.

Paul and Barnabas went from Iconium to Lystra. It was during this time that Timothy became a believer. (Acts 16:1-2) "But Jews came from Antioch and Iconium, and having won over the multitudes, they stoned Paul and dragged him out of the city, supposing him to be dead." (Acts 14:19) When Stephen had been stoned, had Paul made quite certain that he was dead?

Paul arose and went with Barnabas to Derbe to preach the gospel. "They returned to Lystra and to Iconium and to Antioch, strengthening the souls of the disciples...[and] appointed elders for them in every church." (vv.20-23) They preached some more in Perga, and then sailed home to [Syrian] Antioch.

"And when they had arrived and gathered the church together, they began to report all things that God had done with them and how He had opened a door of faith to the Gentiles." (v.27)

God had opened a door of faith to the Gentiles. He had sent Paul through that door, and He had revealed to him the mystery of Messiah. But all the Jewish believers did not yet know or understand this mystery.

"And some men came down [to Antioch] from Judea and began teaching the brethren, 'Unless you are circumcised according to the custom of Moses, you cannot be saved.' And when Paul and Barnabas had great dissension and debate with them, the brethren determined that Paul and Barnabas and certain others of them, should go up to Jerusalem to the apostles and elders concerning this issue.

"Therefore, being sent on their way by the church, they were passing through both Phoenicia and Samaria, describing in detail the conversion of the Gentiles, and were bringing great joy to all the brethren. And when they arrived at Jerusalem, they were received by the church and the apostles and the elders, and they reported all that God had done with them.

"But certain ones of the sect of the Pharisees who had believed, stood up, saying, 'It is necessary to circumcise them, and to direct them to observe the Law of Moses.' And the apostles and the elders came together to look into this matter.

"And after there had been much debate, Peter stood up and said to them, 'Brethren, you know that in the early days God made a choice among you, that by my mouth the Gentiles should hear the word of the gospel and believe. And God, who knows the heart, bore witness to them, giving them the Holy Spirit, just as He also did to us; and He made no distinction between us and them, cleansing their hearts by faith....'

"And all the multitude kept silent, and they were listening to Barnabas and Paul as they were relating what signs and wonders God had done through them among the Gentiles. And after they had stopped speaking, Jacob answered, saying, 'Brethren, listen to me. Simeon has related how God first concerned Himself about taking from among the Gentiles a people for His name. And with this the words of the Prophets agree, just as it is written, *"After these things I will return, and I will rebuild the tabernacle of David which has fallen, and I will rebuild its ruins, and I will restore it, in order that the rest of mankind may seek the Lord, and all the Gentiles who are called by My name, says the Lord, who makes these things known from of old."*

" 'Therefore it is my judgment that we do not trouble those who are turning to God from among the Gentiles, but that we write to them that they abstain from things contaminated by idols and from fornication and from what is strangled and from blood. For Moses from ancient generations has in every city those who preach him, since he is read in the synagogues every Sabbath.' " (Acts 15:1-21)

In Antioch, there was "great dissension and debate." It was not a minor issue. The question could be expressed as: "Do Gentiles have to become Jews first in order to be Christians?" "Will the Church be completely Jewish, or will uncircumcised Gentiles be allowed in?"

The church in Antioch knew how to pray and hear from the Lord. They had remarkable men of God there. (cf. Acts 13:1-3) Their wisdom was to bring the issue before the apostles and elders in Jerusalem.

The apostles and elders in Jerusalem did not demand that the matter be brought before them. The church in Antioch asked them to sit in judgment on the matter. The apostles had been taught by Jesus and the gospel had gone forth from Jerusalem. The Church throughout the world was, and is, the fruit, of their obedience to the Lord.

The believers in Phoenicia and Samaria received with great joy the news of the conversion of the Gentiles. They were happy that Gentiles were getting saved. They just didn't know exactly what to make of it.

In the gathering of the apostles and elders of the church in Jerusalem, there was "much debate." These were proven men of God who had suffered for their faith, and had seen the power of God. They knew the Scriptures and they knew the Lord.

But they were discussing a mystery, one which God was revealing in their midst. Simon Peter related how in the early days God had first begun to gather a people out of the Gentiles, by pouring out His Spirit on Cornelius and his household. Before that, God was only gathering this people within Israel.

The church in Jerusalem had three recognized leaders. Jacob, the brother of Jesus, was one. (cf. Acts 12:17; Gal.2:9) Peter and John were the other two.

Paul later wrote that "when Cephas [i.e. Peter] came to Antioch, I opposed him to his face, because he stood condemned. For prior to the coming of certain men from Jacob, he used to eat with the Gentiles; but when they came, he began to withdraw and hold himself aloof, fearing the party of the circumcision. And the rest of the Jews joined him in hypocrisy, with the result that even Barnabas was carried away by their hypocrisy." (Gal.2:11-13) (Paul and Barnabas parted company shortly after the Jerusalem council. (cf. Acts 15:36-40)

So it seems that when the Jerusalem council began, one of the three leaders of the church, Jacob, favored circumcision. Another, Peter, had been intimidated into vacillation. We do not know what the position of Jacob's brother John was, but even Barnabas, Paul's companion in Gentile ministry, had vacillated.

It is therefore remarkable that the council decided as it did. Peter stood up and declared that God "made no distinction between us and them, cleansing their hearts by faith." Jacob reinforced Simon Peter's declaration by bringing forth support from the prophets.

Then Jacob gave his judgment concerning what should be required of Gentile believers. He listed four things from God's Law. They must abstain from idolatry, immorality, and unbridled appetite. In abstaining from blood, they must respect life.

God had declared in His Law, "And any man from the house of Israel, or from the aliens who sojourn among them, who eats any blood, I will set My face against that person who eats blood, and will cut him off from among his people. For the life of the flesh is in the blood, and I have given it to you on the altar to make atonement for your souls; for it is the blood by reason of the life that makes atonement." (Lev.17:10-11)

Gentile believers were not being called to seek justification through the Law. Nor were they being told to become proselytes. Why the prohibitions from the Law?

Jacob supported his judgment by reminding the council: "For Moses from ancient generations has in every city those who preach him, since he is read in the synagogues every Sabbath." What is the connection? Why should the reading in the synagogue of the Law of Moses affect the Gentile believers?

All the Jewish believers were zealous for the Law. (Acts 21:20) They recognized it as a revelation of God's holiness. They recognized that it explained and defined the gospel.

As Paul later expressed it, "Is the Law then contrary to the promises of God? May it never be!...we were kept in custody under the law... Therefore the Law has become our tutor to lead us to Messiah, that we may be justified by faith." (Gal.3:21-24)

Though salvation is available through the New Covenant, which supercedes the Covenant of the Law, the God who gave Israel's covenants has not changed. He gave the Law to teach Israel of Messiah, the Holy One of Israel. His people must be holy.

Paul knew that "the Law is holy, and the commandment is holy and righteous and good." (Rom.7:12) The Gentile believers were simply being required to be obedient to a God who never changes, to a Lord who is the same yesterday, today, and forever. He is a God who has revealed Himself to the world through His relationship to Israel.

"Then it seemed good to the apostles and the elders, with the whole church, to choose men from among them to send to Antioch with Paul and Barnabas...and they sent this letter by them, '...it seemed good to the Holy Spirit and to us to lay upon you no greater burden than these essentials; that you abstain from things sacrificed to idols and from blood and from things strangled and from fornication; if you keep yourselves free from such things, you will do well. Farewell.' " (Acts 15:22-29)

The Holy Spirit, the apostles, the elders and whole church in Jerusalem agreed. These were "essentials" for Gentiles who received the grace of the Lord unto salvation. God sent the Messiah so that "we being delivered from the hand of our enemies, might serve Him without fear, in holiness and righteousness before Him all our days." (Lk.1:74-75)

After we have finished going through the Book of Acts, we will examine "the mystery of Messiah" in greater detail.

21

"THE GOSPEL IS"

Paul records how the leaders of the church in Jerusalem realized, "that I had been entrusted with the gospel to the uncircumcised, just as Peter with the gospel to the circumcised." (Gal.2:7) Jesus sent Paul to the Gentiles. Paul was accountable before God for the fulfillment of his ministry, which was to reach everyone in the world who was not Jewish with the gospel.

Paul writes to the church at Rome as the apostle to the Gentiles. It is not his "ministry" to preach the gospel to the Jews, but wherever he went he did. And he did it first.

Why did Paul go to the Jews first? Was it merely a practical consideration given the historical circumstances? After all, only the Jews would already understand the context of the gospel. That was not Paul's reason. He said that he preached to the Jews first because "it was necessary" to do so. It was not a circumstantial strategy. It was a divine imperative.

"And when they reached Salamis, they began to proclaim the word of God in the synagogues of the Jews..." (Acts 13:5) "...they arrived at Pisidian Antioch, and on the sabbath day they went into the synagogue and sat down....And Paul stood up, and motioning with his hand, he said..." (Acts 13:14-16)

"And it came about that in Iconium they entered the synagogue of the Jews together, and spoke in such a manner that a great multitude believed, both of Jews and of Greeks." (Acts 14:1) From there, they "...fled to the cities of Lycaonia, Lystra and Derbe, and the surrounding region; and there they continued to preach the gospel." (Acts 14:6-7) We are only told of one incident that occurred during this time, which involved the healing of a lame man, the priest of Zeus, etc.

Yet we know that Paul did preach to the Jews in this region, because on his second missionary journey, "he came also to Derbe and to Lystra. And behold, a certain disciple was there, named Timothy, the son of a Jewish woman who was a believer, but his father was a Greek... Paul wanted this man to go with him; and he took and circumcised him because of the Jews who were in those parts, for they all knew that his father was a Greek." (Acts 16:1,3) Timothy and his mother had become believers as a result of Paul's first missionary journey.

Why did Paul circumcise Timothy before having him join the ministry? Paul did so because he intended to continue to preach the gospel to the Jew first. Timothy's uncircumcision, given his Jewish mother, would have been an unnecessary stumblingblock to the Jews of that region in their consideration of the gospel.

On the second missionary journey, Paul took Silas, and then Timothy, with him. They came to Philippi, "And on the Sabbath day we went outside the gate to a river side, where we were supposing that there would be a place of prayer [προσευχη]; and we sat down and began speaking to the women who had assembled." (Acts 16:13) When there were not enough male Jews to form a synagogue, or if for some other reason there were no synagogue, the Jews living among the Gentiles met at a "proseuche," a place of prayer.

"Now when they had traveled through Amphipolis and Apollonia [after leaving Philippi], they came to Thessalonica, where there was a synagogue of the Jews. And according to Paul's custom, he went to them, and for three Sabbaths reasoned with them from the Scriptures, explaining and giving evidence that the Messiah had to suffer and rise again from the dead, and saying, 'This Jesus whom I am proclaiming to you is the Messiah.' " (Acts 17:1-3)

"And [Jesus] came to Nazareth, where He had been brought up; and as was His custom, He entered the synagogue on the Sabbath, and stood up to read." (Lk.4:16) The custom of the Son of God was to go the synagogue on the Sabbath. Perhaps that was because He was Jewish, and because He "was sent only to the lost sheep of the house of Israel."

Paul, of course, was Jewish too, but he was the Apostle to the Gentiles. Nevertheless, it was the custom, the habitual practice, of the Apostle to the Gentiles to preach the gospel to the Jews first. He believed that, as he had told the Jews in Pisidian Antioch, "It was necessary" to do that.

Paul faced great opposition as he sought to establish that the gospel is "also to the Greek." He faced great opposition as he lived in obedience to the gospel being "to the Jew first." He never backed down or changed his conviction. He knew that the gospel is "to the Jew first and also to the Greek."

Paul was not afraid of confrontation. It only offered greater opportunity to preach the gospel. Some believed and some didn't.

In Thessalonica, as everywhere else, that is what happened. "And some of them were persuaded and joined Paul and Silas, along with a great multitude of the God-fearing Greeks and a number of the leading women. But the Jews [who didn't believe], becoming jealous and taking along some wicked men from the market place, formed a mob and set the city in an uproar; and coming upon the house of Jason, they were seeking to bring them out to the people.

"And when they did not find them, they began dragging Jason and some brethren before the city authorities, shouting, 'These men who have upset the inhabited earth are come here also.' " (Acts 17:4-6) Even their opponents testified that they had "upset the inhabited earth."

Without radio, TV, the printed page, or even the New Covenant

Scriptures, they upset the inhabited earth with the gospel. Without the power of coal or steam, the combustion engine, hydroelectric, photovoltaic, or nuclear devices, they shook the foundation of the world. They were just a handful of people, filled with the Spirit, following God's order.

From Thessalonica, they went to Berea, "...and when they arrived, they went into the synagogue of the Jews." (Acts 17:10) There they preached the gospel. From Berea, they went to Athens.

When Paul was in Athens, "his spirit was being provoked within him as he was beholding the city full of idols. So [ουν] he was reasoning in the synagogue with the Jews and the God-fearing, and in the market place every day with those who happened to be present." (Acts 17:16-17)

Literally, "Paul seeing the city being filled with idols, his spirit was painfully excited in him. He reasoned indeed **therefore** in the synagogue with the Jews ..." The Gentiles in Athens had filled the city with idols and were worshipping them. That bothered Paul so much that he went into the synagogue to preach the gospel.

Why did Paul go into the synagogue? What was the causal relationship between one and the other? What does the "therefore" mean? God created the Jews to be a light to the Gentiles, to bring them, as Paul was doing, to the worship of the true and living God.

As Paul reminded the Gentile believers in Thessalonica, where he had been shortly before coming to Athens, "in every place your faith toward God has gone forth, so that we have no need to say anything. For they themselves report about us what kind of a reception we had with you, and how you turned to God from idols to serve a living and true God, and to wait for His Son from heaven, whom He raised from the dead, that is Jesus, who delivers us from the wrath to come." (1Thes.1:9) Paul was fulfilling the calling of a Jew, and he sought other Jews to join him in that task. This is the reason for the "therefore" [ουν] of going into the synagogue in Athens.

"After these things he left Athens and went to Corinth.... And he was reasoning in the synagogue every Sabbath and trying to persuade Jews and Greeks." (Acts 18:1,4) Paul claimed that doing so delivered him from the bloodguilt of not warning them. (Acts 18:6) Paul knew what God had told Ezekiel: "But if the watchman sees the sword coming and does not blow the trumpet, and the people are not warned, and a sword comes and takes a person from them, he is taken away in his iniquity; but his blood I will require from the watchman's hand." (Ezek.33:6) He understood the God-given responsibility and accountability of those who have been entrusted by God with His message.

Corinth was also filled with idols. That's why Paul wrote to the Gentile believers there about "things sacrificed to idols." (cf. 1Co.8) He also reminded them of another causal relationship: "For if you were to have countless tutors in Messiah, yet you would not have many fathers; for in

Messiah Jesus I became your father through the gospel. I exhort you therefore [ουν], be imitators of me." (1Co.4:15-16) They had seen his faith, observed his conduct, and had been brought into the kingdom of God through his preaching of the gospel (to the Jew first). Paul exhorted them to imitate him.

When Paul told the Jews in the synagogue in Corinth, "from now on I shall go the Gentiles," he did not mean that he would not preach the gospel to Jews anymore. Nor did he mean that in Corinth he would not preach the gospel to Jews anymore.

He was announcing that he was clean — not guilty from failing to warn them. He did **not** say that he would **only** preach to the Gentiles, **but** rather that he would **also** preach to them. We know, in fact, that he continued to preach the gospel to the Jews in Corinth even after he started going to the Gentiles.

"And he departed from there and went to the house of a certain man named Titius Justus, a worshiper of God, whose house was next to the synagogue. And Crispus, the leader of the synagogue, believed in the Lord with all his household, and many of the Corinthians when they heard were believing and being baptized." (Acts 18:7-8) When Paul went to the Gentiles, neither his heart nor his God allowed him to go very far from the synagogue. He moved in next door, continued to preach to his brethren, and the leader of the synagogue and his family believed in Jesus, igniting a revival throughout Corinth.

The new leader of the synagogue in Corinth, Sosthenes, brought Paul before the judgment seat, trying to have him arrested and beaten. Sosthenes wanted to stop Paul from preaching the gospel to the Jews. It didn't work. (Acts 18:12-17) Sosthenes himself later became a believer and accompanied Paul in his preaching of the gospel. (1Co.1:1)

Paul left Corinth, "And they came to Ephesus, and he left them there. Now he himself entered the synagogue and reasoned with the Jews." (Acts 18:19)

"Now a certain Jew named Apollos, an Alexandrian by birth, an eloquent man, came to Ephesus; and he was mighty in the Scriptures....And he began to speak out boldly in the synagogue...." (Acts 18:24,26) This was also the practice of Apollos. It was the practice of Barnabas, Silas, Aquila, and Priscilla. It was the practice of every evangelist of the early Church throughout the Book of Acts. They never changed.

When Paul came again to Ephesus on his third missionary journey, "he entered the synagogue and continued speaking out boldly for three months, reasoning and persuading them about the kingdom of God." (Acts 19:8) "Now after these things were finished, Paul purposed in the spirit to go to Jerusalem after he had passed through Macedonia and Achaia, saying, 'After I have been there, I must also see Rome.' " (Acts 19:21)

From Ephesus, Paul went to Macedonia, exhorted the believers, and took his leave of them. (Acts 20) Then he departed for Jerusalem. In the next section, we will look at what happened there. From Jerusalem, Paul the prisoner sailed to Rome.

Even when Paul was under house arrest in Rome, he adhered to the same order in his evangelism. He could not go to the synagogue, so he asked "the leading men of the Jews" to gather the community to him so that he could proclaim the gospel to them. "And when they had set a day for him, they came to him at his lodging in large numbers; and he was explaining to them by solemnly testifying about the kingdom of God, and trying to persuade them concerning Jesus, from both the Law of Moses and from the Prophets, from morning until evening. And some were being persuaded by the things spoken, but others would not believe." (Acts 28:24)

Paul concluded his remarks that day as he had previously in Pisidian Antioch and Corinth. "Let it be known to you therefore, that this salvation of God has been sent to the Gentiles; they will also listen." (Acts 28:28) Among the Jews who heard Paul, some believed and some didn't. So it was also with the Gentiles, ever since the gospel was **also** sent to them.

22

THE COMMONWEALTH OF ISRAEL

God entrusted the gospel to the Jews, and brought it to the world through them. He did this, not because of any Jewish merit, but because of His eternal, sovereign plan. As Jesus said quite simply, "Salvation is of the Jews."

When God changed Abram's name to Abraham, and made him the father of the Jewish people, He told him that He would also make him "the father of a multitude of Gentiles [goyim]." When God changed Jacob's name to Israel, He promised him the same thing.

"And God said to him, 'Your name is Jacob; you shall no longer be called Jacob, but Israel shall be your name.' God also said to him, 'I am God Almighty; Be fruitful and multiply; A nation and a company [קהל, kahal] of goyim shall come from you, and kings shall come forth from you. And the land which I gave to Abraham and Isaac, I will give it to you, And I will give the land to your descendants after you.' " (Gen.35:10-12)

It is interesting that God here repeats to Jacob the commandment and blessing which had initially been given to Adam (Gen.1:28) — "Be fruitful and multiply." God had repeated the commandment to Noah and his sons: "And God blessed Noah and his sons and said to them, 'Be fruitful and multiply, and fill the earth.' " (Gen.9:1)

In the wilderness, God promised Israel, "If you walk in My statutes and keep My commandments so as to carry them out...I shall also grant peace in the land, so that you may lie down with no one making you tremble. I shall also eliminate harmful beasts from the land, and no sword will pass through your land....

"So I will turn towards you and make you fruitful and multiply you, and I will confirm My covenant with you....I am the Lord your God, who brought you out of the land of Egypt so that you should not be their slaves, and I broke the bars of your yoke and made you walk erect." (Lev.26:3,6,9,13)

In these verses, God gives a picture of the blessing He wants to bestow on His people. He gives a picture of the blessing He **waits** to bestow on His people. The picture envisions a state — a political entity — and a country — a land.

Stephen reminded the Sanhedrin of what God had done with Abraham. "God removed him into this country in which you are now living. And He gave him no inheritance in it, not even a foot of ground; and yet, even when he had no child, He promised that He would give it to him as a possession, and to his offspring after him. But God spoke to this effect, that his offspring would be sojourners in an alien [αλλοτρια] land, and that they would be enslaved and mistreated for four hundred years. 'And whatever nation to which they shall be in bondage, I Myself will judge,' said God, 'and after that they will come out and serve Me in this place.' " (Acts 7:4-7)

Gentiles are naturally "aliens [αλλοτριος] to the commonwealth [πολιτειας] of Israel." (Eph.2:12) They naturally belong to another domain and dominion. They are naturally foreigners, without the rights and responsibilities of citizenship in Israel.

But for Gentiles who repent and believe, that is no longer the case. They have become "fellow-citizens [συμπολιται] of the saints and of the household of God." This is "political" terminology that needs to be understood in its political, but not worldly, sense. Plato's *Republic*, for example, is a "commonwealth" [πολιτειας], a politically distinguished community. Aristotle's *On Politics* is an examination of what the best characteristics of such political communities are.

In *City of God*, Augustine gives the classical meaning of commonwealth. He refers to Scipio, as Cicero presented him. Some of the discussion is helpful to us in understanding these political words as Paul used them.

Scipio "starts by repeating and supporting his brief definition of a commonwealth, that it is 'the weal of the community', and he defines 'the community' as meaning not any and every association of the population, but 'an association united by a common sense of right and a community of interest'. He...derives the proposition that a commonwealth (i.e. 'the weal [well-being] of the community') only exists where there is a sound and just government...And what is called harmony in music answers to concord in a community, and it is the best and closest bond of security in a country. And this cannot possibly exist without justice." [1]

Some of the laws that guaranteed "justice" in the Roman empire, or in ancient Greece, were unjust from a Biblical perspective. But others have important lessons for believers. For example, "the Romans, as Scipio boasts in the discussion *On the Commonwealth*, refused to allow character and reputation to be exposed to the calumnies and libels of poets and imposed the death penalty on anyone who dared to compose verse of this kind." [2] "And the tongue is a fire, the very world of iniquity; the tongue is set among our members as that which defiles the entire body, and sets on fire the course of our life, and is set on fire by hell." (Jacob 3:6)

Augustine concludes, "But true justice is found only in that commonwealth whose founder and ruler is Christ; if we agree to call it a commonwealth, seeing that we cannot deny that it is the 'weal of the community'." [3] "For Scipio gives a brief definition of the state, or commonwealth, as the 'weal of the people'. Now if this is a true definition there never was a Roman commonwealth, because the Roman state was never the 'weal of the people,' according to Scipio's definition. For he defined a 'people' as a multitude 'united in association by a common sense of right and a community of interest.' He explains in the discussion what he means by 'a common sense of right,' showing that a state cannot be maintained without justice, and where there is no true justice there can be no right." [4]

"That being so, when a man does not serve God, what amount of justice are we to suppose to exist in his being? For if a soul does not serve God it cannot with any kind of justice command the body, nor can a man's reason control the vicious elements in the soul. And if there is no justice in such a man, there can be no sort of doubt that there is no justice in a gathering which consists of such men. Here, then, there is not that 'consent to the law' which makes a mob into a people that is said to be a commonwealth." [5]

A man may be legally a part of a community, a citizen with full rights, living in the community, and yet separated from the community by the decisions of his own heart. Likewise, without inner consent to the law of God, a man or a multitude — whether Jewish or Gentile — can find himself in the same paradoxical situation in the commonwealth that God has established.

With the classical definition of commonwealth as background, our clearest understanding of Paul's meaning will come from following him as he encounters issues of citizenship and law. The issues were quite clear to him.

Paul had come to the city of Jerusalem to bring a relief offering from the churches he had established among the Gentiles. Some of the Gentile believers had accompanied him to Jerusalem. "And now the following day Paul went in with us to Jacob, and all the elders were present. And after he had greeted them, he began to relate one by one the things which God had done among the Gentiles through his ministry.

"And when they heard it they began glorifying God; and they said to him, 'You see, brother, how many myriads [μυριαδες, lit. ten thousands] there are among the Jews who have believed, and they are all zealous for the Law; and they have been told about you, that you are teaching all the Jews who are among the Gentiles to forsake Moses, telling them not to circumcise their children nor to walk according to the customs.

" 'What, then, is to be done? They will certainly hear that you have come. Therefore do this that we tell you: We have four men who are under a vow; take them and purify yourself along with them, and pay their expenses in order that they may shave their heads; and all will know that there is nothing to the things which they have been told about you, but that you yourself also walk orderly, keeping the Law.' " (Acts 21:18-24)

Some in the Church were saying that Paul taught the Jews to forsake the Law of Moses. There was no truth to what they were saying. Some in the Church were saying that Paul had forsaken the Law. There was no truth to that either.

So Paul was perfectly willing to do as Jacob and the elders of the church in Jerusalem requested. On a previous occasion, he himself had taken a vow according to the Law. "In Cenchrea he had his hair cut, for he was keeping a vow." (Acts 18:18)

On this occasion in Jerusalem, "Then Paul took the men, and the next day purifying himself along with them went into the temple, giving notice of the completion of the days of purification, until the sacrifice was offered for each one of them. And when the seven days were almost over, the Jews from Asia, upon seeing him in the temple, began to stir up all the multitude and laid hands on him, crying out, 'Men of Israel, come to our aid! This is the man who preaches to all men everywhere against our people, and the Law, and this place; and besides he has even brought Greeks into the temple and has defiled this holy place.'

"For they had previously seen Trophimus the Ephesian in the city with him, and they supposed that Paul had brought him into the temple. And all the city was aroused, and the people rushed together; and taking hold of Paul, they dragged him out of the temple; and immediately the doors were shut." (Acts 21:26-30)

These "Jews from Asia" had their own versions of the false rumors about Paul that were being spread through the Church. None of what they said was true, but they did not give Paul the opportunity to respond.

"And while they were seeking to kill him, a report came up to the commander of the Roman Cohort that all Jerusalem was in confusion. And at once he took along some soldiers and centurions, and ran down to them; and when they saw the commander and the soldiers, they stopped beating Paul.

"Then the commander came up and took hold of him and ordered him to be bound with two chains; and he was asking who he was and what he had done. But among the crowd some were shouting one thing and some another, and when he could not find out the facts on account of the uproar, he ordered him to be brought to the barracks." (Acts 21:31-34)

Paul seized the opportunity and said, in Greek, to the commander, " 'I am a Jew of Tarsus in Cilicia, a citizen [πολιτες] of no insignificant city [πολεως]; and I beg you, allow me to speak to the people.'

"And when he had given him permission, Paul, standing on the stairs, motioned to the people with his hand; and when there was a great hush, he spoke to them in the Hebrew dialect, saying, 'Brethren and fathers, hear my defense which I now offer to you.' And when they heard that he was addressing them in the Hebrew dialect, they became even more quiet; and he said, 'I am a Jew, born in Tarsus of Cilicia, but brought up in this city, educated under Gamaliel, strictly according to the law of our fathers, being zealous for God, just as you all are today.' " (Acts 21:39-22:3)

Before he had come to Jerusalem, the Holy Spirit had warned him several times of what awaited him, lastly through the prophet Agabus. "And coming to us, he took Paul's belt and bound his own feet and hands, and said, 'This is what the Holy Spirit says: "*In this way the Jews at Jerusalem will bind the man who owns this belt and deliver him into the hands of the Gentiles.*"' And when we had heard this, we as well as the local residents began begging him not to go up to Jerusalem. Then Paul answered, 'What are you doing, weeping and breaking my heart? For I am ready not only to be bound, but even to die at Jerusalem for the name of the Lord Jesus.' " (Acts 21:11-13)

Had it not been for the grace of God, Paul would have been one of those actively stirring up the crowd. He had actively sought the death of any Jew like himself who believed in Jesus. Now he was on the other side, and he had the opportunity to speak as he had heard Stephen speak many years before.

In Hebrew, he began, "I am a Jew." Then he told of how he had persecuted the believers until Jesus Himself had appeared to him. "And it came about that when I returned to Jerusalem and was praying in the temple, I fell into a trance, and I saw Him saying to me, 'Make haste, and get out of Jerusalem quickly, because they will not accept your testimony about Me.'

"And I said, 'Lord, they themselves understand that in one synagogue after another I used to imprison and beat those who believed in Thee. And when the blood of Thy witness Stephen was being shed, I also was standing by approving, and watching out for the cloaks of those who were slaying him.' And He said to me, 'Go! For I will send you far away to the Gentiles.' " (Acts 22:17-21)

Up until this point, the whole crowd listened to him in great silence. They were silent when he told how he had persecuted the believers. They were silent when he told how Jesus had appeared to him and brought him to repentance. They were silent when he told how Jesus the Messiah had appointed him to "be a witness for Him to all men of what you have seen and heard." (v.15)

They were silent until he mentioned the Gentiles. "And they listened to him up to this statement, and then they raised their voices and said, 'Away with such a fellow from the earth, for he should not be allowed to live!' And as they were crying out and throwing off their cloaks and tossing dust into the air, the commander ordered him to be brought into the barracks, stating that he should be examined by scourging so that he might find out the reason why they were shouting against him that way." (vv.22-24)

'No Gentiles in the Temple! No uncircumcised men defiling the holy things of God! No Gentiles secretly brought into Israel's holy place!' It was the most volatile issue in the Church. It was also the most volatile issue in Israel.

"And when they stretched him out with thongs, Paul said to the centurion who was standing by, 'Is it lawful for you to scourge a man who is a Roman and uncondemned?' And when the centurion heard this, he went to the commander and told him, saying, 'What are you about to do? For this man is a Roman.'

"And the commander came and said to him, 'Tell me, are you a Roman?' And he said, 'Yes.' And the commander answered, 'I acquired this citizenship [πολιτειαν] with a large sum of money.' And Paul said, 'But I was actually [so] born.' Therefore those who were about to examine him immediately let go of him; and the commander also was afraid when he found out that he was a Roman, and because he had put him in chains." (vv.25-29)

To obtain the privilege to speak, Paul had pointed out that he was a citizen of the city of Tarsus in Cilicia. To avert the scourging, Paul pointed out that he was a Roman citizen.

He was not physically a Roman. He had not been born in Rome, nor was he an inhabitant of the imperial city. But when it came to Roman citizenship, he was as much a citizen as any native-born resident of Rome.

Roman citizenship had its rights and its protections. The centurion and the commander were afraid for their lives, because they had transgressed the rights of a Roman citizen. All the power of the Roman empire could be turned against them.

In Philippi, Paul had cast out a spirit of divination from a slave-girl who kept advertising the devil by putting his seal of approval on their ministry. "But when her masters saw that their hope of profit was gone, they seized Paul and Silas and dragged them into the market place before the authorities, and when they had brought them to the chief magistrates, they said, 'These men are throwing our city into confusion, being Jews, and are proclaiming customs which it is not lawful for us to accept or to observe, being Romans.'

"And the crowd rose up together against them, and the chief magistrates tore their robes off them, and proceeded to order them to be beaten with rods. And when they had inflicted many blows upon them, they threw them into prison, commanding the jailer to guard them securely; and he, having received such a command, threw them into the inner prison, and fastened their feet in the stocks." (Acts 16:19-24)

Some of the Jews in Jerusalem (and in Pisidian Antioch [Acts 13:45] and elsewhere) didn't like hearing about the Gentiles. Some of the Gentiles in Philippi (and Ephesus [Acts 19:34] and elsewhere) didn't like hearing about the Jews.

The masters of the slave-girl put forth their own Roman citizenship as a condemnation of Paul and Silas. The next day the chief magistrates sent word to the jailer to release Paul and Silas. "But Paul said to them, 'They have beaten us in public without trial, men who are Romans, and have thrown us into prison; and now are they sending us away secretly? No indeed! But let them come themselves and bring us out.'

"And the policemen reported these words to the chief magistrates. And they were afraid when they heard that they were Romans, and they came and appealed to them, and when they brought them out, they kept begging them to leave the city." (Acts 16:37-39)

The chief magistrates in Philippi and the Roman army officers in Jerusalem, all feared the power of Rome. All the power of Rome guaranteed the rights of every Roman citizen. On one occasion Paul was beaten, on the other he wasn't. Both times — wherever Rome ruled - his Roman citizenship provoked fear and obedience.

Citizenship brings protection, and it also brings privilege. In the British Commonwealth of Nations — an imperfect analogy — every citizen of the Commonwealth was entitled to a British education, a British passport, and unrestricted travel in the Commonwealth. A Kikuyu in Kenya or a Quebecois in Canada were British citizens fully as much as any lord in London.

Were they British? Well, that depends entirely upon what you mean by "British." From inside the Commonwealth, they were British to the high court, and British to the world, no matter where they lived or what their ancestry. They were grafted in. They were fellow-citizens, fellow-partakers, fellow-members, and fellow-heirs.

Nevertheless, Great Britain was the mother country, and no one could deny the special place of her land and her people. Other countries, to their benefit, were part of the Commonwealth, but it belonged to Britain. To deny that would be to destroy any basis for laying claim to the benefits of belonging. Without Great Britain, there could not be a British Commonwealth. (Without Rome, there could not be a Roman Empire.)

It was there that the Commonwealth began, every day. It was the British people who had brought their cultural, industrial, and intellectual strength to the others. To deny the particular place of the British people in the Commonwealth would be an absurd display of arrogant ingratitude and ignorance.

Paul said that it is "my brethren, my kinsmen according to the flesh, who are Israelites, to whom belongs the adoption as sons and the glory and the covenants and the giving of the Law and the service and the promises, whose are the fathers, and from whom is the Messiah according to the flesh, who is over all, God blessed forever. Amen." (Rom.9:3-5) These are the things that pertain to salvation.

Peter wrote "to those who reside as aliens, scattered throughout Pontus, Galatia, Cappadocia, Asia, and Bithynia, who are chosen." (1Pet.1:1) He said, "Beloved, I exhort you as strangers and sojourners [lit.] to abstain from fleshly lusts, which wage war against the soul. Keep your behavior excellent among the Gentiles, so that in the thing in which they slander you as evildoers, they may on account of your good deeds, as they observe them, glorify God in the day of visitation." (1Pet.2:11-12)

When he said, "the Gentiles...slander you as evildoers," did he mean all Gentiles? No. Some of those to whom he was writing were Gentiles. He meant those Gentiles who do not believe.

Immediately preceding these verses, he wrote, "This precious value, then, is for you who believe, but for those who disbelieve, 'The stone which the builders rejected, this became the very corner stone,' and, 'a stone of stumbling and a rock of offense'; for they stumble because they are disobedient to the word, and to this they were also appointed." (vv.7-8)

Who are these "builders" who rejected the chief corner stone? Jesus made it clear that these were "the chief priests and Pharisees." (Mt.21:42-45) They were Jews, but not all Jews were chief priests or Pharisees.

Some Jews, even most, were among "those who disbelieve." So were some, even most, Gentiles. On the other hand, some Jews and some Gentiles, all by the grace of God, believe.

The covenants and the promises belong to Israel. Peter, like Paul, was part of the chosen faithful remnant which God preserved for Himself in Israel. The covenants and the promises belong to the believing remnant. Gentile believers who are brought into the commonwealth of Israel become fellow-heirs of those covenants and the promises.

Physically, people are either Jewish or Gentile. Since the Tower of Babel and the choosing of Abraham, there are no other possibilities. All peoples are distinguished physically — all peoples except the Church. The Church is Jewish AND Gentile.

Therefore, Peter writes to all believers, "But you are a chosen race, a royal priesthood, a holy nation, a people for God's own possession, that you may proclaim the excellencies of Him who has called you out of darkness into His marvelous light; for you once were not a people, but now you are the people of God; you had not received mercy, but now you have received mercy." (vv.9-10)

Gentile believers share just as much in these promises as their Jewish brethren do. They have been brought out of what they were. They have been brought into something new.

"Now Naaman, captain of the army of the king of Aram, was a great man with his master, and highly respected, because by him the Lord had given victory to Aram. The man was also a valiant warrior, but he was a leper." (2Kings 5:1) He came to Elisha the prophet to be healed of his leprosy.

"And Elisha sent a messenger to him, saying, 'Go and wash in the Jordan seven times, and your flesh shall be restored to you and you shall be clean.' But Naaman was furious and went away and said, '...Are not Abanah and Pharpar, the rivers of Damascus, better than all the waters of Israel? Could I not wash in them and be clean?' So he turned and went away in a rage." (2Kings 5:10-12)

Naaman was furious at the suggestion that the waters of Israel could do for him what the waters of Damascus could not. He went away in a rage, with his leprosy still clinging to him. Had it not been for his servants, who encouraged him to humble himself and forget his Syrian pride, he would have remained a leper to the day of his death. However, Naaman finally humbled himself, obeyed, was healed, and learned that "Salvation is of the Jews."

Pride is not exclusively a Gentile characteristic, nor a Jewish one. It is a human characteristic. That is why Jesus told the other side of the story to those Jews in the synagogue at Nazareth.

" 'And there were many lepers in Israel in the time of Elisha the prophet; and none of them was cleansed, but only Naaman the Syrian.' And all in the synagogue were filled with rage as they heard these things." (Lk.4:25-28)

God's plan of redemption is designed so "that no flesh should boast before God." (1Co.1:29) Gentile believers have been brought into the Commonwealth of Israel. They are fully citizens as much as any physical descendants of Abraham, Isaac, and Jacob. They are not citizens to the exclusion of the children of Israel. They are citizens along with them.

FOOTNOTES

1. St. Augustine, *Concerning THE CITY OF GOD against the Pagans*, trans. by Henry Bettenson, Penguin Books, London, 1984, Bk.2, Ch.21, Pp.72,73
2. ibid., Bk.2, Ch.12, P.60
3. ibid., Bk.2, Ch.22, P.75
4. ibid., Bk.19, Ch.21, Pp.881-882
5. ibid., Bk.19, Ch.21, Pp.883

23

THE MYSTERY OF MESSIAH

Paul explained to the Ephesians that, "To me, the very least of all saints, this grace was given, to preach to the Gentiles the unfathomable riches of Messiah, and to bring to light what is the administration of **the mystery** which for ages has been hidden in God, who created all things." (Eph.3:8-9) He asked them to "pray on my behalf, that utterance may be given to me in the opening of my mouth, to make known with boldness **the mystery** of the gospel." (Eph.6:19)

He told the Colossians, "Of this church I was made a minister according to the stewardship from God bestowed on me for your benefit, that I might fully carry out the preaching of the word of God, that is, **the mystery** which has been hidden from the past ages and generations; but has now been manifested to His saints, to whom God willed to make known what is the riches of the glory of **this mystery** among the Gentiles, which is Messiah in you, the hope of glory." (Col.1:25-27)

He also told them, "Devote yourself to prayer, keeping alert in it with an attitude of thanksgiving; praying at the same time for us as well, that God may open up to us a door for the word, so that we may speak forth **the mystery** of Messiah, for which I have also been imprisoned; in order that I may make it clear in the way I ought to speak." (Col.4:2-4)

Paul concluded his letter to the Romans in praise to God: "Now to Him who is able to establish you according to my gospel and the preaching of Messiah Jesus, according to the revelation of **the mystery** which has been kept secret for long ages past, but now is manifested, and by the Scriptures of the prophets, according to the commandment of the eternal God, has been made known to all the Gentiles, leading to obedience of faith; to the only wise God, through Messiah Jesus, to whom be the glory forever. Amen." (Rom.16:25-27)

Paul was beaten for this mystery. He was imprisoned for it. He suffered greatly to share the revelation of this mystery with others.

Though the prophets had spoken about this mystery, no one understood it until God revealed it to Paul. No one could figure it out. What would be the relationship to Israel of the multitudes of Gentiles who repented and believed? How would God enable the strangers in the camp of Israel to be more numerous than the camp itself?

In writing to the Ephesians, Paul explains what the natural condition of the Gentiles is. "Therefore remember, that formerly you, the Gentiles in the flesh...were at that time separate from Messiah, excluded from the commonwealth of Israel, and strangers to the covenants of promise, having no hope and without God in the world." (Eph.2:11-12)

Then he explains how that is changed in Messiah. The Gentile believers were "separate from Messiah, but they "who formerly were far off, have been brought near by the blood of Messiah. For He Himself is our peace, who made both one, and broke down the dividing wall of the barrier...[to] reconcile them both in one body to God through the cross, by it having put to death the hostility." (Eph.2:13-16)

Far-off Gentile believers have been joined to "those who were near." Abraham, Isaac, and Jacob, Moses, Jeremiah, Anna and Simeon "were near." Peter, Jacob, and John, Paul, Barnabas, and Silas "were near." They were all part of the faithful remnant in Israel. Gentiles who believe are joined to them.

"So then you [Gentile believers] are no longer strangers and aliens [excluded from the commonwealth of Israel, and strangers to the covenants of promise], but you are fellow citizens with the saints [i.e. the Jewish believers], and are of God's household having been built upon the foundation of the apostles and prophets, Messiah Jesus Himself being the cornerstone." (Eph.2:19-20)

The prophets prophesied the New Covenant; the apostles proclaimed it. It is realized in Messiah, the cornerstone. Previously, the Gentile believers were without "hope and without God in the world." Now, they are built upon a foundation, and their lives will be built into something.

"In [Messiah] the whole building, being fitted together is growing into a holy temple in the Lord; in whom you also are being built together into a dwelling of God in the Spirit." (Eph.2:21-22) That is a radical change from their previous condition, when their lives were wasted in vanity and idolatry. They were without hope then, because "Unless the Lord builds the house, they labor in vain who build it." (Ps.127:1)

Gentile believers have become fellow-citizens with the faithful Jewish remnant in the commonwealth of Israel. Consequently they share fully in the New Covenant blessings and responsibilities.

Gentile believers do not take anything from Israel, they are joined to Israel. They are "grafted in among them," among those who are the natural, believing branches. (Rom.11:17) Gentile believers are grafted into what God has given to the Jewish people.

"For this reason I Paul, the prisoner of Messiah Jesus for the sake of you Gentiles — if indeed you have heard of the stewardship of God's grace which was given to me for you; that by revelation there was made known to me **the mystery**, as I wrote before in brief.

"And by referring to this, when you read you can understand my insight into **the mystery** of Messiah, which in other generations was not made known to the sons of men, as it has now been revealed to His holy apostles and prophets in the Spirit; to be specific, that the Gentiles are fellow-heirs and fellow-members of the body, and fellow-partakers of the promise in Messiah Jesus through the gospel." (Eph.3:1-6)

Gentile believers, as Gentiles, become fellow-heirs with the Jewish believers. They now share in Israel's inheritance. They now share in "the adoption as sons."

Gentile believers are fellow-members of the body, the same body. They are not kept as a separate flock. They have been joined to Messiah Jesus, the King of the Jews.

Paul encouraged the Jewish and Gentile believers in Ephesus to be "diligent to preserve the unity of the Spirit in the bond of peace. There is one body and one Spirit, just as also you were called in one hope of your calling; one Lord, one faith, one baptism, one God and Father of all who is over all and through all and in all." (Eph.4:3-6)

Messiah, "From whom the whole body, being fitted and held together by that which every joint supplies, according to the proper working of each individual part, causes the growth of the body for the building up of itself in love. This I say therefore, and affirm together with the Lord, that you walk no longer just as the Gentiles also walk, in the futility of their mind." (Eph.4:16-17)

Along with the faithful Jewish remnant, Gentile believers have become "fellow-partakers of the promise in Messiah Jesus through the gospel." Along with the faithful remnant, they also partake of the promise to Israel that God is fulfilling in Messiah. The promise includes the Holy Spirit (Acts 1:4), Israel's Savior (Acts 13:23), the forgiveness of sin (Acts 13:32-39), the resurrection to life (Acts 26:6-8), and adoption into God's family (2Co.6:17-7:1).

Gentile believers who are joined to Israel through the New Covenant, are not separated by the Covenant of the Law. The wall of physical circumcision and the Law had kept the Gentiles, except for proselytes, separated from Israel and the promises of God. For those in Messiah, the wall of partition is broken down — it no longer divides. The unity of the Church is not physical, but spiritual.

Jewish believers, in fellowshipping with their Gentile brethren on these terms will not be defiled. They will not bring the wrath and judgment of God down upon themselves and upon Israel. In the New Covenant, Gentiles are made acceptable by the sacrificial, atoning death of the King of the Jews.

Inasmuch as the only difference between the believing Jews and their unbelieving brethren was the circumcision of the heart, God sought out for Himself those from the Gentiles who were also willing to have their hearts circumcised. These Gentiles were spiritually joined to the faithful Jewish remnant.

The Church is the New Covenant combination of the believing remnant in Israel and the engrafted believing Gentiles. Scripturally, there are only three kinds of people — Jews, Gentiles, and the Church. (1Co.10:32) Physically, people are either Jewish or Gentile. Those Jews and Gentiles who believe are the Church.

This relationship and its initial development can be simply portrayed by two interlocking circles in **Diagram 3**. One is Israel, within the solid border which represents the physical differences of the covenant which separate Israel from the Gentiles—visible, physical circumcision and the Law. The other circle is the Church, within the dotted border which represents the internal difference which separates believers from unbelievers — the invisible circumcision of the heart.

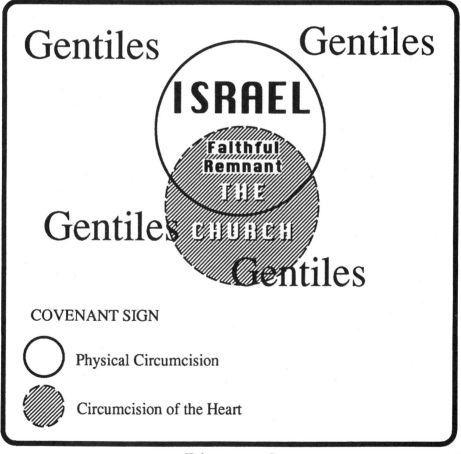

Diagram 3

Within Israel, there were still believers and unbelievers. The area that is common to both circles is the faithful remnant of Israel. They have both physical circumcision and the circumcision of the heart.

The believing Gentiles have become acceptable to God by their faith and the circumcision of their hearts. In the New Covenant, they do not need to be physically circumcised to be joined to Israel.

They are physically the same as their unbelieving Gentile brethren, but they are different in the circumcision of their hearts. In that circumcision of the heart, they are the same as their believing Jewish brethren, though they are different from them in the flesh. Unbelieving Jews and unbelieving Gentiles are physically different, but alike in the uncircumcision of their hearts.

"For you are all sons of God through faith in Messiah Jesus. For all of you who were baptized into Messiah have clothed yourselves with Messiah. There is neither Jew nor Greek, there is neither slave nor free man, there is neither male nor female; for you are all one in Messiah Jesus." (Gal.3:26-28) In the New Covenant, there is no "Court of the Gentiles," or "Court of Women." The physical differences do not disappear, but they no longer affect one's access to God, or those with whom one fellowships or makes a covenant.

These physical differences have become simply part of the individual's calling—i.e. how he, or she, is to specifically serve God in this world. That is why Paul gives specific instructions to those in Messiah who are Jewish, Gentile, slaves, masters, male, or female. See, for example, Rom.11:13 and Eph.5:22-6:9.

"Was any man called circumcised? Let him not become uncircumcised. Has anyone been called in uncircumcision? Let him not be circumcised. Circumcision is nothing, and uncircumcision is nothing, but what matters is the keeping of the commandments of God. Let each man remain in that condition in which he was called." [Literally, "Each in the calling in which he was called, in this let him abide."] (1Co.7:18-20)

For believing Jews, these physical distinctions are not a means of salvation, but simply distinctions of their calling. Had they, or any in Israel, been able to do all that the Covenant of the Law required, then salvation would have been through the Law. "...For if a law had been given which was able to impart life, then righteousness would indeed have been from the Law." (Gal.3:21)

Because they, and all Israel, could not keep their part of the Covenant of the Law, instead of righteousness, they received condemnation. "For as many as are of the works of the Law are under a curse; for it is written, 'Cursed is everyone who does not abide by all things written in the book of the Law, to perform them.' " (Gal.3:10, quoting Dt.27:26)

Paul publicly rebuked Peter for yielding to the pressure of men in separating himself from his uncircumcised brethren: "We are Jews by nature, and not sinners from among the Gentiles," but we know that even we are justified by faith in Messiah and not by works of the law. (Gal.2:14-16) Circumcision and the works of the Law cannot justify anyone, since no one can fulfill the Law.

The death of Jesus satisfies the condemnation of the Law. It is only by faith in that death that anyone can be justified. For "Messiah redeemed us [the Jews who believed] from the curse of the Law, having become a curse for us —for it is written, 'Cursed is everyone who hangs on a tree'— in order that in Messiah Jesus the blessing of Abraham might come to the Gentiles [goyim], so that we might receive the promise of the Spirit through faith." (Gal.3:13-14, quoting, Dt.21:23)

Gentile proselytes had to be physically circumcised to enter into the covenant of the Law which God had made with Israel. That, however, would not justify them before God. The New Covenant, on the other hand, does bring justification to those who believe, without the necessity of physical circumcision.

"And the Scripture, foreseeing that God would justify the Gentiles by faith, preached the gospel beforehand to Abraham, saying, 'All the nations [goyim] shall be blessed in you.' " (Gal.3:8, citing Gen.12:3) It is worth noting that Abraham was not circumcised when God made this promise to him. Therefore, the gospel, which is the proclamation of the New Covenant, does not include a call to physical circumcision. "And he [Abraham] received the sign of circumcision, a seal of the righteousness of the faith which he had while uncircumcised, that he might be the father of all who believe without being circumcised, that righteousness might be reckoned to them." (Rom.4:11)

Paul did not preach that Gentiles had to be physically circumcised to be saved. "But I, brethren, if I still preach circumcision, why am I still persecuted? Then the stumbling block of the cross has been abolished...Those who desire to make a good showing in the flesh try to compel you to be circumcised, simply that they may not be persecuted for the cross of Messiah." (Gal.5:11;6:12)

Those who were still preaching circumcision wanted to be able to boast that the Gentiles had become proselytes, taking upon themselves the Law of Moses. In so doing, those who preached circumcision hoped to escape persecution from their unbelieving Jewish brethren who still believed that they could, and must, be justified through the Law.

The issue for Paul is not circumcision — for he himself circumcised Timothy (Acts 16:3) — but justification. "For neither is circumcision anything, nor uncircumcision, but a new creation. And those who will walk by this rule, peace and mercy be upon them, and upon the Israel of God." (Gal.6:16)

Again, who are these two groups — "those who will walk by this rule...and...the Israel of God" — to whom Paul refers? Paul was writing to Gentile believers in Galatia who had chosen to be circumcised for justification, or who were about to choose to do so. That was his audience and that was the issue he was addressing.

His point was that the Gentile believers could only seek justification in one way. Seeking to be justified by the works of the Law would bring them bondage and disinheritance. Seeking to be justified by faith in Jesus, through His fulfillment of the Law, would bring them eternal life and the blessings of God.

"Those who will walk by this rule" are the Gentile believers who will not seek to be justified by circumcision in the flesh. They will be blessed along with "the Israel of God," i.e. the Israel that belongs to God. Within "the Israel of God" are those Jews, like Paul, who did not seek justification for themselves or for the Gentiles in the works of the Law. To these two groups, "peace and mercy be upon them."

From the beginning, Jesus came to bring this two-fold blessing. "And behold, there was a man in Jerusalem whose name was Simeon; and this man was righteous and devout, looking for the consolation of Israel; and the Holy Spirit was upon him....and when the parents brought in the child Jesus, to carry out for Him the custom of the Law, then he took Him into his arms, and blessed God, and said, 'Now Lord, Thou dost let Thy bond-servant depart, in peace, according to Thy word; for mine eyes have seen Thy salvation, which Thou has prepared in the presence of all peoples, **a light of revelation to the Gentiles, AND the glory of Thy people Israel.'** " (Lk.2:25,27-32)

Paul told the Galatians that he had rebuked Peter for yielding to the Jews who claimed that the Gentiles not only had to believe in Jesus, but also had to be circumcised according to the Law. "The Israel of God" are those Jews who believe in Jesus and do not seek to avoid persecution from their unbelieving brethren by preaching circumcision to the goyim.

This "Israel of God" is those who are both physically and spiritually circumcised. They are both physically and spiritually the seed and the children of Abraham, Isaac, and Jacob. They are like Nathaniel, whom Jesus characterized as "an Israelite indeed, in whom is no guile!" (Jn.1:47)

They are the ones who are of Israel and who are, in every way, truly Israel. (cf. Rom.9:6) God's faithfulness preserved a remnant in Israel to enjoy the spiritual gifts He entrusted to His people. (cf. Rom.9:4-5)

THE SPIRIT OF THE RELATIONSHIP

The interlocking circles portray the structural relationship of Israel and the Church, but there is more to the relationship than structure. The two are part of one family. Though there are men like Cain who do not care about the well-being of their brother, and may even commit fratricide, that was never God's design in creating the family.

Rather it was, and still is, the intention of God that Israel and the Church be willingly bound together by love. In Egypt, before revealing himself to his brothers, Joseph tested their hearts by imprisoning Benjamin. (Gen.44) Did they love him? or would they be concerned only with themselves? Judah spoke for them all and offered to be Joseph's slave in place of Benjamin. He was willing to give his life for his brother.

Judah described to the disguised Joseph what would happen if they returned to their father Jacob without Benjamin. "Now, therefore, when I come to your servant my father, and the lad is not with us, since his soul is bound up with the lad's soul, it will come about when he sees that the lad is not with us, that he will die. Thus your servants will bring the gray hair of your servant our father down to Sheol in sorrow." (Gen.44:30-31) Jacob would die if he lost Benjamin.

Judah, his brothers, and their father Jacob had their faults — as do we all — but the kind of commitment to one another that they expressed here is what the members of every family should have for one another. Though each one must fulfill the particular call that God has on his life, still, the lives of family members are intertwined and inseparable. Each one should be willing to give himself for the other.

Another example of this is the relationship of Jonathan and David. David had just killed Goliath and catalysed a great victory for Israel over the Philistines. Saul had called David to him and asked, " 'Whose son are you, young man?'...Now it came about when he [David] had finished speaking to Saul, that the soul of Jonathan was knit to the soul of David, and Jonathan loved him as himself....Then Jonathan made a covenant with David because he loved him as himself. And Jonathan stripped himself of the robe that was on him and gave it to David, with his armor, including his sword and his bow and his belt." (1Sam.17:58-18:4)

Jonathan willingly gave everything that was rightfully his, including the kingship, to David. He did it for one simple reason, "because he loved him as he loved his own life." (1Sam.20:17) Jonathan chose to become David's servant because he was moved by love.

David had to flee from Saul and go into hiding, "And Jonathan said to David, 'Go in safety, inasmuch as we have sworn to each other in the name of the Lord, saying, *The Lord will be between my descendants and your descendants forever....*" ' " (1Sam.20:42) David vowed to show lovingkindness to Jonathan and his descendants forever.

Jonathan knew that the Lord had chosen David to be king over Israel. (1Sam.23:17) David was a fugitive, but Jonathan could see something that was not visible. He could see the hand of the Lord upon David.

There are different ways that these relationships can be typically understood, but there is something more important than understanding them. That is imitating them. Those who belong to the Lord are commanded, "...you shall love your neighbor as yourself; I am the Lord." (Lev.19:18; cf. the parable of the good Samaritan, Lk.10:25-37)

Jesus commanded His disciples to be a neighbor, and more. "But I say to you, love your enemies, and pray for those who persecute you in order that you may be sons of your Father who is in heaven; for He causes His sun to rise on the evil and the good, and sends rain on the righteous and the unrighteous. For if you love those who love you, what reward have you? Do not even the tax-gatherers do the same?" (Mt.5:44-46) By our behavior, we should show that God is our heavenly Father.

Saul asked David, "Whose son are you?" Though it seems clear that Saul knew the answer, it was a way of giving honor to David's father. It's a very good question, for "By this the children of God and the children of the devil are obvious: anyone who does not practice righteousness is not of God, nor the one who does not love his brother." (1Jn.3:10) How people behave reveals who their father is. Love is the bond of every relationship in the Lord. It is what God has given to be the bond between the Church and Israel.

God is, after all, and perhaps above all, a Father. The people who worship Him in Spirit and in Truth will be a family. He created Adam to be a faithful son in His own image and likeness. (cf. Gen.1:27; Lk.3:38) "Then the Lord God formed the Man of dust from the ground, and breathed into his nostrils the breath of life; and the Man became a living soul." (Gen.2:7) God breathed His own breath [רוח] into Adam. As Adam received the breath of life, he became a living soul.

It is interesting that we do not control our own breath. Ultimately, we cannot hold our breath in, or keep it out. We are not really breathing by ourselves. As long as God breathes in us, we live. When He stops, we die.

God fathered Israel for the same reason that He fathered Adam. He wanted a son in His likeness. God did not father Adam or Israel in a sexual way, but rather in a creative, formative way. "But now, O Lord, Thou art our Father, we are the clay, and Thou our potter; and all of us are the work of Thy hand." (Is.64:8)

God rebuked the unfaithfulness of Israel, "Do you thus repay the Lord, O foolish and unwise people? Is not He your Father who has bought you? He has made you and established you." (Dt.32:6) God's people are made, established, and bought by Him. They doubly belong to Him, since He is both their Creator and their Redeemer.

God told Moses to tell Pharaoh, "Thus says the Lord, 'Israel is My son, My first-born.'" (Ex.4:22) In that God says, "Israel...is My first-born," we know that God has other children as well, gathered from the nations, the Gentiles. Jesus taught His disciples to pray, "Our Father..."

"And a multitude was sitting around Him, and they said to Him, 'Behold, Your mother and Your brothers are outside looking for You.' And answering them, He said, 'Who are My mother and My brothers?' And looking about on those who were sitting around Him, He said, 'Behold, My mother and My brothers! For whoever does the will of God, he is My brother and sister and mother." (Mk.3:32-35) Though the multitude sitting around Him was Jewish, it is clear that Jesus did not have only Jews in mind. "Whoever does the will of God" will include some, but not all, Jews, and some, but not all, Gentiles.

How much will this people/family bear the image of their heavenly Father? Jesus, God's only begotten Son, "is the radiance of His glory and the exact representation of His nature..." (Heb.1:3) He is also the son of Man, i.e. the son of Adam [בֶן אדם].

"See how great a love the Father has bestowed upon us, that we should be called children of God; and such we are. For this reason the world does not know us, because it did not know Him. Beloved, now we are children of God, and it has not appeared as yet what we shall be. We know that when He shall appear, we shall be like Him, because we shall see Him just as He is. And every one who has this hope fixed on Him purifies himself, just as He is pure." (1Jn.3:1-3)

When God created Man, "God blessed them; and God said to them, 'Be fruitful and multiply, and fill the earth, and subdue it; and rule over...' " (Gen.2:28) When Isaiah "saw the Lord sitting on a throne, lofty and exalted," the seraphim cried to each other and said, "Holy, holy, holy is the Lord of hosts, the whole earth is filled with His glory." (Is.6:3) Literally, there will be a day when "the fulness of the whole earth is His glory." God will have a people in His own image; a people who are faithful and true. They will fulfill the purpose for which God created Man.

24

THE MACEDONIAN RESPONSE

As the Jewish apostle to the Gentiles, Paul had the responsibility of bringing the gospel to everyone in the world who was not Jewish. With such a great responsibility, he was careful to be obedient to God's order for world evangelization, knowing that would make his ministry most effective and most honoring to God. That is why he always went to the Jew first. That is why he was the most effective missionary to the Gentiles the world has ever seen.

There was one occasion, however, when Paul was not effective in what he sought to do. He wanted to preach in the province of Asia, but the Holy Spirit would not let him. He then tried to go to the province of Bithynia, but the Spirit of Jesus did not permit him. (Acts 16:6-8)

"And a vision appeared to Paul in the night: a certain man of Macedonia was standing and appealing to him, and saying, 'Come over to Macedonia and help us.' And when he had seen the vision, immediately we sought to go into Macedonia, concluding that God had called us to preach the gospel to them." (Acts 16:9-10) Paul and those who travelled with him arrived in Philippi, "a leading city of the district of Macedonia," and began to preach the gospel.

Philippi was named after Philip of Macedon, the father of Alexander the Great. Alexander conquered the world. Though today we speak of his empire as a "Greek" empire, the ancients spoke of it as a "Macedonian" empire. Thessalonica, and Berea were also in Macedonia.

There were provinces and city-states in ancient Greece, but no united country. The only central government was that established by a conqueror. The heritage of the Macedonians was that they had once conquered not only Greece, but all the world. This was the heritage, and apparently the vision, of the Macedonian believers.

Paul effectively preached the gospel throughout Macedonia so that many Jews and Gentiles believed. More than any other man, he laid the foundation for the churches established there, and elsewhere, among the Gentiles. Then there came a day when he asked something of them in return.

The Jewish believers in Jerusalem, in response to the grace of God in their lives, had sold property and possessions to further the work of the Lord. They brought the money and laid it at the feet of the apostles. (cf. Acts 2:45; 4:34-37) They gave in a powerful way, and the Lord responded in a powerful way: "And with great power the apostles were giving witness to the resurrection of the Lord Jesus, and abundant grace was upon them all." (Acts 4:33)

The Jewish believers in Jerusalem had also suffered great persecution for being faithful to their King. They endured persecution at the hands of such violent fanatics as Saul of Tarsus. They held fast, and they prayed for their persecutors.

They gave their possessions and they gave their life-blood for the gospel. It was from them that the gospel went forth into all the world. Then a famine had come, and they were in greater need than ever before.

So Paul wrote to the churches that he had established among the Gentiles and asked them to give to support their Jewish brethren. (Acts 24:17; Rom.15:25-27; 1Co.16:1-5; 2Co.8 & 9; Gal.2:10) The Macedonians were the first to respond.

Corinth was in the neighboring province of Achaia. So were Athens and Cenchrea. Sparta also, with its heritage of discipline and meagre living in pursuit of victory, was in Achaia. Paul encouraged the Corinthians to give by describing to them what the Macedonian response had been:

"Now, brethren, we wish to make known to you the grace of God which has been given in the churches of Macedonia, that in a great ordeal of affliction their abundance of joy and their deep poverty overflowed in the wealth of their liberality. For I testify that according to their ability, and beyond their ability they gave of their own accord, begging us with much entreaty for the favor of participation in the support of the saints, and this, not as we had expected, but they first gave themselves to the Lord and to us by the will of God." (2 Co.8:1-5)

The Macedonian believers were enduring "a great ordeal of affliction." They were in "deep poverty." Yet they gave in "the wealth of their liberality." They gave more than they were able to give. They gave "beyond their ability."

"They gave of their own accord." No one forced them to give. They simply did not want to miss the blessing of giving to this particular offering. Their desire to give was so great that they begged Paul, "with much entreaty for the favor of participation."

Why did they respond like this? Paul explains, "they FIRST gave themselves to the Lord and to us by the will of God." Having given themselves to the Lord, they were prepared to be obedient to Him. In obedience to the will of God, they gave themselves and whatever they had to sustain and further God's work among the Jews. They gave as the Jewish believers had given.

Paul later wrote to these believers, "I can do all things through Him who strengthens me. Nevertheless, you have done well to share with me in my affliction. And you yourselves know, Philippians, that at the first preaching of the gospel, after I departed from Macedonia, no church shared with me in the matter of giving and receiving but you alone; for even in Thessalonica you sent a gift more than once for my needs.

"Not that I seek the gift itself, but I seek for the profit which increases to your account. But I have received everything in full, and have an abundance; I am amply supplied, having received from Epaphroditus what you have sent, a fragrant aroma, an acceptable sacrifice, well pleasing to God. And my God shall supply all your needs according to His riches in glory in Messiah Jesus." (Phil.4:13-19)

It is to the Macedonians, who gave so freely for his needs and for the needs of the Jewish believers, that Paul promised, "And my God shall supply all your needs according to His riches in glory in Messiah Jesus."

The Corinthian believers, and the others in Achaia, also responded with joy to the opportunity to do the same. Paul wrote to the Gentile believers in Rome, "now I am going to Jerusalem serving the saints. For Macedonia and Achaia have been pleased to make a contribution for the poor among the saints in Jerusalem. Yes, they were pleased to do so, and they are indebted to them. For if the Gentiles have shared in their spiritual things, they are indebted to minister to them also in material things." (Rom.15:25-27)

Paul made his appeal to the Gentile believers in terms of the need of the Jewish believers in Jerusalem. Then he expressed a principle concerning the debt that the Gentile believers owe to the Jewish believers. "For if the Gentiles have shared in their spiritual things, they are indebted to minister to them also in material things."

In Rom.9:4-5, Paul listed some of these spiritual things that belong to Israel — "the adoption as sons and the glory and the covenants and the giving of the Law and the service and the promises, whose are the fathers, and from whom is the Messiah according to the flesh." In Rom.11:24, he talks about unbelieving Jews being "grafted into their own olive tree." Paul makes it clear that the Gentile believers in Rome, and all Gentile believers everywhere, "have shared in their [the Jews'] spiritual things." He makes it clear that they therefore need to give material things in response to this debt.

How much do Gentile believers owe to the Jewish people from whom the gospel went forth? Paul reminded Philemon, "lest I should mention to you that you owe to me even your own self as well." (Philem.19) That is why the Macedonian believers joyfully gave themselves and all they had to repay their debt to the Jewish people.

We do not know for sure whether or not the church at Rome gave anything at all. It seems likely that they did not, for the church at Rome had a different way of looking at things. When Paul was later imprisoned in Rome, he had the opportunity to experience this directly.

He wrote back from Rome to the Macedonian believers, telling them what the Church at Rome was like: "Some, to be sure, are preaching Messiah even from envy and strife...out of selfish ambition, rather than from pure motives, thinking to cause me distress in my imprisonment." (Phil.1:15,17)

He had encouraged the Roman believers to be like the Macedonians. He encouraged the Macedonians not to be as he found the Romans to be: "Do nothing from selfishness or empty conceit, but with humility of mind let each of you regard one another as more important than himself; do not merely look out for your own personal interests, but also for the interests of others." (Phil.2:3-4) The attitude of the Church at Rome seems to be the reason for Paul's letter to them.

25

THE CHURCH AT ROME

Paul's letter to the Romans is generally understood to be a systematic presentation of the doctrinal basis of salvation. It is that, but it is not an abstract theological exposition. Paul is addressing particular errors and sins in the church at Rome.

Rome was a city, but Rome was an empire. Rome ruled the world. All the world bowed to Rome. There had been empires before, but Rome was the greatest of all empires. Romans could, and did, look with condescension and contempt on all other peoples.

The church at Rome seems to have received the spirit of the empire. A more literary title for Paul's letter to them would be "Against Arrogance (and the Ignorance It Breeds)." Though there seem to have been particular problems similar to those in Ephesus and Corinth, Paul's whole letter to the Romans is directed against arrogance - human arrogance, Jewish arrogance, and Gentile arrogance.

Arrogance is not compatible with the gospel. Jesus said, "Take My yoke upon you, and learn from Me, for I am gentle and humble in heart; and you shall find rest for your souls. For My yoke is easy , and My load is light." (Mt.11:29-30) "God is opposed to the proud, but gives grace to the humble." (Jacob 4:6)

How is this demonstrated in Paul's letter to the Romans? It defines the issues Paul raises, the thrust and development of his argument, and the language he uses. It is continually in his thoughts. It is not the sum of what he says, but it provides the motivation and context for the rest. Here are some of the passages where he specifically refers to this problem:

"Therefore **you are without excuse**, every man of you who passes judgment, for in that you judge another, **you condemn yourself**; for you who judge practice the same things....

"And do you suppose this, O man, when you pass judgment upon those who practice such things and do the same yourself, that you will escape the judgment of God? Or **do you think lightly of the riches of His kindness and forbearance and patience**, not knowing that the kindness of God leads you to repentance? But **because of your stubbornness and unrepentant heart you are storing up wrath for yourself** in the day of wrath and revelation of the righteous judgment of God." (2:1,3-5)

"But to those who are **selfishly ambitious** and do not obey the truth, but obey unrighteousness, wrath and indignation." (2:8)

"But if you bear the name 'Jew,' and rely upon the Law, **and boast** in

God...**You who boast in the Law**, through your breaking the Law, do you dishonor God?" (2:17,23)

"What then? **Are we better than they**? Not at all; for we have already charged that both Jews and Greeks are all under sin; as it is written, 'There is none righteous, not even one; there is none who understands, there is none who seeks for God.'...**Where then is boasting? It is excluded**. By what kind of law? Of works? No, but by a law of faith." (3:9-10,27)

"For if Abraham was justified by works, **he has something to boast about; but not before God**." (4:2)

"For I know that **nothing good dwells in me**, that is, in my flesh; for the wishing is present in me, but the doing of the good is not." (7:18)

"You will say to me then, 'Why does He still find fault? For who resists His will?' On the contrary, **who are you, O man, who answers back to God**? The thing molded will not say to the molder, 'Why did you make me like this,' will it?" (9:19-20)

"**Do not be arrogant** toward the branches; but **if you are arrogant**, remember that it is not you who supports the root, but the root supports you. You will say then, 'Branches were broken off so that I might be grafted in.' Quite right, they were broken off for their unbelief, and you stand only by your faith. **Do not be conceited, but fear**...For I do not want you, brethren, to be uninformed of this mystery, **lest you be wise in your own estimation**, that a partial hardening has happened to Israel until the fulness of the Gentiles has come in." (11:18-20,25)

"For through the grace given to me I say to every man among you **not to think more highly of himself than he ought to think**; but to think so as to have sound judgment, as God has allotted to each a measure of faith." (12:3)

"Be devoted to one another in brotherly love; give preference to one another in honor...Be of the same mind toward one another; **do not be haughty** in mind, but associate with the lowly. **Do not be wise in your own estimation**." (12:10,16)

"Therefore **he who resists authority has opposed the ordinance of God**; and they who have opposed will receive condemnation upon themselves." (13:2)

"Now accept the one who is weak in faith, but not for the purpose of passing judgment on his opinions....For not one of us lives for himself, and not one dies for himself...But you, **why do you judge your brother**? Or you again, **why do you regard your brother with contempt**? For we shall all stand before the judgment-seat of God....Therefore let us not judge one another any more, but rather determine this - not to put an obstacle or a stumbling block in a brother's way." (14:1,7,10,13)

"Now we who are strong ought to **bear the weaknesses of those without strength and not just please ourselves**. Let each of us please his neighbor for his good, to his edification....Wherefore, **accept one another**, just as

Messiah also accepted us to the glory of God. For I say that Messiah has become a servant..." (15:1-2,7-8)

"Now I urge you, brethren, **keep your eye on those who cause dissensions and hindrances** contrary to the teaching which you learned, and turn away from them. For such men are slaves not of our Lord Messiah but of **their own appetites**; and by their smooth and flattering speech they deceive the hearts of the unsuspecting." (16:17-18)

The letter, at least through the first eleven chapters, is written to correct some false assumptions which the Roman believers had apparently made. In rhetorical style, Paul confronts, challenges, and disproves these false assumptions. Some of the things that they "know" happen not to be true.

"You therefore who teach another, do you not teach yourself?..." (2:21)

"What then?...May it never be!" (3:3-4)

"May it never be!..." (3:6)

"...May it never be! On the contrary..." (3:31)

"What shall we say then?...May it never be!" (6:1-2)

"Or do you not know...?" (6:3)

"What then?...May it never be!" (6:15)

"Do you not know...?" (6:16)

"Or do you not know...?" (7:2)

"What shall we say then?...May it never be! On the contrary..." (7:7)

"...May it never be!" (7:13)

"What shall we say then?...May it never be!" (9:14)

"What shall we say then?..." (9:30)

"...May it never be!...Or do you not know?" (11:1-2)

"What then?...May it never be!" (11:7,11)

"For I do not want you to be ignorant..." (11:25)

The letter is filled with the contrast between "You will say then..." and "I say then..." Though Paul wrote to other churches about serious sins and errors, the problems in the church at Rome were greatly compounded by their arrogance. Paul battles against it.

It is also remarkable that in Paul's letter to the Romans, he specifically refers to "Jews" and "circumcision" more than he does in his letter to the Galatians. He refers to "Gentiles" more often than he does in all of his other letters combined. This helps us to understand the issues that Paul was addressing.

There are sections, teachings, and rebukes specifically addressed to Jewish believers. (cf. 2:17-; 7:1-6) There are also sections, teachings, and rebukes specifically addressed to Gentile believers. In fact, Paul emphasizes that he is writing as Apostle to the Gentiles.

"Paul, a bond-servant of Messiah Jesus, called as an apostle, set apart for the gospel of God, which He promised beforehand through His prophets in the holy Scriptures, concerning His Son, who was born of the seed of

David according to the flesh...Jesus the Messiah our Lord, through whom **we have received grace and apostleship to bring about the obedience of faith among all the Gentiles,** for His name's sake, among whom you also are the called of Messiah Jesus." (Rom.1:1-6)

Paul reminds the Romans that the gospel is according to "the holy Scriptures" of the Jews. It concerns God's Son, who is the seed of David, king of Israel. It is He who has sent Paul "to bring about the obedience of faith among all the Gentiles...among whom you also are the called of Messiah Jesus."

"And I do not want you to be unaware, brethren, that often I have planned to come to you (and have been prevented thus far) in order that I might obtain some fruit among you also, **even as among the rest of the Gentiles.** I am a debtor both to Greeks and to barbarians, both to the wise and to the foolish. Thus, for my part, I am eager to preach the gospel to you also who are in Rome." (1:13-15)

Again he points to his special apostleship to "obtain some fruit among you also, even as among the rest of the Gentiles." The great apostle comes as a debtor to minister to them. He is "a debtor both to Greeks and to barbarians, both to the wise and to the foolish." He is a debtor to them, not because he has received something from them, but because he has received grace from the Lord.

He does not say here in which category — the wise or foolish — the Gentile believers in Rome are to be found. His debt, however, is his reason for being "eager to preach the gospel to you also who are in Rome." He has received nothing from them, but he wants to impart something to them.

"But **I am speaking to you who are Gentiles.** Inasmuch then as I am an apostle of Gentiles, I magnify my ministry, if somehow I might move to jealousy my fellow-countrymen and save some of them." (11:13-14)

"But **I have written very boldly to you on some points, so as to remind you again,** because of the grace that was given me from God, to be a minister of Messiah Jesus **to the Gentiles,** ministering as a priest the gospel of God, **that my offering of the Gentiles might become acceptable, sanctified by the Holy Spirit.**" (15:15-16)

"Therefore in Messiah Jesus I have found reason for boasting in things pertaining to God. For I will not presume to speak of anything except **what Messiah has accomplished through me, resulting in the obedience of the Gentiles by word and deed.**" (15:17-18)

"Now to Him who is able to establish you according to my gospel and the preaching of Jesus the Messiah, according to the revelation of the mystery which has been kept secret for long ages past, but now is manifested, and by the Scriptures of the prophets, according to **the commandment of the eternal God, has been made known to all the Gentiles, leading to obedience of faith;** to the only wise God, through Messiah Jesus, to whom be the glory forever. Amen." (16:25-27)

This is not the place for another full commentary on Paul's letter to the Romans, but Paul's reason for writing the letter is usually overlooked or treated as if it were insignificant. Paul did not consider it insignificant. He himself said why he wrote the letter: "**I have written very boldly to you on some points, so as to remind you again,...that my offering of the Gentiles might become acceptable, sanctified by the Holy Spirit.**"

What are the points that Paul, the Apostle to the Gentiles, had written boldly to them to seek to make his offering of the Gentiles acceptable? There are four of them. These points form the framework for the entire letter, and reveal Paul's reason for writing the letter. They deal with the height of God's wisdom, power, justice, love, faithfulness, and purpose. They deal with the failure of the Gentile believers in Rome.

Paul tells the Romans: **1. God's order for evangelizing the world; 2. The extent of God's faithfulness to the Jewish people; 3. The way to transform this world from death to life; and 4. A warning for all Gentile believers.**

Paul wants the Gentile believers at Rome to understand these things. He wants them to become obedient, and change their ways. That will make his offering of them "acceptable."

GOD'S ORDER FOR EVANGELIZING THE WORLD

"For I am not ashamed of the gospel, for it is the power of God for salvation to every one who believes, to the Jew first and also to the Greek." (1:16)

"I say then, they [those Jews who did not believe] did not stumble so as to fall, did they? May it never be! But by their transgression salvation has come to the Gentiles, to make them jealous." (11:11)

"For just as you [Gentile believers] once were disobedient to God but now have been shown mercy because of their disobedience, so these also now have been disobedient, in order that because of the mercy shown to you they also may now be shown mercy. For God has shut up all in disobedience that He might show mercy to all....

"I urge you therefore, brethren, by the mercies of God, to present your bodies a living and holy sacrifice, acceptable to God, which is your logical [lit.] service of worship. And do not be conformed to this world, but be transformed by the renewing of your mind, that you may prove what the will of God is, that which is good and acceptable and perfect." (11:30-32; 12:1-2)

What is the gospel? As Paul preached it and lived it, "it is [εστιν] the power of God for salvation [1] to every one who believes, [2] to the Jew first and [3] also to the Greek." For Paul, that was a practical, working definition of the gospel.

[1] "...[T]he gospel...is the power of God for salvation to every one who

believes..." Paul reminds the church in Rome that no one has the power to save himself. Only God has the power to save. Men must choose to believe in what He has done in order to be saved.

This is just as true today as it ever was, because "whoever will call upon the name of the Lord will be saved." (10:13) The gospel does not change. Nor does it lose its power. The verb [εστιν] is in the present tense.

[3] "...[T]he gospel...is the power of God for salvation...also to the Greek." The word "Greek" has different meanings in the New Covenant Scriptures. Here it means non-Jews, i.e. Gentiles. The gospel is not for Jews only, it is also for Gentiles.

"Or is God the God of Jews only? Is He not the God of Gentiles also? Yes, of Gentiles also." (3:29) "...[T]hat He might make known the riches of His glory upon vessels of mercy...even us, whom He also called, not from among Jews only, but also from among Gentiles." (9:23-24)

"For there is no distinction between Jew and Greek; for the same Lord is Lord of all, abounding in riches for all who call upon Him." (10:12) "For I say that Messiah has become a servant to the circumcision on behalf of the truth of God to confirm the promises given to the fathers, and for the Gentiles to glorify God for His mercy..." (15:8-9)

The opportunity for the Gentiles to believe was not a one-time only offer. The gospel IS "also to the Greek." The verb [εστιν] is in the present tense. This is just as true today as it ever was.

[2] "...[T]he gospel...is the power of God for salvation...to the Jew first..." This is God's unchanging order for the evangelization of the world. It is the order which the early Church followed throughout the Book of Acts. It is a priority that God has established, even as He has established priorities in other matters.

"Do not be anxious then, saying, 'What shall we eat?' or 'What shall we drink?' or 'With what shall we clothe ourselves?' For all these things the Gentiles eagerly seek; for your heavenly Father knows that you need all these things. But seek **first** His kingdom and His righteousness; and all these things shall be added to you." (Mt.6:31-33)

It is not that God does not care about our physical needs. He does, but He has established a priority that we need to recognize. Honoring God's priority is the best way to have the assurance that our physical needs will be met. That is why Jesus said, "seek **first** His kingdom and His righteousness."

"Or how can you say to your brother, 'Brother, let me take out the speck that is in your eye,' when you yourself do not see the log that is in your own eye? You hypocrite, **first** take the log out of your own eye, and then you will see clearly to take out the speck that is in your brother's eye." (Lk.6:42)

It is not that God does not care about what our brother is doing wrong.

He does, but He has established a priority that we need to recognize. Obeying God's priority is the best way to make ourselves useful to our brother. That is why Jesus said, "**first** take the log out of your own eye."

God's order is not favoritism, but rather impartiality. He has established an order in the home, in the Church, and in the world. The head of a household is not automatically closer to the Lord than his wife or his children are, but he is given different authority and responsibility. Obedience to the Lord's order brings forth well-being.

Throughout his letter Paul explains to the Gentile believers in Rome some of the reasons why the gospel is to the Jew first. One reason is that judgment is also to the Jew first. "There will be tribulation and distress upon every soul of man who does evil, of the Jew **first** and also of the Greek, but glory and honor and peace to every man who does good, to the Jew **first** and also to the Greek. For there is no partiality with God." (Rom.2:9-11)

The phrase "to [of] the Jew **first** and also to [of] the Greek" means the same here, as it did when Paul wrote it a few minutes earlier in Romans 1:16. It is because there is no partiality with God that tribulation and distress are to the Jew first. It is because there is no partiality with God that glory and honor are to the Jew first. It is because there is no partiality with God that the gospel is to the Jew first. Jews are to receive first, therefore they are to be judged first. It is not possible to consign this order to the past. Is all tribulation, distress, glory and honor to be relegated to the historical past?

God's order is not an expression of identical treatment, but rather of impartial treatment. The two are not the same at all. The demonstration of God's impartiality is that the gospel and judgment are BOTH "to the Jew **first** and also to the Greek."

Jesus said, "And from everyone who has been given much shall much be required; and to whom they entrusted much, of him they will ask all the more." (Lk.12:48) God does not give everyone identical quantities of identical gifts. "But one and the same Spirit works all these things, distributing to each one individually just as He wills." (1Co.12:11)

The assignment to individuals and peoples of tribulation, distress, glory, and honor is solely the domain of God. The proclamation of the gospel, on the other hand, is the responsibility of the Church. Every believer has a responsibility to adhere to God's unchanging, planned priorities, including that for the gospel.

Paul tells the church at Rome that "...the gospel...is [εστιν] the power of God for salvation [1] to every one who believes, [2] to the Jew first and [3] also to the Greek." There is only one verb for the three prepositional phrases. The verb [εστιν] is in the present tense. However one treats the verb, all the prepositional phrases are equally affected. God has not authorized us to change the text back and forth to suit our own preferences.

To change it to the past tense would be to say that the gospel **was** "the power of God for salvation to every one who believes," but it no longer is. To change it to the past tense would be to say that the gospel **was** "the power of God for salvation...**also** to the Greek" but it no longer is. To change it to the past tense would be to say that the gospel **was** "the power of God for salvation...to the Jew first," but it no longer is.

Paul's use of the phrase "to the Jew **first** and **also** to the Greek" in Rom. 2:9-11 clearly indicates a continuing order. It is an ongoing priority that God has established. It applies equally to the past, present, and future of this age. It applies equally to judgment, honor, and the gospel.

This is not simply a description of an historical chronological order. It is just as true today as it ever was. Grammatically and logically, it is impossible to interpret the text in any other way. Biblically, it is impossible to interpret the text in any other way. Paul was telling the Gentile believers at Rome that they, too, should acknowledge and adhere to God's order.

Most of Israel has not yet learned of the salvation that God has entrusted to her. All of Israel did not believe and enter into the offered New Covenant, although a great many did. God kept for Himself a faithful Jewish remnant, but to the rest, "God gave them a spirit of stupor, eyes to see not and ears to hear not, down to this very day." (Rom.11:8)

If all Israel had believed, God's people would have been complete. Salvation would not have become available to the Gentiles, except as proselytes. God sovereignly prevented that from happening by blinding most of the Jewish people to the truth of the gospel. That is why Paul tells the Gentile believers in Rome, "As regards indeed the gospel, they are enemies for your sake, but as regards God's choice, they are beloved for the sake of the fathers [Abraham, Isaac, and Jacob]." (Rom.11:28)

It is only "by their transgression [that] salvation has come to the Gentiles, to make them jealous." (Rom.11:11) Gentile believers have received salvation through the transgression of those Jews who didn't believe. Through the salvation which they have received, they are to make unbelieving Jews jealous. That is God's plan and purpose.

Do the Gentile believers passively or actively provoke them to jealousy? The gospel is never passive. Paul explains, "I magnify my ministry, if **somehow** I might move to jealousy my fellow-countrymen and save some of them." (vv.13-14) Paul did everything he could to move his unbelieving brethren to jealousy and faith. He is asking the Gentile believers to do the same.

He reminds them, "You once were disobedient to God, but now have been shown mercy through their disobedience, so these also now have been disobedient, in order that through the mercy shown to you they also may now be shown mercy." (Rom.11:30-31) He spent the first few chapters of his letter talking about that disobedience. No one can question it.

In God's plan and order, part of Israel did not believe, so that salvation could come to the Gentiles. With patience, God endured unbelieving Israel. "And He did so in order that He might make known the riches of His glory upon vessels of mercy, which He prepared beforehand for glory, even us, whom He also called, not from among Jews only, but also from among Gentiles." (Rom.9:23,24)

It was the Jews who did believe who brought the gospel to the Gentiles. Jesus told Paul that He was sending him to the Gentiles, "To open their eyes so that they may turn from darkness to light and from the dominion of Satan to God, in order that they may receive forgiveness of sins and an inheritance among those who have been sanctified by faith in Me." (Acts 26:18) If the Jewish believers had not been obedient in evangelizing the Gentiles, then the Gentiles would still be in darkness, under the dominion of Satan, and without forgiveness or inheritance.

Gentile believers have the God-given responsibility, because of the mercy they have received, to bring the gospel to those Jews who do not yet believe — to call them to return to the Lord. This is not a responsibility that can be consigned to the past or postponed to the future. It is a continually present command.

Jonah thought, 'God is going to be merciful to the Gentiles anyway in His own time, but I don't want to be part of it. So, I am not going to deliver God's message to them.' Jonah's attitude was wrong. Gentile believers should not imitate it. They should be thankful that Paul and the other early Jewish believers did not imitate it. It is God's plan to use Gentile Christians to bring salvation to the Jewish people.

The chapter divisions in the Bible are very helpful, but they are not part of the text, and occasionally cause a break in continuity which neither the authors nor the Lord intended. The continuity of Paul's teaching here is broken by the "chapter 12" division. Paul continues to explain to the once-disobedient Gentiles how they are to be used of God for the salvation of Israel.

God purposed for the believing Jews to bring salvation to the Gentiles. They could do that because most of Israel did not believe. Now God intends to use the believing Gentiles to bring salvation to the unbelieving Jews.

"You once were disobedient to God, but now have been shown mercy through their disobedience, so these also now have been disobedient, in order that through the mercy shown to you they also may now be shown mercy. For God has shut up all in disobedience that He might show mercy to all. Oh the depth of the riches both of the wisdom and knowledge of God! How unsearchable are His judgments and unfathomable His ways! For who has known the mind of the Lord, or who became His counselor? Or who has first given to Him that it might be paid back to him again? For from Him and through Him and to Him are all things. To Him be the glory forever. Amen. I urge you **therefore,** brethren, by the mercies of God, to present your bodies a living and holy sacrifice, acceptable [well-pleasing] to God, which is your logical [λογικην] service of worship. And do not be conformed to this world, but be transformed by the renewing of your mind, in order to document [δοκιμαζειν] by you what the good and acceptable [well-pleasing] and completed [τελειον] will of God is." (11:30-12:2)

"I urge you **therefore**, brethren" — that is to say, 'because of what I have just told you. You did not give anything to God to make Him your debtor. By His mercy alone, you have received mercy. By God's will, you have received mercy through the disobedience of the Jews who didn't believe, and through the obedience of the Jews who did believe. Through the mercy you have received, the Jews who do not yet believe are to receive mercy. You are God's means of bringing His mercy back to the Jewish people.'

That is well-pleasing to God. It is God's will. The Gentile believers in Macedonia had given themselves to the Lord and to Paul for this purpose, according to the will of God. So Paul tells the Gentile believers in Rome, "I urge you therefore, brethren, by the mercies of God to present your bodies a living and holy sacrifice, **acceptable** to God...so that by you the will of God may be documented."

Paul is willing to give his soul unto eternal death as a sacrifice that his unbelieving brethren might receive mercy. He only asks the Gentile believers in Rome to give their bodies as living sacrifices for the same purpose. Then, his "offering of the Gentiles might become **acceptable**, sanctified by the Holy Spirit."

It is reasonable, it is logical, that they do this. Jews have done it for them. Should they not do the same in return? Obedient Jews brought the Gentiles out of disobedience. Shouldn't those Gentiles then be obedient and bring other Jews out of disobedience? It is logical to God.

"How then shall they call upon Him in whom they have not believed? And how shall they believe in Him of whom they have not heard? And how shall they hear without a preacher? And how shall they preach unless they are sent? Just as it is written, 'How beautiful are the feet of those who bring glad tidings of good things!...Who announces peace and brings good news of happiness, who announces salvation, and says to Zion, "*Your* God *reigns!*" ' " (Rom.10:14-15; Is.52:7)

In His plan of salvation for the world, God used the Jews to bring the gospel to the Gentiles. The Gentiles, in gratitude, are to bring the gospel to the Jews who do not yet believe. In this way, Jews and Gentiles are interdependent, and neither can boast against the other.

"But Zion said, 'The Lord has forsaken me, and the Lord has forgotten me.' Can a woman forget her nursing child, and have no compassion on the son of her womb? Even these may forget, but I will not forget you. Behold I have inscribed you on the palms of My hands; Your walls are continually before Me....

"The children of whom you were bereaved will yet say in your ears, 'The place is too cramped for me that I may live here.' Then you will say in your heart, 'Who has begotten these for me, since I have been bereaved of my children, and am barren, an exile and a wanderer? And who has reared these? Behold I was left alone; from where did these come?' Thus says the Lord God, '**Behold I will lift up My hand to the Gentiles, and set up My standard to the peoples; and they will bring your sons in their bosom, and your daughters will be carried on their shoulders**....And I will feed your oppressors with their own flesh, and they will become drunk with their own blood as with sweet wine; and all flesh will know that I, the Lord, am your Savior, and your Redeemer, the Mighty One of Jacob.' " (Is.49:15-17,20-22,26)

THE EXTENT OF GOD'S FAITHFULNESS TO THE JEWS

"And they also, if they do not continue in their unbelief, will be grafted in; for God is able to graft them in again. For if you were cut off from what is by nature a wild olive tree, and were grafted contrary to nature into a cultivated olive tree, how much more shall these who are the natural branches be grafted into their own olive tree?

"For I do not want you, brethren, to be uninformed of this mystery, lest you be wise in your own estimation, that a partial hardening has happened to Israel until the fulness of the Gentiles has come in; and thus all Israel will be saved....for the gifts and the calling of God are irrevocable." (Rom.11:23-26,29)

What is the difference between a cultivated olive tree and a wild olive tree? A cultivated tree is planted in good soil, situated to receive the proper amount of sunlight, and the surrounding ground is kept clear of weeds, briars, and thorns. It is fertilized and watered. It is pruned and protected. Such a tree should produce good fruit. God exercised that kind of care with Israel. (cf. Is.5:1-7)

A wild tree grows from wherever the seed or sprout happens to take root, no matter what the quality of the soil. It competes with the surrounding vegetation for the necessary sunlight, water, and nutrition. Because it is not pruned, the fruit it produces is small, poorly formed, and of doubtful quality. It has no protection against the ravages of nature or its creatures. This is the natural condition of the Gentiles.

When a branch with a bud is cut off from its own tree and grafted into the stock of another, it will still bear the type of fruit that is natural to its original stock. It uses the life of the new stock to produce its own natural fruit.

Why then would anyone graft a branch from a wild olive tree onto a cultivated olive tree? There would be more life flowing through the branch, but only to produce wild fruit. It would make much more sense to graft a branch from a cultivated tree onto a wild stock. But why perform any grafting at all?

God spent two thousand years cultivating Israel. He gave Himself - His Word, His Presence, His Spirit. He cleared the land for Israel. He pruned away the branches that hindered growth. He did everything He could do to help His cultivated olive tree produce good fruit.

Even so, most of the branches did not produce good fruit. "...Thus He looked for justice, but behold, bloodshed; for righteousness, but behold, a cry of distress....What more was there to do for My vineyard that I have not done in it. Why, when I expected it to produce good grapes did it produce worthless ones?" (Is.5:7,4)

Most of the branches did not produce good fruit because of unbelief — they did not yield to the Lord. So God cut them off. He continued to prune.

In another comparison of Israel to a vine, God told Jeremiah of the continuing destruction of Jerusalem. "Go up through her vine rows and destroy, but do not execute a complete destruction; strip away her branches, for they are not the Lord's." (Jer.5:10) Those branches in Israel that were not faithful to the Lord were cut off. Those branches that were faithful remained. God did not execute a complete destruction.

Then, in Messiah, God did something very strange. Where the unfaithful cultivated branches were cut off, God grafted in faithful wild branches, next to the faithful cultivated branches. Against their nature and against all that is reasonable, God grafted Gentile believers into Israel's cultivated olive tree.

Gentile believers, as wild branches, have been grafted into that which belongs to Israel. For Jews, whether grafted in or cut off, it is still "their own olive tree." (v.24) Normally, it is the nature of the engrafted branch that basically determines the kind of fruit it will bear. In this case, contrary to nature, it is the richness of Israel's cultivated olive tree that determines the kind of fruit the Gentiles will bear.

Paul is explaining the divine pruning process to the Gentile believers in Rome. Those Jews who didn't believe were cut off. Those Gentiles who did believe were grafted in. It is only faith or unbelief that determines whether or not a branch will be grafted in or cut off.

As for those Jews who do not believe, God will still have the last word. "And they also, if they do not continue in their unbelief, will be grafted in; for God is able to graft them in again. For if you were cut off from what is by nature a wild olive tree, and were grafted contrary to nature into a cultivated olive tree, how much more shall these who are the natural branches be grafted into their own olive tree?" (vv23-24)

"How much more...?" It is "contrary to nature" for God to have grafted believing Gentiles into Israel's olive tree. It is much more natural that God should turn the hearts of unbelieving Jews to faith and then graft them back in.

God created nature. The world He created bears witness of Him. "For since the creation of the world His invisible attributes, His eternal power and divine nature, have been clearly seen, being understood through what has been made, so that they are without excuse." (1:20)

God cultivated Israel for His divine purposes of redemption. Those purposes have never changed. God's gifts and calling for Israel are irrevocable. The gifts are given to fulfill the calling. Creation teaches us what to expect.

First there was a mystery that the Jewish believers had to understand. Gentiles can be brought into Israel's New Covenant without entering Israel's Old Covenant. They can become "fellow heirs and fellow members of the body, and fellow partakers of the promise in Messiah Jesus through the gospel." (Eph.3:3-6)

Now, there is also a mystery that all Gentile believers must understand. Paul says, "I do not want you [the plural υμας] brethren to be uninformed [lit., ignorant] of this mystery." What is the mystery which Gentile believers must understand?

It is that this is a time when a partial hardening of Israel has taken place, but this time will not last forever. The partial hardening is "hardness of a part" [πωρωσις απο μερουσ] of Israel. As Paul has just pointed out, the remnant believed, but "the rest were hardened [επωρωθησαν]." (Rom.11:7)

There will be a time when not even a part of Israel is hardened to the gospel. Part of Israel will be hardened "**until** the fulness [πληρωμα, i.e. the full number or measure] of the Gentiles has come in." (v.25) After the fulness of the Gentiles has come in, the fulness [πληρωμα] of Israel (v.12) will come in, bringing life from the dead to the world.

Gentile believers are admonished not to imagine that the kingdom is all theirs to the exclusion of Israel. They are now grafted in among the faithful Jewish remnant, but there is coming a day when no more Gentiles will "come in" — εισελθη, meaning to be brought into that state or condition. The hardening and blinding of a part of Israel to the gospel is God's grace to enable some Gentiles to believe. (Rom.11:7-11,28-30) When God removes that hardness and blindness, no more Gentiles will be saved, but "ALL Israel will be saved."

God is a father to Israel. He longs for His son. David longed even for Absalom. David wept for Absalom. He had no illusions about his son, he just loved him.

The prodigal son came to his senses and decided to come home. "And he got up and came to his father. But while he was still a long way off, his father saw him, and felt compassion for him, and ran and embraced him, and kissed him." (Lk.15:20)

Why did the father see him "a long way off"? The father had been looking down that road for a long time. He was watching and waiting for his son's return. His father's heart longed for that day.

The elder brother was very upset about the welcome that his far-wandering brother received. He reminded the father of his own faithfulness, and complained, "'but when this son of yours came, who has devoured your wealth with harlots, you killed the fattened calf for him.'

"And he said to him, 'My child, you are always with me, and all that is mine is yours. But we had to be merry and rejoice, for this brother of yours was dead and has begun to live, and was lost and has been found.' " (vv.30-32)

What the elder brother said was true. The father knew that. He knew where his son had been and what he had been doing. That only increased his joy at his son's return. Love is strange that way. The Father knows that the sons of Israel have wasted His wealth in harlotry. That is why He is looking down the road, watching and waiting for their return. That is why He rejoices greatly over one lost sheep that is found, over one wayward son who comes home. That may make some in His family jealous, but there is no need for jealousy.

Jesus longs for His brethren even as Joseph in Egypt longed for his. On their first coming to him, he knew them, but they did not know him. On their second coming, he revealed himself to them all.

He hadn't forgotten what they had done, and they hadn't either. "Then Joseph said to his brothers, 'Please come closer to me.' And they came closer. And he said, 'I am your brother Joseph, whom you sold into Egypt. And now do not be grieved or angry with yourselves, because you sold me here; for God sent me before you to preserve life....And God sent me before you to preserve for you a remnant in the earth, and to keep you alive by a great deliverance. Now, therefore, it was not you who sent me here, but God...' " (Gen.45:4-5,7-8)

" 'And as for you, you meant evil against me, but God meant it for good in order to bring about this present result, to preserve many people alive. So therefore, do not be afraid; I will provide for you and your little ones.' So he comforted them and spoke kindly to them." (Gen.50:20-21)

Joseph was not only the savior of all Israel, but also the savior of the goyim round about. He was the only one who had the food necessary to sustain life. In a very strange way, God sent Joseph to Egypt for the salvation of Jews and Gentiles alike.

So it will be with Jesus. "Behold, I have made him a witness to the peoples, a leader and commander for the peoples. Behold, you will call a nation you do not know, and a nation which knows you not will run to you, because of the Lord your God, even the Holy One of Israel; for He has glorified you." (Is.55:4-5)

To Israel, the Lord has promised, "'Fear not for you will not be put to shame; neither feel humiliated, for you will not be disgraced; but you will forget the shame of your youth, and the reproach of your widowhood you will remember no more.

" 'For your husband is your Maker, whose name is the Lord of hosts; and your Redeemer is the Holy One of Israel, who is called the God of all the earth. For the Lord has called you, like a wife forsaken and grieved in spirit, even like a wife of one's youth when she is rejected,' says your God.

" 'For a brief moment I forsook you, but with great compassion I will gather you. In an outburst of anger I hid My face from you for a moment; but with everlasting lovingkindness I will have compassion on you,' says the Lord your Redeemer." (Is.54:4-8)

THE WAY TO TRANSFORM THIS WORLD
FROM DEATH TO LIFE

"I am telling the truth in Messiah, I am not lying, my conscience bearing me witness in the Holy Spirit, that I have great sorrow and unceasing grief in my heart. For I could pray that I myself were accursed, separated from Messiah for the sake of my brethren, my kinsmen according to the flesh, who are Israelites..." (Rom.9:1-4)

"I say then, they did not stumble so as to fall, did they? May it never be! But by their transgression salvation has come to the Gentiles, to make them jealous. Now if their transgression be riches for the world and their failure be riches for the Gentiles, how much more will their fulness be! But I am speaking to you who are Gentiles. Inasmuch then as I am an apostle of Gentiles, I magnify my ministry, if somehow I might move to jealousy my fellow-countrymen and save some of them. For if their rejection be the reconciliation of the world, what will their acceptance be but life from the dead?" (11:11-15)

"For if we live, we live for the Lord, or if we die, we die for the Lord; therefore whether we live or die, we are the Lord's." (14:8)

Paul asked the Macedonian believers in Philippi to pray for him, "according to my earnest expectation and hope, that I shall not be put to shame in anything, but that with all boldness, Messiah shall even now, as always, be exalted in my body, whether by life or by death. For to me, to live is Messiah, and to die is gain....

"Whatever things were gain to me, those things I have counted as loss for the sake of Messiah. More than that, I count all things to be loss in view of the surpassing value of knowing Messiah Jesus my Lord, for whom I have suffered the loss of all things, and count them but rubbish in order that I may gain Messiah." (Phil.1:21; 3:7-8)

For Paul, the only reason he existed was to know and serve the Messiah. He did not desire anyone or anything else. He told the Achaian believers in Corinth, "We are destroying speculations and every lofty thing raised up against the knowledge of God, and we are taking every thought captive to the obedience of Messiah." (2Co.10:5)

The Spirit of Jesus within him gave him love greater than any man can have. The truth in Messiah is that Paul was willing to be anathema, separated from Jesus forever, if it would bring the salvation of all Israel. Paul understood the importance for all the world of the salvation of Israel.

Most of Israel stumbled and did not believe. Even while stumbling, Israel has brought salvation to the Gentiles. Even in transgression, Israel has brought riches to the world. Even in failure, Israel has brought the riches of Messiah to the Gentiles.

"How much more will their fulness be!" If a remnant brought all these blessings to the world, then how much greater will the blessings be when the whole people is faithful? But what could be greater than the riches of salvation becoming available for the world?

Most of Israel rejected their King. That has brought, through the remnant, reconciliation to the world. What could be greater than that?

When all Israel believes, the world will pass from death to life. What does that mean? How can there be such a great contrast between what the world is now and what it will be when all Israel believes?

"For the anxious longing of the creation waits eagerly for the revealing of the sons of God. For the creation was subjected to futility, not of its own will, but because of Him who subjected it, in hope that the creation itself also will be set free from its slavery to corruption into the freedom of the glory of the children of God.

"For we know that the whole creation groans and suffers the pains of childbirth together until now. And not only this, but also we ourselves, having the first fruits of the Spirit, even we ourselves groan within ourselves, waiting eagerly for our adoption as sons, the redemption of our body." (8:20-23)

Jesus said to Jerusalem, "Behold, your house is being left to you desolate. For I say to you, from now on you shall not see Me until you say, 'Blessed is He who comes in the Name of the Lord.' " (Mt.23:38-39) When Jerusalem and her children say, "Blessed is He who comes in the Name of the Lord," Jesus will appear.

Jesus will return to earth. He will rule over all the earth. "Righteousness and justice are the foundation of Thy throne; lovingkindness and truth go before Thee." (Ps.89:14) How different will that be from the way the world is in this age? It will be life from the dead.

Physical creation will be set free from "futility" and from "its slavery to corruption." How different will that be from the way the world is in this age? It will be life from the dead.

For believers? "When Messiah, who is our life, is revealed, then you also will be revealed with Him in glory." (Col.3:4) "When the Lord brought back the captive ones of Zion, we were like those who dream. Then our mouth was filled with laughter, and our tongue with joyful shouting; Then they said among the Gentiles, 'The Lord has done great things for them.' The Lord has done great things for us; We are glad." (Ps.126:1-3)

A WARNING FOR ALL GENTILE BELIEVERS

In the beginning of his letter to the Romans, Paul speaks of the failure of man. He says that, "professing to be wise, they became fools." (1:22) He has a warning for Gentile believers concerning the things they believe and profess about the Jewish people. They should not believe and proclaim what is contrary to the nature of God and to the Word of God. They should not become fools by deceiving themselves with their own professed wisdom.

"I say then, God has not rejected His people, has He? May it never be! For I also am an Israelite, of the seed of Abraham, of the tribe of Benjamin. God has not rejected His people whom He foreknew. Or do you not know what the Scripture says in the passage about Elijah, how he pleads with God against Israel?" (11:1,2)

"But if some of the branches were broken off, and you, being a wild olive, were grafted in among them and became partaker with them of the rich root of the olive tree, do not be arrogant toward the [natural] branches; but if you are arrogant, remember that it is not you who supports the root, but the root supports you.

"You will say then, '[Natural] Branches were broken off so that I might be grafted in.' Quite right, they were broken off for their unbelief, and you stand only by your faith. Do not be conceited, but fear; for if God did not spare the natural branches, neither will He spare you." (11:17-21)

"For I do not want you [the plural υμας] brethren to be ignorant of this mystery, lest you be wise in your own estimation, that a partial hardening has happened to Israel until the fulness of the Gentiles has come in; and thus all Israel will be saved; just as it is written..." (11:25-26)

"Now I am going to Jerusalem serving the saints. For Macedonia and Achaia have been pleased to make a contribution for the poor among the saints in Jerusalem. Yes, they were pleased to do so, and they are indebted to them. For if the Gentiles have shared in their spiritual things, they are indebted to minister to them also in material things." (15:25-27)

Apparently some of the Gentile believers in Rome thought that God had discarded Israel and chosen them instead. Paul seeks to free them from this false teaching, so that they will begin to fulfill their obligations to Israel. Throughout Romans 11:16-24, Paul is warning the **individual** Gentile believer [συ] against arrogance towards the Jews.

Paul points to his own relationship with God as proof of the fact that God has not cast off Israel. When Paul says, "I ALSO am an Israelite," he is identifying himself with his unfaithful, physical brethren. For indeed, Paul himself was once part of unfaithful Israel. That identification is not the same as his identification with the Church.

To substantiate his claim that he is an Israelite, Paul points out that he is "of the seed of Abraham, of the tribe of Benjamin." He refers to his own **physical** descent. It is evident that Paul is an Israelite, because he is "of the tribe of Benjamin."

It is absurd, therefore, to think that God could have cast off Israel. "May it never be!" God kept Paul for Himself. He kept Peter, Jacob, John, and all the early church for Himself. If God cast off Israel, then how did these Gentiles in Rome hear the gospel?

Elijah thought that he alone was left. Elijah was wrong. "What is the divine response to him? 'I have kept for Myself seven thousand men who have not bowed the knee to Baal.' " (v.4)

God kept for Himself a remnant in the past. "In the same way then, there has also come to be at the present time a remnant according to God's choice of grace." (v.5) That faithful remnant is a continuing demonstration of God's fidelity to Israel and to His promise to Abraham.

The fact that the faithful in Israel are a "remnant" indicates, of course, that there is much more of Israel that is not faithful. Within "His people," God has kept for Himself a faithful remnant. The rest of Israel was broken off for unbelief.

The "some [τινες, certain ones] of the branches" that were broken off are the Jews who did not believe. The remaining natural branches are the Jews who did believe, the faithful remnant. The "you [the singular συ], being a wild olive" who were grafted in among them, is the **individual** Gentile believer.

Any individual Jew, though cut off from his own olive tree for his unbelief, can be grafted back in if he believes. The proof of that is that God has grafted, contrary to nature, the wild branch individual Gentile who believes into the cultivated olive tree. If God's grace and mercy are such that He could do that, how much more will He graft back in the natural branches who believe?

He warns the Gentile believers in Rome of the fatal consequence of being arrogant against the natural branches. "Do not be conceited, but fear; for if God did not spare the natural branches, neither will He spare you [singular]." "Or do you think that the Scripture speaks to no purpose...'God is opposed to the proud, but gives grace to the humble.' " (Jacob 4:5-6)

"For the Lord of hosts will have a day of reckoning, against everyone who is proud and lofty, and against everyone who is lifted up, that he may be abased." (Is.2:12) "Everyone who is proud in heart is an abomination to the Lord; assuredly, he will not be unpunished." (Prov.16:5) "Whoever secretly slanders his neighbor, him I will destroy; No one who has a haughty look and an arrogant heart will I endure." (Ps.101:5)

If these Gentile believers are arrogant and ignorant towards the Jews, they are arrogant and ignorant towards their own peril. Paul warns them against being wise in themselves about God's relationship with Israel. "Remember that it is not you who supports the root, but the root supports you."

God planted a root — Abraham, Isaac, and Jacob — from which His people Israel grew. All the Jewish people naturally partake of the richness of God's promises to them. Gentile believers, grafted in by the grace of God, contrary to nature, partake of that Jewish richness too. They should, therefore, seek to repay what they owe for having "shared in their spiritual things."

What are these Jewish spiritual things in which all non-Jewish Christians have shared? It is a familiar list: "the adoption as sons and the glory and the covenants and the giving of the Law and the service and the promises, whose are the fathers, and from whom is Messiah according to the flesh, who is over all, God blessed forever. Amen." (9:4-5) "Salvation is of the Jews." (Jn.4:22)

How much then do Gentile believers owe to the Jewish people? How much have they received? That is how much they owe.

Through Paul's ministry, Philemon had become a believer. Paul wrote to Philemon to ask a favor of him, to graciously receive his slave Onesimus who had become a believer. Paul wrote, "Therefore, though I have enough confidence in Messiah to order you to do that which is proper, yet for love's sake I rather appeal to you...lest I should mention to you that you owe to me even your own self as well." (Philem.8,9,19)

Paul knew what it was to be a debtor. He owed everything to Jesus. He was not ashamed of that. The debt that he owed to Jesus had to be paid through the preaching of the gospel.

The Gentile believers in Macedonia had acknowledged their debt to the Jewish people and had sought to pay some of what they owed. The Macedonian believers joyfully gave *themselves* and all they had to repay their debt to the Jewish people. In their humility they had great joy.

Paul told the church in Corinth about his own sense of debt. "For if I preach the gospel, I have nothing to boast of, for I am under compulsion; for woe is me if I do not preach the gospel....For though I am free from all men, I have made myself a slave to all that I might win the more." (1Co.9:16,19)

In God's design, the Jews brought the gospel to the Gentiles. For God's purposes of redemption, it is essential that Gentile believers pay their debt to the Jewish people. God did not establish a competition between the two. He established a reciprocal obligation.

In a body, the different members are to help each other perform their specific God-designed role. When every member faithfully performs its own specific function, the whole body prospers. When any member refuses or is incapable of performing its own specific function, the whole body suffers.

SECTION D:
THINE IS THE KINGDOM

26

THE RESTORATION OF THE KINGDOM

After His resurrection, Jesus appeared to the apostles and taught them out of the Law, the Writings, and the Prophets. He explained to them how all the Messianic prophecies were about Him. After understanding all these prophecies as Jesus Himself understood and taught them, the disciples had one question burning in their hearts.

"And so when they had come together, they were asking Him, saying, 'Lord, is it at this time You are restoring the kingdom to Israel?' " (Acts 1:6) The prophecies talk about the restoration of the kingdom to Israel. Jesus had just taught the disciples how the prophecies were to be understood and fulfilled. So they asked Him, 'Is this the time for that fulfillment?'

In responding to the apostles' question, "He said to them, 'It is not for you to know times or epochs which the Father has fixed by His own authority." (Acts 1:7) Some people think that Jesus told them, 'There is no kingdom for Israel. Do you not yet understand the spiritual nature of the kingdom?' That is not at all what He said.

Jesus did not disavow the restoration of the kingdom to Israel. He confirmed it. He said that God the Father, by His own unchallengeable authority, has unalterably fixed the date of that restoration. It was not, however, given to His disciples to know when that would be.

Only something that has already been can be restored. The Church was something new, "born" after the resurrection. It is described as "having been built upon the foundation of the apostles and prophets, Messiah Jesus Himself being the cornerstone." (Eph.2:20)

The foundation of a building is laid first. Part of the foundation of the Church was not laid until "the apostles." Since that time, it is in the process of being built.

The Church is an essential part of God's plan for restoring the kingdom to Israel, but it is not of itself the kingdom, nor the restoration of that kingdom. It is never described that way.

Jesus had told the disciples to wait in Jerusalem for the promise of the Father. (Acts 1:4) He did not tell them to wait in Jerusalem for the restoration of the kingdom to Israel. Many understand that day of Pentecost on which the Holy Spirit was poured out to be the birthday of the Church. If the Church were the same as the restoration of the kingdom to Israel, then the two would take place in Jerusalem at the same time.

Instead of equating the two, Jesus distinguished the two. "He said to them, 'It is not for you to know times or epochs which the Father has fixed by His own authority [i.e. the restoration of the kingdom to Israel]; **but** you shall receive power when the Holy Spirit has come upon you; and you shall be My witnesses both in Jerusalem, and in all Judea and Samaria, and even to the remotest part of the earth." (Acts 1:7-8) There is the restoration of the kingdom to Israel, and there is the outpouring of the Spirit on the Church. The two are not the same.

Some people think that Jesus had previously taught the disciples that the kingdom of God would be taken away from Israel. That is not correct. He did not.

In Matthew 21, Jesus has a succession of confrontations with the ruling religious officials. He casts out those who are buying and selling in the Temple and overturns the tables of the moneychangers. He silences the chief priests and the elders of the people when they challenge His authority. He directs a parable to them about a father and his two sons, concluding, "Truly I say to you that the tax-gatherers and harlots will get into the kingdom of God before you." (v.31)

He then tells the parable of the landowner who rented out his vineyard to men who repaid him by beating and killing his servants and his son. Then, "Jesus said to them, 'Did you never read in the Scriptures, *The stone which the builders rejected, this became the chief corner stone; this came about from the Lord, and it is marvelous in our eyes*?

" 'Therefore I say to you, the kingdom of God will be taken away from you, and be given to a nation producing the fruit of it. And he who falls on this stone will be broken to pieces; but on whomever it falls, it will scatter him like dust.' And when **the chief priests and the Pharisees heard His parables, they understood that He was speaking about them**. And when they sought to seize Him, they feared the multitudes, because they held Him to be a prophet." (vv.42-46)

The chief priests and the Pharisees correctly understood that Jesus was speaking about them. Jesus said that the kingdom would be taken away from the chief priests and the Pharisees. They were the builders who had rejected the chief cornerstone. Therefore, they would no longer be keepers of the Lord's vineyard, which is Israel (Is.5:7).

When the lame man was healed at the Temple, a large Jewish crowd gathered. Peter and John preached the gospel to them. "And as they were speaking to the people, the priests and the captain of the temple guard, and the Sadducees, came upon them, being greatly disturbed because they were teaching the people and proclaiming in Jesus the resurrection from the dead. And they laid hands on them, and put them in jail until the next day...Then Peter, filled with the Holy Spirit, said to them, '**Rulers and elders of the people...He [Jesus] is the stone which was rejected by you, the builders**, but which became the very corner stone.' " (Acts 4:1-3,8,11)

Peter cited the same verse as Jesus (Ps.118:22). As a Jew faithful to God, he was rebuking the religious leaders — the "rulers and elders of the people"

— who had trampled the Lord's vineyard. The prophets had similarly rebuked the religious leaders of their day. Their words are living words. They have not passed away.

Saul had been anointed by God as the first king of Israel. He was to protect and rule the people in obedience to God, but he chose to disobey instead. "So Samuel said to him, 'The Lord has torn the kingdom of Israel from you today, and has given it to your neighbor who is better than you.' " (1Sam.15:28) The kingdom was taken away from one ruler in Israel, Saul, who would not obey, and given to another ruler in Israel, David, who would.

Solomon was anointed by God to be king over Israel, but Solomon's heart went after foreign women and their gods. "So the Lord said to Solomon, 'Because you have done this, and you have not kept My covenant and My statutes, which I have commanded you, I will surely tear the kingdom from you, and will give it to your servant.' " (1Kings 11:11) Because of Solomon's unfaithfulness, God took away the fulness of the kingdom from his descendants, "but to his son I will give one tribe, that My servant David may have a lamp always before Me in Jerusalem, the city where I have chosen for Myself to put My name.... Thus I will afflict the descendants of David for this, but not always." (1Kings 11:36,39)

The kingdom was taken away from Solomon and given to another. He was replaced as the leader of Israel. The division of the kingdom also caused all the people of Israel to be diminished and to suffer. And though God Himself decreed the division as his judgment on Solomon, those who were separated from the rightful kings of Israel were not considered innocent in His eyes. He comments, "So Israel has been in rebellion against the house of David to this day." (1Kings 12:19)

Jeremiah declared, "Many shepherds have ruined My vineyard, they have trampled down My field; they have made My pleasant field a desolate wilderness....'Woe to the shepherds who are destroying and scattering the sheep of My pasture!' declares the Lord. Therefore thus says the Lord God of Israel concerning the shepherds who are shepherding My people: 'You have scattered My flock and driven them away, and have not attended to them; behold, I am about to attend to you for the evil of your deeds,' declares the Lord." (Jer.12:10; 23:1-2)

The leaders of the Jewish people were personally judged for the evil of their deeds in destroying and scattering the sheep of God's pasture. However, judgment came upon all the people in the destruction of Judah and Jerusalem, and in the exile to Babylon. The shepherds had exalted themselves above God and His heritage, but the people themselves were not guiltless. They had been abused, but they had also sinned.

In the same way, the rulers of Israel in the time of Jesus were abusing His people. (Jeremiah 23:1-8 prophetically refers to this.) So God took the kingdom away from them and gave it to another. God did not cast off His people, He removed and replaced their leaders. The people also suffered for the sins of the rulers, and for their own sins, in the destruction of Jerusalem and the scattering among the Gentiles.

The kingdom will be restored to Israel, but entrusted to new leaders and shepherds. In the meantime, there is something that the disciples of Jesus must do. 'The Holy Spirit will come upon you and give you power. Then you will testify of Me to all the peoples of the earth.'

27

THE TABERNACLE OF DAVID

At the first Church council, Jacob said, "Brethren, listen to me. Simeon has related how God first concerned Himself about taking from among the Gentiles a people for His name. And with this the words of the Prophets agree, just as it is written, *"'After these things I will return, and I will rebuild the tabernacle* [σκηνην, סכה in the Hebrew] *of David which has fallen, and I will rebuild its ruins, and I will set it straight again* [ανορθωσω], *in order that the rest of mankind may seek the Lord, and all the Gentiles who are called by My Name,"* says the Lord, who makes these things known from of old.' " (Acts 15:13-18, quoting Amos 9:11-12 from the Septuagint)

What is "the tabernacle of David" that is rebuilt "in order that the rest of mankind may seek the Lord?" Paul wrote, "For we know that if the earthly tent [σκηνους] which is our house is torn down, we have a building from God, a house not made with hands, eternal in the heavens." (2Co.5:1)

Peter wrote, "And I consider it right, as long as I am in this earthly dwelling [σκηνωματι], to stir you up by way of reminder, knowing that the laying aside of my earthly dwelling [σκηνωματος] is imminent, as also our Lord Jesus the Messiah has made clear to me." (2Pet.1:13-14) John wrote, "And the Word became flesh, and dwelt [εσκηνωσεν] among us, and we beheld His glory, glory as of the only begotten from the Father, full of grace and truth." (Jn.1:14)

When God brought Israel out of Egypt, He directed His people to build the Tabernacle, a tent in which His presence and glory dwelt. A tabernacle is a temporary dwelling like a tent or a booth. Peter, Paul, and John compared the physical body and its life to a tabernacle.

When David's kingdom was firmly established, he wanted to build a house for the Lord. The Lord responded, "Are you the one who should build Me a house to dwell in? For I have not dwelt in a house since the day I brought up the sons of Israel from Egypt, even to this day; but I have been moving about in a tent, even in a tabernacle... I will make you a great name, like the names of the great men who are on the earth. I will also appoint a place for My people Israel and will plant them, that they may live in their own place and not be disturbed again, nor will the wicked afflict them any more as formerly, ...and I will give you rest from all your enemies. The Lord also declares to you that the Lord will make a house for you. When your days are complete and you lie down with your fathers, I will raise up your descendant after you, who will come forth from you, and I will establish his kingdom...And your house and your kingdom shall endure before Me forever; your throne shall be established forever." (2Sam.7:5-6, 9-12,16)

God promised to build David a house that would endure forever, something much more substantial than a temporary dwelling. The rightful kings of Israel came from the house of David, but David died, and they died, too. With the passage of time, the glorious, royal house of David crumbled in sin and judgment.

King Zedekiah, who did evil in the sight of the Lord, was the last of David's descendants to sit on the throne of Israel. After a long siege, "the army of the Chaldeans pursued the king and overtook him in the plains of Jericho and all his army was scattered from him. Then they captured the king and brought him to the king of Babylon at Riblah, and he passed judgment on him. And they slaughtered the sons of Zedekiah before his eyes, then put out the eyes of Zedekiah and bound him with bronze fetters and brought him to Babylon." (2Kings 25:5-7) Both the house and the kingdom of David had been brought very low. They resembled fallen, broken down, abandoned, little shacks.

The prophet Isaiah described the judgment that came upon Israel for her unfaithfulness: "Your land is desolate, your cities are burned with fire, your fields — strangers are devouring them in your presence, it is desolation, as overthrown by strangers. And the daughter of Zion is left like a shelter [* ηκσ] in a vineyard, like a watchman's hut in a cucumber field, like a besieged city. Unless the Lord of hosts had left us a few survivors, we would be like Sodom, we would be like Gomorrah." (Is.1:7-9)

God had promised David, "your house and your kingdom shall endure before Me forever; your throne shall be established forever." There were still living descendants of David, but their fate was the same as other royal families throughout history who have been impoverished, debased, held captive, or exiled. The royal house had been trodden down, but not totally destroyed. There was a house, but no throne or kingdom.

Sometimes a member of the royal family is raised up, gathers to himself the loyalist remnant, finds favor and support in a foreign land, and seeks to re-establish the kingdom. (e.g., 1Kings 11:14-22) This is what God did with the ruins of "the tabernacle of David." He raised up a member of the royal house, and sent heralds throughout the land to proclaim the legitimate heir — Jesus, the Son of David, the King of the Jews — and to raise up and equip a following for Him. He raised up the house so that one day the kingdom could also be restored.

On the day of Pentecost, when the Holy Spirit empowered the disciples, Peter proclaimed in the royal city, "Brethren, I may confidently say to you regarding the patriarch David that he both died and was buried, and his tomb is with us to this day. And so, because he was a prophet, and knew that God had sworn to him with an oath to seat one of his descendants upon his throne, he looked ahead and spoke of the resurrection of the Messiah, that He was neither abandoned to Hades, nor did His flesh suffer decay. This Jesus God raised up again, to which we are all witnesses. Therefore having been exalted to the right hand of God, and having received from the Father the promise of the Holy Spirit, He has poured forth this which you both see and hear." (Acts 2:29-33)

The loyalists, i.e. the faithful remnant, began to rally to the cause of the King, the Son of David. Directed by the exiled King, these faithful "sons of the kingdom" began to recruit followers in foreign lands, teaching them to observe His commandments, to pray "Thy Kingdom come...in earth as it is in heaven!" He taught them to work for the coming of His kingdom. The great King authorized them to do this work through the issuance of the Great Royal Commission.

To the degree that a people or a nation is in rebellion against the great King, they do not recognize His absolute authority, though they may give lip-service. The same is true of the governments that they establish. Consequently, these governments sometimes do not recognize the legitimacy of the Great Royal Commission.

That is why the loyalists, and all the Gentile believers who are joined to them, must fight to establish the kingdom. We were not given worldly weapons with which to fight on earth, but powerful, spiritual ones with which to fight in heaven. Following His ascension, Jesus began to establish a government in exile. Those who choose to live under His authority await the day when the King Himself will return to destroy all His unrepentant enemies and take up His throne. (cf. 1Th.1:10)

Though we await and pray for the return of our King and the coming of His kingdom, inasmuch as we acknowledge His rule and obey His will, His kingdom has already come into our lives. Even by Himself, the King is the beginning of the kingdom. For the kingdom of God is like a seed, and like a man who casts seed upon the ground. (Mk.4:26-32) And the Word of God is like a seed.

The seed doesn't look like the fruit, but it contains within it the fruit that will one day appear. And the fruit contains within it the seed which one day will bear more fruit. It is God's built-in cycle of increasing seed and fruit. Even as in the beginning of creation, "And the earth brought forth vegetation, plants yielding seed after their kind, and trees bearing fruit, with seed in them, after their kind; and God saw that it was good." (Gen.1:12)

It takes time for the seed of the kingdom to grow, mature, and bear fruit. We are promised that the time will come, but we are not told how long it will be.

As we previously noted, the church in Rome had a serious problem with pride and self-centeredness. Paul told them that they were wrong to consider food and drink more important than their brethren. "So then let us pursue the things which make for peace and the building up of one another.

"Do not tear down the work of God for the sake of food. All things indeed are clean, but they are evil for the man who eats and gives offense. It is good not to eat meat or to drink wine, or to do anything by which your brother stumbles, ...for the kingdom of God is not eating and drinking, but righteousness and peace and joy in the Holy Spirit." (Rom.14:19-21,17)

Paul is telling them the way in which the kingdom of God should be evident in their lives. He is not in any way indicating that Jesus will not return and reign on the earth. Where Jesus is King, there is "righteousness and peace and joy in the Holy Spirit." When Jesus returns and reigns on the earth, all the world will be so blessed.

As Jesus was going towards the Mount of Olives to begin His kingly ride into Jerusalem, He told "a parable, because He was near Jerusalem, and they supposed that the kingdom [βασιλειαν] of God was going to appear immediately. He said therefore, 'A certain nobleman went to a distant country to receive a kingdom [βασιλειαν] for himself, and then return....' " (Lk.19:11-27) Before leaving, the nobleman gave his servants business to fruitfully conduct. While he was gone, his citizens rebelled against Him, saying, "We do not want this man to reign [βασιλευσαι] over us."

Jesus told the parable because "they supposed that the kingdom of God was going to appear immediately." He wanted to correct this incorrect supposition. He wanted them to understand that the kingdom was not going to appear immediately.

"The nobleman" had to go on a long round-trip journey "to a distant country." Jesus knew that He, like the nobleman, would be gone for a long time. Neither His servants nor His citizens would know exactly when He would return "after receiving the kingdom."

Until His return, the disciples, like the servants, were to show themselves faithful and fruitful with what the Lord had entrusted to them. If they do, then when He returns, they will rule with Him in His kingdom. Those who faithfully serve in the government-in-exile, and fight to end the rebellion, will be rewarded with positions of governmental responsibility when the kingdom is secured.

On His return, the King will say, "Well done, good slave, because you have been faithful in a very little thing, be in authority over ten cities." (v.17) As Jesus told the Apostles shortly thereafter at the Passover meal, "And you are those who have stood by Me in My trials; and just as My Father has granted Me a kingdom, I grant you that you may eat and drink at My table in My kingdom, and you will sit on thrones judging the twelve tribes of Israel." (Lk.22:28-30)

In the parable, the citizens of the nobleman's country protested that they did not want Him to "reign" [βασιλευσαι] over them. They realized correctly that when he returned, he would be king [βασιλευσ] over them. Jesus was saying that sometime after He received His kingdom, He would return to Israel to be King in Jerusalem.

The prophet Daniel saw a vision of Jesus receiving His kingdom from the Father: "I kept looking in the night visions, and behold, with the clouds of heaven one like a Son of Man was coming, and He came up to the Ancient of Days and was presented before Him. And to Him was given dominion, glory and a kingdom, that all the peoples, goyim, and men of every language might serve Him. His dominion is an everlasting dominion which will not pass away; and His kingdom is one which will not be destroyed." (Dan.7:13-14)

Having received His kingdom, Jesus will one day return to establish it. Exactly when that will be we do not know, but we do know that it will be. The Apostle John saw visions and heard announcements of it. "And the seventh angel sounded; and there arose loud voices in heaven, saying, 'The kingdom of the world has become the kingdom of our Lord, and of His Messiah; and He will reign forever and ever.' " (Rev.11:15)

28

A NOTE ON PROPHECY

As we begin to discuss events that are still in the future, it is important to keep two things in mind. **First**, God reveals certain things about the future for the understanding of (a) those who live at the time of the prophecy, (b) those who live after the prophecy is given but before it is fulfilled, and (c) those who live in the day of fulfillment. A primary purpose of prophecy is to help those who live in the day of fulfillment recognize what is happening.

Before His crucifixion, Jesus told the apostles of many things that were going to happen in the future. They did not understand much of what He told them. "From now on I am telling you before it comes to pass, so that when it does occur, you may believe that I am He...And now I have told you before it comes to pass, that when it comes to pass, you may believe....But these things I have spoken to you, that when their hour comes, you may remember that I told you of them. And these things I did not say to you at the beginning, because I was with you." (Jn.13:19;14:29;16:4)

God will not give the understanding of some prophecies until the time of their fulfillment. By God's design, our knowledge of the future will remain incomplete. We can build on what is fixed. We can communicate what is revealed. But we cannot force what we do not know to fit into what we do know.

How could the human mind have reconciled in advance the fact that Messiah comes from Bethlehem (Mic.5:2/Mt.2:6), Nazareth (Zech.3:8 [נצר]/ Mt.2:23), and Egypt (Hos.11:1/Mt.2:15)? When it is revealed, we can choose to accept God's revelation. When it is not understood, we have to rest in God's sovereignty. "The secret things belong to the Lord our God, but the things revealed belong to us and to our sons forever, that we may observe all the words of this law." (Dt.29:29)

The **second** thing to keep in mind concerning prophecy is that fulfillment sometimes comes at more than one time, in more than one way. For example, the last prophecy written in Tanakh is "Behold, I am going to send you Elijah the prophet before the coming of the great and terrible day of the Lord. And he will restore the hearts of the fathers to their children, and the hearts of the children to their fathers, lest I come and smite the land with a curse." (Mal.4:5-6)

Gabriel announced the future birth of John, the forerunner of the Lord, by telling Zachariah, "And it is he who will go as a forerunner before Him in the spirit and power of Elijah, to turn the hearts of the fathers back to the children, and the disobedient to the attitude of the righteous; so as to make ready a people prepared for the Lord." (Lk.1:17)

Jesus said about John, "And if you care to accept it, he himself is Elijah, who was to come." (Mt.11:14) John's ministry was a fulfillment of the prophecy in Tanakh.

Sometime after Herod had murdered John, "Jesus took with him Peter and Jacob, and John his brother, and brought them up to a high mountain by themselves....And behold, Moses and Elijah appeared to them, talking with Him....And as they were coming down from the mountain, Jesus commanded them, saying, 'Tell the vision to no one until the Son of Man has risen from the dead.'

"And His disciples asked Him, saying, 'Why then do the scribes say that Elijah must come first?' And He answered and said, 'Elijah is coming and will restore all things; but I say to you, that Elijah already came, and they did not recognize him, but did to him whatever they wished. So also the Son of Man is going to suffer at their hands.' Then the disciples understood that He had spoken to them about John the Baptist." (Mt.17:11-13)

John the Baptist was dead. Elijah the prophet appeared on the earth for a short time to speak with Jesus about a future event — His departure from the earth. (cf. 2Pet.1:15 & Rev.11:3-12 for the departure of Peter and of the two witnesses) Jesus told the disciples, "Elijah is coming and will restore all things." The coming of Elijah himself in fulfillment of the prophecy in Tanakh is still a future event. The same prophecy is fulfilled in two different ways at two different times.

Another aspect of how the same prophecy can apply to two different times can be seen in Isaiah 61:1-3, and on to the end of the chapter. When Jesus spoke in the synagogue in Nazareth, He read only verse one and the first part of verse two: "'The Spirit of the Lord is upon Me, because He anointed Me to preach the gospel to the poor. He has sent Me to proclaim release to the captives, and recovery of sight to the blind, to set free those who are downtrodden, to proclaim the favorable year of the Lord...' ...And He began to say to them, 'Today this Scripture has been fulfilled in your ears.' " (Lk.4:18-19,21)

Verse two continues, "...and the day of vengeance of our God; to comfort all who mourn, [v.3] to grant those who mourn in Zion, giving them a garland instead of ashes, the oil of gladness instead of mourning, the mantle of praise instead of a spirit of fainting. So they will be called oaks of righteousness, the planting of the Lord, that He may be glorified."

Part of the prophecy was fulfilled on that day in Nazareth. The rest of the prophecy has not yet been fulfilled. The first part of the sentence was fulfilled about two thousand years ago. The second part of the same sentence will be fulfilled as the time that is still future becomes the present.

The same prophecy can have a different degree or different nature of fulfillment in different times. The Bible itself shows us this about prophecy.

29

THE FULNESS OF THE GENTILES

Paul said that part of Israel would be blinded until the full number of Gentiles had been brought in. Then the blindness will be lifted, and all Israel will be saved.

John describes that final fulness of the Gentiles. "After these things I looked, and behold, a great multitude, which no one could count, from every nation and all tribes and peoples and tongues, standing before the throne and before the Lamb, clothed in white robes, and palm branches were in their hands; and they cry out with a loud voice, saying, 'Salvation to our God who sits on the throne, and to the Lamb.' " (Rev.7:9-10)

Since this multitude is so great that "no one could count" them, this is the greatest harvest of souls of all time. Since this great multitude is "from every nation and all tribes and peoples and tongues," this is a harvest of all the earth.

"And one of the elders answered, saying to me, 'These who are clothed in white robes, who are they, and from where have they come?' And I said to him, 'My lord, you know.' And he said to me, 'These are the ones who come out of the great tribulation, and they have washed their robes and made them white in the blood of the Lamb.' " (Rev.7:13-14)

This great multitude of believers from all over the earth has come out of the great tribulation. They have been gathered during a particular time. There is no time that has already been when such an event occurred. It is therefore a future event of great suffering.

"For this reason, they are before the throne of God; and they serve Him day and night in his temple; and He who sits on the throne shall spread His tabernacle over them. They shall hunger no more, neither thirst any more; neither shall the sun beat down on them, nor any heat; for the Lamb in the center of the throne shall be their shepherd, and shall guide them to springs of the water of life; and God shall wipe every tear from their eyes." (Rev.7:15-17)

This great multitude has hungered, but they will hunger no more. They have thirsted, but they will thirst no more. The sun has beaten down on them, but it will do so no more. They have wept, but "God shall wipe every tear from their eyes."

Certainly some of these things are true of believers in general, but this is a particular group. "These are the ones who come out of **THE** great tribulation [εκ της θλιψεως της μεγαλης]." Jesus said of this time, "For then there will be a great tribulation [θλιψις μεγαλη], such as has not occurred since the beginning of the world until now, nor ever shall. And unless those days had been cut short, no flesh would have been saved; but for the sake of the chosen ones those days shall be cut short." (Mt.24:21-22)

The devil, the great dragon, is thrown out of heaven and confined to the earth. "...He was a murderer from the beginning..." "The thief comes only to steal, and kill, and destroy...." (Jn.8:44; 10:10) "...Woe to the earth and the sea; because the devil has come down to you, having great wrath, knowing that he has only a short time." (Rev.12:12)

"...And I saw a beast coming up out of the sea, having ten horns and seven heads, and on his horns were ten diadems, and on his heads were blasphemous names....And the dragon gave him his power and his throne and great authority.

"And I saw one of his heads as if it had been slain, and his fatal wound was healed. And the whole earth was amazed and followed after the beast; and they worshiped the dragon, because he gave his authority to the beast; and they worshiped the beast, saying, 'Who is like the beast, and who is able to wage war with him?'

"And he opened his mouth in blasphemies against God, to blaspheme His name and His tabernacle, those who tabernacle in heaven. And it was given to him to make war with the saints and to overcome them; and authority over every tribe and people and tongue and nation was given to him. And all who dwell on the earth will worship him, every one whose name has not been written from the foundation of the world in the book of life of the Lamb who has been slain." (13:1-5,7-8)

This beast is the anti-Messiah, the anti-Christ. He is against everything that Jesus is. He seeks to murder everyone who will not worship him. He has a false prophet.

"And he [the false prophet] deceives those who dwell on the earth because of the signs which it was given him to perform in the presence of the beast, telling those who dwell on the earth to make an image to the beast who had the wound of the sword and has come to life. And there was given to him to give breath to the image of the beast, that the image of the beast might even speak and cause as many as do not worship the image of the beast to be killed." (13:14-15)

Before the Devil is cast out of heaven, and before the beast rules over the earth, John "...saw underneath the altar the souls of those who had been slain because of the word of God, and because of the testimony which they had maintained; and they cried out with a loud voice, saying, 'How long, O Lord, holy and true, wilt Thou refrain from judging and avenging our blood on those who dwell on the earth?'

"And there was given to each of them a white robe; and they were told that they should rest for a little while longer, until the number of their fellow-servants and their brethren who were to be killed even as they had been, should be completed also." (6:9-11)

Much of the "great multitude, which no one could count, from every nation and all tribes and peoples and tongues" comes "out of the great tribulation" through death. The souls under the altar must wait for God to judge and avenge their blood until this great multitude is killed, "even as they had been."

"And I heard a voice from heaven, saying, 'Write, "*Blessed are the dead who die in the Lord from now on!*"' 'Yes,' says the Spirit, 'that they may rest from their labors, for their deeds follow with them.'

"And I looked, and behold, a white cloud, and sitting on the cloud was one like a son of man, having a golden crown on His head, and a sharp sickle in His hand. And another angel came out of the temple, crying out with a loud voice to him who sat on the cloud, 'Put in your sickle and reap, because the hour to reap has come, because the harvest of the earth is ripe.' And He who sat on the cloud swung His sickle over the earth; and the earth was reaped." (14:13-16)

Some Gentiles will come against Jerusalem and reap judgment. Others will find salvation and be joined to Israel. "For thus says the Lord of hosts, 'After glory He has sent Me against the Gentiles which plunder you [Zion], for he who touches you, touches the pupil of His eye.... Sing for joy and be glad, O daughter of Zion; for behold I am coming and I will dwell in your midst,' declares the Lord. And many Gentiles will join themselves to the Lord in that day and will become My people. Then I will dwell in your midst, and you will know that the Lord of hosts has sent Me to you. And the Lord will possess Judah as His portion in the holy land, and will again choose Jerusalem." (Zech.2:8,10-12)

This triumphant command — "**Sing for joy and be glad, O daughter of Zion; for behold I am coming**" — is a Messianic promise similar to Zech.9:9,"**Rejoice greatly, O daughter of Zion**! Shout in triumph, O daughter of Jerusalem! **Behold, your king is coming to you...**" Messiah, the King of Israel, is also the Lord of the harvest.

30

THE LAST REMNANT

What is the means by which this great multitude hears and believes the gospel? John said that he saw this great multitude "After these things." After what things? What are the things that take place before this great multitude comes out of the great tribulation?

"And I looked when He broke the sixth seal, and there was a great earthquake; and the sun became black as sackcloth made of hair, and the whole moon became like blood; and the stars of the sky fell to the earth, as a fig tree casts its unripe figs when shaken by a great wind. And the sky was split apart like a scroll when it is rolled up; and every mountain and island were moved out of their places.

"And the kings of the earth and the great men and the commanders and the rich and the strong and every slave and free man, hid themselves in the caves and among the rocks of the mountains; and they said to the mountains and to the rocks, 'Fall on us and hide us from the presence of Him who sits on the throne, and from the wrath of the Lamb; for the great day of their wrath has come; and who is able to stand?' " (6:12-17)

The fulness of God's wrath is about to be poured out upon the earth. Before that happens, John "saw another angel ascending from the rising of the sun, having the seal of the living God; and he cried out with a loud voice to the four angels to whom it was granted to harm the earth and the sea, saying, 'Do not harm the earth or the sea or the trees, until we have sealed the bond-servants of our God on their foreheads.'

"And I heard the number of those who were sealed, one hundred and forty-four thousand sealed from every tribe of the sons of Israel: from the tribe of Judah, twelve thousand were sealed, from the tribe of Reuben twelve thousand, from the tribe of Gad twelve thousand,...from the tribe of Zebulon twelve thousand, from the tribe of Joseph twelve thousand, from the tribe of Benjamin, twelve thousand were sealed." (7:2-8)

Before the wrath of God is poured out, and before the great multitude is saved out of the great tribulation (7:9-19), a select remnant in Israel is sealed. How is the text that describes this sealed company to be understood? There are obvious reasons for understanding the text in its ordinary normal sense.

John hears that a specific number of the bond-servants of God, 144,000, are sealed. This specific number is given in contrast to the "great multitude which no one could count." An exact number is given in contrast to an innumerable multitude.

These bond-servants of God are "sealed from every tribe of the sons of Israel." Each of the twelve tribes is then mentioned by name. Twelve thousand from each of the tribes of "the sons of Israel" are sealed. This is in sharp contrast to the "great multitude which no one could count, from every nation and all tribes and peoples and tongues." An exact number is given from the specific tribes of "the sons of Israel".

Some have "spiritualized" the 12,000 bond-servants from each of the twelve tribes of the sons of Israel to mean an indefinite number of believers from all the peoples of the world. There is no textual basis for doing that. The specific number is given in contrast to the indefinite number of the great multitude. The tribes of Israel are specifically mentioned in contrast to the "every nation and all tribes and peoples and tongues" of the great multitude.

There is no principle of interpretation for making the text mean the opposite of what it says. If one chooses to do that, despite the clear meaning of the text, it would then be just as consistent to "spiritualize" the "great multitude which no one could count, from every nation and all tribes and peoples and tongues" to mean 12,000 from each of the twelve tribes of Israel.

There is nothing in the text that suggests or demands treating it in such a strange way. The text is very specific. It is meant to be.

There are some parallels in Tanakh that can help us to understand why the text says what it says, and means what it says. There are three things to look at: 1) the sealing; 2) the number; and 3) the naming of each tribe.

Ezekiel saw a similar vision in which some of the sons of Israel are sealed. "Then [the Lord] cried out in my hearing with a loud voice saying, 'Draw near, O executioners of the city, each with his destroying weapon in his hand.' And behold, six men came from the direction of the upper gate which faces north, each with his shattering weapon in his hand; and among them was a certain man clothed in linen with a writing case at his loins. And they went in and stood beside the bronze altar.

"Then the glory of the God of Israel went up from the cherub on which it had been, to the threshold of the temple. And He called to the man clothed in linen at whose loins was the writing case. And the Lord said to him, 'Go through the midst of the city, even through the midst of Jerusalem, and put a **mark** on the foreheads of the men who sigh and groan over all the abominations which are being committed in its midst.'

"But to the others He said in my hearing, 'Go through the city after him and strike; do not let your eye have pity, and do not spare. Utterly slay old men, young men, maidens, little children, and women, but do not touch any man on whom is the **mark**; and you shall start from My sanctuary.' So they started with the elders who were before the temple." (Ezek.9:1-6)

God was about to pour out His wrath on Jerusalem. Before He did that, He sealed some of the sons of Israel. He sealed, with a mark on their foreheads, "the men who sigh and groan over all the abominations which are being committed in its midst." They did not partake of the immorality of the rest, they grieved over it.

The word translated "mark" is Tav/ת, the last letter of the Hebrew alphabet. Each of those sealed had a "ת" on his forehead. The letter is originally a cross of one kind or another, like a "+" or "x". In the time of Ezekiel, the letter had approximately this shape: ╳ [1] The Lord commanded that each of those in Jerusalem who was to be preserved should receive the mark of this cross on his forehead.

God told the angelic executors of His wrath that the judgment was to begin at "My sanctuary." God revealed the same principle to Peter. "For it is time for judgment to begin with the household of God..." (1Pet.4:17) Even in judgment, God has an order.

The sealing that John saw is parallel to the sealing that Ezekiel saw. The wrath of God is about to be poured out. There are those of the sons of Israel who are protected by God from that wrath. This remnant has kept itself from immorality.

Later on, John is told of the 144,000 that "These are the ones who have not been defiled with women, for they are virgins. These are the ones who follow the Lamb wherever He goes. These have been purchased from among men as first fruits to God and to the Lamb. And no lie was found in their mouth; they are blameless." (Rev.14:4-5)

Towards the end of the wandering in the wilderness, the sons of Israel defeated some of the Amorite tribes that came to fight against them. When Balak, king of Moab, and the Midianites heard of what Israel had done, they were afraid. So they sought for some way to defeat Israel.

"So the elders of Moab and the elders of Midian departed with the fees for divination in their hand; and they came to Balaam..." (Num.22:7) Balaam was a Gentile prophet who knew the voice of God, but he did not belong to God. He was hired to curse the Jews.

Balaam sought the word of the Lord. "Then the Lord put a word in Balaam's mouth and said, 'Return to Balak, and you shall speak thus, ...From Aram Balak has brought me, Moab's king from the mountains of the East, *"Come curse Jacob for me, and come, denounce Israel!"*

" 'How shall I curse, whom God has not cursed? And how can I denounce, whom the Lord has not denounced?...Let me die the death of the upright, and let my end be like his!' " (Num.23:5,7,8,10)

Balaam saw what the final end of the Jewish people would be, and he desired it for himself. He did not, however, "die the death of the upright." Nor will he share in the glorious end that God has reserved for Israel.

Balaam did continue to listen to God, and God would not let him curse Israel. Nevertheless, Balaam still wanted his reward from Balak. So he counselled Balak and the Midianites to seduce Israel into immorality.

"While Israel remained at Shittim, the people began to play the harlot with the daughters of Moab....So Moses said to the judges of Israel, 'Each of you slay his men who have joined themselves to Baal of Peor.' Then behold, one of the sons of Israel came and brought to his relatives a Midianite woman, in the sight of Moses and in the sight of all the congregation of the sons of Israel, while they were weeping at the doorway of the tent of meeting.

"When Phinehas the son of Eleazar, the son of Aaron the priest, saw it, he arose from the midst of the congregation, and took a spear in his hand; and he went after the man of Israel into the tent, and pierced both of them through, the man of Israel and the woman, through the body, So the plague on the sons of Israel was checked. And those who died by the plague were 24,000." (Num.25:1,5-9)

There were those in Israel then who indulged in idolatry and immorality. God sent a plague among the people to bring judgment on them. There were also those who kept themselves pure.

"Then the Lord spoke to Moses saying, 'Take full vengeance for the sons of Israel on the Midianites; afterward you will be gathered to your people.' And Moses spoke to the people, saying, 'Arm men from among you for the war, that they may go against Midian, to execute the Lord's vengeance on Midian. **A thousand from each tribe of all the tribes of Israel you shall send to the war.' So there were furnished from the thousands of Israel, a thousand from each tribe, twelve thousand armed for war.**" (Num.31:1-5)

For the war against the Midianites, a war against immorality and idolatry, one thousand men were chosen out of each of the tribes of Israel. The one thousand from each tribe, twelve thousand in all, were chosen for the Lord according to the nature of the war. They could not be men who would be seduced.

It is the same with the 12,000 from each tribe who are sealed for the Lord before the fulness of the wrath of God is poured out. They do battle for the Lord in a world of idolatry and immorality. (cf.Rev.8:20-21) They cannot be men who will be seduced or defiled by "Midianite women." They cannot be drawn away from their task.

That is why, "These are the ones who have not been defiled with women, for they are virgins....These have been purchased from among men as first fruits to God and to the Lamb. And no lie was found in their mouth; they are blameless." (Rev.14:4-5)

They have "put on the full armor of God, that [they] may be able to stand firm against the schemes of the devil." (Eph.6:11) "For the weapons of [their] warfare are not of the flesh, but divinely powerful for the destruction of fortresses." (2Co.10:4)

All the works of God are done in Truth. (cf.Ps.111:8) As for the 144,000

Israelites, we are told, "And no lie was found in their mouth." Literally, "And in their mouth, guile [δολος] was not found." That is how Jesus described Nathaniel when He saw him. "Behold, an Israelite indeed, in whom is no guile [δολος]!" (Jn.1:47)

Zephaniah prophesied for the Lord, "But I will leave among you a humble and lowly people, and they will take refuge in the name of the Lord. The remnant of Israel will do no wrong and tell no lies, nor will a deceitful tongue [The Septuagint has γλοσσα δολια] be found in their mouths; for they shall feed and lie down with no one to make them tremble." (Zeph.3:12-13)

Isaiah prophesied of the Lamb who leads them, "His grave was assigned to be with wicked men, yet with a rich man in His death; although He had done no violence, nor was there any deceit [The Septuagint has δολον] in His mouth." (Is.53:9) Peter told "those who reside as aliens," "For you have been called for this purpose, since Messiah also suffered for you, leaving you an example for you to follow in His steps, who committed no sin, nor was any deceit [δολος] found in His mouth." (1Pet.2:20-21)

The 144,000 without guile are a chosen, representative remnant out of all Israel. "These are the ones who follow the Lamb wherever He goes." They have His mark on them. That mark preserves them.

After the war against Midian, "the officers who were over the thousands of the army, the captains of thousands and the captains of hundreds, approached Moses; and they said to Moses, 'Your servants have taken a census of men of war who are in our charge, and **no man of us is missing**.' " (Num.31:49-50) They knew that the hand of God had been upon them and preserved them all throughout the battle. (cf. Rev.7:3; 9:4)

The 144,000 sons of Israel bring the greatest fulfillment in this age of the calling of Israel, which is to be "a light to the Gentiles." They are the primary means by which the great multitude from "every nation and all tribes and peoples and tongues" is saved out of the great tribulation.

Immediately after describing the remnant, John says, "And I saw another angel flying in midheaven, having an eternal gospel to preach to those who live on the earth, and to every nation and tribe and tongue and people; and He said with a loud voice, 'Fear God, and give Him glory, because the hour of His judgment has come; and worship Him who made the heaven and the earth and sea and springs of waters.' " (14:6-7)

The activity of angels in heaven is related to the activity of men upon the earth. As the gospel goes forth in heaven, it goes forth on the earth. What is loosed in heaven is loosed on the earth. What takes place in the "spiritual" realm also takes place in the physical realm.

FOOTNOTE

1. "Taw," *Encyclopedia Judaica Jerusalem, Vol.15,* The MacMillan Co., NY, 1971, P.835

31

THE LAST WAR IN HEAVEN

"And there was war in heaven, Michael and his angels waging war with the dragon. And the dragon and his angels waged war, and they were not strong enough, and there was no longer a place found for them in heaven. And the great dragon was thrown down, the serpent of old who is called the Devil and Satan, who deceives the whole world; he was thrown down to the earth, and his angels were thrown down with him.

"And I heard a loud voice in heaven, saying, 'Now the salvation, and the power, and the kingdom of our God and the authority of His Messiah have come, because the accuser of our brethren has been thrown down, who accuses them before our God day and night.' " (Rev.12:7-10)

This is a very important war. Actually, it is the final battle of a war that has been going on in heaven for a long time. The end result is that the Devil and his angels are cast down, "and there was no longer a place found for them in heaven." The Devil will never again have access before God to accuse and to seek to destroy. The end result is also that "the salvation, and the power, and the kingdom of our God and the authority of His Messiah have come."

The Scriptures indicate that the Devil was cast down from heaven a long time ago, in the beginning: "Thus says the Lord God, 'You had the seal of perfection, full of wisdom and perfect in beauty. You were in Eden, the garden of God...You were the anointed cherub who covers; and I placed you there. You were on the holy mountain of God; you walked in the midst of the stones of fire. You were blameless in your ways from the day you were created, until unrighteousness was found in you. By the abundance of your trade you were internally filled with violence, and you sinned; therefore **I have cast you as profane from the mountain of God**. And I have destroyed you, O covering cherub, from the midst of the stones of fire.

" 'Your heart was lifted up because of your beauty; you corrupted your wisdom by reason of your splendor. **I cast you to the ground**; I put you before kings, that they may see you.' " [Ezek.28:12-17] "**How you have fallen from heaven**, O star of the morning, son of the dawn! **You have been cut down to the earth**, you who have weakened the nations!" [*Is.14:12*]

The Devil was cast out of heaven to the earth back in the beginning, but he still had access into the heavenlies. The book of Job gives us an interesting view of events taking place in heaven. Job did not see or know what was going on in heaven, but it certainly affected his life.

"Now, there was a day when the sons of God came and presented themselves before the Lord. And Satan also came among them. And the

Lord said to Satan, 'From where do you come?' Then Satan answered the Lord and said, 'From roaming about on the earth and walking around on it.' " (Job 1:6-7)

The sons of God, His created angels, were out ministering. Satan, "the adversary," also had been busy seeking to kill, to steal, and to destroy. "Devil" means "the accuser." When he comes before God, he comes to accuse. He came to accuse Job.

God showed Zechariah some similar events in heaven: "Then he showed me Joshua, the high priest standing before the angel of the Lord, and Satan standing at his right hand to accuse him. And the Lord said to Satan, 'The Lord rebuke you, Satan! Indeed, the Lord who has chosen Jerusalem rebuke you! Is this not a brand plucked from the fire?' Now Joshua was clothed with filthy garments and standing before the angel." (Zech.3:1-2)

In the vision, Joshua, as the high priest of Israel, is representing his people. He stands before God to intercede for Jerusalem and her children. Joshua is clothed in filthy garments. He is representing a people who are acknowledged to be guilty and unclean.

Centuries before, Isaiah had prayed, "For all of us have become like one who is unclean, and all our righteous deeds are like a filthy garment; and all of us wither like a leaf, and our iniquities, like the wind, take us away." (Is.64:6) The iniquities of the Jewish people took them away into captivity in Babylon. It was the faithfulness of God that restored them to the land.

Zechariah and Joshua the high priest were part of the returned remnant. So was Ezra. Ezra had prayed, "O Lord God of Israel, Thou art righteous, for we have been left an escaped remnant, as it is this day; behold, we are before Thee in our guilt, for no one can stand before Thee because of this." (Ez.9:15)

In the vision that God gave to Zechariah, we are told that Joshua the high priest symbolizes the Messiah. (Zech.3:8) In Hebrew, the name "Joshua" is "Jehoshua/Yehoshua/יהושע." The name "Jesus/Jeshua/Yeshua/ישוע" is a shortened form of "Joshua/Jehoshua/Yehoshua." ("Jesus" comes from the Greek transliteration, Iesous/Ιησους.)

Throughout the book of Ezra, this same Joshua the high priest is called by the shortened form, "Jesus/Jeshua/Yeshua/ישוע." God is very clearly indicating, in this vision that He gave to Zechariah, that Messiah Jesus, the high priest of Israel, is interceding for Jerusalem and her children.

Satan, on the other hand, is seeking to accuse, and thereby destroy, Jerusalem and the Jewish people. They are as a burning brand, about to be consumed. But it is the Lord Himself who says, "The Lord rebuke you, Satan! Indeed, the Lord who has chosen Jerusalem rebuke you!" The Lord has chosen a city, and He has chosen a people. "Behold, He that guards Israel will neither slumber nor sleep." (Ps.121:4)

The Lord Himself promises to pull that brand out of the fire. It is the

Lord Himself who takes away the filthy garments of Joshua the high priest, the representative of Israel. " 'See, I have taken your iniquity away from you and will clothe you with festal robes.

" '...I will remove the iniquity of that land in one day. In that day,' declares the Lord of hosts, 'every one of you will invite his neighbor to sit under his vine and under his fig tree.' " (Zech.3:4,9,10) The Lord of hosts [i.e. the Commander of the armies of God] will intervene in that future day. That is the promise given in Zechariah's vision.

When Jesus appointed seventy disciples, He sent them out before Him to heal and to announce the coming of the kingdom of God. "And the seventy returned with joy, saying, 'Lord, even the demons are subject to us in Your name.' And He said to them, 'I was watching Satan fall from heaven like lightning.' " [Lk.10:17-18]

Satan was in heaven again, but the ministry of the seventy, empowered by the Holy Spirit, caused him to "fall from heaven like lightning." What they did on earth made a difference in the heavenlies. The battle in the heavenlies is affected by what believers do on the earth. It parallels the battle on earth.

Though Satan was cast out of heaven in the beginning, and again when the seventy ministered in power, that result was not final. He still has access to accuse and to seek to destroy. The last war in heaven will put an end to that.

The Lord revealed to the prophet Daniel some vital aspects of that war in heaven. Daniel was a godly man, faithful to pray. Nothing — not the business of the kingdom, not even the threat of being thrown to the lions — could stop him from praying. Towards the end of that faithful life, he was mourning, fasting and praying before the Lord. He was praying, as always, for Jerusalem, for Israel, for the Jewish people. He was praying for their restoration.

Daniel had "observed in the books the number of the years which was revealed as the word of the Lord to Jeremiah the prophet for the completion of the desolations of Jerusalem, namely, seventy years. So I set my face to the Lord God to seek Him by prayer and supplications, with fasting, sackcloth, and ashes." (9:2-3)

Daniel did not sit back to observe the fulfillment of prophecy, he set his face to pray for the restoration of Jerusalem. In response to his prayers, God sent Gabriel who told him, "O Daniel, I have now come forth to give you insight with understanding. At the beginning of your supplications the command was issued, and I have come to tell you..." (Dan.9:22-23)

In response to Daniel's prayer, Gabriel gave him wisdom and understanding direct from God. Daniel wanted more than that. He continued to pray and fast for the restoration of Jerusalem, Israel, and the Jewish people.

Someone else came from heaven in response to his prayers. "And I lifted up my eyes and looked, and behold, there was a certain man, dressed in linen, whose waist was girded with a belt of pure gold of Uphaz. His body also was like beryl, his face had the appearance of lightning, his eyes were like flaming torches, his arms and feet like the gleam of polished bronze, and the sound of his words, like the sounds of a tumult." (Dan.10:5-6)

At the beginning of the book of Revelation, the Apostle John describes Jesus in much the same way. "And I turned to see the voice that was speaking with me. And having turned I saw seven golden lampstands; and in the middle of the lampstands one like a son of Adam, clothed in a robe reaching to the feet, and girded across His breasts with a golden girdle. And His head and His hair were white like white wool, like snow; and His eyes were like a flame of fire; and His feet were like burnished bronze, when it has been caused to glow in a furnace, and His voice was like the sound of many waters. And in His right hand He held seven stars; and out of His mouth came a sharp two-edged sword; and His face was like the sun shining in its strength.

"And when I saw Him, I fell at His feet as a dead man. And He laid His right hand upon me, saying, 'Do not be afraid; I am the first and the last, and the living One; and I was dead, and behold, I am alive forevermore, and I have the keys of death and of Hades.' " (Rev.1:12-18) It seems that John is describing the same one that Daniel saw.

The one Daniel saw said to him, "Do not be afraid, Daniel, for from the first day that you set your heart on understanding this and on humbling yourself before your God, your words were heard, and I have come in response to your words. But the prince of the kingdom of Persia was withstanding me for twenty-one days; then behold, Michael, one of the chief princes, came to help me, for I had been left there with the kings of Persia. Now I have come to give you an understanding of what will happen to your people in the latter days, for the vision pertains to the days yet future." (Dan.10:12-14)

Gabriel was commanded to come because Daniel prayed. This "certain man" does not mention a command, He simply says, "I have come in response to your words." He came out of the heavens because Daniel prayed, and because of what Daniel prayed. He seems to be the same One who appeared to John — the Lord Jesus Himself.

However, a demonic power tried to prevent Him from getting through to Daniel. But as Daniel kept praying, Michael, "one of the chief princes," came and fought against this demonic power, enabling the man to get through to Daniel with His message about "what will happen to your people in the end of the days [literal]."

"And behold, one as a likeness of sons of Adam was touching my lips...Then this one with human appearance touched me again and strengthened me....Then he said, 'Do you know why I came to you? But I shall now return to fight against the prince of Persia; so I am going forth, and behold, the prince of Greece is about to come. However, I will tell you what is inscribed in the writing of truth. Yet there is no one who shows himself strong with me against these forces except Michael your prince.' " (Dan.10:16,18-21)

Michael, like Gabriel, is "one of the chief princes," a commander of angels, an archangel. In fact, Gabriel and Michael are the only chief princes of the angels mentioned in the Bible. The spiritual forces involved in this battle are the highest and most powerful that there are. The commander of the armies of heaven and his two chiefs-of-staff come to Daniel in response to his prayers for the restoration of Israel.

But how is it possible that the Lord Himself could be resisted for twenty-one days — the time Daniel had been praying — by a demonic prince? When Jesus was in Nazareth, "He did not do many miracles there because of their unbelief." (Mt.13:58) Both faith and unbelief make a difference in what God does. Daniel was praying in faith that God would break open the mightiest kingdoms for the sake of His people Israel, but Daniel was only one man.

The Lord told Daniel about the end of this age: "Now at that time Michael, the great prince who stands guard over the sons of your people, will arise. And there will be a time of distress such as never occurred since there was a nation until that time; and at that time your people, everyone who is found written in the book, will be rescued.

"And many who sleep in the dust of the ground will awake, these to everlasting life, but the others to disgrace and everlasting contempt. And those who have insight will shine brightly like the brightness of the expanse of heaven, and those who lead the many to righteousness, like the stars forever and ever. But as for you, Daniel, conceal these words and seal up the book until the end of time; many will go back and forth, and knowledge will increase." (Dan.12:1-4)

The Septuagint calls this, " a time of tribulation [θλιψεως], such tribulation [θλιψις] as has not been from the time that there was a nation on the earth until that time." The Apostle John was told it would be "the great tribulation [της θλιψεως της μεγαλης]." (Rev.7:14) This time of tribulation is worse than any that the Jewish people have yet endured.

Michael is the archangel who has been given by God the specific responsibility of protecting the Jewish people. He is the one who "stands guard over the sons of your people." Michael arises to fight for Israel, in her darkest hour ever. That is why he is the one who is waging this war in heaven against the Devil.

It is the war to end all wars in heaven. The Devil is personally fighting this war with all of his angels. All the forces of hell are fighting against the restoration of Israel, knowing that when they lose, they lose everything. They are forever cast out of heaven. The salvation, power, and kingdom of God and His Messiah follow this victory. The resurrection of the dead follows it.

Michael does not, however, fight this last of all wars in heaven alone. John saw "**Michael AND his angels** waging war with the dragon." Michael has received reinforcements. Where did his reinforcements come from?

Previously, as Daniel continued to pray, Michael himself was sent to reinforce the "certain man" who came to Daniel. **Daniel chose to give himself to bring about God's appointed purpose.** He "set his face to the Lord God to seek Him by prayer and supplications, with fasting, sackcloth, and ashes." He did not stop after five, ten, or fifteen days. Things happened in heaven as he prayed. He kept praying until the answer came. Gabriel came. Jesus came. Michael came.

When righteous men and women of God pray, God moves in the heavenlies. He sends angels to their appointed tasks. "Are they not all ministering spirits, sent out to render service for the sake of those who will inherit salvation?" (Heb.1:14) Even the Lord Himself goes forth.

That is why Paul reminds all believers to put on the full armor of God, "For **our** struggle is not against flesh and blood, but against the rulers, against the powers, against the world-forces of this darkness, against the spiritual forces of wickedness in the heavenly places." [Eph.6:12] The Devil was cast out of heaven in the beginning, yet today there are still "spiritual forces of wickedness in the heavenly places." **OUR** struggle is against them.

Michael receives reinforcements because people who belong to God have been praying for the restoration of the Jewish people, Jerusalem, and the land of Israel. Their prayers affect what happens in heaven. What happens in heaven determines what happens on the earth.

The battle will be won in heaven because people have prayed on earth. Then the Lord of hosts, the Supreme Commander of the armies of God, will descend from heaven to the earth to destroy the nations gathered together against Jerusalem and the Jewish people.

"Therefore say to them, 'Thus says the Lord of hosts, Return to Me, declares the Lord of hosts, *that I may return to you*, says the Lord of hosts.' " (Zech.1:3) The Lord of hosts will return to Israel when Israel returns to the Lord.

Jesus said to Jerusalem, "Behold, your house is being left to you desolate. For I say to you, from now on you shall not see Me until you say, 'Blessed is He who comes in the Name of the Lord.' " (Mt.23:38-39) Those who pray now as Daniel did will have a part in bringing the return of the Lord.

"On your walls, O Jerusalem, I have appointed watchmen. All day and night they will never keep silent. You who remember the Lord, take no rest for yourselves; and give Him no rest until He establishes and makes Jerusalem a praise in the earth." (Is.62:6-7)

Whoever remembers the Lord — the Lord who has chosen Jerusalem — is to pray as Daniel did for the restoration of the Jewish people. When that happens, Michael will have enough reinforcements to defeat the Devil. The Devil and his angels, i.e. the very gates of hell, will not be strong enough to resist this onslaught. When that happens, the One whose voice is as the sound of many waters will come. He said to Daniel, "**I have come in response to your words.**" (Dan.10:12)

32

ALL ISRAEL SHALL BE SAVED

The battle that John sees is won in heaven, and the Devil is cast down to the earth. Then John hears: "For this reason, rejoice, O heavens and you who dwell in them. Woe to the earth and the sea; because the devil has come down to you, having great wrath, knowing that he has only a short time." (Rev.12:12)

The Devil has "only a short time" after he has been cast down out of heaven to the earth. It is the return of the Lord that brings an end to this short time. John was later shown a vision of what takes place in heaven just before the Lord returns.

"And I heard, as it were, the voice of a great multitude and as the sound of many waters and as the sound of mighty peals of thunder, saying, 'Hallelujah! For the Lord our God, the Almighty, reigns. Let us rejoice and be glad and give the glory to Him, for the marriage of the Lamb has come and His bride has made herself ready.' And it was given to her to clothe herself in fine linen, bright and clean; for the fine linen is the righteous acts of the saints." (Rev.19:6-8)

The marriage of the Lamb takes place in heaven. The believers are there clothed in bright and clean fine linen, which represents the righteous deeds they have done. They are joined in marriage to the Lamb, the Lion of the tribe of Judah.

"Wives, be subject to your own husbands, as to the Lord. For the husband is the head of the wife, as Messiah also is the head of the church, He Himself being the Savior of the body. But as the church is subject to Messiah, so also the wives ought to be to their husbands in everything.

"Husbands, love your wives, just as Messiah also loved the church and gave Himself up for her; that He might sanctify her, having cleansed her by the washing of water with the word, that He might present to Himself the church in all her glory, having no spot or wrinkle or any such thing; but that she should be holy and blameless." (Eph.5:22-27) Even so, the bride of the Lamb is joined to her Husband and subject to Him.

John describes what he sees immediately after the marriage supper of the Lamb: "And I saw heaven opened; and behold, a white horse, and He who sat upon it is called Faithful and True; and in righteousness He judges and wages war. And His eyes are a flame of fire, and upon His head are many diadems; and He has a name written upon Him which no one knows except Himself. And He is clothed with a robe dipped in blood; and His name is called The Word of God.

"And the armies which are in heaven, clothed in fine linen, white and clean, were following Him on white horses. And from His mouth comes a sharp sword, so that with it He may smite the Gentiles; and He will rule them with a rod of iron; and He treads the wine press of the fierce wrath of God, the Almighty..." (Rev.19:12-15)

The armies are the saints, i.e. those who have been sanctified by the blood of the Lamb. They are the bride of the Lamb, His body. "Clothed in fine linen, white and clean," they return with Him to wage war, triumph, and reign. They return to earth with Jesus to do battle for Israel.

Some have mistakenly thought that Jesus returns to earth for the Church. That is not what the Bible teaches. The Church meets Jesus in the air. The Apostle Paul wrote, "For the Lord Himself will descend from heaven with a shout, with the voice of the archangel, and with the trumpet of God; and the dead in Messiah shall rise first. Then we who are alive and remain shall be caught up together with them in the clouds to meet the Lord in the air, and thus we shall always be with the Lord." (1 Thes.4:17)

Jesus does not return to earth for the Church. Sometime before that return, the Church meets Him in the air. Sometime before that return, the marriage of the Lamb takes place. Jesus returns to earth **with** the Church. Together, **He AND the Church return to earth for Israel,** to re-establish the kingdom of David.

John had heard a loud voice in heaven saying, "the accuser of **our brethren** has been thrown down." Those who are saying this are not angels or heavenly beings. They are brethren of those who are being accused. They are children of Adam.

At the time that the Devil is cast down, there is a multitude of the redeemed in heaven. It is their loud voice that John hears.

Remember Elijah and Elisha. Before Elijah was taken from the earth, he was told to anoint Elisha as prophet in his place. Elisha had walked with Elijah and had learned from him. This is like the Church and the 144,000 sons of Israel.

The ministry of Elijah did not end when he was taken up. He will return to the earth to complete his ministry as one of the two witnesses spoken of in Revelation 11. The ministry of the Church does not end when it is taken up. It will return to earth to complete its ministry — to fight for the salvation of Israel — but there is something significant that takes place in heaven, which prepares the Church for its return.

The marriage of the Lamb is the complete and intimate joining of the Church to Jesus, but to a Jesus who was prophesied, announced, and crucified as King of the Jews; to a Jesus who ministered and who is returning as King of the Jews — the despised and rejected King of the despised and rejected people.

The Church is joined to a Jesus who is the same yesterday, today, and forever. He is the One who said, "For I, the Lord, do not change; therefore you, O sons of Jacob, are not consumed." (Mal.3:6)

The 144,000 are Jewish followers of their King. They are part of the Church, but they must remain behind, even as Elisha had to remain behind. The young "street gang" taunted him, "Go up baldhead. Go up." The remnant of Israel will face similar gangs, taunts, and much worse.

When Elijah was taken up, Elisha received a double portion of the spirit which the Lord had placed upon him. (cf. 2Kings 2:9-14) The 144,000 remain behind with a double portion anointing — the mantle of the Church and the calling of Israel.

During the time of the return from Babylon, the Lord told Zechariah what the time of Israel's repentance would be like. "The burden of the word of the Lord concerning Israel. Thus declares the Lord who stretches out the heavens, lays the foundation of the earth, and forms the spirit of man within him: 'Behold, I am going to make Jerusalem a cup that causes reeling to all the peoples around; and when the siege is against Jerusalem, it will also be against Judah. And it will come about in that day that I will make Jerusalem a heavy stone for all the peoples; all who lift it will be severely injured. And all the goyim of the earth will be gathered against it....

" 'And it will come about in that day that I will set about to destroy all the goyim that come against Jerusalem. And I will pour out on the house of David and on the inhabitants of Jerusalem the Spirit of grace and of supplication, so that they will look on Me whom they have pierced; and they will mourn for Him, as one mourns for an only son, and they will weep bitterly over Him, like the bitter weeping over a first-born.' " (Zech.12:1-3,9-10)

There is a time when all the goyim are gathered to destroy Israel. It is the time of the greatest tribulation that the Jewish people have ever known. "Alas! for that day is great, there is none like it; And it is the time of Jacob's distress, but he will be saved from it." (Jer.30:6)

"But immediately after the tribulation of those days the sun will be darkened, and the moon will not give its light, and the stars will fall from the sky, and the powers of the heavens will be shaken, and then the sign of the Son of Adam will appear in the sky, and then all the tribes of the earth will mourn, and they will see the Son of Adam coming on the clouds of the sky with power and great glory. And He will send forth His angels with a great trumpet and they will gather together His chosen ones from the four winds, from one end of the sky to the other." (Mt.24:30-31)

The Lord showed Zechariah that the appearance of the sign of the Son of Adam in the sky will cause all Israel to repent and return to the Lord. John said, "Behold, He is coming with the clouds, and every eye will see Him, even those who pierced Him; and all the tribes of the earth will mourn over Him. Even so. Amen." (Rev.1:7)

As all the tribes of the earth are mourning, Jesus gathers "together His chosen ones from the four winds, from one end of the sky to the other." "These are the ones who come out of the great tribulation, and they have washed their robes and made them white in the blood of the Lamb." (Rev.7:14)

As Israel faces the wrath of the Devil on the earth, the whole earth faces the wrath of the Lamb. Isaiah describes the time of shaking on the earth in this way: "The earth is broken asunder, the earth is split through, the earth is shaken violently. The earth reels to and fro like a drunkard, and it totters like a shack, for its transgression is heavy upon it, and it will fall, never to rise again.

"So it will happen in that day, that the Lord will punish the host of heaven, on high, and the kings of the earth, on earth. And they will be gathered together like prisoners in the dungeon, and will be confined in prison; and after many days they will be punished. Then the moon will be abashed and the sun ashamed, for the Lord of hosts will reign on Mount Zion and in Jerusalem, and His glory will be before His elders." (Is.24:19-23) There will be judgment on angels and judgment on men.

As all the goyim are gathered together to fight against Jerusalem, "Then the Lord will go forth and fight against those nations, as when He fights on a day of battle. And in that day His feet will stand on the Mount of Olives, which is in front of Jerusalem on the east..." (Zech.14:3-4; cf. Acts 1:11-12)

At the Temple in Jerusalem, Peter preached to unbelieving Israelites and told them, "Repent therefore and return, that your sins may be wiped away, in order that times of refreshing may come from the presence of the Lord; and that He may send Him who was proclaimed to you before, Jesus the Messiah, whom heaven must receive until the times of restoration of all things, about which God spoke by the mouth of His holy prophets from ancient time." (*Acts 3:19-21*)

With the repentance of Israel, Jesus the Messiah will descend from heaven to restore the kingdom to Israel. From ancient time, God has spoken through the mouth of His holy prophets, saying that it would be so. The Son of Adam will come at the precise time, season, day, and hour that God the Father has fixed by His own authority. The Church will come with Him.

"And about these also Enoch, in the seventh generation from Adam, prophesied, saying, 'Behold, the Lord came with His holy ten thousands to execute judgment upon all, and to convict all the ungodly of all their ungodly deeds which they have done in an ungodly way, and of all the harsh things which ungodly sinners have spoken against Him.' " (Judah 14-15)

As the apostles watched Jesus ascend from the Mount of Olives into heaven, after He had responded to their question about the restoration of the kingdom to Israel, two men in white clothing appeared beside them.

These men said to the apostles, "Men of Galilee, why do you stand looking into heaven? This Jesus who was taken up from you into heaven will come in just the same way as you have watched Him go into heaven." (Acts 1:11)

From the Mount of Olives Jesus ascended into heaven. To the Mount of Olives He will descend from heaven (Zech.14:4), to restore the kingdom to Israel. The same Jesus of whom the prophets prophesied, the same Jesus who was crucified for being the King of the Jews, the same Jesus who ascended from the Mount of Olives; that is the Jesus who will return there.

"And God said to Abram, 'Know for certain that your descendants will be strangers in a land that is not theirs, where they will be enslaved and oppressed four hundred years. But I will also judge the nation whom they will serve; and afterward they will come out with great possessions....Then in the fourth generation they shall return here, for the iniquity of the Amorite is not yet complete.' " (Gen.15:13-14,16) When the iniquity of the Amorites was full, God brought judgment upon them.

Before His crucifixion, Jesus had told the disciples, "Jerusalem will be trampled under foot by the Gentiles until the times of the Gentiles be fulfilled [πληρω–θωσιν, fully stored up]." (Lk.21:24) When the time given to the Gentiles to trample Jerusalem is completed, God will bring judgment upon them. When the time of the Gentiles is fulfilled, Jerusalem will no longer be trampled down by them.

Jesus is coming to "reign over the house of Jacob forever; and His kingdom will have no end." (Lk.1:33) He is coming to bring to Israel "salvation from our enemies, and from the hand of all who hate us; to show mercy toward our fathers, and to remember His holy covenant, the oath which He swore to Abraham our father, to grant us that we, being delivered from the hand of our enemies, might serve Him without fear." (Lk.1:71-74)

Jesus has come to reign. "You say correctly that I am a king. For this I have been born, and for this I have come into the world..." (Jn.18:37)

"Hosanna! Blessed is He who comes in the Name of the Lord; Blessed is the coming kingdom of our father David. Hosanna in the highest." (Mk.11:9,10) The time and season which the Father fixed by His own authority has come.

33

THE COMPLETED RELATIONSHIP

When that happens, the relationship between Israel and the Church will be like that in **Diagram 4**. All of physical Israel will have believing, circumcised hearts, just like their Gentile brethren in the Church.

This is the completed revelation of "the mystery of Messiah." (Eph.3:4-6) "For He Himself is our peace, who made both groups into one... that in Himself He might make the two into one new man, thus establishing peace, and might reconcile them both in one body to God through the cross..." (Eph.2:14-16) Jesus reconciles Jew and Gentile to each other and to God through His atoning death.

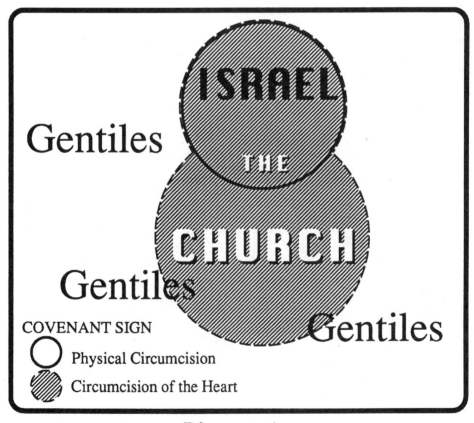

Diagram 4

It is a spiritual unity, not a physical loss of identity. "For even as the body is one and yet has many members, and all the members of the body, though they are many, are one body, so also is Messiah. For by one Spirit we were all baptized into one body, whether Jews or Greeks, whether slaves or free, and we were all made to drink of one Spirit. For the body is not one member, but many." (1Co.12:12-14)

Diagram 5 presents an alternate way of portraying the same relationship.

God had told Ezekiel that He would one day take the two kingdoms of Judah and Israel and make them one. "Behold, I will take the sons of Israel from among the goyim where they have gone, and I will gather them from every side and bring them into their own land; and I will make them one nation in the land, on the mountains of Israel; and one king will be king for all of them; and they will no longer be two nations, and **they will no longer be divided into two kingdoms...**

"And My servant David will be king over them, and they will all have

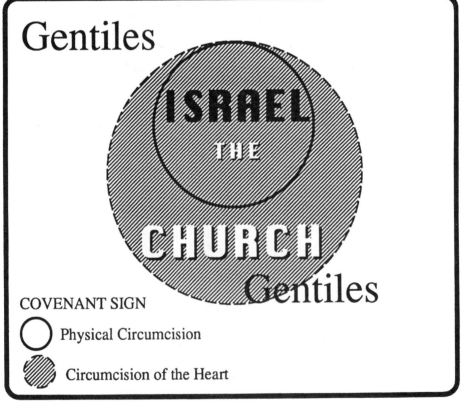

Diagram 5

one shepherd; and they will walk in My ordinances, and keep My statutes, and observe them. And they shall live on the land that I gave to Jacob My servant, in which your fathers lived; and they will live on it, they, and their sons, and their sons' sons, forever; and David My servant shall be their prince forever. And I will make a covenant of peace with them; it will be an everlasting covenant with them. And I will place them and multiply them, and will set My sanctuary in their midst forever. My dwelling place also will be with them; and I will be their God, and they will be My people. And the Gentiles will know that I am the Lord who sanctifies Israel, when My sanctuary is in their midst forever." (Ezek.37:21-22,24-28)

This is representative of another unification which Jesus had told His Jewish fold to expect. "And I have other sheep, which are not of this fold; I must bring them also, and they shall hear My voice; and **they shall become one flock with one Shepherd.**" (Jn.10:16)

Ruth was as completely grafted into Israel as anyone could be. She committed herself to her Jewish mother-in-law saying, "Do not urge me to leave you or turn back from following you; for where you go, I will go, and where you lodge, I will lodge. Your people shall be my people, and your God, my God. Where you die, I will die, and there I will be buried. Thus may the Lord do to me, and worse, if anything but death parts you and me." (Ruth 1:16-17) The choice that she had made was both clear and final.

Boaz saw her faithfully gleaning in the fields to provide for her mother-in-law and herself. "And Boaz answered and said to her, 'All that you have done for your mother-in-law after the death of your husband has been fully reported to me, and how you left your father and your mother and the land of your birth, and came to a people that you did not previously know. May the Lord reward your work, and your wages be full from the Lord, the God of Israel, under whose wings you have come to seek refuge.' " (Ruth 2:11-12).

Boaz was willing to fulfill the role, according to custom and law, of kinsman-redeemer. "Then Boaz said to the elders and all the people, 'You are witnesses today that I have bought from the hand of Naomi all that belonged to Elimelech and all that belonged to Chilion and Mahlon. Moreover, I have acquired Ruth the Moabitess, the widow of Mahlon, to be my wife in order to raise up the name of the deceased on his inheritance, so that the name of the deceased may not be cut off from his brothers or from the court of his birth-place; you are witnesses today.'

"And all the people who were in the gate, and the elders, said, 'We are witnesses. May the Lord make the woman who is coming into your home like Rachel and Leah, both of whom built the house of Israel; and may you achieve wealth in Ephrathah and become famous in Bethlehem.' " (Ruth 4:9-11)

Legally, the descendants of Ruth would carry the name of her deceased husband. The people and elders of Bethlehem asked a blessing for Ruth, that she would be "like Rachel and Leah, both of whom built the house of Israel." God answered their prayer. David, his descendants, and Messiah, the Son of David — the royal house in Israel — came forth from Ruth. So, "Ruth the Moabitess" became great in Israel.

In Paul's rebuke of Peter in Antioch, he said, "We are Jews by nature, and not sinners from among the Gentiles; nevertheless knowing that a man is not justified by the works of the Law but through faith in Messiah Jesus, even we have believed in Messiah Jesus, that we may be justified by faith in Messiah, and not by the works of the Law; since by the works of the Law shall no flesh be justified." (Gal.2:15-16)

"For the Scripture says, 'Whoever believes in Him will not be disappointed.' For there is no distinction between Jew and Greek; for the same Lord is Lord of all, abounding in riches for all who call upon Him; for 'Whoever will call upon the name of the Lord will be saved.' " (Rom.10:11-13)

In Jerusalem, "The commander came and said to him [Paul], 'Tell me, are you a Roman?' And he said, 'Yes.' And the commander answered, 'I acquired this citizenship with a large sum of money.' And Paul said, 'But I was actually born a citizen.' " (Acts 22:27-28)

In the Commonwealth of Israel, there are some who "are Jews by nature," and others who are not. There are some who are born citizens and others who are not. There are differences, but there is no difference in standing.

'Well then,' you will say, 'are the natives of the commonwealth nations British or not?' Or you might say, 'Are Gentile Christians Israel or not?' The answer depends upon what is meant by the question, or by who is asking and why.

Certainly they are not Israel to the exclusion of the Jews. 'Are they then Israel with the inclusion of the Jews?' Asking the question that way distorts the issue. The appropriate question is, 'Are the Jews with the inclusion of the believing Gentiles still Israel?' Of course.

" 'And it will come about that you shall divide it by lot for an inheritance among yourselves and among the aliens who stay in your midst, who bring forth sons in your midst. And they shall be to you as the native-born among the sons of Israel; they shall be allotted an inheritance with you among the tribes of Israel. And it will come about that in the tribe with which the alien stays, there you shall give him his inheritance,' declares the Lord God." (Ezek.47:22-23)

Remember, man looks at the outward appearance, but God looks at the heart. If there is arrogance in the heart of a man, be he Jew or Gentile, then he is cut off. If there is humility in the heart of a man, be he Jew or Gentile, then he is included.

"And it came about while He [Jesus] was on the way to Jerusalem, that He was passing between Samaria and Galilee. And as He entered a certain village, there met Him ten leprous men, who stood at a distance; and they raised their voices, saying, 'Jesus, Master, have mercy on us!'

"And when He saw them, He said to them, 'Go and show yourselves to the priests.' And it came about that as they were going, they were cleansed. Now one of them, when he saw that he had been healed, turned back, glorifying God with a loud voice, and he fell on his face at His feet, giving thanks to Him. And he was a Samaritan.

"And Jesus answered and said, 'Were there not ten cleansed? But the nine — where are they? Were none found who turned back to give glory to God, except this foreigner?' And He said to him, 'Rise, and go your way; your faith has saved you.' " (Lk.17:11-19)

The point that Jesus made is similar to the one He made in the synagogue in Nazareth: "And there were many lepers in Israel in the time of Elisha the prophet; and none of them was cleansed, but only Naaman the Syrian." (Lk.4:27) Jews should not think themselves to be better than Gentiles. And Naaman was only healed when he humbled himself and washed in the waters of Israel.

The actions of the Samaritan leper make the same point. Samaritans should not think themselves to be better than Jews. Jesus recognized what was in the man's heart.

Samaria was populated by Samaritans, Galilee by Jews. Jesus passed between them, on His way to Jerusalem. Ever since His ascension, Jesus has been headed to Jerusalem.

These ten lepers didn't live anywhere. They didn't belong anywhere. They were all outcasts. They were alive but dead.

The Law of God prescribed: "As for the leper who has the infection, his clothes shall be torn, and the hair of his head shall be uncovered, and he shall cover his mustache and cry 'Unclean! Unclean!' He shall remain unclean all the days during which he has the infection; he is unclean. He shall live alone; his dwelling shall be outside the camp." (Lev.13:45-46)

When Isaiah saw the Lord, he said, "Woe is me, for I am ruined! Because I am a man of unclean lips, and I live among a people of unclean lips; for my eyes have seen the King, the Lord of hosts." (Is.6:5) "What then? Are we better than they? Not at all; for we have already charged that both Jews and Greeks are under sin." (Rom.3:9) We are all, by nature, unclean.

Some of the lepers were Jews. At least one was a Samaritan. They were outcasts together. When they saw Jesus, they cried out, "Jesus, Master, have mercy on us!" They recognized who He was, and what they needed.

The Samaritan leper cried out to the Jewish Messiah for mercy. He had no time for, "Our fathers worshiped in this mountain; and you Jews say that in Jerusalem is the place where men ought to worship." (Jn.4:20) He wanted to be cleansed, and he knew Who could do it.

Jesus told the ten, "Go and show yourselves to the priests." The Samaritan leper didn't say, 'Which priests? Where should we go?' He knew. He headed towards the Temple in Jerusalem along with the other nine. Pride was not his problem.

"When he saw that he had been healed, [he] turned back, glorifying God with a loud voice, and he fell on his face at His feet, giving thanks to Him." Humility preceded his being healed and restored to the land of the living. Gratitude followed it.

The other nine would have done well to follow his example. Jesus healed them all because they humbled themselves before Him. Being healed, or being "saved," is no reason to forget humility. The mercy of the Lord is always reason enough to be humble before God and man.

34

THEY WILL REIGN UPON THE EARTH

Jesus told the church in Thyatira, "Nevertheless what you have, hold fast until I come. And he who overcomes, and he who keeps My deeds until the end, to him I will give authority over the Gentiles; and he shall rule them with a rod of iron, as the vessels of the potter are broken to pieces, as I also have received authority from My Father; and I will give him the morning star. He who has an ear, let him hear what the Spirit says to the churches." (Rev.2:26-29)

To the one who overcomes, Jesus has promised to "give authority over the Gentiles; and he shall rule them with a rod of iron." **The Gentiles will be upon the earth. Those who rule over them will do so on the earth.**

What Gentiles will these be? Jesus spoke of how He would judge the Gentiles when He returns. He said, "But when the Son of Man comes in His glory, and all the angels with Him, **then He will sit on His glorious throne**.

"And all the Gentiles will be gathered before Him; and He will separate them from one another, as the shepherd separates the sheep from the goats; and He will put the sheep on His right, and the goats on the left. Then the King will say to those on His right, 'Come you who are blessed of My Father, inherit the kingdom prepared for you from the foundation of the world.'...Then He will also say to those on His left, 'Depart from Me, accursed ones, into the eternal fire which has been prepared for the devil and his angels.' " (Mt.25:31-34,41)

These are Gentiles still alive on the earth when Jesus returns with the Church to fight for Israel. Those on the right are brought into the kingdom. Those on the left are sent into the eternal fire.

What is the basis for this judgment? Jesus explains that the basis for this judgment is what they have done or failed to do to Him. These Gentiles will ask Him, 'When did we ever serve (or fail to serve) You?'

Then Israel's returned King will answer these Gentiles by pointing to another group that is also gathered before Him at His return. He will say, "Truly I say to you, to the extent that you did it to one of these brothers of Mine, even the least of them, you did it to Me." (Mt.25:40,45) These brothers of His, even the least of them, are the Jews whom He has just delivered.

When Jesus returns to earth, He destroys those Gentiles who had sought to destroy His city and His people. He gathers the remaining Gentiles before Him for judgment — a judgment according to His promise to Abraham, Isaac, Jacob, and all Israel: "I will bless those who bless you and curse those who curse you."

The individual surviving Gentiles who in some way ministered to the Jews will receive the blessing of the Father for what they have done to Israel, His first-born son. They will have done so at great personal risk, even as it was during the Holocaust. It is these Gentiles who will enter in to the kingdom of the Lord. It is these Gentiles over whom the disciples will rule on earth.

God caused John to see that only the Lion of Judah, the root of David, could "overcome so as to open the book and its seven seals....And they [the four living creatures and the elders] sang a new song, saying, 'Worthy art Thou to take the book, and to break its seals; for Thou wast slain, and didst purchase for God with Thy blood men from every tribe and tongue and people and nation. And Thou hast made them to be a kingdom and priests to our God; and **they will reign upon the earth.**' " (5:9-10)

Who are those who have been purchased for God by the blood of the Lion of Judah, the Lamb that was slain? They are those redeemed "from every tribe and tongue and people and nation." Certainly, this must apply to the Church.

"And Thou hast made them to be a kingdom and priests to our God; and they will reign upon the earth." Where will they reign? "They will reign upon the earth."

Paul encouraged Timothy during a time when Rome reigned over the earth: "It is a trustworthy statement: for if we died with Him, we shall also live with Him. If we endure, we shall also reign with Him..." (2Tim.2:11-12) Where will Jesus be reigning? Those who endure will also reign with Him there.

A rich young man came to Jesus, asking, "'Teacher, what good thing shall I do that I may obtain eternal life?'...And He said to him, '...if you wish to enter into life, keep the commandments.'...

"The young man said to Him, 'All these things I have kept; what am I still lacking?' Jesus said to him, 'If you wish to be complete, go and sell your possessions and give to the poor, and you shall have treasure in heaven; and come, follow Me.' But when the young man heard this statement, he went away grieved; for he was one who owned much property.

"And Jesus said to His disciples, 'Truly I say to you, it is hard for a rich man to enter the kingdom of heaven. And again I say to you, it is easier for a camel to go through the eye of a needle, than for a rich man to enter the kingdom of God.'

"And when the disciples heard this, they were very astonished and said, 'Then who can be saved?' And looking upon them Jesus said to them, 'With men this is impossible, but with God all things are possible.'

"Then Peter answered and said to Him, 'Behold, we have left everything and followed You; what then will there be for us?' And Jesus said to them, 'Truly I say to you, that you who have followed Me, in the regeneration when the Son of Man will sit on His glorious throne, you also shall sit upon twelve thrones, judging the twelve tribes of Israel.' " (Mt.19:16-28; cf. Mt.12:27)

The issue concerned the relationship of material possessions and eternal life, entering the kingdom of heaven, and entering the kingdom of God. Jesus said that abundant material possessions made it difficult for a man to inherit eternal life, the kingdom of heaven, and the kingdom of God.

Then Peter said, "Behold, we have left everything and followed You; what then will there be for us?" Jesus told them that in the age to come, they would "sit upon twelve thrones, judging the twelve tribes of Israel." **The tribes of Israel will be upon the earth. Those who judge them, those who exercise God's rule over them, will do so upon the earth.** (The sense of "judging" here is that of a continuing administration for God, as in the ministry of Samuel and the other "judges.")

Jesus told His disciples much the same thing at the Passover table before His death. "And there arose also a dispute among them as to which one of them was regarded to be the greatest. And He said to them, 'The kings of the Gentiles lord it over them; and those who have authority over them are called *"Benefactors."*

" 'But not so with you, but let him who is the greatest among you become as the youngest, and the leader as the servant. For who is greater, the one who reclines at table, or the one who serves? Is it not the one who reclines at table? But I am among you as the one who serves.

" 'And you are those who have stood by Me in My trials; and just as My Father has granted Me a kingdom, **I grant you that you may eat and drink at My table in My kingdom, and you will sit on thrones judging the twelve tribes of Israel.'** " (Lk.22:24-30)

Jesus was telling them that when they rule, they should not do it the way the kings of the Gentiles do. When the disciples rule, they are to serve others. He told them on many occasions, "...whoever wishes to become great among you shall be your servant." (Mt.20:27)

Then He told them when it was that they would rule. **When His kingdom comes,** they "will sit on thrones judging the twelve tribes of Israel." The twelve tribes, the thrones, and the disciples will be upon the earth.

Moses told Israel of the requirements for a God-ordained king. Among other requirements, he mentioned, "you shall surely set a king over you whom the Lord your God chooses, **one from among your countrymen you shall set as king over yourselves**; you may not put a foreigner over yourselves who is not your countryman." (Dt.17:15) Inasmuch as "the word of the Lord abides forever," the Lord will fulfill this, His Word, when His Kingdom comes. He will fulfill it for Israel and for all those who have been purchased for God by the blood of the Lamb.

God promised Israel, "Moreover, I will give you a new heart and put a new spirit within you; and I will remove the heart of stone from your flesh and give you a heart of flesh. And I will put My Spirit within you and cause you to walk in My statutes, and you will be careful to observe My ordinances. And **you will live in the land that I gave to your forefathers**; so you will be My people, and I will be your God." (Ezek.36:26-28)

The intersection of time and eternity cannot be understood from the perspective of time alone. There are eternal things that exist in time. At some point in the future, time will be swallowed up by eternity. Before that happens, there are occasions when eternity breaks in and disrupts time.

When Jesus died, "Behold, the veil of the temple was torn in two from top to bottom, and the earth shook; and the rocks were split, and the tombs were opened; and many bodies of the saints who had fallen asleep were raised; and coming out of the tombs after His resurrection they entered the holy city and appeared to many." (Mt.27:51-53)

Many believers who had died before Jesus did were raised out of their graves at His resurrection. In a special way, they shared in His resurrection. When Jesus ascended into heaven after His resurrection, they ascended with Him. In a special way, they shared in His ascension.

"Therefore it says, 'When He ascended on high, He led captive a host of captives, and He gave gifts to men.' (Now this expression, 'He ascended,' what does it mean except that He also had descended into the lower parts of the earth? He who descended is also He who ascended far above all the heavens, that He might fill all things." (Eph.4:8-10)

Sometime in the future, the sign of the Son of Adam will appear in the heavens. "For the Lord Himself will descend from heaven with a shout, with the voice of the archangel, and with the trumpet of God; and the dead in Messiah shall rise first. Then we who are alive and remain shall be caught up together with them in the clouds to meet the Lord in the air, and thus we shall always be with the Lord." (1Thes.4:16-17)

"The dead in Messiah," those who were not previously resurrected with Him, will then share in His resurrection. Both they and "we who are alive and remain" will also share in His ascension in a particular way.

When the Lord returns to the earth, He returns with His bride to establish His kingdom and reign over all the earth. As part of establishing His kingdom upon the earth, Jesus judges the Gentiles, and then entrusts various kingdom responsibility to those who have suffered, died, risen, and ascended with Him.

The Lord revealed to John much that focused on the final destruction of the Devil's kingdom on the earth. That destruction climaxes with the return of the Lord and the armies of heaven, the casting of the Beast and the false prophet into the lake of fire, and the binding of the Devil for a thousand years.

God gives John a brief view of the time which follows this triumphant return of Messiah to Jerusalem. "And **I saw thrones, and they sat upon them, and judgment was given to them**. And I saw the souls of those who had been beheaded because of the testimony of Jesus and because of the word of God, and **those who had not received the mark upon their forehead and upon their hand; and they came to life and reigned with Messiah for a thousand years**.

"The rest of the dead did not come to life until the thousand years were completed. This is the first resurrection. Blessed and holy is the one has a part in the first resurrection; over these the second death has no power, but they will be priests of God and of Messiah and will reign with Him for a thousand years." (Rev.20:4-6)

Those who held fast to the testimony of Jesus and the word of God, and would not receive the mark of the beast were killed during the great tribulation. As Jesus sets up His kingdom on the earth, they are resurrected to life. They join those who were resurrected before and those who were raised to meet Him in the air. Then they reign with Jesus for a thousand years.

During that time, the Gentiles will come again to Jerusalem, but it will be for worship. "In the last days, the mountain of the house of the Lord will be established as the chief of the mountains, and will be raised above the hills; and all the Gentiles will stream to it. And many peoples will come and say, 'Come, let us go up to the mountain of the Lord, to the house of the God of Jacob; that He may teach us concerning His ways, and that we may walk in His paths. For the law will go forth from Zion, and the word of the Lord from Jerusalem.' " (Is.2:2-3)

"And it will be that whichever of the families of the earth does not go up to Jerusalem to worship the King, the Lord of hosts, there will be no rain on them." (Zech.14:17) The King, the Lord of hosts, will be ruling from Jerusalem.

35

OUT OF HEAVEN

Jesus prayed to His Father, "I manifested Thy name to the men whom Thou gavest Me out of the world [εκ του κοσμου]; Thine they were, and Thou gavest them to Me, and they have kept Thy word....I have given them Thy word; and the world has hated them, because they are not of the world [εκ του κοσμου], even as I am not of the world [εκ του κοσμου]. I do not ask Thee to take them out of the world [εκ του κοσμου], but to keep them from the evil one." (Jn.17:6,14-15)

Jesus, of course, was praying in the Hebrew/Aramaic of the day, not in Greek. Nevertheless, the Greek accurately presents His prayer, and helps us understand an important aspect of His kingdom.

His disciples have been given to Jesus by the Father, "out of the world." The substance of their lives was composed of worldly things, but it no longer is. Having been redeemed, their life is not "out of the world" — it does not come from the world — even as Jesus Himself is not "out of the world."

Jesus said to a group of Pharisees, "You are from below, I am from above; you are of this world [εκ του κοσμου]; I am not of this world [εκ του κοσμου]. I said therefore to you, that you shall die in your sins; for unless you believe that I am, you shall die in your sins." (Jn.8:23-24) If they believe, and are therefore born from above, then they, too, will be "not of this world."

Jesus prayed for His disciples that they not be taken "out of the world," but rather that they remain in it. Their life is not composed of worldly things, but they are to live in the world to be witnesses for Him. They are to be living as Jesus did. Their life is from above, but they live it on the earth.

Jesus told Pilate, "My kingdom is not of this world [εκ του κοσμου]. If My kingdom were of this world [εκ του κοσμου], then My servants would be fighting, that I might not be delivered up to the Jews; but as it is, My kingdom is not from here [εντευθεν]." (Jn.18:36) If the kingdom of Jesus were a worldly kingdom, then it would have to be established by worldly means. His Jewish disciples would have to physically fight against the Jewish leaders and the Roman rulers in order to establish it.

Since His kingdom is not a worldly kingdom, it cannot be established by worldly means. That does not mean that it cannot be established upon the earth. It can be, and it will be, but not by worldly means.

That is why Jesus taught His disciples to pray, "Thy kingdom come, Thy will be done, in earth as it is in heaven." The kingdom that is in heaven is to be established upon the earth.

Heaven and earth are different realms, but God is One. God is over all, and the Creator of all. The will of the One who rules heaven and earth is to be done in both heaven and earth.

Jesus said, "I am the living bread that **came down out of heaven**...For the bread of God is **that which comes down out of heaven**, and gives life to the world." (Jn.6:51,33) He was in heaven, but He came down to the earth. "For **I have come down from heaven**, not to do My own will, but the will of Him who sent Me." (Jn.6:38)

"By faith Abraham, when he was called, obeyed **by going out to a place which he was to receive for an inheritance**; and he went out, not knowing where he was going. By faith **he lived as an alien in the land of promise, as in a foreign land, dwelling in tents** with Isaac and Jacob, fellow-heirs of the same promise; for he was looking for the city which has foundations, whose architect and builder is God." (Heb.11:8-10)

Abraham went to the "place which he was [one day] to receive for an inheritance." "He lived as an alien in the land of promise." Isaac and Jacob, "fellow-heirs of the same promise," also lived as aliens in that land. What land? The land of Canaan.

The patriarchs had the promise of God concerning the land of Canaan, but there was more to the promise than the land they saw. They were not looking for something that existed upon the earth, but "for the city which has foundations, whose architect and builder is God." What city is that? The new Jerusalem.

"All these died in faith, without receiving the promises, but having seen them and having welcomed them from a distance, and having confessed that they were strangers and exiles on the earth. For those who say such things make it clear that they are seeking a country of their own. And indeed if they had been thinking of that country from which they went out, they would have had opportunity to return. But as it is, they desire a better country, that is a heavenly one. Therefore God is not ashamed to be called their God; for He has prepared a city for them." (Heb.11:13-16)

The patriarchs saw the promises. They welcomed them. But they did not receive them. Instead, they lived as "strangers and exiles on the earth," aliens in the land of promise.

They were seeking a country of their own. They saw it, but they did not possess it. There is a time still to come when they will possess it, when the land of promise will be transformed.

Paul tells believers, "Set your mind on the things above, not on the things that are on earth." (Col.3:2) "For our citizenship is in heaven, from which also we eagerly wait for a Savior, the Lord Messiah Jesus." (Phil.3:20) Our Savior comes from heaven.

Our citizenship also comes from heaven. We are not children of any city made by men, but rather one made by God. The Hebrew for citizens is "sons of the city" [בני עיר]. "The Jerusalem above is free, which is our mother."

(Gal.4:26) But our Savior did not and will not stay in heaven. Neither will our city.

"And I saw a new heaven and a new earth; for the first heaven and the first earth passed away, and there is no longer any sea. And I saw the holy city, new Jerusalem, **coming down out of heaven** [εκ του ουρανου] from God, made ready as a bride adorned for her husband. And I heard a loud voice from the throne, saying, 'Behold, **the tabernacle of God is among men**, and He shall dwell among them, and they shall be His peoples, and God Himself shall be among them.' " (Rev.21:1-3)

John sees a new heaven and a new earth. The new Jerusalem comes down out [εκ] of heaven. Where does it come to? There is only one other place in existence, the new earth. The new Jerusalem comes down out of heaven to the new earth.

It is the city that Abraham, Isaac, Jacob, and their faithful descendants had been seeking all along. They had lived "as aliens in the land of promise." Now, in the ultimate fulfillment of God's promise and purpose for the land, the new Jerusalem comes down out of heaven. The "place which he [Abraham] was to receive for an inheritance" is theirs to possess.

God brought His people out of Egypt in the ex-odus [εκ/ξ–οδυς], the journey out. He brought them out of Egypt to bring them into the place He had prepared for them. God was preparing His people for the land. "Then I will let you dwell in this place, in the land that I gave to your fathers forever and ever." (Jer.7:7)

In preparing them for the land, God gave specific instructions to Moses concerning the building of a tabernacle: "Tell the sons of Israel to raise a contribution for Me; from every man whose heart moves him you shall raise My contribution....And let them construct a sanctuary for Me, that I may dwell among them. According to all that I am going to show you, as the pattern of the tabernacle and the pattern of all its furniture, just so you shall construct it." (Ex.25:2,8,9)

God showed Moses the pattern for making an earthly tabernacle, which would serve as a copy and shadow of the heavenly tabernacle. (cf.Heb.8-10) God dwelt in the earthly tabernacle between the cherubim over the ark. (Ex.25:22) How much more does He dwell in the heavenly tabernacle!

God will then dwell among His peoples in a special way. "So then you are no longer strangers and aliens, but you are fellow-citizens with the saints, and are of God's household, having been built upon the foundation of the apostles and prophets, Messiah Jesus Himself being the cornerstone, in whom the whole building, being fitted together is growing into a holy temple in the Lord; in whom you also are being built together into a dwelling of God in the Spirit." (Eph.2:19-22)

"And coming to Him as to a living stone, rejected by men, but choice and precious in the sight of God, you also, as living stones, are being built up as a spiritual house for a holy priesthood, to offer up spiritual sacrifices acceptable to God through Messiah Jesus." (1Pet.2:4-5)

"Therefore, holy brethren, partakers of a heavenly calling, consider Jesus, the Apostle and High Priest of our confession. He was faithful to Him who appointed Him, as Moses also was in all His house. For He has been counted worthy of more glory than Moses, by just so much as the builder of the house has more honor than the house. For every house is built by someone, but the builder of all things is God." (Heb.3:1-4)

"...For we are the temple of the living God; just as God said, 'I will dwell in them and walk among them; and I will be their God, and they shall be My people.' " (2Co.6:16) There was a pattern, there was a type. There will come a day when the reality in all its fulness will be visible upon the earth.

"And He shall wipe away every tear from their eyes; and there shall no longer be any death; there shall no longer be any mourning, or crying, or pain: the first things have passed away. And He who sits on the throne said, 'Behold, I am making all things new.' And He said, 'Write, for these words are faithful and true.' " (Rev.21:4-5)

God is not making all new things, He is making all things new. There is an important difference. Heaven is made new. The earth is made new. Jerusalem is made new.

It is similar to the change that takes place when someone repents, believes, and enters into the New Covenant. "Therefore if any man is in Messiah, he is a new creature; the old things passed away; behold, new things have come." (2Co.5:17)

God gives a "new" spirit and a "new" heart. (e.g. Ezek.11:19) "Therefore, we have been buried with Him through baptism into death, in order that as Messiah was raised from the dead through the glory of the Father, so we too might walk in newness of life." (Rom.6:4)

A man dead in the sins of the world is transformed into a new creature alive to God. He is the same man, but he is not the same man at all. He has been made new. The totality of the difference has not yet appeared.

"Beloved, now we are children of God, and it has not appeared as yet that we shall be. We know that, if He should appear, we shall be like Him, because we shall see Him just as He is." (1Jn.3:2)

When the totality of that difference appears, those who overcome will receive "a new name." (Rev.2:17) Jerusalem will receive "a new name." (Is.62:2) Still, it is Jerusalem.

"And he carried me away in the Spirit to a great and high mountain, and showed me the holy city, Jerusalem, coming down **out of heaven** [εκ του ουρανου] from God, having the glory of God....It had a great and high wall, with twelve gates...and names were written on them which are those of the twelve tribes of the sons of Israel....And the wall of the city had twelve foundation stones and on them were the twelve names of the twelve apostles of the Lamb." (Rev.21:10-12,14)

All of Jerusalem's children, those who have been redeemed, will walk through the gates under the names of the twelve tribes of Israel. Considering the sins of the different sons of Jacob, there would be ample reason for blotting out at least some of those names. But God promised Abraham, Isaac, Jacob, and all Israel that He would be their God and God of their children, too. God is faithful to the Jewish people, no matter what men think or do. The very gates of the new Jerusalem declare that.

Both the natural and the engrafted children of Jerusalem will rejoice with her. Jews and Gentiles who have received the message declared through the twelve apostles have been made her fellow-citizens. The very foundation stones of the city declare that.

"For behold, I create [בורא] new heavens and a new earth; and the former things shall not be remembered or come to mind. But be glad and rejoice forever [עדי עד] in what I create [בורא]; for behold, I create [בורא] Jerusalem for rejoicing, and her people for gladness. I will also rejoice in Jerusalem, and be glad in My people; and there will no longer be heard in her the voice of weeping and the sound of crying." (Is.65:17-19) The new Jerusalem is a new creation, not made of the things of this world or this age.

"For the anxious longing of the creation waits eagerly for the revealing of the sons of God. For the creation was subjected to futility, not of its own will, but because of Him who subjected it, in hope that the creation itself also will be set free from its slavery to corruption into the freedom of the glory of the children of God.

"For we know that the whole creation groans and suffers the pains of childbirth together until now. And not only this, but also we ourselves, having the first fruits of the Spirit, even we ourselves groan within ourselves, waiting eagerly for our adoption as sons, the redemption of our body." (Rom.8:19-23)

36

CONCLUSION

The children of Adam were once unified in their rebellion against God. God divided them into nations to break that rebellion. Each nation then individually rebelled against the Lord. So God created Israel, a new people, for the purpose of breaking those multiple national rebellions against Him. Israel was not chosen from among the nations, as though in a beauty contest; rather it was Abraham alone who was chosen out of the goyim.

Through Jesus, the King of the Jews, God has made Abraham, the first Jew, the Father of many Gentiles. All the true children of Abraham, whether they be Peter and Paul or Rahab and Ruth, walk with God as Abraham did. They leave everything behind to follow God.

Through Israel, the New Covenant, and the Church, God is fulfilling His promise to Messiah: "Ask of Me, and I will surely give the Gentiles as Thine inheritance, and the very ends of the earth as Thy possession." (Ps.2:8) If there had not been those from Israel to proclaim the message of redemption, the Gentiles would have continued to be in darkness, "hopeless and without God in the world."

If there had not been those of the house of Israel and the house of Judah who received the New Covenant, Gentiles could not have been brought into it. If there had not been believing Jews to make up the original Church, there would have been no one to testify of the crucifixion and resurrection. There would not be any New Covenant Scriptures.

On the other hand, Israel also needs the Church. Who else can bring good news, announce peace and salvation, and say to Zion, "Your God reigns!"? (Is.52:7) Even the faithful remnant by itself, like Joshua and Caleb, would be unable to enter the Promised Land. God has prepared a place for a people, not a handful. The Church is the way in which all the nations can be brought to bow before the living God, the God of Israel.

In God's plan, Israel and the Church are complementary, not competitive and irreconcilable. Neither is or will be complete without the other, "because God had provided something better for us, so that apart from us they should not be made perfect." (Heb.11:40) Together, Israel and the Church are made complete in God.

Paul reminded the Gentile believers in Ephesus that they had been hopelessly estranged from God and the commonwealth of Israel, until the blood of Jesus the Messiah brought them near. (Eph.2:11-22) He explains to them that **their being grafted in was a mystery** "which in other generations was not made known to the sons of men, as it has now been revealed to His holy apostles and prophets in the Spirit....

"To me, the very least of all saints, this grace was given, to preach to the Gentiles the unfathomable riches of Messiah, and to bring to light what is the administration of the mystery which for ages has been hidden in God, who created all things; **in order that the manifold wisdom of God might now be made known through the church to the rulers and the authorities in the heavenly places.** This was **in accordance with the eternal purpose which He carried out in Messiah Jesus our Lord.**" (Eph.3:5,8-11)

The mystery of the gospel is that Gentiles who believe are brought near in Messiah, joined to the commonwealth of Israel, and made one with the faithful in Israel. A Church that does not understand, appreciate, and proclaim this mystery of the gospel is not living in accordance with God's eternal purpose. It cannot fulfill God's eternal purpose.

That is why Paul encourages the Ephesian believers to grow in their understanding of what Messiah has done, and to live accordingly. (Eph.3:12 to the end of the chapter) "I, therefore, the prisoner of the Lord, entreat you to walk in a manner worthy of the calling with which you have been called, with all **humility** and **gentleness**, with **patience**, showing **forbearance** to one another in **love**, being **diligent** to preserve the **unity** of the Spirit in the bond of **peace**. There is one body and one Spirit, just as also you were called in one hope of your calling: one Lord, one faith, one baptism, one God and Father of all who is over all and through all and in all." (Eph.4:1-6)

God's eternal purpose will be accomplished. The King of the Jews will have an obedient bride. The time is at hand.

The success of God's plan and purpose can be seen in the final outcome. "Behold a great multitude, which no one could count, from every nation and all tribes and peoples and tongues, standing before the throne and before the Lamb, clothed in white robes, and palm branches in their hands; and they cry out with a loud voice, saying, 'Salvation to our God who sits on the throne, and to the Lamb.' " (Rev.7:9-10)

In the end, as in the beginning, there is a people all of one kind, but they are not from only one nation, tribe, people or tongue. Their oneness does not extend to these things. Their hearts overflow in praise of God and His Lamb for the grace and mercy of their salvation. They are united in their worship in Spirit.

In the beginning, the nations were united in their rebellion against God. When this age is over, they will be united in their obedience to Him. They are united in their worship in Truth. God will then have what He has long been seeking, "a people to worship Him in Spirit and in Truth."

"And he showed me a river of the water of life, clear as crystal, coming from the throne of God and of the Lamb, in the middle of its street. And on either side of the river was the tree of life, bearing twelve kinds of fruit, yielding its fruit every month; and the leaves of the tree were for the healing of the goyim.

"And there shall no longer be any curse; and the throne of God and of the Lamb shall be in it, and His bondservants shall serve Him; and they shall see His face, and His name shall be on their foreheads. And there shall no longer be any night; and they shall not have need of the light of a lamp nor the light of the sun, because the Lord God shall illumine them; and they shall reign forever and ever." (Rev.22:1-5)

PART THREE:

THE TRADITIONS OF MEN

SECTION A:
AUGUSTINE AND AQUINAS

37

AUGUSTINE'S *CITY OF GOD*

We have examined the Biblical teaching concerning the relationship of the Church and the Jews. We have also examined the development of the historical deviation from the Biblical teaching. Now it is time to examine the theological enshrinement of that deviation.

Even as Origen became the new guide to interpreting the Bible, so Augustine became the theologian of the new order. In about 426 A.D., Augustine wrote what he himself calls an "immense work" [1] — *Concerning the City of God* against the Pagans. It has provided the framework for almost all Church theology down to this day. It contains some great truths, but it also contains some great errors, especially in terms of the relationship of the Church and the Jewish people.

"The controversy over 'Origenism' had flared up shortly before St. Augustine started the *City of God*, and in A.D. 400 a council at Alexandria condemned certain doctrines ascribed to Origen. There was further controversy during the sixth century, and 'Origenism' was finally repudiated at the Second (Oecumenical) Council of Constantinople in 543." [2]

The wildest of Origen's speculations were condemned, but his system of interpretation, at least as far as it defined the Church as Israel, was maintained. Augustine distanced himself from Origen on some issues,[3] but *City of God* is conceptually dependent upon an acceptance of Origen's definition of the Church. Before we look at how Augustine viewed the relationship of the Church and the Jewish people, we need some background on his method of interpretation.

Augustine's basic approach to interpretation is sound. In discussing the garden of Eden, Augustine rejects the views of those who understand the scriptural account only symbolically. He says, "It is, however, arbitrary to suppose that there could not have been a material paradise, just because it can be understood also in a spiritual significance; it is like the assumption that there were not two wives of Abraham, named Hagar and Sarah, who bore two sons, one a slave's son, the other the son of a free woman, just because the Apostle finds in them the prefiguration of the two covenants; or that there was no rock from which water flowed when Moses struck it, just because it can be interpreted in a symbolic sense, as prefiguring Christ; which is how the same Apostle takes it when he says, 'Now the rock was Christ.'

"...This is the kind of thing that can be said by way of allegorical interpretation of paradise; and there may be other more valuable lines of interpretation. There is no prohibition against such exegesis, provided that we also believe in the truth of the story as a faithful record of historical fact." [4]

Concerning the flood in the time of Noah, he writes, "No one ought to imagine, however, that this account was written for no purpose, or that we are to look here solely for a reliable historical record without any allegorical meaning, or, conversely, that those events are entirely unhistorical, and the language purely symbolical." [5]

Augustine occasionally strays into symbolic fantasy. For example, in discussing the symbolical meaning of the dimensions of the ark, Augustine demonstrates how arbitrary such a system of interpretation can be. "It may be, for example, that someone will prefer a different interpretation to the one that I have given in the above-mentioned work of this passage, 'You will make it with lower, second, and third storeys.' I suggested that the Church is said to have two storeys because it is assembled from all nations, having two classes of men, the circumcised and the uncircumcised, or, as the Apostle puts it in another way, Jews and Greeks; and that it is called three-storeyed because all nations were re-established after the Flood from the three sons of Noah.

"But my critic must suggest some other interpretation which is not at variance with the Rule of Faith.

"For instance, God wanted the ark to have living-quarters not only on the lowest level but on the higher level (which he called the second storey) and on the level above that (the third storey) so that a dwelling-place should rise up, the third from the bottom upwards. Now this could be interpreted as illustrating the three virtues extolled by the Apostle: faith, hope, and charity.

"Again, three storeys could be much more appropriately explained as standing for the three abundant harvests in the Gospel, 'thirty fold, sixty fold, and a hundred fold.' Married chastity, on this interpretation, would inhabit the lowest level, widowed chastity the floor above, and virginal purity the top storey.

"And there may be other explanations and better ones, that could be advanced, which would be in harmony with the faith of this City. I would be prepared to say the same about all the other interpretations which can be put forward on this topic. Different suggestions may be made; but they must be checked by the standard of the harmonious unity of the Catholic faith." [6]

This is not really interpretation, because there is nothing in the text that actually signifies the point being made. How do three levels in the ark actually signify a thirty fold harvest which is married chastity, a sixty fold harvest which is widowed chastity, and an hundred fold harvest which is virginal purity? There is nothing in the text that signifies this, there is only something in the author's mind. The only thing in common between the text and the interpretation is that there are three of something.

However, in this portion, Augustine correctly recognizes the Church as being a joining together of Jews and Gentiles. He is in error though in saying that "all nations were re-established after the Flood." The nations did not come into existence until the later destruction of the tower of Babel.

Augustine is always willing to accept a variety of interpretations, provided that they are "not at variance with the Rule of Faith." This is very important in understanding him. For Augustine, "the Rule of Faith" is "the traditional orthodoxy governing the interpretation of Scripture. It is not identical with any accepted formula." [7]

In the midst of the Passover controversy of the second century, Polycrates had written to Victor, bishop of Rome. In refusing to submit and conform to Victor and the Roman church, he spoke of those who "observed the fourteenth day of the passover according to the gospel, deviating in no respect, but following **the rule of faith**." [8] For Polycrates, the Scriptures had provided the rule of faith. For Augustine, "the Rule of Faith" was determined by Church orthodoxy.

In another example of allegorical interpretation, Augustine "interprets" a phrase in the Septuagint rendering of Habakkuk. "'Between the two living creatures you will be recognized' can surely only mean between the two covenants, or between the two thieves, or between Moses and Elijah conversing with him on the mountain." [9] He tells us three things which it "can surely only mean." And again, there is nothing in the text that actually points to any of the three "interpretations." The only thing in common between the text and the interpretation is that there are two of something.

Augustine's only restriction on such imaginings is that "they must be checked by the standard of the harmonious unity of the Catholic faith." Whatever that may be, it is not the Scriptures themselves. In the time of Augustine, "the harmonious unity of the Catholic faith" had been established by threatenings, excommunications, exile and execution through the power of the Imperial decree. In the case of the date of Passover/Easter and the related issues, as well as in other cases, it had been established in direct opposition to the teaching of the Scriptures. It is this "standard of the harmonious unity of the Catholic faith" that causes havoc in the *City of God*.

Unfortunately for Augustine, historical events of the previous century had created a standard and framework that greatly distorted the nature of the Biblical relationship between the Church and Israel. He seems to go back and forth between declaring what the Scriptures actually say and declaring what the Constantinian Church had imposed upon them.

Augustine does not, however, share the views or the spirit of Eusebius and Constantine towards the Jews. Eusebius and Constantine were only able to speak of the Jews as evil creatures. Though Augustine had some negative things to say about the Jews, he had some positive things to say as well. In this very important respect, Augustine differs greatly from Eusebius and Constantine.

For example, in several sections Augustine discusses the discrepancies between the Hebrew text and the Septuagint, from which the Latin version, which the Church of the Roman Empire used, was derived. He notes that there are some who "refuse to question the reliability of the text which is accepted by the Church and is thus given a wider authority; and they believe that it is the version of the Jews and not the other text which contains inaccuracies.

"These people will not allow that it is more likely that we have here a mistake on the part of the translators, than that there should be a false statement in the language from which the Scriptures themselves were translated, through the Greek version, into our tongue. They assert that it is unbelievable that seventy translators who made their translation at one and the same time and produced one and the same meaning, could have made a mistake, or should have deliberately uttered a falsehood on a point of no importance to them. But they maintain that the Jews, in their jealousy at the transference to us, through translation, of the Law and the prophets, altered some passages in their own texts to diminish the authority of our version." [10] "Now these seventy (who were themselves Jews) had been assembled in one place, because Ptolemy, king of Egypt, had appointed them to this task." [11]

"But in fact it is unthinkable that any sensible person should suppose either that the Jews, whatever their perversity and malice, could have achieved such a feat in so many texts, so widely dispersed; or that those seventy men of reknown should have united in a common plan to deprive the Gentiles of the truth, because of jealousy. It would be more plausible, therefore, to suggest that when the text began to be transcribed for the first time from the copy in Ptolemy's library, some inaccuracy of this sort might have happened in one copy.

"...the divergence of the numbers given in the Latin and Greek versions from those appearing in the Hebrew, should not be ascribed either to Jewish malice or to a carefully thought-out plan on the part of the seventy translators. It should be put down to the mistake of the scribe who first received the text from the library of the aforesaid King Ptolemy to transcribe." [12]

Concerning God's promise of the land of Canaan to Abraham and his seed, Augustine says, " 'Then the Lord appeared to Abram, and said to him: *I shall give this land to your seed.*' There is nothing said here about that seed in respect of which he became the father of all nations; the only seed mentioned is that by which he is the father of the one nation of Israel; for it was this seed that took possession of that land." [13]

Augustine does not evidence any desire to condemn the Jewish people and then claim for the Church everything that God has given to them. Within the limits of his historical framework, Augustine was simply interested in knowing the truth. He comes very close to expressing it.

We have already noted how he correctly viewed the Church as a joining together of Jews and Gentiles, rather than as a Gentile entity. [14] He understood that to be the continuing nature of the Church, not just its beginning. In another passage, he says, "As for 'the sons of Levi,' and 'Judah,' and 'Jerusalem,' we ought to take those as standing for the Church of God itself, assembled not only from the Hebrews but from other nations also. And we should understand not the Church in its present state, when 'if we say that we have no sin we are fooling ourselves and we are strangers to the truth,' but the Church as it will be then, purified by the last judgement..." [15]

Augustine often notes the existence and nature of the remnant within Israel. He says, "And yet there was even there an Israel 'in whom there was no trickery,' like some grain among that chaff. For the apostles, as we know, came from Israel, as did all those martyrs, of whom Stephen was the first; and so did all those churches, which the apostle Paul mentions as giving glory to God for his conversion.

"I have no doubt that the next words are to be interpreted along these lines. 'And Israel will be divided into two' must mean, into Israel the enemy of Christ, and Israel which attaches itself to Christ — the Israel connected with the maidservant, and the Israel connected with the free woman. For these two kinds of Israel were at first together..." [16]

Augustine speaks of the judgment that came upon "the earthly Jerusalem," and says, "All this came upon Jerusalem the maidservant, in which there reigned also some sons of the free woman, holding that kingdom on a temporary lease, while possessing, by true faith, the kingdom of the Heavenly Jerusalem, whose sons they were, and placing their hope in the true Christ."[17]

"In fact, very many of the Jews, thinking over those prophecies both before his passion and more particularly after his resurrection, have come to believe in him." [18]

To these Jews who believed were added the Gentiles who believed. "Now it is a fact that there was no other people to bear the distinctive title of the people of God; for all that, the Jews cannot deny that in other nations also there have been some men who belonged not by earthly but by heavenly fellowship to the company of the true Israelites, the citizens of the country that is above. In fact, if the Jews deny this, they are very easily proved wrong by the example of Job, that holy and amazing man. He was neither a native of Israel nor a proselyte (that is, a newly admitted member of the people of Israel)...I have no doubt that it was the design of God's providence that from this one instance we should know that there could also be those among other nations who lived by God's standards and were pleasing to God, as belonging to the spiritual Jerusalem." [19]

Augustine also looked forward to the future salvation of all Israel. "The belief that in the final period before the judgement this great and wonderful prophet Elijah will expound the Law to the Jews, and that through his activity the Jews are destined to believe in our Christ, this is a very frequent subject in the conversation of believers, and a frequent thought in their hearts. The expectation that he will come before the coming of the Saviour in judgement is certainly not without good reason, since there is good reason for the belief that he is still alive; for he was carried up from the world of men in a fiery chariot, as holy Scripture testifies most explicitly.

"Well then, when he comes, he will explain in a spiritual sense the Law which the Jews now take in a material sense, and by so doing he will 'turn the heart of the father toward the son'...The meaning, then, is that the sons, that is, the Jews, will interpret the Law as their fathers – that is, the prophets, including Moses himself – interpreted it." [20]

He discusses the prophecy of Zechariah 12 in its literal fulfillment. "Now can we think that it is in the power of anyone but God to remove all the nations hostile to the holy city of Jerusalem and all who 'come against her', that is, to subject her to themselves? And 'to pour out over the house of David and the inhabitants of that city the spirit of grace and mercy'? This is without doubt an act of God...For on that day even the Jews will certainly repent, even those Jews who are to receive 'the spirit of grace and mercy.' " [21]

"There is also that statement of the Apostle, 'God has confined them all in unbelief, so that he may show mercy to them all.'...For the Apostle was speaking to the Gentiles about the Jews who were destined to believe later..." [22] Augustine believed that the Scriptures clearly taught that "the Jews were destined" to come to faith in the future. Their hearts would, at that future time, be restored to the Lord.

Unfortunately, as we will see shortly, Augustine discusses most of the end-times in symbolical language, rejecting any literal interpretation. His conclusions, or lack of them, do not really leave him any place to fit in this restoration of Israel. In fact, the consistent application of his allegorical system of interpretation leads to the disinheritance of all Israel. "Augustine's exegesis [system of interpretation] left Jewish Christians without Biblical or historical support for their actions, and they could only henceforth be considered, like Jews and heretics, as altogether outside the church." [23]

But before we look at his discussion of the end-times, we need to understand Augustine's concept of the "City of God." It is a concept that he draws from the allegory which Paul explains in Galatians 4:21-31.

THE ALLEGORY OF GALATIANS 4:21-31

Paul's allegory in Galatians 4:21-31 is misunderstood by some to teach the replacement of national Israel by the Church. That is not at all what it teaches.

Peter reminds us that in the letters of Paul, there "...are some things hard to understand...." (2Pet.3:16) To understand Paul, we must first understand 1) to whom he is writing, 2) the issue he is addressing, and then 3) the point he is making.

In Galatians, Paul is writing primarily to Gentile believers who have submitted, or who are considering submitting, to physical circumcision in order to be righteous before God. That is his audience, and that is the issue. Paul proceeds very logically, step by step, to build an irrefutable case against requiring Gentile believers to be physically circumcised. That is the point he is making.

He bases his case on the Tanakh, which is unimpeachable. In particular, he refers to the Torah, the Law, the five books of Moses. Paul does not, however, always write down every step that he takes. That is what gives the superficial appearance of his sometimes jumping from one thing to another. It is also what gives rise to much misunderstanding of what he is saying.

In 4:21-31, he is appealing to the Gentile believers in Galatia out of the law which they have taken, or are considering taking, upon themselves. For Paul, the allegory that he presents is not a fable (something that never really happened), but a spiritual lesson from the actual history of Israel. If they will properly understand the primary, physical reality, it will give light to them for their own lives.

Paul does not interpret the scripture allegorically as Augustine did. He simply explains that the real, natural events present an allegorical lesson. It is not greatly different from the method Paul used in describing the exodus to the Corinthians, e.g. the cloud and baptism, and then concluding: "Now these things happened as examples for us..." (1Co.10:6) The history of God's dealings with Israel contains lessons for the Church.

Throughout Galatians, Paul is comparing law as opposed to grace, and justification by the works of the law as opposed to justification by faith. That is what he is doing in chapter 4 as well. He does it through the comparison of a series of related pairs: 2 mothers, 2 sons, 2 cities, 2 mountains, 2 conditions, 2 destinies, and 2 covenants. He indicates to which column (v.25 sustoicei, "as soldiers in rank") each member belongs, but he does not write out both sides of all of the comparisons or even name all that is being compared. The reader is assumed to know the history and to be able to fill in what is obvious but left out.

Filled in, the comparisons are these: Abraham had two sons — Isaac is named, but Ishmael is not. Isaac was promised by God, born of a free woman, persecuted, and Abraham's heir. Ishmael was born of the flesh, born of a bondwoman, a persecutor, and cast out.

The two women are wives of Abraham — Hagar is named, but Sarah is not. Hagar was a bondwoman, compared to the Covenant of the Law which can be represented by Mount Sinai, which bears its children into bondage, and corresponds to the present (earthly) Jerusalem. Sarah was the free woman, compared to the New Covenant of grace and faith which can be represented by Mount Zion (unnamed, but see Hebrews 12:18-23), which bears its children into freedom, and corresponds to the (future) heavenly Jerusalem.

What then is the point that Paul is making? Is he saying that the Jews are cast out and that the Church is now the heir? It is important to remember that the opposite of "Jew" is "Gentile," and the opposite of "the Church" is "unbelievers."

COMPARISONS IN GALATIANS 4:21-31

TWO MOTHERS
Sarah	Free Woman
Hagar	Bondwoman

TWO CITIES
Heavenly Jerusalem	Future
Earthly Jerusalem	Present

TWO MOUNTAINS
Mt. Zion	Her Children are Free
Mt. Sinai	Her Children are Enslaved

TWO COVENANTS
New, of Grace & Faith	To Freedom
Old, of Law	To Bondage

TWO SONS
Isaac	Promised, Persecuted
Ishmael	Born of the Flesh, Persecutor

TWO CONDITIONS
Freedom	Born of covenant of Grace
Slavery	Born of covenant of Law

TWO DESTINIES
Heir	Born of the Free Woman
Cast Out	Born of the Bondwoman

Paul himself was a persecutor of those who believed in Jesus. He was then, like Ishmael, born of the flesh, and destined to be cast out. When he became a believer, he became like Isaac, a persecuted child of promise, destined to be an heir. As a believer, Paul had been persecuted in Corinth by Sosthenes, the leader of the synagogue. (Acts 18:17) Sosthenes later became a believer and ministered with Paul. (1Co.1:1)

Paul and Sosthenes, and many others, had been on one side of the allegory and were transferred by the grace of God to the opposite side. Paul reminded the believers in Corinth of how much the same thing had happened to them: "Or do you not know that the unrighteous shall not inherit the kingdom of God? Do not be deceived; neither fornicators, nor idolaters, nor adulterers, nor effeminate, nor homosexuals, nor thieves, nor the covetous, nor drunkards, nor revilers, nor swindlers, shall inherit the kingdom of God. And such were some of you; but you were washed, but you were sanctified, but you were justified in the name of the Lord Messiah Jesus, and in the Spirit of our God." (1Co.6:9-11)

He told Titus to remind the believers "to malign no one, to be uncontentious, gentle, showing every consideration for all men. For we also once were foolish ourselves, disobedient, deceived, enslaved to various lusts and pleasures, spending our life in malice and envy, hateful, hating one another." (Titus 3:2-3) He reminded the believers in Ephesus that, "you formerly walked according to the course of this world, according to the prince of the power of the air, of the spirit that is now working in the sons of disobedience. Among them we too all formerly lived in the lusts of our flesh, indulging the desires of the flesh and of the mind, and were by nature children of wrath, even as the rest." (Eph.2:2-3)

"We too all formerly...were by nature children of wrath..." The point is not that one's physical ancestry necessarily leads to bondage, for neither Gentiles nor Jews need to remain in a lost state. It is the quest for justification through the works of the law, rather than through grace and faith, that leads to bondage. Paul was writing to Gentiles in Galatia who were making the wrong choice, which would lead them back into bondage and a disinherited state, and eventually turn them into persecutors.

AUGUSTINE'S CITY

Augustine's interpretation of Galatians 4:21-31 is the basis for *City of God*. Augustine seems to have clearly understood and accepted the point that Paul was making. "Thus the prophecies refer in part to the maidservant whose children are born into slavery, that is, the earthly Jerusalem, who is in slavery, as are also her sons; but in part they refer to the free City of God, the true Jerusalem, eternal in heaven, whose sons are the men who live according to God's will in their pilgrimage on earth. There are, however, some prophecies which are understood as referring to both; literally to the bondmaid, symbolically to the free woman." [24]

But then Augustine takes two "spiritual" steps beyond Paul. He takes one step with each city. "I undertook after that to write about the origin, the development, and the destined ends of the two cities. One of these is the City of God, the other the city of this world; and God's City lives in this world's city, as far as its human element is concerned; but it lives there as an alien sojourner." [25]

"The other city, the Heavenly City on pilgrimage in this world, does not create false gods. She herself is the creation of the true God, and she herself is to be his true sacrifice. Nevertheless, both cities alike enjoy the good things, or are afflicted with the adversities of this temporal state, but with a different faith, a different expectation, a different love, until they are separated by the final judgement, and each receives her own end, of which there is no end." [26]

Here, the two steps that Augustine took beyond Paul are evident.

Step #1: In the allegory, the earthly Jerusalem is one city. In City of God, the earthly Jerusalem is only a symbol for "the city of this world." In this sense, the Scriptures present Babylon, not the earthly Jerusalem, as "the city of this world." In part, that is what Augustine is referring to, but his primary identification of "the city of this world" is everyone who is not a believer in Jesus.

While there is much that can be learned from some of the comparisons that Augustine makes, his comparisons are not the subject of the allegory in chapter 4 of Galatians. Augustine is talking about something different than Paul did. That does not mean that what Augustine says cannot contain any truth. It simply means that Augustine's cities are different than the cities of which Paul writes in Galatians chapter 4.

Paul is exhorting Gentile believers not to subject themselves to the yoke of the Law. Their relationship with God is not through the Covenant of the Law, which proceeded from Mt. Sinai, but rather through the New Covenant. Both covenants were made with the Jewish people. When Paul says "the present Jerusalem," he explicitly means the earthly Jewish city of Jerusalem.

Step #2: In the allegory, the Jerusalem above is the other city. In City of God, the Jerusalem above is on the earth. "It lives there as an alien sojourner." When Paul writes, in contrast, "the Jerusalem above," he does not mean the Church on the earth. He means a city named Jerusalem that is in heaven.

Abraham looked for that city. If Abraham, Isaac, and Jacob were the new Jerusalem on the earth, then they would not have needed to look. They were not the Jerusalem above "in pilgrimage on earth." They were not "the Heavenly City on pilgrimage in this world." They themselves were in pilgrimage on the earth, looking for the Jerusalem above, of which they were citizens.

For Augustine, the fact that either and both of the cities are named "Jerusalem" is irrelevant. That was not so for Paul. Nor is it so for God, who caused the two cities to be named that. "Jerusalem" is a word that has meaning. It designates a particular city.

The allegory itself only has meaning because of the relationship between the two Jerusalems. Augustine's *City of God*, for all the truth that it contains, ignores the specifics of Paul's comparison.

Augustine then imposes his own allegory back on the Scriptures. He quotes the Septuagint of Jer.31:31-34, and concludes, "This is, without doubt, a prophecy of the Jerusalem above, whose 'reward' is God himself; and to possess him, and to be his possession, is the Highest Good, and the Entire Good, in that City." [27]

Having previously decided that the actual words of the text do not determine its meaning, he simply ignores the words. He does not even try to give alternate meanings for them — "house of Israel and house of Judah...their fathers...out of the land of Egypt...My covenant which they broke" — he simply ignores them. He then concludes, "without doubt," that the prophecy is to be understood according to his own assumptions.

Having replaced the words of the prophecy with his own assumptions, he seeks to interpret other prophecy in the same way. This becomes painfully evident in his discussion of the Millennium, where he finds himself unable to make sense out of the text.

THE MILLENNIUM

The Millennium was anathema to Eusebius because it meant the restoration of Israel. Though Augustine initially believed in a millennial kingdom, he later changed his views. He does not give the reasons for this change, but faith in the Millennium had been declared to be outside the established orthodoxy, and Augustine believed that it was necessary to accept the established orthodoxy — "the Rule of Faith."

Consequently, *City of God* became the basis for much anti-Judaic theology. It "de-Judaizes" the Bible and (some of) the promises of God. Thus it distorts the nature and destiny of the Church.

Augustine speaks of those who "have been particularly excited, among other reasons, by the actual number of a thousand years, taking it as appropriate that there should be a kind of Sabbath for the saints for all that time, a holy rest, that is, after the labours of the six thousand years since man's creation, when in retribution for his great sin he was expelled from paradise into the troubles of this moral condition...

"This notion would be in some degree tolerable if it were believed that in that Sabbath some delights of a spiritual character were to be available for the saints because of the presence of the Lord. I also entertained this notion at one time. But in fact those people assert that those who have risen again will spend their rest in the most unrestrained material feasts, in which there will be so much to eat and drink that not only will those supplies keep within no bounds of moderation but will also exceed the limits even of incredibility. But this can only be believed by materialists; and those with spiritual interests give the name 'Chiliasts' to the believers in this picture, a term which we can translate by a word derived from the equivalent Latin, 'Millennarians'. It would take too long to refute them in detail; we ought instead to show how this scriptural passage is to be taken...." [28]

Augustine says that faith in the Millennium was an error caused by carnal desires. Yet, he also says that when he believed in the millennial reign of Messiah on the earth, he did not have those carnal desires. He did not believe in those "materialist" things. He himself believed that "some delights of a spiritual character were to be available for the saints because of the presence of the Lord."

Augustine still personally found that a "notion...in some degree tolerable." It was not, however, theologically tolerable to the Church that was built on the Constantinian foundation.

Whether there actually were "Chiliasts" or "Millennarians" who believed as Augustine said they did is not historically evident. It is certainly not what the writers of the New Covenant Scriptures, like John or Paul, believed or taught. It is not what those they taught, like Papias or Polycarp, believed or taught to others. It is not what the Church prior to Origen, as Justin Martyr testifies, believed or taught.

So, in a sense, Augustine's rejection of such a belief is beside the point. Such belief should be rejected. It is not what the Scriptures teach. The question is, what do they teach? How does Augustine deal with the Scriptures?

Revelation 19 describes the marriage supper of the Lamb, where the Church is joined to Messiah. Then Messiah descends from heaven to the earth with the Church following Him. "And from His mouth comes a sharp sword, so that with it He may smite the goyim; and He will rule them with a rod of iron; and He treads the wine press of the fierce wrath of God, the Almighty. And on His robe and on His thigh He has a name written, 'King of Kings, and Lord of Lords.' And I saw an angel standing in the sun; and he cried out with a loud voice, saying to all the birds which fly in midheaven, 'Come, assemble for the great supper of God; in order that you may eat the flesh of kings and the flesh of commanders and the flesh of mighty men and the flesh of horses and of those who sit on them and the flesh of all men, both free men and slaves, and small and great.'

"And I saw the beast and the kings of the earth and their armies, assembled to make war against Him who sat upon the horse, and against His army. And the beast was seized and with him the false prophet who performed the signs in his presence, by which he deceived those who had received the mark of the beast and those who worshiped his image; these two were thrown alive into the lake of fire which burns with brimstone. And the rest were killed with the sword, which came from the mouth of him who sat upon the horse, and all the birds were filled with their flesh.

"And I saw an angel coming down from heaven, having the key of the abyss and a great chain in his hand. And he laid hold of the dragon, the serpent of old, who is the Devil and Satan, and bound him for a thousand years, and threw him into the abyss, and shut it and sealed it over him, so that he should not deceive the Gentiles any longer, until the thousand years were completed; after these things he must be released for a short time.

"And I saw thrones, and they sat upon them, and judgment was given to them. And I saw the souls of those who had been beheaded because of the testimony of Jesus and because of the word of God, and those who had not worshiped the beast or his image, and had not received the mark upon their forehead and upon their hand; and they came to life and reigned with Messiah for a thousand years." (Rev.19:15-20:4)

Following Origen's method of interpretation, Augustine explains the thousand-year reign in this way:

"In the meantime, while the Devil is bound for a thousand years, the saints reign with Christ, also for a thousand years; which are without doubt to be taken in the same sense, and denoting the same period, this is, the period beginning with Christ's first coming. We must certainly rule out any reference to that kingdom which he is to speak of at the end of the world, in the words, 'Come, you that have my Father's blessing, take possession of the kingdom prepared for you;' and so, even now, although in some other and far inferior way, his saints must be reigning with him, the saints to whom he says, 'See, I am always with you, right up to the end of the world;' for otherwise the Church could surely not be called his kingdom, or the kingdom of heaven...." [29]

"It follows that the Church even now is the kingdom of Christ and the kingdom of heaven. And so even now his saints reign with him, though not in the same way as they will then reign...Ultimately, those people reign with him who are in his kingdom in such a way that they themselves are his kingdom." [30]

Augustine is saying that "Christ's first coming" began the period of a thousand years in which "the saints reign with Christ...[in a] far inferior way" and in which "the Devil is bound." The thousand years is the period of time from "Christ's first coming" to "the end of the world." At "the end of the world," the saints will reign with Christ in a greater way. If they are not reigning now, Augustine says, then "the Church could surely not be called his kingdom, or the kingdom of heaven."

Some passages in Revelation, and throughout the Scriptures for that matter, are difficult to understand, but still the words must have some meaning. If they do not mean what their normal meaning is, then they must mean something else. In this portion of scripture, there is no problem with understanding the words in their normal sense.

Augustine rejects their normal sense, because the normal sense cannot be reconciled with his concept of the Church as the kingdom of God. His interpretation is not based on the text, but on his previous alteration of Paul's allegory. There are many insurmountable problems with Augustine's "spiritual" interpretation, which many others following him adopted.

If the thousand years begins with "Christ's first coming," then whatever happens before the thousand years begins must have happened before "Christ's first coming." These things would include the marriage supper of the Lamb; the return of Jesus with the Church to the earth for battle against the goyim; the destruction in the lake of fire of the beast, the false prophet, and those who received the mark of the beast or worshipped his image; and the beheading of those who, for the testimony of Jesus (who had not yet come and died), did not receive the mark of the beast or worship his image. It also would mean that before "Christ's first coming," the Devil was bound with a great chain, thrown into the abyss, which is then shut and sealed over him so that he cannot deceive the Gentiles any more.

When did these things happen before "Christ's first coming"? The words must have some meaning. To what events do they refer? For Augustine's explanation to be an actual interpretation, there must be some way in which all these things happened before "Christ's first coming." But all of these are unanswered questions for Augustine. In fact, they do not even arise, because he ignores the words of the text.

Who are those who were beheaded for the testimony of Jesus (before His first coming)? Augustine takes it to be a symbol for believers of all times. But, according to Augustine, all this happens before "Christ's first coming." Have all believers of all times been beheaded? for refusing to take the mark of the beast? **Only** those who were beheaded by the beast come to life at the beginning of the thousand years and then reign with Messiah. (20:4)

In what way can it be said that, before "Christ's first coming," "the Devil was bound with a great chain, thrown into the abyss, which is then shut and sealed over him so that he cannot deceive the Gentiles any more"? Augustine goes to great lengths to try to explain, but often contradicts himself, and occasionally admits the contradiction. It is worth the time to look at some of the details of his explanation, since it is the basis for all amillennial and post-millennial theology:

" 'And he threw him,' says John, 'into the abyss', meaning, clearly, that he cast the Devil into the abyss; and 'the abyss' symbolizes the innumerable multitude of the impious, in whose hearts there is a great depth of malignity against the Church of God. Not that the Devil was not in them before; but the reason why he is said to be thrown there is that when he is excluded from believers he starts to have a greater hold on the irreligious. For any person is more securely in the Devil's possession when he is not only estranged from God but goes on to conceive a gratuitous hatred for God's servants.

" 'And he shut it up,' it continues, 'and sealed it over him, so that he could no more lead astray the nations until the thousand years should be ended.' 'Shut it up' means that 'the angel put a ban on the Devil, so that he could not come out,' he was forbidden to pass the barrier — to 'transgress.' While the addition of 'and sealed it' seems to me to signify that God wished it to be kept a secret who belongs to the Devil's party, and who does not. For in this world, to be sure, this is kept a secret, since it is uncertain whether he who seems to be standing firm is destined to fall and whether he who seems to lie fallen is destined to rise again.

"Now because he is bound and shut up by this ban the Devil is prohibited and inhibited from leading astray the nations which belonged to Christ but were in time past led astray by him or held in his grip...This, then, is the purpose for which the Devil is bound and shut up in the abyss; so that he may no longer lead astray the nations of which the Church is made up, nations whom he led astray and held in his grip before they were a Church...

" 'After this', the narrative continues, 'the Devil must be unloosed for a short time.' Now if the binding and shutting up of the Devil means that he cannot lead the Church astray, will his unloosing mean that he can do so again? God forbid! For he will never seduce that Church which was predestined and chosen before the foundation of the world, the Church of which it is said that 'the Lord knows those who belong to him.' And yet there will be a Church on earth at that time also when the Devil is due to be unloosed, just as there has been a Church on earth from the time of the world's foundation, and as there will always be, represented by its members as each new generation succeeds the generation that passes away.

"In fact, a little after this John says that when the Devil has been unloosed he will lead nations astray throughout the world and draw them into waging war on the Church, and that the number of the Church's enemies will be as the sands of the sea. 'And they went up,' he says, 'over the breadth of the land, and surrounded the camp of the saints and the beloved city; and fire came down on them from heaven and devoured them. And the Devil, who seduced them, was thrown into the lake of fire and sulphur, where the beast and the false prophet are; and they will be tormented day and night for ever.'

"..And so the Devil is bound throughout the whole period embraced by the Apocalypse, that is, from the first coming of Christ to the end of the world, which will be Christ's second coming, and the meaning of the binding is not that he ceases to seduce the Church during that interval called 'the thousand years,' as is shown by the fact that when unloosed he is evidently not destined to lead it astray. For assuredly if his binding meant that he is unable, or not allowed, to lead it astray, his unloosing can only mean that he is now able, or permitted, to do so. But God forbid that this should be the case! Instead, what the binding of the Devil means is that he is not permitted to exert his whole power of temptation either by force or by guile to seduce men to his side by violent compulsion or fraudulent delusion.

"For if he were permitted for so long a time, a time when so many were so insecure, he would overthrow very many of the faithful or prevent very many from believing, and those would be the kind of men to whom God did not will that this should happen. It was to prevent his achieving this end that he was bound." [31]

The Devil is bound with a great chain and thrown into the abyss, which is then shut up and sealed over him so that he can't deceive the nations [εθνη, Gentiles]. According to Augustine, this only means that the Devil is not allowed to deceive the nations [εθνη, Gentiles] which are the Church and might otherwise be deceived. According to Augustine, the Devil can still deceive the nations [εθνη, Gentiles] who are unbelievers so that they don't believe, except that some, as he acknowledges later, do believe.

Augustine has overlooked some details. First, he says that "'the abyss' symbolizes the innumerable multitude of the impious, in whose hearts there is a great depth of malignity against the Church of God." But according to his own interpretation, the Devil is thrown into the abyss before "the first coming of Christ," that is, before the Church existed.

Second, he says that the nations [Gentiles] whom the Devil can't deceive are the Church. He has overlooked the fact that the Church is made up of Jews as well as Gentiles [nations]. It was John, one of those Jewish believers, who received the Revelation from the Lord. Can the Devil still deceive Jewish believers like John, Peter, Paul, etc.?

Third, Augustine says that the Devil can deceive the unbelieving nations [Gentiles] during this time, "from the first coming of Christ to the end of the world, which will be Christ's second coming." Does that mean that he can't deceive Jewish unbelievers during this time? Wasn't the Devil able to deceive Jews like Judas Iscariot, Caiaphas, and the leaders of the Great Revolt in 70 A.D.? and all those who haven't believed?

Would the Devil still be able to deceive Jews like that enemy of God and persecutor of the Church, Saul of Tarsus? Wasn't Saul of Tarsus deceived? Aren't there at least some believers, whether Jewish or Gentile, who were unbelievers first? like Augustine himself? Wasn't Augustine deceived before he became a believer?

When the Devil is loosed, Augustine says, he can then deceive the nations [εθνη, Gentiles], which he has been doing all along anyway. But he can't deceive the nations [εθνη, Gentiles] which are the Church. What then does the Devil being loosed mean? According to Augustine, he was bound so that he couldn't deceive the Church. Now he is loosed so that he can deceive the unbelieving nations.

It cannot be stated too emphatically that this is not interpretation. There is nothing in the text that gives rise to, or supports, Augustine's explanation. Augustine's explanation turns the words into nonsense. It is, therefore, not an interpretation, but an imposition.

Augustine then enters into a discussion of how the thousand years in which the Devil is bound is not exactly the same as the thousand years in which the saints reign with the Lord. He gets into the discussion because he understands the three and a half years mentioned in Rev.12 and Dan.9&12 [the second half of the seventieth week] in their literal, obvious sense. "This last persecution, which is to be inflicted by Antichrist, will last for three years and six months; I have already stated this, and it is also laid down earlier in the Apocalypse and in the book of the prophet Daniel." [32]

Augustine understands this time period to be the persecution from the Antichrist at the end of the thousand years. Rev.19:20 says that the reign of the Antichrist is ended as he is thrown into the lake of fire, which happens before the saints reign with the Lord for a thousand years. Augustine does not notice the chronological impossibility of the scenario he has created. He is concerned with where to place the three and a half years.

"Then the time of the persecution belongs, we believe, neither to the reign of the saints nor to the imprisonment of Satan — both lasting a thousand years — but is to be reckoned as an additional period. But on this supposition we shall be forced to admit that the saints will not reign with Christ in that time of persecution. Yet who would dare to say that his members will not reign with him at that time when they will cleave to him most closely and strongly and at a time when the fiercer the assault of war the greater the glory of refusal to yield, and the richer the martyr's crown?

"Alternatively, if they are not to be accounted as destined to reign, because of the tribulations they are to endure, it will follow that in earlier times also, during those thousand years, all the saints who suffered tribulation must not be accounted as having been reigning with Christ during the actual time of their tribulation. Accordingly, those whose souls the author of the Apocalypse writes that he beheld, those who were 'killed because of their witness to Jesus and because of the word of God,' and did not reign with Christ when they were suffering persecutions, and they themselves were not the kingdom of Christ, although Christ possessed them in a preeminent sense. Now this, to be sure, is utterly absurd, a conclusion to be repudiated at all costs....

"Hence the reign of the saints with Christ will last for more years than the Devil's imprisonment in chains, because they will reign with their King, God's Son, during the three and a half years also when the Devil is no longer bound. The conclusion is, then, that when we hear these words: 'The priests of God and of Christ will reign with him for a thousand years; and when the thousand years are ended Satan will be unloosed from his prison,' we should take it in one of two ways: either the thousand years of the reign of the saints is not ended, but the imprisonment of the Devil in chains is at an end, so that both sides have their thousand years, that is, their particular totality of years, though the length of the periods differs, the reign of the saints being longer, while the imprisonment of the Devil is shorter in duration; or else, since three years and six months is a very short space of time, it may be assumed that it does not require taking into account..." [33]

For Augustine then, the thousand years for the binding of the Devil and the thousand years for the reigning of the Church are the same, or else not exactly the same. In any case, the former is three and a half years shorter than the latter. And anyway, at the end of the thousand years or so, however long it actually is, the dead do not really come to life and reign with the Lord, for they have been reigning with Him all along.

Thus, in effect, the words have no meaning at all. Augustine's dilemma comes solely from the fact that he has "spiritualized" the thousand years to some perfect "totality of years," and then tries to fit a literal event into it.

The established orthodoxy of the Church declared that the Millennium had to be allegorized and "spiritualized." Augustine accepted the established orthodoxy of the Church as the "Rule of Faith" by which the Scriptures had to be interpreted. If we were to cut out from City of God this "spiritualization" of the Millennium, we would find that Augustine actually understands the Biblical sequence quite well. The confusion and perplexity disappear quite quickly.

In another portion, he says, "That last persecution, to be sure, which will be inflicted by Antichrist, will be extinguished by Jesus himself, present in person. For the Scripture says that 'he will kill him with the breath of his mouth and annihilate him by the splendour of his coming.' [2Thes.2:8] Here the usual question is, 'When will this happen?' But the question is completely ill-timed. For had it been in our interest to know this, who could have been a better informant than the master, God himself, when the disciples asked him? For they did not keep silent about it with him, but put the question to him in person, 'Lord, is this the time when you are going to restore the sovereignty to Israel?' But he replied, 'It is not for you to know the times which the Father has reserved for his own control.' " [34]

Augustine understands that "Jesus himself, present in person," will return to earth "to restore the sovereignty to Israel," and to destroy the Antichrist. We previously noted Augustine's treatment of the prophecies of Zechariah concerning the salvation of all Israel, the gathering of the nations [goyim] against Jerusalem for battle, and the return of the Lord to destroy them. [35] In fact, despite his extended "spiritualization" of the events of the last days, Augustine actually believed in their literal fulfillment.

"There is no one therefore who denies or doubts that the last judgement, as foretold in holy Scriptures, is to be executed by Jesus Christ, unless it is someone who, with an unbelievable kind of animosity or blindness, does not believe in those sacred writings, which have by now demonstrated their truth to the whole world. And so in that judgement, or in connection with that judgement, we have learnt that those events are to come about: Elijah the Tishbite will come; Jews will accept the faith; Antichrist will persecute; Christ will judge; the dead will rise again; the good and the evil will be separated; the earth will be destroyed in the flames and then will be renewed. All those events, we must believe, will come about; but in what way, and in what order they will come, actual experience will then teach us with a finality surpassing anything our human understanding is now capable of attaining. However, I consider that these events are destined to come about in the order I have given." [36]

Augustine understood the Scriptures. He knew what they taught. But he also embraced the traditional teaching, the accepted orthodoxy of the Church. He simply was unable to reconcile the two.

FOOTNOTES

1. St. Augustine, *Concerning THE CITY OF GOD against the Pagans,* trans. by Henry Bettenson, Penguin Books, London, 1984, Bk.15, Ch.14, P.620
2. ibid., P.455n
3. ibid., e.g. Book 11, chapter 23 on "The mistake of Origen"
4. ibid., Bk.13, Ch.22, Pp.534-535
5. ibid., Bk.15, Ch.27, P.645
6. ibid., Bk.15, Ch.26, Pp.644-645
7. ibid., Bk.15, Ch.7, P.603n
8. Ecclesiastical History, op.cit., P.209
9. St. Augustine, *Concerning THE CITY OF GOD against the Pagans,* op.cit., Bk.18, Ch.32, P.800
10. ibid., Bk.15, Ch.11, P.612
11. ibid., Bk.15, Ch.11, P.615
12. ibid., Bk.15, Ch.13, P.616
13. ibid., Bk.16, Ch.18, P.677
14. ibid., Bk.15, Ch.26, P.644
15. ibid., Bk.20, Ch.25, P.952
16. ibid., Bk.17, Ch.7, P.732
17. ibid., Bk.17, Ch.11, P.739
18. ibid., Bk.18, Ch.46, P.827

19. ibid., Bk.18, Ch.47, P.829
20. ibid., Bk.20, Ch.29, P.957
21. ibid., Bk.20, Ch.30, P.960
22. ibid., Bk.21, Ch.24, P.1007
23. "Attitudes of the Fathers toward Practices of Jewish Christians," R.E. Taylor, in *Studia Patristica*, Vol.IV, Berlin, 1961, P.511
24. St. Augustine, *Concerning THE CITY OF GOD* against the Pagans, op.cit., Bk.17, Ch.4, P.714
25. ibid., Bk.18, Ch.1, P.761
26. ibid., Bk.18, Ch.54, P.842
27. ibid., Bk.17, Ch.4, P.714
28. ibid., Bk.20, Ch.7, P.907
29. ibid., Bk.20, Ch.9, P.914
30. ibid., Bk.20, Ch.9, P.915
31. ibid., Bk.20, Chs.7-8, Pp.908-911
32. ibid., Bk.20, Ch.13, P.921
33. ibid., Bk.20, Ch.13, Pp.922-923
34. ibid., Bk.18, Ch.53, P.838
35. ibid., Bk.20, Ch.30, P.960
36. ibid., Bk.20, Ch.30, P.963

THOMAS AQUINAS' *SUMMA THEOLOGICA*

The *Summa Theologica* of Thomas Aquinas has been described as, "what must be the most unified comprehensive theology in Christian history." [1] Aquinas intended it to be the framework for all that his theological students at Rome would ever learn. He began work on it in 1265, "was to work on it for the next seven years and leave it unfinished; even so, it comprises, as did his commentary on the *Sentences*, over 1,500,000 words.

"Gradually, but only gradually, the *Summa* became the accepted textbook of theology in the Catholic church; it is said to have lain on the altar alongside the scriptures during the Council of Trent [1545], a symbol of orthodoxy to Catholics, of the adulteration of the pure word of God to Protestants." [2]

Aquinas' procedure is to present a question that contains several parts, which he calls "articles." He takes the first article and presents several reasoned objections to it, giving various evidence in support of the objection. Then he states his conclusion, replying to each objection in turn, supporting his view from the classics, or from traditionally approved church writings, or from the Bible. He continues in this way with each of the articles in the question, and then proceeds to the next question.

The deciding argument may be superior logic, classical philosophical or legal authority, church tradition, or the Scriptures. Any one of these can be equally decisive. "The Philosopher," Aquinas' term for Aristotle, is cited more than any other author. For Aquinas, Aristotle, correctly understood, is the end to an argument.

"The *Summa* then is written in a different sort of language from the scriptures, the literal language of argument, the analytic and technical language that aiming at clarity in argument necessarily develops. In large part this language is learned from Aristotle and echoes his ideas, but it is employed in the service of other ideas which spring from a tradition nurtured on the metaphor and typology of the scriptures...It would, for example, be perfectly possible to treat the Summa as though it was simply a sort of Christian supplement to Aristotle: the first part adding to Aristotle's theology of divine thought at the eternal centre of the ever-turning world, the Christian notion of a personal providence, and to Aristotle's psychology of man the Christian concept of bodily resurrection; the second part adding divine friendship and a life to come to Aristotle's ethics. But in this way of looking at the Summa the core is Aristotelian and scripture contributes the extras. This is not how the work is really structured. Despite all the difference in style, what guides the structure of the Summa is the structure of the scriptures themselves and their fundamental theme. That theme might briefly be expressed as one of creation, un-creation and re-creation, or of creation, collapse and salvage, finally leading to the building of a house for all." [3]

In the *Summa Theologica*, Aquinas presents a reasonable, philosophical defense of "Christianity," a Christianity based more on accumulated Church tradition than on the Biblical teachings themselves. It is not a Biblical theology, because the Bible is not **THE** standard to which he appeals for proof. Aquinas maintains that, "The greatest authority of all is church tradition, which should always be jealously observed. Even the teaching of the great Catholic theologians gets its authority from the church, the authority of which is greater than that of Augustine or Jerome or any other thinker." [4]

That is to say that the teachings of Augustine and Jerome are authoritative because the Church has traditionally accepted them. The Bible itself is subjugated to Church tradition. Aquinas follows in the steps decreed by Constantine: "For what was approved by 300 bishops can only be considered as the pleasure of God, especially as the Holy Spirit, dwelling in the minds of so many and such worthy men, has clearly shown the divine will." [5] (The teachings of Aristotle become authoritative because they are supremely reasonable.)

The *Summa Theologica* does not actually follow "the structure of the scriptures themselves and their fundamental theme." Most of the Bible speaks of God's relationship with Israel — this is how God reveals Himself to the world. Almost none of the *Summa Theologica* does.

The questions that are raised are philosophical ones more than Biblical ones. The proofs are philosophical more than Biblical. It is all understood in terms of tradition.

Still, in the abstract, Aquinas has a basically healthy approach to the interpretation of scripture. He says that "Poets use imagery for the sake of representation itself in which men take a natural delight; this teaching uses it as a necessary means towards something else. But what scripture says symbolically in one place it always explains more expressly in another, and the symbols are drawn from humble things so as not to mislead us into taking their application to God literally. Imagery reveals what God is not, rather than what he is, and this fits the way we know God in this life.

"St Gregory says that *scripture transcends all other sciences by the way it uses one and the same discourse to tell history and reveal mystery*. The author of the scriptures is God, who has power to endow with significance not only words but also things themselves. In every science words have meaning; in this science alone what is meant by the words has further meaning. We call the first meaning of the words the *historical* or *literal* meaning; and the further meaning, based on the literal meaning, we call the *spiritual* meaning. The spiritual meaning can itself be multiple: the Old Testament prefigures the New, and the deeds of Christ and what prefigured them symbolize how we ought to behave today and the eternal glory to come. There can also be more than one literal meaning of a scriptural text: for literal meaning is meaning intended by the author, and the author of scripture is God whose mind grasps all things at once. Every spiritual meaning is founded on a literal meaning, and from that alone should we argue, not from allegory. Moreover, anything necessary for faith contained in a spiritual meaning is conveyed clearly and literally in some other place in scripture. We must not forget that the literal meaning of a parable or figure of speech is not the figure of speech itself but what it is used to say." [6]

Unfortunately, this approach of Aquinas only holds true in the abstract. The agenda and content of Aquinas' theology does not come from the teaching of the Bible, but from the teaching of the Church. The *Summa Theologica* is not an examination of the Scriptures to establish what the Bible teaches. Instead, it calls upon the Scriptures intermittently to support a chosen philosophical or traditional view.

Additionally, Aquinas superimposes the philosophy of Athens and the imperial law of Rome over the Holy One of Israel. A thousand years earlier, Tertullian had observed that Athens and Jerusalem could not agree. "Tertullian was right in proclaiming that Athens can never agree with Jerusalem — even though for two thousand years the foremost thinkers of the Western world have firmly believed that a reconciliation is possible and have bent their strongest and most determined efforts toward effecting it." [7] "What for Athens is wisdom is for Jerusalem foolishness: Tertullian said nothing else." [8]

This is not the place for an extended examination of the irreconcilable antagonism between Greek philosophy and Biblical faith, but how the Scriptures are to be understood is a critical question. Must man's reason submit to God and His Word, or must God and His Word submit to man's reason? Those who are interested in a very comprehensive examination of this issue should read Lev Shestov's *Athens and Jerusalem*.

Shestov observes, "Reason, I repeat, has ruined faith in our eyes; it has 'revealed' in it man's illegitimate pretension to subordinate the truth to his desires, and it has taken away from us the most precious of heaven's gifts — the sovereign right to participate in the divine 'let there be'— by flattening out our thought and reducing it to the plane of the petrified 'it is.' " [9]

On what plane did Aquinas operate? "Thomas perhaps can't help thinking of revelation as teaching in the manner of the medieval schools, with God as the great schoolman expounding truth to his students: Abraham, Moses and the prophets, who, but for the needs of the ordinary people without education, might have written it all down in the analytic language of the great philosophers rather than the metaphor and symbolism of the poets. In this he is in one sense a child of his time, but in another he is in fact dissociating himself from much contemporary barren typology that could read anything into anything." [10]

Of course, the prophets and the apostles were not noted for their education. In many cases, they were noted for their lack of education. Jesus said, "I praise Thee, O Father, Lord of heaven and earth, that Thou didst hide these things from the wise and intelligent and didst reveal them to babes." (Mt.11:25)

Paul wrote to the believers in Corinth, "**For** the word of the cross is to those who are perishing foolishness, **but** to us who are being saved it is the power of God. **For** it is written, 'I will destroy the wisdom of the wise, and the cleverness of the clever I will set aside.' Where is the wise man? Where is the debater of this age? Has not God made foolish the wisdom of the world?

"**For** since in the wisdom of God the world through its wisdom did not come to know God, God was well pleased through the foolishness of the message preached to save those who believe. **For** indeed Jews ask for signs, and Greeks search for wisdom; **but** we preach Messiah crucified, to Jews a stumbling block, and to Gentiles foolishness, **but** to those who are the called, both Jews and Greeks, Messiah the power of God and the wisdom of God. **Because** the foolishness of God is wiser than men, and the weakness of God is stronger then men.

"**For** consider your call, brethren, that there were not many wise according to the flesh, not many mighty, not many noble; **but** God has chosen the foolish things of the world to shame the wise, and God has chosen the weak things of the world to shame the things which are strong, and the base things of the world and the despised, God has chosen, the things that are not, that He might nullify the things that are, that no flesh should boast before God." (1Co.1:26-29)

That is not to say, of course, that learning has no place in the service of God. Quite the contrary, "disciples" are learners. But, as Paul continues in writing to the Corinthians, "And my message and my preaching were not in persuasive words of wisdom, but in demonstration of the Spirit and of power, that your faith should not rest on the wisdom of men, but on the power of God...Now we have received, not the spirit of the world, but the Spirit who is from God, that we might know the things freely given to us by God, which things we also speak, not in words taught by human wisdom, but in those taught by the Spirit, communicating spiritual thoughts with spiritual words." (1Co.2:4-5,12-13)

The theology and the authority of the *Summa Theologica* does not lie in the "demonstration of the Spirit and of power, ...the power of God," but in philosophical proof. Reason is the arbiter and judge. Aquinas did recognize that human reason will often lead to different conclusions than Divine revelation, but he did not recognize that as the case in his own theology.

He said, "The standards set by human reason and divine law are different, e.g. in moderation of pleasure in food. Human reason commands us not to harm our health or hinder our reasoning powers; whereas divine law requires us to *chasten our body and make it our servant*, by abstaining from food and drink. Instilled moral virtue aims at making us good *fellow-citizens with the saints and members of God's household*; whereas the acquired moral virtues aim at good human order. If God was merely causing miraculously the same virtues we usually have to acquire, we would not distinguish a special group of instilled virtues." [11]

Luther later complained of Aquinas that he "wrote many heretical things and is the originator of the now ruling pious doctrine of the awful Aristotle."[12] "In all his works Luther speaks again and again of the *malleus Dei*, the hammer of God, which breaks the trust that man puts in his own knowledge and in the virtue founded on the truths furnished by this knowledge." [13]

Shestov notes that, "Within the 'limits of reason' one can create a science; a sublime ethic, and even a religion; but to find God one must tear oneself away from the seductions of reason with all its physical and moral constraints and go to another source of truth. In Scripture this source bears the enigmatic name 'faith,' which is that dimension of thought where truth abandons itself fearlessly and joyously to the entire disposition of the Creator: 'Thy will be done!' The will of Him who, on his side, fearlessly and with sovereign power returns to the believer his lost power:...'what things soever ye desire...ye shall have them.'

"It is here that there begins for fallen man the region, forever condemned by reason, of the miraculous and of the fantastic. And, indeed, are not the prophecy of the 53rd chapter of Isaiah, 'the Lord hath laid upon him the iniquity of us all,' and what the New Testament tells of the fulfillment of this prophecy, fantastic?...

"Can we 'understand,' can we grasp, what the prophets and the apostles announce in Scripture? Will Athens ever consent to allow such 'truths' to come into the world?" [14]

What does natural, or Aristotelian, reason tell us about God becoming man? or about Jesus dying for the sins of the world? or the resurrection? or walking on water? What does reason tell us about the blood of the Lamb on the doorposts and lintel of every Jewish house in Egypt? What does it tell us about the parting of the Red Sea?

The ten spies who returned from Canaan said, "We are not able to go up against the people, for they are too strong for us." (Num.13:31) The ten were the reasonable ones. Joshua and Caleb, on the other hand, had faith in God for what was otherwise not possible.

Was it reasonable for Abraham to sacrifice Isaac? We are called to follow Abraham in his faith, not in his logic. What would Gideon have done if he had let his reason be his guide? In God's Book, the notable men and women are not those distinguished by their reason, but rather those distinguished by their faith. Natural reason does not accept God's revelation.

God's revelation is not received or understood by natural reason. Jesus said to Peter, "Blessed are you, Simon Barjonas, because flesh and blood did not reveal this to you, but My Father who is in heaven." (Mt.16:17) The greatest of all commandments begins, "HEAR, O Israel..." God is saying something, man must listen.

THE OLD LAW AND THE NEW LAW

"**The Old Law**. St Paul says the *law itself is holy and the commandment is holy, right and good*. There can indeed be no doubt that the Old Law was good, since it was reasonable." [15] Aquinas errs in two ways here. First, the Law of God is not good because man finds it reasonable, it is good because God, who is good, says it is good. Second, the Law of God does, in fact, contains many things that are impenetrable to human reason. "But a natural man does not accept the things of the Spirit of God; for they are foolishness to him, and he cannot understand them, because they are spiritually appraised." (1Co.2:14)

Aquinas says of the Law, "And it was bestowed together with other special advantages on the people of the Jews, because of the promise made to their forefathers that Christ should be born from them. This promise was made to Abraham not because Abraham earned it but because God freely chose him. And if you press the question as to why he chose this people rather than any other for Christ to be born from, then Augustine's answer will have to do: *why he attracts this one rather than that don't try to decide — you will only make mistakes*....certain other injunctions of the Old Law were peculiar to it and obliged only the people of the Jews: designed to give that people a special holiness out of reverence for Christ who was to be born from them. The special worthiness of the Jewish people as opposed to others lay in their consecration to the worship of God: the same sort of worthiness attaches today to the clerical state as distinct from that of the laity, and to the religious state [i.e. monks, nuns, etc.] as distinct from that of the non-religious. Non-Jews could however be admitted to the observances of the law, since they could be saved more perfectly and safely in that way than by simply following the law that was in them by nature. Just as today laity become clerics and non-religious religious, though they could be saved without doing so." [16]

Aquinas correctly notes that, the Law "was bestowed together with other special advantages on the people of the Jews." He correctly notes that, "This promise was made to Abraham not because Abraham earned it but because

God freely chose him." Aquinas also correctly notes that man is not in a position to understand God's reasons for His choices.

But then Aquinas introduces the concept of "The special worthiness of the Jewish people as opposed to others." He does this to justify the non-Biblical Church structure of his own time. He compares Gentile proselytes under the Law to "clerics" and the "religious" in that "they could be saved more perfectly and safely in that way."

Aquinas' argument depends upon the "special worthiness of the Jewish people," but the Bible does not teach that. It teaches that the Jewish people have a special calling, "because God freely chose [them]." Nor does the Bible teach that that special calling was solely for "Christ to be born from them."

Half a century after Messiah was born from the Jews," Paul told the Gentile believers in Rome that "the gifts and the calling of God [for the Jewish people] are irrevocable." (Rom.11:29) These gifts and calling were according to God's design, not according to any "special worthiness" of the Jewish people. Aquinas' argument concerning "clerics" and the "religious" is based on this "special worthiness." Without it, his argument collapses.

Aquinas did have a high regard for "The Old Law." He believed that, "The Old Law is one law with one goal, but issues different commands to cover the different steps to be taken towards that goal. *The goal of the law is the love of charity*, for all law aims at friendship of men with each other and with God."[17]

"But inasmuch as the whole state of that people was figurative, judicial injunctions also were. God chose the Jews as the people from whom Christ would be born; so their judicial injunctions are more figurative than other peoples'. Even their wars and history have figurative meanings, whereas those of the Assyrian and Roman peoples, though humanly more famous, have none."[18]

He understands the distinction between Israel and the Gentiles before the death of Jesus. He comments, " '*I was sent only to the lost sheep of Israel.*' It was appropriate that Christ's preaching — his and his apostles' — started with the Jews alone, so as to show that his coming fulfilled the ancient promises made, not to the Gentile peoples, but to the Jews. By the victory of his cross Christ would win power and dominion over the Gentiles, so, although before his passion he did not wish his teaching preached to them, afterwards he told his disciples: Go and teach all nations. This is also why shortly before his passion, when certain Gentile disciples wished to see Jesus, he answered, '*Unless the grain of wheat falls on the ground and dies it remains a single grain, but if it dies it yields much fruit: here he calls himself a grain which is to die in the Jews' lack of faith in order to multiply in the faith of the Gentiles.*' "[19]

"**The New Law.** The law of the New Covenant is implanted in people's hearts: *The days are coming, says the Lord, when I will draw up a new covenant with the people of Israel: I will put my laws in their minds and write them on their hearts*. The New Law is first and foremost the gracious gift of the Holy Spirit to those who believe in Christ....No one ever had this grace of the Holy Spirit except by believing in Christ, explicitly or implicitly. To have the law of grace implanted in one is to belong to the New Covenant." [20]

"The house of Judah" and "the house of Israel" have disappeared from Aquinas' shortened version of the text of Jer.31:31-33. The fact that the New Covenant is promised to Israel has no significance for him. He does not see it. He does not see God's faithfulness to Israel, nor the thrust of His ongoing plan and purpose in the earth.

Aquinas does touch on an important issue: Jesus, implicitly or explicitly, has always been the proper object of faith for all men, but the New Covenant was not presented until the end of Jesus' life on the earth. Nor did men receive the Holy Spirit until the fulness of Pentecost came. How then are believers of all times related? Aquinas says, "To have the law of grace implanted in one is to belong to the New Covenant." He adds, "So the New Law is to be proclaimed in all places, though it was not proclaimed at all times. At all times nevertheless some men have belonged to the New Covenant." [21]

This view of the relationship of believers of all times is not systematically developed throughout *Summa Theologica*. However, since we will look further at this issue when we examine the theology of John Calvin, it will be worthwhile here to slightly extend Aquinas' view to encompass some of the issues that Calvin raises.

Aquinas seems to have recognized, though he does not state it explicitly, that the Church did not come into being until the New Covenant was presented. He believed, "At all times **nevertheless** some men have belonged to the New Covenant." Individual believers of all times, therefore, would also be considered part of the Church after the Church has come into existence. In their own time however, they were not the Church, since the Church did not exist then.

THE CHURCH OF THE INQUISITION

Aquinas does not have much to say about the Biblical relationship of the Church and the Jews. It is not really an issue for him. He does have some important things to say about the relationship that the Church historically established with the Jews. Aquinas became the theologian of the Inquisition, even as Luther later became the theologian of the Holocaust. Neither recognized any debt, obligation, or relationship to the Jewish people.

Given the official attitude of the Constantinian Church towards the Jewish people, there is no reason to expect any Jews to have believed in Jesus after the Council of Nicea. This is especially true inasmuch as the Church itself did not have a good grasp of the gospel or of what a life of service to God entailed. Nevertheless, contrary to reason, there were some Jews who actually believed, even in the centuries preceding Thomas Aquinas.

"With all the persecuting of the Jews, efforts were made time and again to win them to Christian truth. One means of this was the religious discussion. Far too often, it is true, this became an argument or dispute in which the important thing was to vanquish the opponent rather than to understand and win him over. Occasionally, especially in the earlier Middle Ages, there were real discussions. Abbot Gilbert Crispin of Westminster (1084-1117) tells that he had engaged in one with a friendly London Jew and thereupon another Jew of the city had been converted and had entered a monastery. In discussions of this sort Archbishop Bruno of Trier (1102-24) succeeded in convincing his Jewish physician Josuah and in inducing him to be baptized. The most celebrated example of such a conversion was Hermann Judaeus. He had money transactions with the Archbishop of Cologne and thereby came into contact with Abbot Rupert of Deutz. This led to exhaustive religious discussions. After severe struggles he had himself baptized, became a Premonstratensian at Kappenberg, and finally was made first prior of Scheda, founded in 1143. In his account of his conversion he laments that Christians' hatred for Jews kept Jews from belief in Christ." [22]

Accounts like this reveal much about that very different time — the society, its commerce, and its religious conceptions. The monastery and the priory were institutions of the time. So entering one was an unquestioned, acceptable choice for those who were serious about their faith. Consequently, some Jews made that choice.

When such a Jewish believer "laments that Christians' hatred for Jews kept Jews from belief in Christ," it speaks volumes about the condition of the Church. It is a lament that indicates the believer's genuine relationship with Jesus. It is a lament over "Christians" who live in ignorance of and in opposition to the real "Christ."

This was the world in which Aquinas lived. The Inquisition was initially instituted in 1208 by Pope Innocent III. Its ostensible purpose was to keep the Church free from heresy. It followed the Constantinian path. The *Summa Theologica* (1265) presents theological justification for the Inquisition and similar measures.

What people believe affects the way they act. The particulars of a person's faith will justify some acts and condemn others. Theology has consequences. Jesus said, "You will know them by their fruits. Grapes are not gathered from thornbushes, nor figs from thistles, are they?" (Mt.7:16)

William Lecky, a leading nineteenth century rationalist, wrote, "Almost all Europe, for many centuries, was inundated with blood, which was shed at the direct instigation or with the full approval of the ecclesiastical authorities, and under the pressure of a public opinion that was directed by the Catholic clergy, and was the exact measure of their influence.

"That the Church of Rome has shed more innocent blood than any other institution that has ever existed among man-kind, will be questioned by no Protestant who has a competent knowledge of history. The memorials, indeed, of many of her persecutions are now so scanty, that it is impossible to form a complete conception of the multitude of her victims, and it is quite certain that no powers of imagination can adequately realise their sufferings.

"Llorente, who [as one time secretary in the Inquisition] had free access to the archives of the Spanish Inquisition, assures us that by that tribunal alone more than 31,000 persons were burnt, and more than 290,000 condemned to punishments less severe than death. The number of those who were put to death for their religion in the Netherlands alone, in the reign of Charles V, has been estimated by a very high authority at 50,000, and at least half as many perished under his son.

"...For these atrocities were not perpetrated in the brief paroxysms of a reign of terror, or by the hands of obscure sectaries, but were inflicted by a triumphant Church, with every circumstance of solemnity and deliberation. Nor did the victims perish by a brief and painless death, but by one which was carefully selected as among the most poignant that man can suffer. They were usually burnt alive. They were burnt alive not unfrequently by a slow fire....One of the advantages of this being that the victim had more time for repentance." [23]

"Upon the 16th of February, 1568, a sentence of the Holy Office condemned all the inhabitants of the Netherlands to death as heretics. From this universal doom only a few persons especially named were excepted. A proclamation of the king, dated ten days later, confirmed this decree of the Inquisition, and ordered it to be carried into instant execution....Three millions of people, men, women and children, were sentenced to the scaffold in three lines." [24]

In our day, it is necessary to say that the totalitarian state, the child of the rationalists of the French Revolution and their Marxist heirs, has far exceeded the Church in this regard. However, the point here — and it is important to make it — is that the fruit of such a Church does not speak well for the tree from which it came. Such a Church shows no evidence of having been produced by a living relationship with Jesus, the King of the Jews. Such a Church, whatever it was, was not part of the bride of the Lamb.

The "Church Triumphant," married to the State by Constantine, was a persecutor, a murderer, an enemy of Truth. That marriage created a great confusion of identity; the fruit of a theology that taught that the Church had replaced Israel in the plan and purpose of God. The Church-State therefore sought to put heretics and witches to death, and exercise ecclesiastical authority over all the earth.

Until the Inquisition, the Crusades had been the most visible abominations that resulted. The Crusades were characterized by greed, lust, and indiscriminate slaughter of "Christians," Muslims, and Jews. Actually, the slaughter was not indiscriminate. The Jews were a special target. There was nothing godly or good about the Crusades. Nothing. Aquinas lived in the time of both the Crusades and the Inquisition.

One of the major justifications for killing the Jews was the charge that they had killed God. Aquinas, writing according to his own reason, said, "The Jews sinned in this way, crucifying Christ not only as man but as God. The Jewish leaders' sin was the greatest, both because of what they did and because it was done with malice. More excusable was the sin of the pagans at whose hands Christ was crucified, for they had no knowledge of the Law." [25]

The most comprehensive list of those responsible for the death of Jesus is given in Acts 4:27-28. The Jewish believers in Jerusalem were praying and praising God after the release of Peter and John by the Sanhedrin. They mention five different parties who bear the responsibility.

"For truly in this city there were gathered together against Thy holy Servant Jesus, whom Thou didst anoint, both Herod and Pontius Pilate, along with the Gentiles and the peoples of Israel, to do whatever Thy hand and Thy purpose predestined to occur." The five parties mentioned who bear responsibility for the crucifixion of Jesus are 1) Herod, 2) Pontius Pilate, 3) the Gentiles, 4) the peoples of Israel, and 5) God. We could also single out Judas and the religious leaders to be added to this list.

Certainly, the greatest responsibility is God's, for He planned it from the beginning. Though He sent His Son expressly for that purpose, He does not bear any guilt. Isaiah prophesied of Messiah, "But the Lord was pleased to crush Him, putting Him to grief; If He would render Himself as a guilt offering...By His knowledge the Righteous One, My Servant, will justify the many, as He will bear their iniquities." (Is.53:10)

The specific individuals who were responsible bear their own particular guilt. What about the people who are mentioned, "the Gentiles and the peoples of Israel"? Aquinas says, "The Jews sinned in this way, crucifying Christ not only as man but as God." Did the Jews crucify God, but the Gentiles only crucify a man? The cross is where the ways of men and the Way of God meet. Only those who are guilty can receive God's forgiveness there.

Peter preached at the Temple, "The God of Abraham, Isaac, and Jacob, the God our fathers, has glorified His Servant Jesus, the one whom you delivered up, and disowned in the presence of Pilate, when he had decided to release Him. But you disowned the Holy and Righteous One, and asked for a murderer to be granted to you, but put to death the Prince of life, the one whom God raised from the dead, — a fact to which we are witnesses....And now brethren, **I know that you acted in ignorance, just as your rulers did also**. But the things which God announced beforehand by the mouth of all the prophets, that His Messiah should suffer, He has thus fulfilled. Repent therefore and return, that your sins may be wiped away..." (Acts 3:13-15,17-19)

There are several things to note in what Peter preached. The first is that he is speaking as a Jew to fellow Jews. He is not setting himself outside of Israel, *Contra Judaeos* and *Adversus Judaeos*. He is a Jew whose heart is controlled by the God of Israel, and who, like all prophets of God, loves the people whom he is rebuking.

The second thing to note is that Peter is not holding himself guiltless. Twice he says, "you disowned" Jesus. This is the same Peter who disowned Jesus three times in one night. We can be fairly certain that he never forgot it, especially after the passage of less than two months.

This is the same Peter whom Paul later condemned as a hypocrite in Antioch. This same Peter had withdrawn himself from the Gentiles, despite what he had experienced with Cornelius. After Peter had been born of the Spirit and after he had become a pillar of the church, Peter turned away, out of fear of men, from belief in salvation by faith.

So when Peter says, "Repent therefore and return, that your sins may be wiped away," we can rest assured that he was not speaking abstractly. He knew and had experienced what he was talking about. Those who do not know their own guilt are in no position before God to point to the guilt of others.

The third thing to note is that Peter says, "And now brethren, I know that you acted in ignorance, just as your rulers did also." He is preaching as Jesus prayed on the cross, "Father forgive them; for **they do not know what they are doing**." (Lk.23:34) He is seeking reconciliation.

This is the same Peter who rebuked the Lord when "Jesus the Messiah began to show His disciples that He must go to Jerusalem, and suffer many things from the elders and chief priests and scribes, and be killed, and be raised up on the third day." (Mt.16:21) Peter, in ignorance, had rejected God's eternal plan of salvation.

Paul could speak so strongly about the sins of others because he knew his own. "I was formerly a blasphemer and a persecutor and a violent aggressor....It is a trustworthy statement, deserving full acceptance, that Messiah Jesus came into the world to save sinners, among whom I am foremost of all." (1Ti.1:12,15)

Every man bears the guilt. Every man can receive the forgiveness. Jesus rebuked those who said, "If we had been living in the days of our fathers, we would not have been partners with them in shedding the blood of the prophets [or of the Lord]." (Mt.23:31) Those who say such things are only deceiving themselves. Peter, Paul, and Jesus did not see it the way that Aquinas, the Crusaders, and the Inquisitors did.

Aquinas takes great care to distinguish the differing magnitude of error and sin of which pagans, Jews, and heretics are guilty: "And if men who lack faith in this sense are lost, that is because of other sins that cannot be forgiven without faith, rather than because their disbelief is sinful. Strict disbelief, like faith, is a disposition of mind under the influence of will. It distances us from God by depriving us of true knowledge of him, and as such is a greater sin than any moral wrongdoing, though not than wrong against the other theological virtues. There are several types of disbelief: pagans resist a faith they have never accepted, Jews a faith they accept in figure, and heretics a faith that was clearly revealed to them....

"Disbelief of heretics, who resist and distort a gospel they once professed, is a worse sin than the disbelief of Jews who never accepted it; but because Jews accept the gospel faith in figure in the Old Testament, but distort it by bad interpretation, their disbelief is worse than that of pagans who have never accepted the gospel at all. Nevertheless pagans are more mistaken than Jews, and they than heretics: except perhaps for the Manichean heresy which is more mistaken about the faith than even pagans are." [26]

For Aquinas, it is important to distinguish the different measures of error and guilt. It is important because that enables him to then distinguish the different ways in which the Church should treat pagans, Jews, and heretics.

He writes, "In Luke we are told: *Go out into the country roads and lanes and compel people to come in, that my house may be full.* So **some people are to be compelled to believe and enter the church.** But only people who had once accepted the faith: pagans and Jews can't be forced to believe, since believing is a matter of will. The faithful, if they have the power, may use it to stop such disbelievers hindering the faith by blasphemy or propaganda or openly persecuting it. **This is the reason Christians frequently wage war on disbelievers**: not to force them to believe (because even if conquered and held captive they must be left their freedom to believe or not as they will), but **to stop them hindering the faith.** However, disbelievers who once accepted and professed the faith — heretics and apostates — can be compelled, even physically, to fulfil their promises and hold to what they once professed. For even though making a vow is a voluntary matter, keeping it is an obligation. So **adopting the faith is voluntary, but sticking to it once adopted is obligatory.** As Augustine says, none of us would want a heretic to die. *But the house of David could not have had peace if Absalom had not died in the war he waged against his father. And in the same way, if the catholic church loses some in gathering others, freeing the many heals the wound in her maternal heart.*" [27]

Aquinas explains that, "Christians frequently wage war on disbelievers [i.e. Jews and pagans]...to stop them hindering the faith." **The justification,** therefore, for the Crusades is that the Jews and Muslims in "the Holy Land" are "hindering the faith." In this view, only the Church has a right to "the Holy Land," because the Church has inherited all the promises made to the Jews.

He maintains that, "The faithful, if they have the power, may use it to stop such disbelievers [i.e. Jews and pagans] hindering the faith by blasphemy or propaganda or openly persecuting it." The Church, therefore, had a right to burn Jewish books, i.e. "faith-hindering propaganda." Constantine would have approved, even as he approved of the burning of the writings of Arius.

We will look at the matter of forcing people to believe when we get to the end of Aquinas' argument. He continues:

"The faithful are forbidden communication with certain persons partly to punish those persons and partly to safeguard the faithful. The church therefore visits the penalty of excommunication on heretics and apostates, but not on disbelievers who have never accepted the Christian faith — Jews and pagans — since over them she has no spiritual jurisdiction, and temporal jurisdiction only if they live in a Christian community and when in fault are punishable by Christians. But as regards the safety of the faithful: if their faith is strong enough one can hope more for conversion of the disbelievers than subversion of believers, and in this case the faithful should not be forbidden communication with Jews or pagans. But if the faithful are weak and uneducated they should be forbidden such communication, especially in intimate or unnecessary ways.

"Authority is instituted by human law, but believers and disbelievers are distinguished by God's law. Since the law of grace does not abrogate human law based on reason, being believers does not as such exempt us from the already established authority of disbelievers. **The church, however, does have God's authority to take authority away from disbelievers, since their disbelief makes them unworthy to exercise power over believers, who have become sons of God.** And sometimes the church exercises this right, sometimes not. As regards disbelievers subject to the temporal authority of the church or its members, church law states that slaves of Jews must be freed immediately on becoming Christians, with no ransom paid if they were born slaves or sold into slavery. But if in the market they must be offered for ransom within three months. **The church has the right to dispose of the Jew's goods since he is subject to the church.** And secular princes have enacted similar laws for their own subjects, favoring freedom. But as regards disbelievers not subject to the church's temporal authority the church — in order to avoid scandal — has made no such law, though it has the right to. The church permits Christians to work Jewish lands, because that doesn't involve living together; but if such contact did hold dangers for the faith of Christians it would be altogether forbidden."[28]

Such a theology puts to death both the Great Commission and the greatest commandment. They are unrelated to this kind of Church.

However, "Pagans and Jews can't be forced to believe, since believing is a matter of will." They can't be forced to believe, but the Church can destroy anything that hinders the faith. They can't be forced to believe, but they can be removed from any positions of authority, "since their disbelief makes them unworthy to exercise power over [any] believers." They can't be forced to believe, but they can be forbidden contact with the community at large. They can be isolated, as in ghettos. They can't be forced to believe, but their property can be confiscated.

In fact, however, they **were** forced to believe. Not only were they forced to attend preaching sessions, they were, not infrequently, forced to be baptised or be expelled from the domain. Occasionally the choice was baptism or death.

Aquinas did not favor this, but he provided the "theological" justification for it. In some places the forcible baptism of Jewish children was advocated and practiced. The baptism was to insure their salvation. Aquinas speaks out against this practice, but not because it is totally contrary to the Spirit of Jesus and has nothing to do with salvation. He speaks out against it because the children might commit apostasy later in life, and because "it is also repugnant to natural justice."

He says, "...Now it has never been the church's custom to baptize Jewish children without their parents' permission; though in past ages many powerful Catholic princes with holy bishops as their friends — Constantius with Sylvester, Theodosius with Ambrose — would surely have claimed authority to do it if they had thought they reasonably could. But it is a practice dangerous to the faith, for when the children grow up their parents will easily persuade them to abandon what they unknowingly received. And it is also repugnant to natural justice, since children belong by nature to their parents, and to remove them from their parents' care or arrange things against their parents' wishes while the children are still without use of their own reasons is an offence against natural justice. When children start to use their own free will they begin to belong to themselves, and then they can be brought to believe — but by persuasion, not by coercion — and be baptized without their parents' permission." [29]

The problem with Aquinas' reasons is that they did not seem reasonable to everyone. Justice based on the reason of man often changes - only God and His Word remain the same. So when the Church felt that it had an adequate way of handling apostasy, its concept of "justice" changed. It found a new way to serve God in addition to theft and murder — kidnapping.

Every tradition starts some time. New traditions were added to the old. Aquinas' highest authority, Church tradition, was the means of bringing destruction rather than salvation to the Jewish people. Reason, his arbiter and judge, informed by hatred and fear, was the means of justifying the destruction.

"After the expulsion from Spain, 80,000 Jews took refuge in Portugal, 'relying on the promise of the king. Spanish priests lashed the Portuguese into fury, and the king was persuaded to issue an edict which threw even that of Isabella into the shade [i.e. it shone much more brightly]. All the adult Jews were banished from Portugal; but first of all their children below the age of fourteen were taken from them to be educated as Christians. Then, indeed, the serene fortitude with which the exiled people had borne so many and such grievous calamities gave way, and was replaced by the wildest paroxysms of despair.' " [30]

The Church of that time had a strange Christianity. Some traditional sacramental things were very important, but it had neither love nor good fruit. It certainly did not worship God in Spirit and Truth. There was no Biblical way in which it was the Church.

"**Mediaeval theologians and canonists forbade Jews to attend Christian worship.** For Thomas Aquinas it was not fitting that infidels and Jews should look at the sacred Host. **Jews were, however, allowed to hear sermons.**...Only in Spain did persons go to great trouble from the thirteenth century to convert Muslims and Jews and to fit them into Christian society. **Since they did not come voluntarily, the authorities resorted to force.** These compulsory sermons, occurring several times a year in churches, public squares, or even in synagogues, had, understandably, only slight and, for the most part, merely external success, especially when the preachers, annoyed by their failure, began to revile the Jews...

"Under the influence of Spanish bishops, the Council of Basel decreed in 1434 that several times a year bishops should have the Christian faith preached to the Jews; all Jews should be compelled under penalties to hear these sermons....

"If the number of converts remained extremely slight, the explanation is not to be sought only in the curious missionary methods or lack of a genuine missionary spirit in accord with the Gospel among Christians nor in the loyalty and love of the Jews for the faith of their ancestors and their tradition. Not the least important reason is the fact that their conversion was opposed to the financial interests of the princes, not excluding the bishops, and these made it almost impossible by legal measures. The source of revenue which every Jew represented on the basis of the right of protection and especially of the cameral servitude dried up with his baptism. To balance matters converts were to renounce their property. Already in 1090 the Emperor Henry IV had demanded this of the Jews of Worms and Speyer who desired to become his brothers in the faith. In his privilege for the Jews of Vienna Frederick II decreed: 'If one, for his part, desires baptism,...he shall give up his inheritance just as he has abandoned the law of his fathers.'

"Naturally, this total loss of property kept many from being baptized. That from Alexander III in 1179 the Popes took measures against this practice and threatened excommunication for those who caused converts to lose their inheritances or confiscated their property seems to have had little effect....Cardinal d'Ailly protested that people did not leave the converted Jews even the necessities of life, with the result that they fell away and accused the Christians of uncharitableness." [31]

If the Jews didn't believe, they were accursed outcasts, whose employment, property, children, and lives could be taken from them. If they did believe, or if they were baptised, their property was often still taken from them, making it impossible for them to provide for their families. Perhaps worst of all, they then became subject to the Inquisition for being Christians with Jewish ideas.

According to Aquinas, heretics can expect much worse treatment from the Church than can disbelieving Jews: "Even doctors of the church have disagreed about matters of no consequence to the faith or not yet decided by the church; but when such matters are decided by the authority of the universal church (vested principally in the Pope) anyone who stubbornly resists the decision must be adjudged a heretic. About heretics there are two things to say. Their sin deserves banishment not only from the church by excommunication but also from the world by death. But the church seeks with mercy to turn back those who go astray, and condemns them not immediately but only after a first or second warning. If, however, a heretic remains stubborn, the church, despairing of his conversion, takes care of the salvation of others, separates the heretic from the church with a sentence of excommunication, and delivers him to the secular courts to be removed from the world by death." [32]

A heretic, i.e. someone who did not accept the decisions of the pope and the papal system, could be restored once. "...But if they lapse again, on their second return they are admitted to repentance but not delivered from sentence of death. God can read the heart and knows those genuinely returning and always receives them. But the church is not able to imitate this, and presumes that those who lapse a second time did not genuinely return. So though it does not deny them the way to salvation, it does not save them from death. Our Lord told Peter we should forgive *seventy times seven times* — meaning always — offences committed against ourselves; but that does not mean we are free to forgive offences against God and our fellowmen: there the law sets the standard, taking into account God's honour and our fellowmen's well-being." [33]

This Church claimed all the authority of God in determining doctrine, worship, and practice. How odd that such an ecclesiastical system could find justification to act in God's behalf by putting a man to death, but not to restore him to life. It claimed to exercise that power. It claimed the authority to define and to punish sins, but, for "God's honour and our fellowmen's well-being," it could not forgive them.

The proper thrust of theology is not the absurd and the irrelevant. Its proper thrust is the definition of a godly life. Sometimes the Church has made that thrust with a sword. There is no Biblical justification for that. There is Biblical condemnation for it.

What were the signs that such a system or its leaders belonged to the Lord? A spiritually similar, but less accomplished, system had demanded the death of Jesus. God brought an end to that system. In response to an ecclesiastical system which exalted the traditions and cruelties of men above the Word and love of God, the Spirit of God began what has become known as the Reformation.

FOOTNOTES

1. St. Thomas Aquinas, *Summa Theologiae, A Concise Translation*, edited by Timothy McDermott, Christian Classics, Westminster, MD., 1989, P.xxiii
2. ibid., P.xxii
3. ibid., P. lvi-lvii
4. ibid., Bk.2, Ch.10, 10.8-12, P.341
5. *The Ecclesiastical History of Eusebius Pamphilus*, translated by Christian Frederick Cruse, op. cit., P.51, following the ecclesiastical history.
6. ibid., Introduction, 9, P.4
7. Bernard Martin in his introduction to Lev Shestov, *Athens and Jerusalem*, translated by Bernard Martin, Ohio U. Press, Athens, OH, 1966, P.31
8. ibid., Lev Shestov, P.287
9. ibid., P.70 Shestov is really an apostle to the philosophers.
10. St. Thomas Aquinas, *Summa Theologiae, A Concise Translation*, op.cit., P.lvi
11. ibid., Bk.2, Ch.8, 62.2&4, P.241
12. Shestov, *Athens and Jerusalem*, P.354
13. ibid., P.200
14. ibid., Pp.67-68
15. ibid., Bk.2, Ch.9, 98.1, P.294
16. ibid., Bk.2, Ch.9, 98.2, Pp.295-6
17. ibid., Bk.2, Ch.9, 99.1, P.296
18. ibid., Bk.2, Ch.9, 104.2, P.302
19. ibid., Bk.3, Ch.14, 42.1, P.518
20. ibid., Bk.2, Ch.9, 105.1, P.303
21. ibid., Bk.2, Ch.9, 105.3, P.303
22. *History of the Church, Vol.IV*, ed. by Hubert Jedin & John Dolan, translated by Anselm Biggs, Crossroad Publishing Co., NY, 1986, P.610
23. W.E.H. Lecky, *History of the Rise and Influence of the Spirit of Rationalism in Europe, Vol.II*, D.Appleton & Co., NY, 1867, Pp.40-41 and Note 3
24. Motley's *Rise of the Dutch Republic, Vol.II*. p.155, quoted in Lecky, P.41, Note 2
25. *Summa Theologiae, A Concise Translation*, op.cit., Bk.3, Ch.14, 47.1, P.527
26. ibid., Bk.2, Ch.10, 10.1-6, Pp.339-340
27. ibid., Bk.2, Ch.10, 10.8-12, P.340
28. ibid., Bk.2, Ch.10, 10.8-12, Pp.340-341
29. ibid., Bk.2, Ch.10, 10.8-12, Pp.341-342
30. Lecky, quoted in *The Pentateuch and Haftorahs*, ed. by Dr. J.H. Hertz, Soncino Press, London, 1956, P.249
31. *History of the Church, Vol.IV*, ed. by Jedin & Dolan, op. cit., Pp.612-613
32. *Summa Theologiae, A Concise Translation*, op.cit., Bk.2, Ch.10, 11.2-3, P.342
33. ibid., Bk.2, Ch.10, 11.4, P.343

SECTION B:
THE PARTIAL REFORMATION

39

THE PARTIAL REFORMATION

The Reformation was a recognition that for many, many centuries there had been great and grievous errors in the doctrine and practice, worship and vision of the Church. The Reformation was a call for radical change, a demand that the Church return to its Biblical roots, identity, and purpose. More than a thousand years of the accumulation of commandments and traditions of men had once more made void the Word of God.

What we call the Reformation was a beginning. Some indispensable changes were made in critical areas, returning the Church to its Biblical foundation. There were particular issues on which the Reformers focused. They expressed their Biblical convictions in opposition to the accepted doctrine of the Church.

They were considered heretics and outlaws, and their very lives were in danger. In that hostile environment, they sought to know and to systematically teach the Word of God. What they understood and what they accomplished is amazing.

Yet in other areas, the Reformers did not return to the Biblical teaching. They accepted the traditions they had received without question. They were not infallible, and it is a mistake to think that they were. There are indispensable changes that still need to be made to return the Church to its Biblical foundation.

Because it was an important issue for Calvin, he noticed, for example, Eusebius' misrepresentation concerning Peter and the Church at Rome. "However, I do not see how their account of Peter's presiding over the church at Rome has any credibility. Surely, what is said in Eusebius - that he ruled there for twenty-five years — is easily refuted...." [1]

Calvin does not, however, notice Eusebius' related misrepresentation concerning the Millennial reign of Jesus. That was not, as we shall see, an important issue for Calvin. He seems simply to have followed the general view of Augustine.

As far as the relationship of the Church and the Jews is concerned, both Calvin and Luther followed the traditional teaching of men. In particular, they followed the teachings of Augustine. Some of Augustine's errors they recognized and rejected. Some of Augustine's errors they perpetuated and built upon.

"Throughout the *Institutes* Calvin's self-confessed debt to Augustine is constantly apparent....It has been said that 'the Reformation, inwardly considered, was just the ultimate triumph of Augustine's doctrine of grace over Augustine's doctrine of the church.' The measure of dependence of

Luther and Calvin upon Augustine cannot easily be stated, but certainly both Reformers were frank to recognize their debt to him, without in the least exempting his opinions from the test of Scripture. Calvin may be said to stand at the culmination of the later Augustinianism." [2]

In general, the leaders of the Reformation continued to hold on to the belief that the Church had replaced Israel in the plan and purpose of God. Consequently, they built their theologies on the Constantinian foundation. They are still children of the marriage of Church and State. The confusion of identity and purpose continued.

"The right of the civil magistrate to punish heresy was maintained by the Helvetic, Scottish, Belgic, and Saxon Confessions. Luther, in reply to Philip of Hesse, distinctly asserted it; Calvin, Beza, and Jurieu, all wrote books on the lawfulness of persecution. Knox, appealing to the Old Testament, declared that those who were guilty of idolatry might justly be put to death. Cranmer and Ridley, as well as four other bishops, formed the commission in the reign of Edward VI for trying Anabaptists; and, if we may believe Fox, it was only by the long and earnest solicitation of Cranmer that Edward consented to sign the warrant that consigned Joan Bocher to the flames." [3]

The historical conflict with the papacy was irreconcilable. The popes and their followers were not willing to accept the Bible as the ultimate standard of Truth. Calvin, Luther, and others were not willing to forsake it. The very nature of this conflict, however, distorted their theology and understanding of the mission of the Church. They continually read their own historical situation into the Scriptures.

Calvin maintains, "That embassy which Paul so glowingly extols — 'I beseech you in Christ's name, be reconciled to God' [2Cor.5:20p.] — is directed not to outsiders, but to those who have already been reborn. But having bidden farewell to satisfactions, he relegates them to the cross of Christ. So where Paul writes to the Colossians that Christ has 'reconciled all things that are on heaven or earth...by the blood of the cross' [Col.1:20p], he does not confine this to the moment we are received into the church, but extends it throughout life. This is readily apparent from the context, where he says that believers have redemption through the blood of Christ, that is, the forgiveness of sins [Col.1:14]." [4]

The literal text of 2Co.5:18-20 is: "And all things are of God, who reconciled us to himself by Messiah Jesus, and gave to us the service [διακονιαν] of reconciliation: how that God was in Messiah reconciling the world to Himself, not reckoning to them their offences, and having put in us the word of reconciliation. For Messiah therefore we are ambassadors, as it were God exhorting by us, we beseech for Messiah, 'Be reconciled to God.' "

Calvin is incorrect in limiting the believer's ministry of reconciliation to other believers only. Clearly, God is seeking to reconcile the world, i.e. unbelievers also, to Himself. Paul's point is that as God reconciled us to Himself (through others who believed), so we are to seek to be His means for reconciling others who do not yet believe. Believers are His ambassadors to the world, bringing "the word of reconciliation," which He has "put in us." Because Paul brought "the word of reconciliation" to Corinth, there were believers there for him to write to.

David said, "O taste and see that the Lord is good; How blessed is the man who takes refuge in Him!" (Ps.34:8) All believers have eaten of that sweet fruit, and "tasted that the Lord is kind." (1Pet.2:3) The seed is in the fruit. All believers have the responsibility to sow that seed in the lives of others.

God is "in Messiah reconciling the world to Himself, **not reckoning to them their offences**." Believers have a ministry of reconciliation to "them." It is historically understandable why the initial reformers did not embrace this outward thrust of the believer's ministry. Nevertheless, they seriously distorted the nature of the ministry of reconciliation.

To correctly understand this ministry of reconciliation is to understand why the gospel is to the Jew first. In the misunderstanding of the initial reformers, there was no purpose or place for the reconciliation of Israel to the Lord.

Calvin's *Institutes* which is a systematic presentation of his theology, was written (initially) in 1536, twenty years after Luther's *Commentary on Romans*. We will look at Calvin first, however, since he more closely follows Augustine in his attitude toward the Jews and in some of his views on Israel.

FOOTNOTES

1. *Calvin:Institutes of the Christian Religion, Vol.1 & 2*, Trans. by Ford Lewis Battles, The Library of Christian Classics, Vol.XXI, Ed. by John T. McNeill, The Westminster Press, Philadelphia, 1960, Bk.4, Ch.14, P.1114
2. ibid., Pp.lvii-lviii, citing "Augustine," by B.B.Warfield, in Hasting's Dictionary of Religion and Ethics, II. 224
3. Lecky, *Rationalism in Europe*, Vol.II, op.cit., Pp.50-51
4. *Calvin:Institutes of the Christian Religion, Vol.1 & 2*, Trans. by Ford Lewis Battles, op. cit., Bk.3, Ch.4.27, P.654

40

CALVIN'S *INSTITUTES OF THE CHRISTIAN RELIGION*

A major issue for Calvin was the authority of Scripture. He recognized that if the authority of Scripture were not first established, it would be impossible to demonstrate the errors of the Church.

In the first part of his *Institutes*, Calvin wrote, "Before I go any farther, it is worth-while to say something about the authority of Scripture, not only to prepare our hearts to reverence it, but to banish all doubt. When that which is set forth is acknowledged to be the Word of God, there is no one so deplorably insolent — unless devoid also both of common sense and of humanity itself — as to dare impugn the credibility of Him who speaks. Now daily oracles are not sent from heaven, for it pleased the Lord to hallow his truth to everlasting remembrance in the Scriptures alone (cf. John 5:39). Hence the Scriptures obtain full authority among believers only when men regard them as having sprung from heaven, as if there the living words of God were heard...

"But a most pernicious error widely prevails that Scripture has only so much weight as is conceded to it by the consent of the church. As if the eternal and inviolable truth of God depended upon the decision of men!...

"Thus these sacrilegious men, wishing to impose an unbridled tyranny under the cover of the church, do not care with what absurdities they ensnare themselves and others, provided they can force this one idea upon the simple-minded: that the church has authority in all things...It is utterly vain, then, to pretend that the power of judging Scripture so lies with the church that its certainty depends upon churchly assent." [1]

As to how Scripture is to be interpreted, Calvin gives only a very small place to allegory. He comments on a traditional allegory that many in the Church had created for the parable of the good Samaritan: "First, suppose I do not want to accept their allegory. What, pray, will they do? For no doubt the fathers devised this interpretation without regard to the true meaning of the Lord's words. Allegories ought not to go beyond the limits set by the rule of Scripture, let alone suffice as the foundation for any doctrines." [2] **Calvin replaced Augustine's "Rule of Faith" with "the rule of Scripture."**

In another place, he declares, "They derive a second argument from the same source, that is from an allegory — as if allegories were of great value in confirming any dogma! But, let them be of value, unless I show that I can apply those very allegories more plausibly than they...Now let them go and peddle their allegories." [3]

Given this necessary firm reliance upon a non-allegorical reading of the

Bible as the ultimate standard of truth, let's examine where and why Calvin departs from its teaching concerning Israel and the Church. He begins with the scriptural truth that salvation is of the Jews, and for both Jews and Gentiles, but then he makes five distinct, though related, errors that lead him away from the Biblical teaching to the traditions of men.

These five errors of Calvin are: 1) The Covenant of the Law brings condemnation for all men. 2) The faithful in any particular time are the Church. 3) The New Covenant is made with the Church. 4) Individuals are grafted into the Church. 5) There is no future restoration of the Jews or any Millennial kingdom, since the Church is the kingdom.

These errors are not insignificant, since much of Calvin's doctrines of election and perseverence are based on these points. His concept of the covenant community — which leads to his doctrine on infant baptism and to his doctrine of reprobation - is also built on this faulty foundation. It is not our purpose here to discuss these doctrines, but simply to point out Calvin's errors in understanding the relationship of the Jewish people and the Church.

In different sections, Calvin tends to slightly, but significantly, vary the point that he is making. So, it will be occasionally necessary to include quotations from these different sections to show the variation.

ERROR #1: THE COVENANT OF THE LAW
BRINGS CONDEMNATION FOR ALL MEN

Calvin understood that there were many different religions in the world, but only one that was true. He states, "Besides this, Christ answered the Samaritan woman: 'You worship what you do not know; we worship what we know; for salvation is from the Jews' (John 4:22). In these words he both condemns all pagan religions as false and gives the reason that under the law the Redeemer was promised to the chosen people alone. From this it follows that no worship has ever pleased God except that which looked to Christ. On this basis, also, Paul declares that all heathen were 'without God and bereft of hope of life' (Eph.2:12)." [4]

Calvin well understood that the Covenant of the Law was only made with Israel. In fact, he firmly maintains that the salvation in the New Covenant is as much of and for the Jews as anything in the Old. "Let no one perversely say here that the promises concerning the gospel, sealed in the Law and the Prophets, were intended for the new people. For the apostle, shortly after saying that the gospel was promised in the law, adds: 'Whatever the law contains is without doubt intended specifically for those under the law' (Rom.3:19p).

"I admit that Paul said this in another context. But when he said that whatever the law teaches applies properly to the Jews, he was not so forgetful as to overlook what he had affirmed a few verses before concerning the gospel promised in the law (Rom.1:2; cf. ch.3:21). When the apostle says that the promises of the gospel are contained in it, he proves with utter clarity that the Old Testament was particularly concerned with the future life...

"Who, then, dares to separate the Jews from Christ, since with them, we hear, was made the covenant of the gospel, the sole foundation of which is Christ? Who dares to estrange from the gift of free salvation those to whom we hear the doctrine of the righteousness of faith was imparted? Not to dispute too long about something obvious — we have a notable saying of the Lord: 'Abraham rejoiced that he was to see my day; he saw it and was glad' (John 8:56).

"And what Christ there testified concerning Abraham, the apostle shows to have been universal among the believing folk when he says: 'Christ remains, yesterday and today and forever' (Heb.13:8). Paul is not speaking there simply of Christ's everlasting divinity but of his power, a power perpetually available to believers. Therefore, both the blessed Virgin and Zacharias in their songs called the salvation revealed in Christ the manifestation of the promises that the Lord had formerly made to Abraham and the patriarchs (Luke 1:54-55, 72-73). If the Lord, in manifesting his Christ, discharged his ancient oath, one cannot but say that the Old Testament always had its end in Christ and in eternal life." [5]

Calvin recognizes God's singular choice of Israel as His people, the people with whom He established His covenant. "And because, passing by all others, he chose this one nation in which to confine his grace for a time, he called it his own (Ex.19:5) and his purchased (Ex.15:16) people." [6]

"The fifth difference [between the two covenants], which may be added, lies in the fact that until the advent of Christ, the Lord set apart one nation within which to confine the covenant of his grace...Israel was then the Lord's darling son; the others were strangers. Israel was recognized and received into confidence and safekeeping; the others were left to their own darkness. Israel was hallowed by God; the others were profaned. Israel was honored with God's presence; the others were excluded from all approach to him." [7]

Yet Calvin often disregards this evident scriptural reality in order to make his own point. For example, in discussing the differences between the Old Covenant and the New Covenant, he remarks, "The Old brings death, for it can but envelop the whole human race in a curse....The Old is the ministry of condemnation, for it accuses all the sons of Adam of unrighteousness." [8]

This, of course, is not true, because the Covenant of the Law was not made with "the whole human race," or with "all the sons of Adam," but with Israel alone. Therefore, neither "the whole human race" nor "all the sons of Adam" can break the Covenant of the Law or be condemned by it.

Calvin maintains, "The fact, then, remains that through the law the whole human race is proved subject to God's curse and wrath, and in order to be freed from these, it is necessary to depart from the power of the law and, as it were, to be released from its bondage into freedom." [9] That is, in fact, not a fact at all. Paul writes, as Calvin notes above, "Now we know that whatever the Law says, it speaks to those who are under the Law..." (Rom.3:19) "For all who have sinned without the Law will also perish without the Law; and all who have sinned under the Law will be judged by the Law." (Rom.2:12)

The Old Covenant cannot bring condemnation for those with whom it was not made. The Covenant of the Law was not made with Adam and all his descendants. It was not made with Gentiles, although they could be grafted into it by becoming proselytes. It was not made with the Jewish people who lived before the covenant was given at Mt. Sinai.

Calvin says, "We must also note this about the holy patriarchs: they so lived under the Old Covenant as not to remain there but ever to aspire to the New, and thus embraced a real share in it." [10] However correctly Calvin may understand the aspirations of the patriarchs, the fact remains that they did not live under the Old Covenant. To paraphrase Paul, "What I am saying is this: the Law, which came four hundred and thirty years later..."(Gal.3:17) did not apply to the patriarchs.

Throughout the *Institutes*, Calvin emphasizes God's continuity in His dealings with men. Sometimes he emphasizes a continuity that is not there. Such is the case here, and in his second error as well.

ERROR #2: THE FAITHFUL IN ANY PARTICULAR TIME ARE THE CHURCH

Calvin asserts that the Covenant of the Law applies to all men so that he can eliminate the difference between Israel and the Church. Without doing this, he cannot establish his point that the faithful in any particular time are the Church. His **ENTIRE** theology depends upon this point.

The assertion often appears, but only as an assertion. Since it is contrary to the clear teaching of the Bible, there is no scriptural evidence to support it. Calvin frequently asserts this erroneous belief.

"In Isaiah's day, there was a church at Jerusalem which God had not yet forsaken...The church also endured to the time of Jeremiah." [11] This is critical for Calvin, because he intends to show that the New Covenant is made with the Church. If previous believers in Israel are identified as the Church, then he can take the promise made to Israel of a New Covenant and transfer it to the Church.

He recognizes that it is only chronologically after the crucifixion that Gentiles too can enjoy the blessings of Abraham. "After the wall was broken down (as the apostle elsewhere writes [Eph.2:14]) which separated Gentiles from Jews, the Gentiles too were given access to God's Kingdom, and Abraham became their father — and that apart from the sign of circumcision..." [12]

This new condition gave rise to a new people, the Church. Calvin, however, asserts that the believers of any time period are the Church. That is not scriptural. The very concept of the Church was an unrevealed mystery before Cornelius, Paul, and the Council at Jerusalem.

Calvin is well aware of this, but he does not seem to notice the contradiction of calling believers of any previous time "the Church": "But however many testimonies of Scripture proclaimed the calling of the Gentiles, when the apostles were about to undertake it the call seemed so new and strange to them that they shrank back from it as a monstrous thing. At last they set about it tremblingly and not without misgiving. And no wonder! For it seemed completely unreasonable that the Lord, who for so many ages had singled out Israel from all other nations, should suddenly change his plan and abandon that choice. Prophecies had indeed foretold this. But men could not heed these prophecies without being startled by the newness of the thing that met their eyes. And these evidences of the future calling of the heathen which God had given them of old were not sufficient to convince them. Besides the fact that he had called very few, he in a manner engrafted them into Abraham's family, thus adding them to his people. But by this public calling the Gentiles not only were made equal to the Jews, but it also was manifest that they were, so to speak, taking the place of dead Jews. Besides this, all those strangers whom God had previously received into the body of the church had never been made equal to the Jews. Paul with good reason, therefore, proclaims this a great 'mystery hidden for ages and generations' (Col.1:26; cf. Eph.3:9), and says that it is wonderful even to the angels (cf. 1Peter 1:12)." [13]

It was a new thing, something that had not been before. It was a mystery, something that had not been known before. Paul explains that the death of Jesus in the flesh enables Jew and Gentile to become one. God did it so "that the two he might **create** in Himself into one new man, making peace." (Eph.2:15, lit.) The Church is something that God **created** after the death of Jesus in the flesh. The Bible does not offer any support for calling previous believers "the Church."

Calvin does not, but others have suggested Acts 7:38 as support. In Acts 7:38, Stephen was speaking to the Sanhedrin about Moses: "This is the one who was in the congregation in the wilderness..."

The Greek word used for "congregation" is ekklesia [εκκλησια], the same word used to signify "church." But the word only signified a called-out assembly. It was not then a theological or religious term. That is why it is also used in Acts 19:39,41 to refer to the riotous gathering of the Ephesians.

The townclerk quieted the screaming multitude, rebuked them, and said,

" 'But if you want anything beyond this, it shall be settled in the lawful assembly [εκκλησια]. For indeed, we are in danger of being accused of a riot in connection with today's affair, since there is no real cause for it; and in this connection we shall be unable to account for this disorderly gathering.' And after saying this he dismissed the assembly [εκκλησιαν].' "

Calvin, of course, uses the term in the theological sense which it gained with the passage of time. In that sense, there is no support for calling previous believers prior to the fulness of Pentecost "the church." There is a clear and compelling reason not to do so. The Church that the New Covenant Scriptures describe was something new.

There is a special aspect of Calvin's error that requires some particular attention. This concerns his development of his doctrine of election and reprobation. Part of the development of that doctrine is based on assumptions that are clearly false.

"We must now add a second, more limited degree of election, or one in which God's more special grace was evident, that is, when from the same race of Abraham God rejected some but showed that he kept others among his sons by cherishing them in the church. Ishmael had at first obtained equal rank with his brother, Isaac, for in him the spiritual covenant had been equally sealed by the sign of circumcision. Ishmael is cut off; then Esau; afterward, a countless multitude, and well-nigh all Israel." [14]

It is very strange that Calvin, of all people, should so misrepresent the election of God. Ishmael never "obtained equal rank with his brother, Isaac." Before they were born, God chose Isaac. God told Abraham, "And I will establish My covenant between Me and you and your seed after you throughout their generations for an everlasting covenant, to be God to you and to your seed after you. And I will give to you and to your descendants after you, the land of your sojournings, all the land of Canaan, for an everlasting possession; and I will be their God." (Gen.17:7-8)

Then God told Abraham that Sarah would have a son. (vv.15-16) "Then Abraham fell on his face and laughed...And Abraham said to God, 'Oh that Ishmael might live before Thee!' But God said, 'No, but Sarah your wife shall bear you a son, and you shall call his name Isaac; and I will establish My covenant with him for an everlasting covenant for his seed after him.

" 'And as for Ishmael, I have heard you; behold, I will bless him, and will make him fruitful, and will multiply him exceedingly. He shall become the father of twelve princes, and I will make him a great nation. **But My covenant I will establish with Isaac**, whom Sarah will bear to you at this season next year.' " (vv.17-21)

Ishmael was circumcised, but the covenant was never made with Ishmael. Paul makes this very clear in Romans 9:7-9. Likewise, the covenant was never made with the sons of Keturah, the woman whom Abraham married after Sarah's death. (Gen.25:1-6)

The same holds true concerning Esau. Esau was circumcised, but the covenant was never made with Esau. God chose Jacob before they were born.

God told Rebekah, "Two nations are in your womb; and two peoples shall be separated from your body; and one people shall be stronger than the other; and the older shall serve the younger." (Gen.25:23) Before Jacob and Esau were born, they were two different peoples. The covenant was only made with Jacob. Paul reiterates this as well. (Rom.9:10-13)

Calvin continues, "By their own defect and guilt, I admit, Ishmael, Esau, and the like were cut off from adoption. For the condition had been laid down that they should faithfully keep God's covenant, which they faithlessly violated." [15]

Calvin is wrong. Ishmael and Esau were not cut off by "their own defect and guilt." They were never heirs of the covenant. As Paul writes concerning Jacob and Esau, "For though they were not yet born, and had not done anything good or bad, in order that God's purpose according to His choice might stand, not because of works, but because of Him who calls, it was said to her, 'The older will serve the younger.' " (Rom.9:11-12)

In opposition to Paul, Calvin writes, "For God takes it for granted that, as both [Jacob and Esau] had been begotten of a holy father, were successors of the covenant, and in short, were branches of a sacred root, the children of Jacob were now under extraordinary obligation, having been received into that dignity; but after the first-born, Esau, had been rejected, and their father, who was inferior by birth, had been made heir, God accuses them of being doubly thankless, and complains that they were not held by that double bond." [16]

It is true that Esau was rejected, and it is true that the children of Jacob should, therefore, be doubly thankful. But it is not true that Esau was a "successor of the covenant." He never was.

Calvin continues his argument, building on the false foundation which he has laid. "It is easy to explain why the general election of a people is not always firm and effectual: to those with whom God makes a covenant, he does not at once give the spirit of regeneration that would enable them to persevere in the covenant to the very end." [17]

He has misrepresented believers of all time as being the Church. He has misrepresented the covenant people as including Ishmael and Esau. Now he draws the conclusion that "to those with whom God makes a covenant, he does not at once give the spirit of regeneration." Calvin is maintaining that people can enter into the New Covenant and be members of the Church without having received from God "the spirit of regeneration." That is to say, unbelievers can be part of the Church too.

Neither Ishmael nor Isaac were members of the Church. Paul does not say that they were. By definition, the Church is the combined called-out assembly of Jews and Gentiles who believe in Jesus.

It is true that in some covenants God "does not at once give the spirit of regeneration." In some covenants He never gives "the spirit of regeneration." He does not say that He will. That, however, is not true of the New Covenant.

The Spirit of God is part of the New Covenant promise. There is nothing in the Bible that indicates a person can enter into the New Covenant without receiving the Spirit of God.

Nicodemus was a righteous man. He was seeking the kingdom of God. He was a man of Israel. When he came to Jesus, he had not entered into the New Covenant.

"Jesus answered, 'Truly, truly, I say to you, unless one is born of water and the Spirit, he cannot enter into the kingdom of God. That which is born of the flesh is flesh; and that which is born of the Spirit is spirit.' " (Jn.3:5-6) The only way to enter the kingdom of God, which Calvin maintains is the Church, is to be "born of water and the Spirit."

"By this we know that we abide in Him and He in us, because He has given us of His Spirit." (1Jn.4:13) "...if anyone does not have the Spirit of Messiah, he does not belong to Him." (Rom.8:9) "And because you are sons, God has sent forth the Spirit of His Son into our hearts, crying, 'Abba! Father!' " (Gal.4:6)

When Jesus said, "I will build My church; and the gates of Hades shall not overpower it" (Mt.16:18), He was **not** including unbelievers in the Church. Paul exhorted the elders of the church in Ephesus, "Be on guard for yourselves and for all the flock, among which the Holy Spirit has made you overseers, to shepherd the church of God which He purchased with His own blood." Paul did **not** include unbelievers in the Church.

When Paul told the church at Rome, "So we, who are many, are one body in Messiah, and individually members of one another," he was **not** including unbelievers in the body of Messiah. The body of Messiah and the Church are the same. "And He put all things in subjection under His feet, and gave Him as head over all things to the church, which is His body, the fulness of Him who fills all in all." (Eph.1:22-23)

Paul was **not** including unbelievers in the Church when he wrote to the church at Ephesus: "For the husband is the head of the wife, as Messiah also is the head of the church, He Himself being the Savior of the body. But as the church is subject to Messiah, so also the wives ought to be to their husbands in everything. Husbands, love your wives, just as Messiah also loved the church and gave Himself up for her; that He might sanctify her, having cleansed her by the washing of water with the word, that He might present to Himself the church in all her glory, having no spot or wrinkle or any such thing; but that she should be holy and blameless." (Eph.5:23-27)

At one point in his argument against the Roman Church, Calvin says, "He [Paul] speaks somewhat more explicitly in the letter to the Galatians, where, in comparing Ishmael with Isaac, he states that many have a place in the church to whom the inheritance does not apply, for they are not the offspring of a free mother (Gal.4:22ff.). From this, Paul goes on to the comparison of the two Jerusalems. For just as the law was given on Mt. Sinai, so the gospel came forth from Jerusalem. Thus, many born and brought up as slaves boast without hesitation that they are children of God and of the church. Indeed, they haughtily despise God's real children, even though they themselves are bastards." [18]

Here, Calvin denies that "many born and brought up as slaves" are really "children of God." He should have also denied that they are "of the church."

Calvin is wrong in his identification of the Church. All of his theology is built upon that incorrect identification.

ERROR #3: THE NEW COVENANT IS MADE WITH THE CHURCH

Here as in the previous two errors, Calvin seems to be aware of the correct Biblical teaching. Here as in the previous two errors, he again ignores it, or simply does not grasp its significance. In its place, he substitutes a teaching that helps the flow of his theology.

Calvin gives the First Commandment as, "I am Jehovah, your God, who brought you out of the land of Egypt, out of the house of bondage. You shall have no other gods before my face." Then he discusses the different phrases.

In discussing "I am Jehovah your God," he says, "God first shows himself to be the one who has the right to command and to whom obedience is due. Then, in order not to seem to constrain men by necessity alone, he also attracts them with sweetness by declaring himself God of the church. For underlying this expression is a mutual correspondence contained in the promise: 'I will be their God, and they shall be my people' (Jer.31:33)." [19]

First, Calvin calls the people whom God brought out of Egypt "the church." Then he refers to Jeremiah's prophecy concerning the New Covenant. Since the New Covenant is promised to the people whom God brought out of Egypt, Calvin is then able to speak of the New Covenant as being made with the Church.

"But even though I believe I have already more than fully confirmed this, I shall add certain other testimonies by which these wriggling snakes may be so held fast that after this they will be unable to coil up even the tip of their tail. This is the new covenant that God in Christ has made with us, that he will remember our sins no more (Jer.31:31,34)." [20]

Though Calvin often refers to the New Covenant and parts of Jeremiah's prophecy, he never examines the text itself. That is unfortunate, because the text itself makes it clear that the New Covenant is made with the Jewish people. Paul also refers to this in Rom.9:4. Calvin comes close to recognizing this, but then ignores it, and finally contradicts it.

Calvin acknowledges that there is, by God's choice, a remnant of Israel that is kept faithful to the Lord. He acknowledges it, but then he ignores it. In Rom.11:16-24, Paul presents his analogy of the cultivated olive tree, the wild olive tree, and their branches.

Calvin comments, "Nevertheless, when Paul cast them down from vain confidence in their kindred, he still saw, on the other hand, that the covenant which God had made once for all with the descendants of Abraham could in no way be made void. Consequently, in the eleventh chapter he argues that Abraham's progeny must not be deprived of their dignity. By the virtue of this, he teaches, the Jews are the first and natural heirs of the gospel, except to the extent that by their ungratefulness they were forsaken as unworthy — yet forsaken in such a way that the heavenly blessing had not departed utterly from their nation. For this reason, despite their stubbornness and covenant-breaking, Paul still calls them holy (Rom.11:16) (such great honor does he give to the holy generation whom God had held worthy of his sacred covenant); but he calls us (if we are compared with them [the Jews]), as it were, posthumous or even abortive children of Abraham — and that by adoption, not by nature — as if a sapling broken from its tree were grafted upon the trunk of another (Rom.11:17).

"Therefore, that they might not be defrauded of their privilege, the gospel had to be announced to them first. For they are, so to speak, like the first-born in God's household. Accordingly, this honor was to be given them until they refused what was offered, and by their ungratefulness caused it to be transferred to the Gentiles. Yet, despite the great obstinacy with which they continue to wage war against the gospel, we must not despise them, while we consider that, for the sake of the promise, God's blessing still rests among them. For the apostle indeed testifies that it will never be completely taken away: 'For the gifts and the calling of God are without repentance.' (Rom.11:29, Vg.)." [21]

In this selection, Calvin is correct in six points. 1. Paul "cast them down from vain confidence in their kindred." 2. "He still saw, on the other hand, that the covenant which God had made once for all with the descendants of Abraham could in no way be made void"; 3. "Jews are the first and natural heirs of the gospel, except to the extent that by their ungratefulness they were forsaken as unworthy — yet forsaken in such a way that the heavenly blessing had not departed utterly from their nation." [Who, for that matter, is not unworthy?]

4. "Paul still calls them holy." 5. "That they might not be defrauded of their privilege, the gospel had to be announced to them first. For they are,

so to speak, like the first-born in God's household." 6. Gentiles "must not despise them, while we consider that, for the sake of the promise, God's blessing still rests among them. For the apostle indeed testifies that it will never be completely taken away: 'For the gifts and the calling of God are without repentance.' "

Calvin is incorrect in four points. 1. Romans 11 was not written so that "Abraham's progeny must not be deprived of their dignity." It was written so that they might be saved. Dignity without salvation is of no eternal worth. Paul's exhortation to the Gentile believers is for their own well-being, and for the salvation of Israel.

2. Calvin does not incorporate the reality that the Church is not Gentile only. "But he calls us [Gentiles] (if we are compared with them [the Jews]), as it were, posthumous or even abortive children of Abraham — and that by adoption, not by nature." "We [Gentiles] must not despise them [the Jews]."

Where does a Jewish believer belong in this analysis? Not with the "us" that is Gentile believers, and not with the "them" that is Jewish unbelievers. Calvin, unconsciously no doubt, is presenting the Church as Gentile, as opposed to the Jews, who are unbelievers. But the Church is not Gentile, and not all Jews are unbelievers. The Church is Jewish and Gentile believers made one in Messiah.

3. Calvin changes Paul's analogy. Paul said that the believing Jewish branches still abide in the tree. The unbelieving Jewish branches were broken off, and believing Gentiles were engrafted in their place. In Paul's analogy, the Church can be said to be all the branches, whether Jewish or Gentile, that receive their life from the tree. The main trunk of the tree is not cut at all.

Calvin says, it is "as if a sapling broken from its tree were grafted upon the trunk of another." In Calvin's analogy, the main trunk is cut off, and the Church is a sapling broken from another [Gentile] tree. Calvin radically changes the analogy to make it appear that all Israel was broken off, and then replaced by the Gentiles.

Calvin's analogy teaches the opposite of Paul's analogy. It teaches the opposite of what Paul is saying throughout Romans 11. Calvin's analogy also contradicts his own doctrine that believers of any time are the Church. Why would the trunk be cut? What, in his analogy, is cut off? If believing Gentiles have always been part of the Church, then why was it necessary to cut off the natural branches? For that matter, what then would be natural about the natural branches, if Gentiles, as Gentiles, have always been part of the tree?

4. In speaking of the necessity of bringing the gospel to the Jew first, Calvin says, "Accordingly, this honor was to be given them until they refused what was offered, and by their ungratefulness caused it to be

transferred to the Gentiles." First, whether or not it was an "honor" [Calvin's term], it was "necessary" [the Scriptural term]. Second, most Jews refused the gospel the first time it was preached to them on the day of Pentecost, and everywhere thereafter, but the order never changed. It was not "transferred to the Gentiles." It became "also to the Gentile."

In another place, Calvin shows that he mentally knew what the Scriptures actually taught concerning Gentiles who believed: "When Paul would assure the Ephesians of their adoption into the fellowship of Israel, he teaches that the hindrance which once held them back has now been removed." [22] That is to say that Paul taught the Gentile believers in Ephesus that they were adopted into the fellowship of Israel. The concept, however, was so far removed from Calvin's context and the thrust of his theology that he did not grasp its significance. Instead, he perpetuated the erroneous traditions of men.

ERROR #4: INDIVIDUALS ARE GRAFTED INTO THE CHURCH

In Paul's olive tree analogy, individual believers are represented by the individual branches that are grafted into Israel's "own olive tree." (v.24) Calvin identifies the olive tree in various ways; "Christ," "the body of Christ," "the church," "the people of God," etc.

"We also, in turn, are said to be 'engrafted into him' (Rom.11:17), and to 'put on Christ' (Gal.3:27)..." [23] "...that thus engrafted into him (cf. Rom.11:19) we are already, in a manner, partakers of eternal life, having entered in the Kingdom of God through hope." [24]

The olive tree can be understood to be Messiah Himself. The root would still represent the fathers — Abraham, Isaac, and Jacob — from whom Messiah, the King of Israel, came. Israel, and the Church, must draw life from Him. This makes the analogy of Paul more similar to the vine analogy which Jesus presented in John 15.

In his commentary on Romans, Calvin says, "It follows that the calling of the Gentiles resembled an ingrafting, and that they grew together into the people of God only as they struck root in the stock of Abraham." [25] If Calvin had stopped there, he would have avoided the error of saying that individuals are grafted into the Church. Instead, he replaces Israel's olive tree with the Church. He replaces "Christ" with "the body of Christ." The two are closely related, but they are not the same.

"Among the 'multitude' I include even certain distinguished folk, until they become engrafted into the body of the church." [26] "Moreover, it is quite unfitting that those not engrafted into the body of the only-begotten Son are considered to have the place and rank of children." [27] "Indeed, Paul himself also dissuades us from overassurance: 'Let him,' he says, 'who stands well, take heed lest he fall' (1Co.10:12). Again: You are grafted into the people of God? 'Be not proud but fear' (Rom.11:20). For God can cut you off again that he may engraft others (cf. Rom.11:21-23)." [28]

Calvin well understands, as we shall soon see, that there is a difference between the body of Christ and Christ Himself. Yet he maintains that individuals are grafted into the body of Christ, the Church. He even maintains that the patriarchs were grafted into the Church. There is no basis for this in Paul's analogy.

Calvin maintains that, "The adoption was put in Abraham's hands. Nevertheless, because many of his descendants were cut off as rotten members, we must, in order that election may be effectual and truly enduring, ascend to the Head, in whom the Heavenly Father has gathered his elect together, and has joined them to himself by an indissoluble bond. So, indeed, God's generous favor, which he has denied to others, has been displayed in the adoption of the race of Abraham; yet in the members of Christ a far more excellent power of grace appears, for, engrafted to their Head, they are never cut off from salvation." [29]

Calvin's point is that many Jews were cut off because they were not grafted into Christ, the Head. The "members of Christ," since they are "engrafted to their Head, they are never cut off from salvation." Being grafted into Christ, the Head, not the body of Christ, is what gives the Church its security.

Calvin extends this contrast between the Church and the Jews, ignoring the fact that the "signatories" to the New Covenant are the same as with the Old. He looks at Paul's exhortation to Gentile believers and concludes that the Gentiles have corporately replaced the Jews.

"And while he takes from the fall of the Jews the basis for his exhortation that 'he who stands take heed lest he fall' (1Cor.10:12p; Rom.11:20), he is not bidding us to waver, as if we were unsure of our steadfastness. Rather, he is merely taking away arrogance and rash overconfidence in our own strength so that after the Jews have been rejected, the Gentiles, received into their place, may not exult more wildly. Yet, he there not only addresses believers but in his prayer includes also the hypocrites, who gloried only in outward show.

"And he does not admonish individual men, but makes a comparison between Jews and Gentiles; and he shows that the Jews in being rejected underwent the just punishments of their unbelief and ingratitude. He then also exhorts the Gentiles not to lose, through pride and self-display, the grace of adoption recently transferred to them. Just as in that rejection of the Jews some of them remained who had not fallen away from the covenant of adoption, so from the Gentiles some might arise who, without true faith, would only be puffed up with stupid confidence of the flesh, and thus, to their own destruction, would abuse God's generosity. But even if you take this statement to apply to the elect and believers, this will cause no discomfiture. For it is one thing to restrain presumption, which sometimes creeps upon the saints from the vestiges of the flesh, in order that it may not play the wanton in vain confidence. It is another thing so to dishearten the conscience with fear that it cannot rest with full assurance in God's mercy." [30]

Calvin repeats the point: "For Paul tells the Gentiles, whom he is teaching, not to vaunt it proudly and inhumanly over the Jews because they have been introduced in place of the latter who have defected (cf. Rom.11:18ff.). He also requires fear, not that we may be dismayed and waver but that, as we have stated elsewhere, in preparing us humbly to receive God's grace, our trust in him may in no wise be diminished. Furthermore, he is not speaking to men individually but to the sects generally. For after the church had been divided into two parts, and rivalry gave rise to schism, Paul warned the Gentiles, who were put in the place of a peculiar and holy people, that this ought for them to be reason for fear and modesty. Yet among them many were puffed up, whose empty boasting it was useful to check." [31]

Calvin is incorrect in asserting that Paul "is not speaking to men individually but to the sects generally," and that "he does not admonish individual men, but makes a comparison between Jews and Gentiles." This is a point that Calvin repeats continually in his *Commentary on Romans*, when discussing chapter 11:16-24:

"Let us remember that in this comparison Paul is contrasting nation with nation, not man with man." [32] "We ought particularly to notice and recall what I have just stated, that Paul's remarks are directed not so much to individuals as to the whole body of the Gentiles...This proves again more clearly that Paul is speaking generally to the body of the Gentiles, for the breaking off which he mentions could not apply to individuals, whose election is unchangeable, since it is based on the eternal purpose of God." [33]

"Paul does not address each of the godly separately (as we have said before), but compares the Gentiles and the Jews...Paul adds the condition, *if thou continue in His goodness*, because he is not arguing about individuals who are elected, but about the whole body." [34] "We should, however, bear in mind the solution which I have mentioned, that Paul is not discussing here the special election of each individual, but is setting the Gentiles and Jews in opposition to one another." [35]

Calvin proposes his "solution" — that Paul is not speaking to individual Gentiles, but to Gentiles as a whole — because Paul's words create problems for Calvin's doctrine of election. Calvin's solution, however, no matter how often it is repeated, stands in opposition to the text.

Paul does use the plural in verse 13 where he emphasizes his right as the apostle to the Gentiles to teach all the Gentile believers. He uses the plural in verse 25 where he is exhorting all Gentile believers not to be ignorant of God's faithfulness to Israel.

But Paul uses the singular in verses 17, 18, 19, 20, 21, 22 and 24 where he issues his warning against Gentile arrogance towards those Jews who have not yet believed. He is warning individual men. He is warning individual Gentiles, because it is as individuals that they were grafted in. It is only as individuals that Gentiles are grafted in, not corporately. And it is as individuals that they can be cut off.

One final comment should be made concerning this error of Calvin. He discusses in different places the origin, nature, and election of angels. At one point, he makes a rather strange statement which he does not explain: "Hence, it ought not to be doubted that Jacob was, with the angels, engrafted into the body of Christ that he might share the same life." [36]

Calvin says that "Jacob was...engrafted into the body of Christ," though the Church did not yet exist on the earth. The strange part of the statement though is Calvin's assertion that, "Jacob was, **with the angels**, engrafted into the body of Christ." Calvin does speak of angels in terms of election, reprobation, and representation by their head — either Satan or Christ. [37] He does treat all "the elect" the same.

Did Calvin believe that "the elect angels" were "engrafted into the body of Christ"? It is not possible to say for sure on the basis of Calvin's *Institutes*, but such a belief would be clearly contrary to Scripture. The Bible says, "For assuredly He does not give help to angels, but He gives help to the seed of Abraham. Therefore, He had to be made like His brethren in all things, that He might become a merciful and faithful high priest in things pertaining to God, to make propitiation for the sins of the people." (Heb.2:16-17)

As for angels, "Are they not all ministering spirits, sent out to render service for the sake of those who will inherit salvation?" (Heb.1:14)

ERROR #5: THERE IS NO FUTURE RESTORATION OF THE JEWS OR ANY MILLENNIAL KINGDOM

As with Augustine, there are places that show that Calvin understood God's faithfulness to Israel. For example, Calvin shows his understanding that the New Covenant is made with the Jewish people.

"The apostle writes that 'Christ' is 'a minister of the circumcision, to fulfill the promises which had been given to the fathers' (Rom.15:8p.). Speaking thus, he does not philosophize as subtly as if he had spoken in this fashion: 'Inasmuch as the covenant made with Abraham applies to his descendants, Christ, to perform and discharge the pledge made once for all by his Father, came for the salvation of the Jewish nation.' Do you see how, after Christ's resurrection also, he thinks that the promise of the covenant is to be fulfilled, not only allegorically but literally, for Abraham's physical offspring? To the same point applies Peter's announcement to the Jews (Acts 2:39) that the benefit of the gospel belongs to them and their offspring by right of the covenant; and in the following chapter he calls them 'sons of the covenant' (Acts 3:25), that is, heirs." [38]

Calvin also demonstrates an understanding of the spiritual fulness of God's promise and purpose for Israel. He argues against those who deride the inheritance of the Jews as being merely material and carnal.

"The point of our quarrel with men of this sort is this: they teach that the Israelites deemed the possession of the Land of Canaan their highest and ultimate blessedness, and that after the revelation of Christ it typified for us the heavenly inheritance. We contend, on the contrary, that, in the earthly possession they enjoyed, they looked, as in a mirror, upon the future inheritance they believed to have been prepared for them in heaven." [39]

Yet at the same time, Calvin contradicts himself and places the Jews in opposition to the Church. Unfortunately, he did not integrate the ongoing reality of the faithful remnant into his theology. "And Christ, quoting Isaiah's prophecy, 'They shall all be taught by God' (John 6:45; Isa.54:13), means only that the Jews are reprobate and alien to the church because they are unteachable. And He offers no other reason than that God's promise does not pertain to them." [40]

Jesus continued in John 6:45, "...Every one who has heard and learned from the Father comes to Me." Of course, the tens of thousands of Jews in Jerusalem who believed and came to Jesus, and the tens of thousands of Jews elsewhere who believed and came to Him cannot be considered "reprobate and alien to the church because they are unteachable." They are the ones who went forth and taught the Gentiles.

As for their being "alien to the church," Paul, in Romans 11, maintains that it is natural for Jews to believe in Jesus and "be grafted into their own olive tree." In Romans 9, Paul maintains that the covenants, the promises, and the fathers belong to them. Calvin's statements are false.

In Ephesians 2 and 3, Paul makes it clear that Gentiles are aliens to the promise, not Jews. It is, after all, Gentiles who were aliens, but who, through faith, have now been brought into the commonwealth of Israel. If "God's promise does not pertain to them [the Jews]," the natural branches, then, assuredly, it does not pertain to anyone. As Calvin elsewhere remarked, "The apostle writes that 'Christ' is 'a minister of the circumcision, to fulfill the promises which had been given to the fathers' (Rom.15:8)."

There are three general ways in which Calvin interprets the scriptures that speak of the Jewish people and their restoration. One, he interprets them correctly in one place, but contradicts that interpretation in another. Two, he interprets them correctly, at least partially, but then ignores the interpretation, its application to the Jewish people, and the significance of that application. Three, he interprets incorrectly.

Let's look at an example of a partially correct interpretation that ignores its application to the Jewish people, and the significance of that application. Calvin notes that "In the examples of Moses and Paul, we see that it was not grievous for them to turn their minds and eyes away from themselves and to long for their own destruction with fierce and burning zeal in order that, despite their own loss, they might advance God's glory and Kingdom (Ex.32:32; Rom.9:3)." [41]

He correctly understands that Moses and Paul were both willing "to long for their own destruction with fierce and burning zeal in order that, despite their own loss, they might advance God's glory and Kingdom." Calvin recognizes their "fierce and burning zeal," but ignores the object of it. The object of their "fierce and burning zeal" cannot be separated from its purpose, i.e. that "they might advance God's glory and Kingdom."

They were both willing to be damned forever for the forgiveness and salvation of Israel. They understood how the immediate and ultimate advancement of God's glory and Kingdom was, by God's design, dependent upon the fate of Israel. Paul makes it very clear that the salvation of Israel will bring much more blessing than the "riches of the world" and the "riches of the Gentiles" which the gospel initially brought.

He makes it very clear that the acceptance of all Israel will be more than the "reconciliation of the world" that has already come through the gospel. It will be "life from the dead." To Calvin, on the other hand, what Moses and Paul were willing to be accursed for has no significance at all. He does not even mention it.

Let's look at an example of an incorrect interpretation. Calvin understood that there is a remnant, but does not grasp its significance. He ignores Romans 11:1, and misinterprets the following verse. "Therefore we must come to that lesser people, of whom Paul elsewhere writes that they were foreknown of God (Rom.11:2). ...The people foreknown, then, mean for Paul only a small portion mixed with the multitude, which falsely claims the name of God." [42]

Paul identifies the "Israel" he is talking about in both verse 1 and verse 2 as the whole nation. Paul is speaking about Israel when he says, "God has not rejected His people whom He foreknew." He is not speaking about the remnant. The remnant is not a people. It is part of a people. That is why it is called a remnant. "Israel" is a people.

"Hear this word which the Lord has spoken against you, sons of Israel, against the entire family which He brought up from the land of Egypt, 'You only have I known [lit.] of all the families of the earth; therefore, I will punish you for all your iniquities.' " (Am.3:2) Whom did God know? "The sons of Israel...the entire family which He brought up from the land of

Egypt." Did He *really* mean that He only knew the faithful remnant? No, for He says, "therefore, I will punish you for all your iniquities." He will punish the unfaithful in Israel whom He has known.

Paul distinguishes the faithful remnant in Israel from the rest of Israel who were hardened. "Until the fulness of the Gentiles has come in," only the faithful remnant will believe. There will be a point in time when "the fulness of the Gentiles has come in." Then, not even a part of Israel will be blinded. "All Israel will be saved," because "God has not rejected His people whom He foreknew."

In his introduction to his *Commentary on Romans*, Calvin writes, "God's covenant has not wholly departed from the seed of Abraham, for the Jews are at length to be provoked to jealousy by the faith of the Gentiles, so that God may gather all Israel to Himself." [43] Calvin seems to be expressing a faith in the restoration of the Jewish people, as a people, to God.

Yet when it comes to commenting on the verse itself (11:26), where the Apostle Paul writes, "and thus all Israel will be saved...," Calvin cannot accept the only and obvious meaning of Paul's words. He writes, "*and so all Israel shall be saved*. Many understand this of the Jewish people, as if Paul were saying that religion was to be restored to them again as before. But I extend the word *Israel* to include all the people of God." [44] Calvin rejects the Millennial reign of Messiah, so he has to change Paul's meaning by "extend[ing] the word *Israel* to include all the people of God."

Frederic Louis Godet, in his *Commentary on Romans*, says, "It is almost incredible how our Reformers could have held out obstinately, as they have done, against a thought so clearly expressed. But they showed themselves in general rather indifferent about points of eschatology, and they dreaded in particular everything that appeared to favor the expectation of the thousand years' reign which had been so much abused in their time. " [45]

For the most part, Calvin ignores the scriptures that speak of the restoration of the Jewish people and the Millennial reign of Jesus on the earth. For that matter, he generally ignores anything in the Messianic prophecies that speak of the Jewish people. That part of the Bible simply does not fit in his theology.

He gives, for example, an extended list of different Messianic prophecies that refer to David, his kingdom, and the Jewish people. But, for Calvin, the fact that the prophecies clearly express God's faithfulness to Israel has no meaning.

"In short, to show God merciful, all the prophets were constantly at pains to proclaim that kingdom of David upon which both redemption and eternal salvation depended. Thus Isaiah says: 'I will make with you a...covenant, my steadfast mercies for David. Behold, I made him a witness to the peoples' (Isa.55:3-4). That is, under such adverse conditions believers could have no hope except when this witness was put forward that God would be compassionate to them. In the same way to lift up the despairing, Jeremiah says: 'Behold, the days are coming when I will raise up for David a righteous Branch...and then Judah will be saved, and Israel will dwell securely' (Jer.23:5-6). Ezekiel, moreover, says: 'I will set over my sheep one shepherd,...namely, my servant David....I, Jehovah, will be their God, and my servant David shall be shepherd...and I will make with them a covenant of peace.' (Ezek.34:23-25p.) Elsewhere, likewise, after discussing this incredible renewal, he says: 'David, my servant, shall be their king, and shall be the one shepherd over all, ...and I will make an everlasting covenant of peace with them.' (Ezek.37:24,26p.)

"Here I am gathering a few passages of many because I merely want to remind my readers that the hope of all the godly has ever reposed in Christ alone. All the other prophets also agree. For example, in Hosea it is said: 'And the children of Judah and the children of Israel shall be gathered together, and they shall appoint for themselves one head' (Hos.1:11). This he afterward explains more clearly: 'The children of Israel shall return and seek Jehovah their God, and David their king' (Hos.3:5). Micah, also, referring to the people's return, clearly expresses it: 'Their king will pass on before them, Jehovah at their head' (Micah 2:13). So, too, Amos — meaning to foretell the renewal of the people — says: 'In that day I will raise up the tent of David that is fallen, and repair its breaches, and raise up its ruins' (Amos 9:11). This signifies: 'I will raise up once more the royal glory in the family of David, the sole standard of salvation, now fulfilled in Christ.' Hence, Zechariah, as his era was closer to the manifestation of Christ, more openly proclaims: 'Rejoice, daughter of Zion! Be jubilant, daughter of Jerusalem! Lo, your king comes to you; righteous and unharmed is he' (Zech.9:9, cf. Comm.). This agrees with the verse of the psalm already quoted: 'Jehovah is...the saving power of his Christ. Save, ...O Jehovah' (Ps.28:8-9, cf. RV marg.). Here salvation flows from the Head to the whole body." [46]

Calvin has no further comment. For him, it all refers to the Church. The apostles, on the other hand, after Jesus Himself had explained these very prophecies and more to them, asked in response, "Lord, is it at this time You are restoring the kingdom to Israel?"

Calvin ignores the apostles' question and the response of the Lord. He also deletes or ignores the references to Israel in the prophecies he quotes. He also tends to ignore all the references in the New Covenant Scriptures that indicate Messiah's special relationship with the Jewish people — e.g., Mt.2:2 where the Gentile wise men seek to find and worship the King of the Jews; Lk.1:33 where Gabriel announces that Jesus will reign over the house of Jacob forever; the identification on the cross of who Messiah crucified is, i.e.King of the Jews; etc.

For that matter, Calvin ignores the actual text of Jer.31:31-34 and Heb.8:6-

13 concerning the New Covenant. For him, there is no real content to the words of these scriptures. The reader can pretend that the words say whatever he wants. It is as though they were not really in the Bible at all.

He treats Rom.1:16, which states that the gospel is to the Jew first, and 2:9-10, which state that judgment and honor are to the Jew first, in the same way. He ignores the text. He has no comment. Likewise, he ignores Rom.9:1-5, where Paul expresses his anguish and willingness to be accursed for the salvation of Israel, and 15:25-27, where he states the principle that Gentile believers have a debt to pay for the salvation they have received through the Jewish people.

Calvin ignores altogether Rom.11:11-15, which proclaims that the salvation of all Israel will bring life from the dead to the world. He ignores 11:24-28, which exhorts Gentile believers not to be ignorant of the future salvation of all Israel. He ignores 11:30-31 which remind Gentile believers of their responsibility in the plan of God to bring salvation to those Jews who do not yet believe.

In Rom.10:15, Paul refers to Is.52:7-9, which declares,"How lovely on the mountains are the feet of him who brings good news, who announces salvation, and says to Zion, 'Your God reigns!' Listen! Your watchmen lift up their voices, they shout joyfully together; for they will see with their own eyes when the Lord restores Zion. Break forth, shout joyfully together, you waste places of Jerusalem; for the Lord has comforted His people, He has redeemed Jerusalem."

Paul, like Isaiah, is encouraging those who know the good news of salvation to bring it to the Jewish people. Paul also, like Isaiah, is affirming God's promise of restoration and redemption for Israel.

Calvin cites the same portion of the text, but relates it to the respect that is due to ministers of the gospel. [47] He eliminates both the restoration of the Jewish people and the means by which they are to be restored. He eliminates any Gentile responsibility to the Jewish people. Though he has some comments on these verses in his *Commentary on Romans*, such teachings do not fit with his theology, so they are not part of the *Institutes of the Christian Religion*. Calvin does not find them relevant to his formulation of the Christian faith. In one way or another, he treats them as though they do not exist.

CALVIN'S VIEW OF THE MILLENNIUM

What then is Calvin's view of the kingdom and the Millennium? In an extended discussion of the Lord's Prayer, he concisely presents his view of the kingdom. On the phrase, "Thy Kingdom come," he says, "But even though the definition of this Kingdom was put before us previously, I now briefly repeat it: God reigns where men, both by denial of themselves and by contempt of the world and of earthly life, pledge themselves to his righteousness in order to aspire to a heavenly life. Thus there are two parts to this Kingdom: first, that God by the power of his Spirit correct all the desires of the flesh which by squadrons war against him; second, that he shape all our thoughts in obedience to his rule." [48]

"The third petition is: that God's will may be done on earth as in heaven [Matt.6:10p.]. Even though it depends upon his Kingdom and cannot be separated from it, still it is with reason added separately on account of our ignorance, which does not easily or immediately comprehend what it means that 'God reigns in the world.' It will therefore not be absurd to take it as an explanation that God will be King in the world when all submit to his will." [49]

Calvin did not deny that the Lord would actually return to the earth and reign upon it. He believed that Jesus would return, judge, and rule. He did not, however, believe in a thousand-year reign of any kind. He believed that the return of the Lord would be followed by an eternal reign on the earth.

"It is right, therefore, that faith be called to ponder that visible presence of Christ which he will manifest on the Last Day. For he will come down from heaven in the same visible form in which he was seen to ascend (Acts 1:11; Matt.24:30). And he will appear to all with the ineffable majesty of his Kingdom, with the glow of immortality, with the boundless power of divinity, with a guard of angels. From thence we are commanded to await him as our Redeemer on that day when he will separate the lambs from the goats, the elect from the reprobate (Matt.25:31-33). No one — living or dead — shall escape his judgment. The sound of the trumpet will be heard from the ends of the earth, and by it all will be summoned before his judgment seat, both those still alive at that day and those whom death had previously taken from the company of the living (1Thess.4:16-17)." [50]

"As far as I am concerned, I not only refrain personally from superfluous investigation of useless matters, but I also think that I ought to guard against contributing to the levity of others by answering them....In short, they leave no corner of heaven exempt from their search. Then it occurs to them to ask what purpose is to be served by a restoration of the world, since the children of God will not be in need of any of this great and incomparable plenty but will be like the angels (Matt.22:30), whose abstinence from food is the symbol of eternal blessedness. But I reply that in the very sight of it there will be such pleasantness, such sweetness in the knowledge of it alone, without the use of it, that this happiness will far surpass all the amenities that we enjoy. Let us imagine ourselves set in the richest region on earth, where we lack no pleasure. Who is not from time to time hindered or prevented from enjoying God's benefits by his own illness? Who does not often have the even tenor of his life broken by his own intemperance? From this it follows that an enjoyment, clear and pure from every vice, even though it makes no use of corruptible life, is the acme of happiness." [51]

In formulating this view of an eternal earthly reign of the Lord that begins with His return, Calvin ignores Rev.19 and 20:1-5, except, in passing, as appears below. In speaking of "The error of the chiliasts," Calvin seems to simply present his contemporary adaptation of what Augustine had previously written. Calvin borrowed the term "Chiliasts" from Augustine, to signify those who believed in a one thousand year [Greek, χιλια ετη; Latin, *mille annum*] reign of Jesus upon the earth.

Calvin said that these Chiliasts "limited the reign of Christ to a thousand years. Now their fiction is too childish either to need or to be worth a refutation...Those who assign the children of God a thousand years in which to enjoy the inheritance of the life to come do not realize how much reproach they are casting upon Christ and his Kingdom. For if they do not put on immortality, then Christ himself, to whose glory they shall be transformed, has not been received into undying glory (1 Cor.15:13ff.). If their blessedness is to have an end, then Christ's Kingdom, on whose firmness it depends, is but temporary. In short, either such persons are utterly ignorant of everything divine or they are trying by a devious malice to bring to nought all the grace of God and power of Christ, the fulfillment of which is realized only when sin is blotted out, death swallowed up, and everlasting life fully restored!

"Even a blind man can see what stupid nonsense these people talk who are afraid of attributing excessive cruelty to God if the wicked be consigned to eternal punishment! If the Lord deprives of his Kingdom those who through their ungratefulness have rendered themselves unworthy of it — that, forsooth, will be too unjust!...This blasphemy is not to be borne, when God's majesty is so little esteemed, when the contempt of it is valued less than the loss of one soul. But let us pass over these triflers, lest, contrary to what we have previously said, we seem to judge their ravings worth refuting." [52]

These Chiliasts believed, or at least Calvin said that they believed, that there was only a thousand years to the kingdom of God. They did not believe in immortality. Nor did they believe in the eternal punishment of the wicked.

If those were their views, then there is ample reason for Calvin to speak out against them. Those views, however, are significantly different from those of the apostles and the early Church which they instructed.

There is the inescapable historical fact that those who wrote the New Covenant Scriptures believed in and taught a thousand-year corporeal reign of Messiah on this earth in a restored Jerusalem and Israel. No matter how people in the intervening centuries or people today interpret these scriptures, what the Biblical authors believed and meant is indisputable.

The faithful disciples who were taught by them testify that the authors of the New Covenant Scriptures taught this doctrine in their preaching and in their writings. There is no evidence to the contrary. The New Covenant Scriptures teach what those who wrote them believed and taught.

Papias tells us that they believed in the restoration of the kingdom to Israel, with Jesus reigning from Jerusalem over all the earth. Irenaeus bears witness of the same thing. So does Apollinarius. So do, according to Eusebius, "most of the ecclesiastical writers." So do, according to Jerome, "the others." The evidence is unanimous. There is none to the contrary.

As Justin told Trypho, "For it is not men, or the doctrines of men, that I choose to follow, but God and the doctrines that come from Him.

"For even if you yourselves have ever met with some so-called Christians, who yet do not acknowledge this, but even dare to blaspheme the God of Abraham, and the God of Isaac, and the God of Jacob... But I, and all other entirely orthodox Christians, know that there will be a resurrection of the flesh, and also a thousand years in a Jerusalem built up and adorned and enlarged, as the prophets Ezekiel and Isaiah, and all the rest, acknowledge." [53]

"And, further, a man among us named John, one of the apostles of Christ, prophesied in a Revelation made to him that they who have believed our Christ will spend a thousand years in Jerusalem, and that afterwards the universal, and, in one word, eternal resurrection of all at once, will take place, and also the judgment." [54] Justin's language is unequivocal.

There is no question about what the writers of the New Covenant Scriptures and those who accepted their instruction believed. A denial of the millennial reign of Messiah is a denial of the apostolic New Covenant teaching.

Inasmuch as Calvin does not comment in his *Institutes* on the particularly relevant scriptures, there is not much more that can be said here about his views on the end of the age. There are, however, three related aspects on which he does comment. It will be helpful to look at these.

"But when Christ was no longer far off, a time was appointed for Daniel 'to seal both vision and prophet' (Dan.9:24), not only that the prophetic utterance there mentioned might be authoritatively established, but also that believers might patiently go without the prophets for a time because the fullness and culmination of all revelations was at hand." [55]

Though Daniel was instructed to seal up part of his own prophecy [Dan.12:4], he was not told "to seal both vision and prophet." The text says, "Seventy weeks have been decreed for your people and your holy city...to seal up vision and prophet..." (Dan.9:24) Sometime before the end of the seventy weeks both vision and prophet are sealed up, but it did not happen during Daniel's time.

Believers did not need to "patiently go without the prophets for a time because the fullness and culmination of all revelations was at hand." By "the fullness and culmination of all revelations" Calvin meant the first coming of Jesus, which took place almost five hundred years after Daniel. Closely following Daniel were Ezra, Nehemiah, Esther, Haggai, Zechariah, and Malachi. Vision and prophet were not sealed up in their time.

Nor were they sealed up after the first coming of Jesus. The New Covenant Scriptures contain vision and prophecy in numerous places in the gospels and the epistles. The Apostle John was told, "Write therefore the things which you have seen, and the things which are, and the things which shall take place after these things." [Rev.1:19] The things which he wrote, from Rev.1:1 to 22:21, describe events in this age, in the Millennium, and beyond.

The seventy weeks of Dan.9:24 are decreed by God for Israel. Gabriel is telling Daniel of final, not temporary, events. Before the end of the seventieth week, all of them will have taken place.

The second point concerns the great tribulation. In his argument against the practice of "indulgences" which had been established by the Roman Church, Calvin again demonstrates his abuse of scripture as he, in passing, seeks to further his own theology. "Indulgences" are "the distribution of the merits of Christ and the martyrs, which the pope distributes by his bulls [decrees]." [56]

"Indulgences declare: 'Paul and others died for us.' Elsewhere Paul says, 'Christ acquired the church with his own blood.' (Acts 20:28p.) Indulgences establish another purchase price in the blood of martyrs. 'By a single offering Christ has perfected for all time those who are sanctified.' Indulgences proclaim: Sanctification, otherwise insufficient, is perfected by the martyrs. John says that 'all the saints have washed their robes....in the blood of the Lamb.' (Rev.7:14) Indulgences teach that they wash their robes in the blood of the saints." [57]

There can be no disagreement with Calvin's rebuke and refutation of the practice of indulgences. He battled against " a deep night of errors [in which] men were immersed for centuries." But there is an interesting error in his argument.

John does **not** say that "all the saints have washed their robes....in the blood of the Lamb." (Rev.7:14) He says, "These are the ones who come out of the great tribulation, and they have washed their robes and made them white in the blood of the Lamb." It is not critical to his particular argument against indulgences, but Calvin first changes the text, and then deletes the reference to "the great tribulation."

If only a particular group of saints, at a particular time, go through the Great Tribulation, then the Great Tribulation is obviously a particular, literal period of time. If the Great Tribulation is a particular, literal period of time, then it is preceded and followed by other particular, literal events, like the return of the Lord with the saints for Israel, events which Calvin had "spiritualized."

A literal Great Tribulation was therefore not acceptable to Calvin. There is no place for it in his theology. He did not want to deal with it in context. So he deletes it.

The third point concerns the Antichrist. "Daniel (Dan.9:27) and Paul (2Thess.2:4) foretold that Antichrist would sit in the Temple of God. With us, it is the Roman pontiff we make the leader and standard bearer of that wicked and abominable kingdom. The fact that his seat is placed in the Temple of God signifies that his reign was not to be such as to wipe out either the name of Christ or of the church." [58]

"To some we seem slanderers and railers when we call the Roman pontiff 'Antichrist.' But those who think so do not realize they are accusing Paul of intemperate language, after whom we speak, indeed, so speak from his very lips. And lest anyone object that we wickedly twist Paul's words (which apply to another) against the Roman pontiff, I shall briefly show that these cannot be understood otherwise than of the papacy. Paul writes that Antichrist will sit in God's temple...Since, therefore, it is clear that the Roman pontiff has shamelessly transferred to himself what belonged to God alone and especially to Christ, we should have no doubt that he is the leader and standard-bearer of that impious and hateful kingdom."[59]

"Indeed, Paul plainly shows that the Antichrist will sit in no other place than the temple of God (2Thess.2:4). By this he means that the terrible calamity of which he there speaks will come from no other source than from those who will sit as pastors in the church." [60]

Calvin rejects the idea of a physical temple, but he accepts the idea of a physical Antichrist. He rejected the idea of a physical temple, because he did not believe in a future restoration of the Jewish people to the land of Israel, and a subsequent rebuilding of the Temple. He accepted the idea of a physical Antichrist, because he was faced with particular individuals whom he perceived as evil incarnate. Because of his historical circumstances, "pastors in the church" became Antichrist in the temple.

He distorts the Scriptures to make them fit his own historical situation. Luther shared this same selective belief and general practice.

FOOTNOTES

1. *Calvin:Institutes of the Christian Religion*, op. cit., Bk.1, Ch.7.1-2, Pp.74-76
2. ibid., Bk.2, Ch.5.19, P.339
3. ibid., Bk.3, Ch.4.5, Pp.628-629
4. *Calvin:Institutes of the Christian Religion*, op. cit., Bk.2, Ch.6.1, P.342
5. ibid., Bk.2, Ch.10.3-4, Pp.431-432
6. ibid., Bk.4, Ch.16.13, P.1335
7. ibid., Bk.2, Ch.11.11, Pp.460-461
8. ibid., Bk.2, Ch.11.8, P.457

9. ibid., Bk.3, Ch.17.1, P.803
10. ibid., Bk.2, Ch.11.10, P.460
11. *Calvin:Institutes of the Christian Religion*, op. cit., Bk.4, Ch.9.3, Pp.1168
12. ibid., Bk.4, Ch.16.13, Pp.1335-1336
13. ibid., Bk.2, Ch.11.12, Pp.461-462
14. ibid., Bk.3, Ch.21.6, P.929
15. ibid., Bk.3, Ch.21.6, P.929
16. ibid., Bk.3, Ch.21.6, Pp.929-930
17. ibid., Bk.3, Ch.21.6, P.930
18. ibid., Bk.4, Ch.2.3, P.1044
19. *Calvin:Institutes of the Christian Religion*, op. cit., Bk.2, Ch.8.14, P.365
20. ibid., Bk.3, Ch.4.29, P.656
21. ibid., Bk.4, Ch.16.14, Pp.1336-1337
22. ibid., Bk.2, Ch.7.17, P.365
23. *Calvin:Institutes of the Christian Religion*, op. cit., Bk.3, Ch.1.1, P.537
24. ibid., Bk.3, Ch.15.5, P.793
25. *Calvin's Commentaries, The Epistles of Paul the Apostle to the Romans and to the Thessalonians*, Translated by Ross Mackenzie, Edited by David W. Torrance & Thomas F. Torrance, Oliver and Boyd, Edinburgh, 1961, P.250
26. ibid., Bk.1, Ch.7.5, P.81
27. ibid., Bk.3, Ch.6.1, P.342
28. ibid., Bk.3, Ch.24.6, P.972
29. ibid., Bk.3, Ch.6, P.930
30. ibid., Bk.3, Ch.2.22, P.569
31. ibid., Bk.3, Ch.24.7, P.974
32. *Calvin's Commentaries, The Epistles of Paul the Apostle to the Romans and to the Thessalonians*, op. cit., P.248
33. ibid., P.251
34. ibid., P.252
35. ibid., P.253
36. *Calvin:Institutes of the Christian Religion*, op. cit., Bk.3, Ch.22.6, P.938
37. ibid., cf. Bk.1, Ch.14.14, P.174; Bk.1, Ch.14.15, P.175; Bk.3, Ch.23.4, P.952
38. *Calvin:Institutes of the Christian Religion*, op. cit., Bk.4, Ch.16.14, P.1337
39. ibid., Bk.2, Ch.11.1, Pp.450-451
40. ibid., Bk.3, Ch.24.14, P.981
41. ibid., Bk.3, Ch.20.35, P.898
42. ibid., Bk.3, Ch.22.6, P.939
43. *Calvin's Commentaries, The Epistles of Paul the Apostle to the Romans and to the Thessalonians*, op. cit., P.10
44. ibid., P.255
45. Frederic Louis Godet, *Commentary on Romans*, Kregel, Grand Rapids, 1977, P.410
46. *Calvin:Institutes of the Christian Religion*, op. cit., Bk.2, Ch.6.3, Pp.345-346
47. ibid., Bk.4, Ch.3.3, P.1055-1056
48. *Calvin:Institutes of the Christian Religion*, op. cit., Bk.3, Ch.20.42, P.905

49. ibid., Bk.3, Ch.20.43, P.906
50. ibid., Bk.2, Ch.16.17, P.525
51. ibid., Bk.3, Ch.25.11, Pp.1006-1007
52. ibid., Bk.3, Ch.25.5, Pp.995-996
53. Justin Martyr, *The Dialogue with Trypho*, translated by A. Lukyn Williams, S.P.C.K., London, 1930, P.169, Sec. 80.1-5
54. ibid., P.172, Sec. 81.4
55. ibid., Bk.2, Ch.15.1, P.495
56. ibid., Bk.3, Ch.5.1, P.670
57. ibid., Bk.3, Ch.5.2, P.672
58. ibid., Bk.4, Ch.3.12, P.1052
59. ibid., Bk.4, Ch.7.25, Pp.1144-1145
60. ibid., Bk.4, Ch.9.4, Pp.1168-1169

LUTHER'S *COMMENTARY ON ROMANS*

Martin Luther's *Commentary on Romans* is considered one of the most influential books of all time. It formed a major part of the foundation on which the Reformation was built. It was written from sermons which Luther delivered in 1515-1516, a year or two before he nailed "The Ninety-five Theses" to the Wittenberg church door. It reveals both his strengths and his weaknesses.

Concerning the scriptures in Romans that speak of a continuing role for the Jewish people in God's plan of redemption for the world, Luther responds in basically two ways. He says nothing at all, or he greatly distorts the text, sometimes maintaining that it means the opposite of what it says. Two preliminary examples will show how pronounced this tendency is. Then we can proceed through his *Commentary* from the beginning, noting some of his anti-Biblical, anti-Judaic remarks.

First, an example of his silence: Luther's *Commentary on Romans* begins with an introductory summation of the content of Romans, chapter by chapter. He devotes only three paragraphs to chapters nine, ten, and eleven. He summarizes the content of these three chapters without once mentioning Israel or the Jewish people. Considering the content of these chapters, that is more than amazing.

His commentary on Rom.11:28 provides a clear example of how he distorts the text and maintains that it means the opposite of what it actually says. The verse is: "From the standpoint of the gospel they are enemies for your sake, but from the standpoint of God's choice they are beloved for the sake of the fathers."

Luther comments: "*As concerning the gospel, they are enemies for your sakes* (11:28). The word 'enemies' must here be taken in a passive sense; that is, they deserve to be hated. God hates them, and so they are hated by the Apostles and all who are of God." [1]

Paul says that the Jews who do not yet believe are beloved of God. Luther says the opposite. We'll look at this again when we get to his comments on chapter 11, but here it serves to highlight a serious aberration in Luther's theology.

After his introduction, Luther begins a general commentary on Romans before he proceeds to a verse by verse commentary. Wherever they appear, the notes of the modern editor are given in *italic* in parentheses (). There are some remarks that Luther makes in this general commentary that help us to understand his whole approach to the letter.

"There are many who indeed for God's sake, regard temporal blessings as nothing and gladly renounce them, as, for example, Jews and heretics. But there are very few who regard also their spiritual gifts and good works as nothing, seeking to obtain only the righteousness of Christ. Of this Jews and heretics are incapable, though without this no one can be saved." [2]

When Luther says "heretics," he is essentially referring to "the papists," the followers of the papal system. He generally places Jews and heretics in the same category (sometimes including "Turks," i.e. Muslims, also). In this case, he is saying that Jews and heretics are incapable of "seeking to obtain only the righteousness of Christ."

In saying this, he obviously is forgetting that Moses and David, for example, are Jews. He is also forgetting that all the early Church was Jewish. And, of course, he is forgetting that the author of Romans is Jewish.

So, forgetting all the Jews who have believed since God created the Jewish people, Luther maintains that Jews are "incapable" of "seeking to obtain only the righteousness of Christ." The reality of believing Jews — "the remnant according to God's gracious choice" — cannot be reconciled with Luther's theology, and so the reality does not exist for him.

Luther comments on Paul's motive for writing the letter: "Regarding the Epistle, I do not believe that its recipients, who are addressed as 'beloved of God' and 'called saints,' were in such a situation that the Apostle found it necessary to intervene because of existing dissensions and to regard them all as (*gross*) sinners. If really they were Christians, they knew this, (*the need of peace and concord*), as believers. I rather think that he used the opportunity of writing to them because they were Christian believers. They were to have a testimony of their faith and doctrine from the pen of the great Apostle for their controversies with Jews and Gentiles." [3]

Paul wrote the letter to believers in Rome, primarily to Gentile believers. "Paul, a bond-servant of Messiah Jesus, ...through whom we have received grace and apostleship to bring about the obedience of faith among all the Gentiles, for His name's sake, among whom you also are the called of Messiah Jesus." (Rom.1:1,5-6) His main audience are those who are the object of his ministry, "the Gentiles...among whom you also are..." That is what Paul says.

He addresses certain sections of the letter to Jewish believers, and he greets some of them by name in the close of the letter. "Greet Prisca and Aquila [16:3, cf. Acts 18:2]...Greet Andronicus and Junias, my kinsmen [16:7]...Greet Herodion my kinsman [16:11]..." There are things that he wants them to know, too, but that was not his motivation in writing.

Paul explicitly declares why he has written this letter to the Romans. "But I have written very boldly to you on some points, so as to remind you again, because of the grace that was given me from God, to be a minister of Messiah Jesus to the Gentiles, ministering as a priest the gospel of God, that my offering of the Gentiles might become acceptable, sanctified by the Holy Spirit." (15:15-16)

Why did Paul write his letter to the Romans? Luther thinks Paul wrote it so the Roman believers might "have a testimony of their faith and doctrine from the pen of the great Apostle for their controversies with Jews and Gentiles." Luther thought that Paul was writing to give the Roman believers theological ammunition against their unbelieving adversaries.

Though Paul's letter to the Romans is certainly helpful in presenting a defense of the faith, as are his other letters, that was not his purpose in writing it. Luther has imposed his own historical situation — his controversy with his theological adversaries — upon Paul. Luther is incorrect.

Paul himself says, "I have written very boldly to you on some points...that my offering of the Gentiles might become acceptable, sanctified by the Holy Spirit." There are some things that the Gentile believers in Rome are not doing that they need to do to make Paul's offering of them to God acceptable. There are some things that the Gentile believers in Rome are doing that they need to stop doing. Otherwise, Paul's offering of them to God will not be acceptable. That is why he wrote to them. He did not want his labors to be in vain.

Because Luther did not correctly perceive Paul's audience or purpose, he often did not correctly perceive either the issues that Paul was addressing or the points he was making. This will become more evident as we look at some of his commentary.

CHAPTERS 1 THROUGH 4

Luther makes no comment on the particularity of Paul's "apostleship for obedience to the faith **among all Gentiles** (1:5)," or his desire to "have some fruit among you also, even as **among other Gentiles**." (1:13) He speaks at length about 1:16, but has no comment at all on the last part of the verse — "to the Jew first, and also to the Greek."

He has an interesting comment on the phrase in 1:25, "Who is blessed for ever. Amen." He begins by saying, "The Apostle evidently adds this blessing because of his Jewish piety; for whenever the Jewish teachers mention God, they supplement it with such terms as the 'Holy One,' or the 'Blessed One,' as Caiaphas did when he asked: 'Art thou the Christ, the Son of the Blessed?' (Mark 14:61)

"But alas, most people even today entertain unworthy thoughts of God and assert in a bold, not to say, arrogant way that God is so or so. They do not do Him the honor to admit that the glorious God is supremely exalted over their reason and judgment, but they elevate their own opinions so highly that they have no more difficulty or fear to judge God than they judge the leather of a poor shoemaker. They think that God's righteousness and mercy are just so as they imagine them to be; and although they are without the Spirit who knows even the deep things of God, in their arrogance they boast as though they were full, yes, more than full of Him.

"So do the heretics, the Jews, and all men of conceited mind, all indeed who are outside divine grace." [4] Luther begins by praising Paul's Jewish piety and closes by condemning "heretics, the Jews, and all men of conceited mind" who do not honor God and are therefore "outside divine grace."

Luther does not notice the contradiction between his praise and his condemnation. On the one hand, Luther says that Paul's traditional Jewish piety causes him to honor God. On the other, he says that Jews are incapable of honoring God or receiving His grace.

Is it not the Jews who brought the Scriptures to the world? Is it not the Jews who brought the gospel to the Gentiles? Is it not a Jew who wrote the letter to the Romans (and to the Galatians, etc.) to teach the Gentiles about the nature of "divine grace"?

In his closing comments on chapter one, Luther characterizes the ingratitude of man. In doing so, he describes his own behavior toward the Jewish people: "*Being filled with...maliciousness* (1:29). Maliciousness is the perverse tendency in man to do evil despite the good which he has received; indeed he abuses even the good things which God gives him in the service of evil. Conversely, goodness is the right disposition in man to do good even when his effort is hindered or checked by some wrong done to him...

"...in Luke 6:35:'But love ye your enemies, and do good, and lend, hoping for nothing again; and your reward shall be great, and ye shall be children of the Highest: for he is kind unto the unthankful and to the evil.' Malevolence, on the contrary, is the perverse, hateful tendency to hurt or harm others. In his total depravity man does injury even to those who are grateful and good, and not merely to the evil...

"*Being filled with...malignity* (1:29). Malignity is the perverse tendency willfully to omit what is good and to hinder what is evil. Some act in this way because of envy, but others from an impudence that cries to high heaven." [5]

He continues the theme in his opening comments on 2:1. "This mistake (*of condemning others though guilty themselves*) is committed by all who are outside of Christ; for, while the righteous (*true believers*) make it a point to accuse themselves in thought, word and deed, the unrighteous (*unbelievers*) make it a point always to accuse and judge others, at least in their hearts. For this (*fact*) there is an explanation. The righteous invariably try to see their own faults and overlook those of others. Again, they are eager to recognize the good things in others and to disregard those of their own. On the other hand, the unrighteous look for good in themselves and for evil in others....

"The Apostle therefore at the beginning of the chapter stresses the thought that in his accusation he has in mind mainly the Jews. To them we may compare, in a special degree, the heretics and hypocrites as also our modern jurists and priests, and lastly also those who quarrel among themselves and judge one another, while they do not regard themselves as offenders.

Indeed they boast of their being right and even invoke God's wrath upon their adversaries..." [6]

Luther correctly characterizes the way a believer should behave, and the way unbelievers do behave, but he does not act the way he says a believer should. It can easily be seen that throughout his *Commentary on Romans*, Luther seems to "make it a point always to accuse and judge others." He tends to "look for good in [himself]and for evil in others." He "boast[s] of [his] being right and even invoke[s] God's wrath upon [his] adversaries."

That sometimes makes his silence preferable to his comments. The text of 2:9-10 is, "Tribulation and distress for every soul of man who does evil, of the Jew first and also of the Greek, but glory and honor and peace to every man who does good, to the Jew first and also to the Greek." On 2:9, Luther cuts off "of the Jew first and also of the Greek" before commenting. He ignores 2:10 altogether. There is nothing that he can say. The text cannot be fit into his theology.

The rest of his comments on chapter two, as well as his comments on chapter three and four, are fairly straightforward and well related to the text. He continues, however, to understand "Jews" as referring only to unbelievers. Though most Jews are not believers, some, like the apostle writing the letter, are. The same is true of Gentiles, too.

Luther's comments on chapters five through eight do not directly relate to the relationship of the Jewish people and the Church. So we will skip over them to his comments on chapters nine and ten.

CHAPTERS 9 AND 10

Luther takes the strange position that Paul is addressing this chapter to unbelieving Jews, though in his introduction he claimed that Paul wrote the letter to provide theological ammunition against unbelieving Jews. By taking this strange position, Luther is able to evade the cry of Paul's heart. (Calvin does much the same in his commentary on Romans.)

Luther quotes part of the third verse and comments, "*I could wish that myself were accursed from Christ for my brethren.* (9:3) The Apostle begins this chapter with a strong affirmation and oath, moved to this by an irrepressible urgency. With these words he desires to win their confidence; for he was regarded by the Jews as one who was not at all interested in their salvation; indeed, as one who above all others persecuted them and destroyed their salvation...." [7]

Luther makes multiple errors here. First, Paul wrote the letter, and addressed his remarks, "to all who are beloved of God in Rome, called saints. Grace to you and peace from God our Father and the Lord Jesus the Messiah." (1:7) Paul is not writing to unbelieving Jews, he is writing to believers. Paul's language and the content of his remarks do not indicate that he is speaking to unbelieving Jews, but rather that he is speaking **about** them.

Second, Paul would not gain the confidence of unbelieving Jews by being willing to be "accursed from Christ" for their sake. Those who were hostile towards him would desire of him nothing more than that he be accursed and separated from Christ.

Third, Luther's comment — "he was regarded by the Jews as one who was not at all interested in their salvation; indeed, as one who above all others persecuted them and destroyed their salvation" — is a strange invention.

What exactly does Luther mean? Does he mean that unbelieving Jews had the same concept of salvation, but saw Paul as indifferent to it? That was not the case. Some had a different concept of salvation. They could have considered Paul hostile to the true well-being of Israel, but not indifferent.

Does Luther then mean that unbelieving Jews saw Paul as being "not at all interested in," or hostile to, the national salvation of Israel? Certainly that was not the case, but there is no evidence that anyone in the first century thought that Paul persecuted unbelieving Jews.

In the Temple, there were Jews from Asia who cried, "Men of Israel, come to our aid! This is the man who preaches to all men everywhere against our people, and the Law, and this place; and besides he has even brought Greeks into the temple and has defiled this holy place." (Acts 21:28) They were, of course, wrong on all counts.

The Jews from Asia made four charges: 1. "This is the man who preaches to all men everywhere against our people." 2. "This is the man who preaches to all men everywhere against...the Law" 3. "This is the man who preaches to all men everywhere against...this place." 4. "He has even brought Greeks into the temple and has defiled this holy place."

If these charges are what Luther had in mind, then Paul's response should reveal the motivation that Luther says he had. It does not. Instead, Paul used the incident as an opportunity to speak of how he came to believe in Jesus.

Paul knew how to address each of the charges. He did so later in his defense to Felix before Ananias, Tertullus, and the Jewish elders: "You can take note of the fact that no more than twelve days ago I went up to Jerusalem to worship. [a response to charge #3] And neither in the temple, nor in the synagogues, nor in the city itself did they find me carrying on a discussion with anyone or causing a riot. [a response to charge #4]...But this I admit to you, that according to the Way which they call a sect I so serve the God of our fathers, believing everything that is in accordance with the Law, and that is written in the Prophets. [a response to charge #2]...Now after several years I came to bring alms to my nation and to present offerings; in which they found me occupied in the temple, having been purified, without any crowd or uproar. [a response to charges #1&4]..." (Acts 24:14,17)

If Paul wanted to tell his unbelieving brethren what Luther suggests, then this would have been the ideal opportunity to do it. Paul did not seek to assure the unbelieving Jews who were there that he was concerned about their salvation. Nor would testifying of his willingness to be "accursed from Christ" have spoken to their fears, doubts, or anger. It would only have further provoked them.

In Romans 9, Paul is not speaking to unbelieving Jews. He is speaking to the church at Rome. That is what he himself says. He is trying to communicate to the church the intensity and urgency of his desire to see the salvation of "my brethren, my kinsmen according to the flesh, who are Israelites."

Luther continues, *"My brethren, my kinsmen according to the flesh: who are Israelites; to whom pertaineth the adoption (9:3-4)*...He desires for the Jews the greatest salvation, and he is willing to lose his own salvation if only they would gain theirs. He says the same thing in II Corinthians 12:15: 'I will very gladly spend and be spent for you.'

"For those who truly love God with a love that comes from the Holy Spirit these words are most wonderful. Such (*consecrated and loving Christians*) never seek what is their own, but they are willing to suffer hell and damnation, in order that God's will might be accomplished (*in the salvation of others*). So also Christ was condemned and forsaken more than all His saints." [8]

What Paul says in Rom.9:3-4 is **not** "the same thing [that he says] in 2 Corinthians 12:15." The two statements are similar, they both speak of giving of self, but they are not at all the same. In 2 Co.12:15, Paul is expressing his willingness to pour out his life for believers.

He wrote to the Corinthians, "For in what respect were you treated as inferior to the rest of the churches, except that I myself did not become a burden to you? Forgive me this wrong! Here for this third time I am ready to come to you, and I will not be a burden to you; for I do not seek what is yours, but you; for children are not responsible to save up for their parents, but parents for their children. And I will most gladly spend and be expended for your souls. If I love you the more, am I to be loved the less? But be that as it may, I did not burden you myself...Certainly I have not taken advantage of you through any of those whom I sent to you, have I?...Titus did not take any advantage of you, did he?..." (2Co.12:13-18)

What Paul is saying is certainly "wonderful." It certainly should be an example for all "who truly love God." But it is certainly not the same as what he is saying in Rom.9:1-5. What he says there is in another realm altogether.

In Rom.9:3-4, Paul is expressing his willingness to be accursed forever — he is willing to lose his own salvation and be damned for eternity — for the salvation of his unbelieving brethren. There is a tremendous difference between this and what he says in 2Co.12:15.

Luther comes very close to grasping what Paul is saying, but he seems to want to get away from it. With pointed editing, Luther says, "He desires for the Jews the greatest salvation, and he is willing to lose his own salvation if only they would gain theirs...in order that God's will might be accomplished." Paul is saying, 'The salvation of Israel is so much the will and desire of God that I would choose an eternity of torment in order to bring it about.' To grasp what Paul is saying means to be grasped by it, and that Luther is unprepared and unwilling to do.

Luther's comments on chapter ten are fairly accurate, but, in some places, his tendency to avoid the implications of what Paul is saying comes through. He begins, "*Brethren, my heart's desire and my prayer to God for Israel is, that they might be saved.* (10:1) Here, according to St. Augustine, the Apostle begins to speak of the hope of the Jews, in order that the heathen might not exalt themselves over the Jews. For as he had to reject the arrogance of the Jews inasmuch as they gloried in their works, he now must oppose the Gentiles, in order that they might not be overbearing as though God preferred them to the Jews." [9]

Paul is against arrogance, whether Jewish or Gentile, whether in Rome, Jerusalem, or any place else. He is continually exposing and denouncing it in this letter. From prison in Rome, Paul wrote to the saints in Philippi. He told them that because of his imprisonment many of the believers in Rome have begun to boldly preach the gospel. "Some, to be sure, are preaching Messiah even from envy and strife, but some also from good will...What then? Only that in every way, whether in pretense or in truth, Messiah is proclaimed; and in this I rejoice, yes, and I will rejoice." (Phil.1:15,18)

Paul is against arrogance, but what is it that he wants from the church at Rome? He has been praying, preaching, and pouring out his life so that those Jews who do not yet believe might be saved. He is expressing his heart's desire so that the believers in Rome will embrace the same desire. If they have the same desire, they will do as he does. Luther has sidestepped the point.

The parts of the Scriptures that he does not want to see have become invisible. On 10:12 — "For there is no distinction between Jew and Greek; for the same Lord is Lord of all, abounding in riches for all who call upon Him" — Luther ignores the first part of the verse. He previously ignored 3:29 altogether where Paul is making a similar point.

Paul is making the point that Jews and Gentiles are both saved in the same way. Luther seems not to like to think about Jews being saved, so he ignores it as much as possible. He doesn't mind if they are saved, in fact he would like to see it happen, but he prefers to think that a Jew who believes is no longer a Jew. He states this fairly explicitly in his *Commentary on Galatians*.

In Gal.3:28, Paul writes, "There is neither Jew nor Greek, there is neither slave nor free man, there is neither male nor female; for you are all one in Messiah Jesus." Paul is not maintaining that those distinctions are obliterated, he is emphasizing that all are made one by coming to God in the same way. There is one new man, Messiah, whose body has many different members.

Luther comments, "The Apostle speaketh not here of the Jew according to his nature and substance: but he calleth him a Jew, who is the disciple of Moses, is subject to the law, is circumcised, and with all his endeavour keepeth the ceremonies commanded by the law. For Christ hath abolished all the laws of Moses that ever were. Wherefore, the conscience believing in Christ must be so surely persuaded that the law is abolished, with its terrors and threatenings, that it should be utterly ignorant whether there were ever any Moses, any law, or any Jew. For Christ and Moses can in no wise agree. Moses came with the law, with works, and with ceremonies; but Christ came without law, or works, or ceremonies, giving grace and righteousness, remission of sins and eternal life: 'For the law was given by Moses, but grace and truth came by Jesus Christ' (St. John i.17)." [10] [There is no "but" in the text of John 1:17.]

Luther makes five serious errors in this one comment. First, he says, "The Apostle speaketh not here of the Jew according to his nature and substance," but that is exactly what the apostle is speaking of. As Paul notes earlier in Gal.2:15-16, he had said to Peter, "**We are Jews by nature**...even we have believed in Messiah Jesus, that we may be justified by faith in Messiah..." Paul and Peter are believers, but they are still Jews by nature.

Second, Luther asserts that "Christ hath abolished all the laws of Moses that ever were." But Jesus said, "Do not think that I came to abolish the Law or the Prophets; I did not come to abolish, but to fulfill." (Mt.5:17)

Third, Luther says that "the conscience believing in Christ must be so surely persuaded that the law is abolished, with its terrors and threatenings, that it should be utterly ignorant whether there were ever any Moses, any law, or any Jew." But Paul's conscience did not operate that way. By Moses and the law, he was led to Messiah. (Gal.3:24) In Messiah he became fully Jewish. (Rom.2:28-29) Luther previously commented on chapter 2, "Only he is a genuine Jew who is one inwardly (v.29), that is, who believes in Christ." [11] And this Christ, in whom Paul believes, is the Son of David, the King of Israel. (Rom.1:3)

Fourth, Luther claims that, "Christ and Moses can in no wise agree." But Jesus said, "For if you believed Moses, you would believe Me; for he wrote of Me." (Jn.5:46) And Paul notes, "So then, the Law is holy, and the commandment is holy and righteous and good...For we know that the Law is spiritual..." (Rom.7:12,14) In his commentary on Romans chapter 7, Luther ignores these verses. In his theology, "Jews" are inseparably linked to "Law," and therefore opposed to "Christ."

Fifth, Luther maintains that, "Christ came without law or works, or ceremonies." Jesus said, "But the witness which I have is greater than that of John; for the works which the Father has given Me to accomplish, the very works that I do, bear witness of Me, that the Father has sent Me....If I do not do the works of My Father, do not believe Me; but if I do them, though you do not believe Me, believe the works; that you may know and understand that the Father is in Me, and I in the Father...For if you believed Moses, you would believe Me; for he wrote of Me...Which one of you convicts Me of sin?..." (Jn.5:36; 10:37-38; 5:46; 8:46)

Jesus came as a Jew, did the works of the Law, and observed the ceremonies which God had prepared before the foundation of the world. If Jesus had come without works, then all the children of Adam would still be lost. "So then as through one transgression there resulted condemnation to all men; even so through one act of righteousness there resulted justification of life to all men. For as through the one man's disobedience the many were made sinners, even so through the obedience of the One the many will be made righteous." (Rom.5:18-19)

Luther is not able to read the Scriptures as Paul wrote them. He imposes upon them his own conflict with the Roman Catholic Church, believing that Paul's conflict with "the Judaizers" was exactly the same. That was not so.

Paul also sought to establish that one must be justified by faith and not by works, but Paul was not hostile to the Law. It had not saved him, but it had led him to Messiah. Paul kept the ceremonies — Passover, Pentecost, Yom Kippur, etc. He purified himself, paid the expenses of sacrifice for others, and went to the Temple to demonstrate, in Jacob's words, "that you yourself also walk orderly, keeping the Law." (Acts 21:20-26)

Paul himself, as a Jew, did things that he knew should not be imposed on Gentiles. The issue for Paul was twofold: 1. No one can be justified before God by the Law — "by the works of the Law no flesh will be justified in His sight;" and 2. Gentiles do not need to be circumcised and become proselytes — "how is that you compel the Gentiles to live like Jews?" Luther, on the other hand, de-Judaizes Paul, turning him into a Gentile and separating him from the Jewish people.

Luther distorts Paul's point in 10:13-15. *"How shall they call on him in whom they have not believed* (10:14) Here the Apostle meets the arrogance of the proud Jews; indeed, the arrogance of all who teach falsely and are of a haughty mind. Oh, that the false prophets only would heed these words!

"How shall they believe in him of whom they have not heard? and how shall they hear without a preacher? (10:14) Even though they say that they hear, they boast in vain, unless they hear true preachers; for to hear false prophets means as much as not to hear. They hear and they do not hear; they have ears, but do not hear, nor do they preach (*the Word of God*). This is a striking statement against all conceited and arrogant hearers and students (*of the Bible*).

"How shall they preach, except they be sent? (10:15). This is directed against all conceited teachers and arrogant instructors...So, then, the entire source and origin of salvation rests on this, that God sends out someone. If He does not send out any, then they who preach preach falsely, and their preaching is no preaching at all. In fact, it would be better for them not to preach. Then also they who hear, hear error, and it would be better for them not to hear. Then also they who believe, would believe false doctrine, and it would be better for them not to believe. Then also they who call upon Him would call falsely, and it would be better for them not to call. For such preachers do not preach; such hearers do not hear; such believers do not believe; such callers do not call; they will be damned because they would be saved (*by falsehood*).

"How beautiful are the feet of them that preach the gospel of peace (10:15). By this quotation the Apostle shows that only those can preach truly who are sent (*by God*). Those cannot preach the divine Word and be messengers of God whom He has not sent and to whom He has not entrusted His Word." [12]

Luther's statements may well contain some truth — they may even be good preaching — but they are not what Paul is writing about. Paul begins chapter 10 by expressing his heart's desire for the salvation of all Israel. In chapter 11, he explains why this is so important.

In this section, Paul is not rebuking unbelievers, he is showing the necessity of preaching the gospel to them. He is not pointing out differences between true and false ministers, messages, and faiths. He is encouraging believers to send forth God's messenger with God's message.

Luther has presented Paul's appeal as though the apostle intended it to be a method for distinguishing between papists and Reformers. While it may be possible to draw such an application, there is nothing in the text that supports such an "interpretation."

CHAPTER 11

"I say then, Hath God cast away his people? God forbid (11:1). The Apostle now reaches the end of his discussion and concludes what he began in Chapter 9, where he said: 'Not as though the word of God hath taken none effect (v.6)'. Or, already in Chapter 3, where he said: 'Shall their unbelief make the faith of God without effect (3:3)?' He treats this subject with such

great earnestness in order that he may destroy the arrogant boasting of the Jews regarding their merits by emphasizing the firm and immutable faithfulness of God...

"*I also am an Israelite* (11:1). Here the Apostle concludes from the smaller to the greater; for had God cast away His people, then above all He would have cast away the Apostle Paul, who had opposed Him with all his might. But now, to prove that he does not reject His people, God accepted even one who was hopelessly lost. In this way the Apostle shows how firm God's predestination and election stands, for not even the most desperate circumstances could hinder it (*God's plan of salvation*). So, very rightly, the Apostle adds: 'God hath not cast away his people which he foreknew (v.2).' He means to say: This He has proved in my own case, for He has not cast away me; much less has He cast away the others who did not depart from Him.

"*I am left alone and they seek my life* (11:3). The Apostle argues against them (the Jews) with a most effective illustration. He means to say: If you believe that either God is a liar or that none of you is cast away, what are you going to say regarding the case where something similar actually took place? If then it was foolish to think that God will not cast away His people, it is foolish at this time, when experience teaches the same thing. The Jews arrogantly assumed that they were God's people, simply because the heathen were not His people." [13]

Is Paul, in these verses, arguing against the Jews? Is he saying to unbelieving Jews, "it is foolish...to think that God will not cast away His people"? Is he trying to destroy their "arrogant boasting"?

That is not what Paul is talking about at all. As he points out in v.13, he is addressing himself to Gentile believers. It is to Gentile believers that he is saying, "it is foolish...to think that God **will** cast away His people." Luther is saying the opposite of what Paul is saying.

Luther seeks to cut off Israel by equating the remnant with "His people which He foreknew." He is suggesting that only the elect remnant was foreknown, i.e. chosen by "predestination." There are two problems with Luther's attempt.

First, the word [προεγνω] that is translated "foreknew" (v.2) means those whom He "knew before." Paul uses it in his defense before King Agrippa: "So then, all Jews know my manner of life from my youth up...who before knew [προγινωσκοντες] me from the first..." (Acts 26:4-5) Peter tells believers of events to come, and then says, "You therefore, beloved, knowing beforehand [προγινωσκοντες], beware..." (2Pet.3:17)

It is not a word that denotes "predestination and election." It denotes prior knowledge. God told Israel long before, "You only have I known of all the families of the earth..." (Am.3:2)

Luther says, "The Jews arrogantly assumed that they were God's people, simply because the heathen were not His people." Luther is wrong. It is God who told the Jews that they were His people. As Moses told Israel, "For you are a holy people to the Lord your God; the Lord your God has chosen you to be a people for His own possession out of all the peoples who are on the face of the earth." (Dt.7:6)

Second, Paul points to the chosen remnant as proof that God has not cast away Israel. He is not pointing to the remnant as proof that God has not cast away the remnant. A remnant is not a people. It is a part of a people.

Paul is not saying that God did not cast away those who believe in Him. He points to physical descent to delineate the people who have not been cast away. God did not cast away the people, Israel, that He created for His ongoing purposes of redemption.

"Have they stumbled that they should fall? God forbid: but rather through their fall salvation is come unto the Gentiles, for to provoke them to jealousy (11:11). 'Now if the fall of them be the riches of the world, and the diminishing of them the riches of the Gentiles; how much more their fulness' (v.12)? That means: If faith has come to the heathen, because the Jews fell, how much more would it have come to them (*the heathen*), had they stood firm. Hence they, (*the Jews*), did not fall merely 'to fall,' but rather that they should rise again, encouraged by the example of the Gentiles." [14]

Translations sometimes obscure the fact that Paul used different words for "stumbled," "fall," and "offense." "Have they stumbled [επταισαν] that they should fall [πεσωσιν]? God forbid: but rather through their offense [παραπτωματι] salvation is come unto the Gentiles..." It was not "because the Jews fell," but rather because those Jews who did not believe offended/ transgressed that salvation has come to the Gentiles.

Paul is explaining that, in the sovereignty of God, the blinding of the rest of Israel was necessary for the salvation of the Gentiles. Their stumbling caused the people that God was seeking to worship Him in Spirit and in Truth to remain incomplete. Their stumbling is one of the twin means through which salvation became available to the Gentiles. The other is through the obedience of the remnant. Both were necessary. Luther seeks to eliminate the causal relationship.

Paul goes on to say, "how much more will their fulness be...[than the current] riches of the world, and...the riches of the Gentiles." Luther twists this to "how much more would it [salvation] have come to them (*the heathen*), had they stood firm." That eliminates the prophetic thrust of Paul's statement.

Luther did correctly understand from this verse that "they [those Jews who did not believe] did not fall merely 'to fall,' but rather that they should rise again." In God's plan, there is a time for the restoration of all Israel. Unfortunately, Luther later rejected what he clearly saw in the Scriptures here.

"Inasmuch as I am the apostle of the Gentiles, I magnify mine office: if by any

means I may provoke to emulation them which are of my flesh, and might save some of them (11:13,14). The Apostle preached to the Jews and was rejected (Acts 13:46). Therefore he magnifies his office among the Gentiles, in order that they (the Jews), might be provoked to emulation." [15]

Luther's statement — "The Apostle preached to the Jews and was rejected" — is incorrect. The Apostle preached to the Jews and was accepted by some and rejected by others, even as he was accepted by some Gentiles and rejected by others. Luther has again forgotten the remnant.

"If the casting away of them be the reconciling of the world (11:15). This is not to be understood causally, but it follows as a consequence; for upon the unbelief of these *(the Jews)* followed the reconciliation of the world. But this would have followed no less, had they stood firm, as we clearly learn from Acts 10:44-48. There we see that the grace of the Holy Spirit was poured out upon the heathen at which the Apostles, who as yet were not sure of the rejection of the Jews, were greatly astonished." [16]

What is the meaning of "This is not to be understood causally, but it follows as a consequence"? How can something be a consequence if there is no causal relationship? Does not Paul intend for this to "be understood causally"?

Luther denied the causal relationship expressed in v.11. He ignored its continuing future effect — the "how much more" — in v.12. If something greater than "the reconciliation of the world" is to come from the receiving of all Israel, how is it possible not to understand this causally?

Luther's comment on Acts 10:44-48 is quite strange. "There we see that the grace of the Holy Spirit was poured out upon the heathen at which the Apostles, who as yet were not sure of the rejection of the Jews, were greatly astonished." When did the Jewish Apostles become "sure of the rejection of the Jews"? Only when they became sure of their own rejection.

This chapter of Romans begins with Paul's emphatic declaration, "God has not rejected His people whom He foreknew." Even with Luther's attempt to redefine "His people" to mean the remnant, that still would not change the fact that the remnant is Jewish.

Paul never became "sure of the rejection of the Jews." Nor did Peter, nor any of the Apostles. How could they? They were Jewish. They would have been "greatly astonished" by Luther's comments.

Luther continues, "Behold therefore the goodness and severity of God (11:22). From this passage we learn that when we see the fall of the Jews, heretics, and others, we should not so much regard them that fall, as rather the work of God which He does regarding them, so that we may learn from the example of misfortune befalling others to fear God and not boast arrogantly in any way. In contradistinction to this *(lesson)* many exalt themselves in an amazingly stupid manner and call the Jews either dogs or accursed, or they insult them with other abusive words, though they themselves do not know what kind of people they are and what is their standing in God's sight. They want to convert the Jews by force or invective. May God resist them." [17]

This is an interesting comment. Luther desired that Jews 'convert and become Christians,' and recognized that the Church was the greatest obstacle to that happening. In a pamphlet entitled "Jesus Christ was Born a Jew," Luther stated, "If the apostles, who were also Jews, had dealt with us Gentiles as we Gentiles have dealt with the Jews, no Christians would ever have emerged from among the Gentiles." [18]

"For our fools, the popes, bishops, sophists, and monks — the gross asses' heads — have treated the Jews to date in such fashion that he who would be a good Christian might almost have to become a Jew. And if I had been a Jew and had seen such oafs and numbskulls governing and teaching the Christian faith, I would have rather become a sow than a Christian." [19]

Yet Luther himself is well known for his abusive insults and curses directed at the Jewish people, and for his appeals for their destruction. He far surpassed those whom he criticized. He far surpassed Eusebius and Constantine. There is no one who exceeded him in this regard.

He attributed his curses and judgments on the Jews to the Lord. "Everything concurs with Christ's judgment that the Jews are venomous, bitter, vengeful, slimy snakes, assassins and devil's children, who steal and wreak havoc on the sly because they cannot afford to do so in the open. A Christian has, next to the devil, no more venomous, bitter enemy than the Jew...(The Jews ought to convert,) but if they refuse, we should neither tolerate nor suffer their presence in our midst!" [20]

"If thou wert cut out of the olive tree which is wild by nature, and wert graffed contrary to nature into a good olive tree; how much more shall these, which be the natural branches, be graffed into their own olive tree? (11:24) That the seed of the olive tree does not produce a good olive tree, illustrates that the children born of flesh are not the children of God, and that the Jews did not possess the glory — (*the glorious promise and adoption*) of the Fathers simply because they were the seed of the Fathers. The contrary rather is true. As the wild olive tree becomes a good branch, not by nature, but by the art of grafting, so also the heathen become God's people, not by their natural righteousness, or virtue, but by the grace implanted into them." [21]

None of Luther's comments relate to the verse. It is hard to know what some of these comments actually do relate to, since they do not relate to Paul's analogy. Luther has created his own different analogy so that he can say whatever he wants to say.

What does Luther mean when he says, "the seed of the olive tree does not produce a good olive tree"? Does he mean that a good olive tree cannot be produced from seed, but only from a transplanted root or by cultivation? Perhaps he means that, but then how does he get from there to "the children born of flesh are not the children of God"? Paul is saying that the Jews are the natural branches of the good olive tree.

Paul's point is clear: If Gentiles, wild by nature, can be grafted contrary to nature into a good olive tree, how much more can Jews, the natural branches of the good olive tree, be grafted into their own olive tree. Paul is telling the Gentile believers that they should not think it hard for God to save the Jews who do not yet believe. "How much more" can God do that than save Gentiles. Luther ignores the text and simply uses the occasion to speak against the Jews.

"*I would not, brethren, that ye should be ignorant of this mystery, lest ye should be wise in your own conceits* (11:25). From this passage it is generally concluded that the Jews at the end of the world will be converted to faith. However, it is true that this passage is so obscure that hardly anyone will be persuaded with absolute clarity, unless he follows the verdict of the Fathers (*Augustine, Chrysostom, Theodoret*) who interpret the Apostle in this sense. The meaning then, is: The Jews who are now fallen, will be converted and saved, after the heathen according to the fulness of the elect are come in. They will not remain outside forever, but in their own time they will be converted.

"*So all Israel shall be saved...for this is my covenant unto them, when I shall take away their sins* (11:26,27)...The purpose of the whole passage is to incite the people (*the Jews*) to repentance. To understand the Apostle rightly, we must bear in mind that his statement extends to the whole lump of the Jewish people. Even if some among them are cast away, nevertheless, the lump must be honored because of the elect. So we must respect any community because of the good in it, even when they are in the minority over against the wicked. In this sense the Jewish people is a 'holy lump,' namely, because of the elect, but the Jews are 'cut off branches' as regards the castaways. Thus the Jews are both 'fulness' and 'emptiness.' He calls them 'lump' to show that he is speaking not of individual persons, but of the whole people, in which there may not be many that are holy.

"(*Luther at first wavered with regard to the conversion of 'all Israel.' In Romans he at times speaks as though he believed in the final conversion of all Jews, though he also emphasizes the fact that only the elect will be saved. Later he definitely accepted the opinion of Origen, Theophylact, Jerome, and others, who identified 'all Israel' with the number of the elect, to which corresponds the expression 'the fulness of the Gentiles.' The leading Lutheran exegetes have followed this interpretation and taught that while the elect from among the Gentiles are being brought in through the preaching of the Gospel before Judgment Day, so also are the elect from among the Jews.*)" [22]

Luther says that vv.25-26 are "so obscure that hardly anyone will be persuaded with absolute clarity, unless he follows the verdict of the Fathers." Paul did not mean for it to be obscure. He was explaining something that every Gentile believer needed to know. No Gentile believer should be ignorant of what Paul was saying. Otherwise they might be arrogant towards the Jews who did not yet believe.

The early Church did not think that what Paul was saying was obscure. They thought it meant that at some future point in time there would be the salvation of all the Jews on the earth at that time. All the early Church Fathers thought the same. They did not find it obscure.

Augustine did not find it obscure. He said, "The belief that in the final period before the judgement this great and wonderful prophet Elijah will expound the Law to the Jews, and that through his activity the Jews are destined to believe in our Christ, this is a very frequent subject in the conversation of believers, and a frequent thought in their hearts." [23]

There are no words in the passage that are difficult to understand. It is not difficult to follow Paul's reasoning. The only thing that makes the passage obscure is a theology that has cut off the Jewish people.

Why did Luther find the passage obscure? His difficulty with the text does not seem to be with understanding it, but rather with believing it. There is no place for it in Luther's theology. So he dismisses it as "obscure." Later in his life, the obscurity vanished, and he found it to clearly speak of the Church.

As for obscurity, what is the meaning of Luther's phrase, "after the heathen according to the fulness of the elect are come in"? "The fulness of the elect"? Paul talks about "the fulness of the Gentiles" (v.25), and he talks about "the fulness" of Israel (v.12). He talks about the faithful Jewish remnant as "the elect" (v.7).

None of Paul's phrases fit what Luther is trying to say. What is "the heathen according to the fulness of the elect"? Luther seems to be saying again that the Gentiles are the elect, and the Jews are rejected. It seems that Luther is again removing all Jews from the Church.

Luther says, "The purpose of the whole passage is to incite the people (the Jews) to repentance." If that is its purpose, then Paul is very confused and misguided, for he has stated that he is speaking to Gentile believers. He tells Gentile believers that they should not be ignorant of God's faithfulness to the Jews. He tells them that they should not be arrogant towards the Jews. Paul is trying to incite the **Gentile believers** to repentance.

Luther seems to be trying to find some way to understand "the lump" as meaning something other than all Israel. He is unsuccessful, but he tries one thing more. He says, "Thus the Jews are both 'fulness' and 'emptiness.' " He is trying to find some other meaning for "fulness," so that he does not have to believe in the future salvation of all Israel. He simply does not want to accept the text for what it says.

Luther adamantly maintained that, "The promises made to Abraham do not refer literally to Abraham's blood and seed, nor is the biblical prophecy of salvation addressed to the Jews as Jews: Christians may 'despair of the

Jews with a clear conscience.' The Jews have been rejected by God. The homelessness of the Jews provides Luther with such overwhelming proof of this that he feels safe to take an oath: If it should happen that the diaspora comes to an end and the Jews are led back to Jerusalem, then we Christians will follow on their heels and ourselves 'become Jews.' " [24]

A natural question would be: 'If the biblical prophecies of salvation addressed to the Jews are not addressed to the Jews as Jews, then what about the biblical prophecies of judgment that are addressed to the Jews?' If the Church appropriates one, should not the Church also appropriate the other?' For those scriptures that promise judgment for the Jews, Luther saw a dual application to both the Jews and the imperfect church (i.e. papists et.al.). The scriptures that promised salvation belonged only to the true Church.

Luther saw confirmation of his theology in the Diaspora. "In brief: Because you see that after fifteen hundred years of misery (when no end is certain or will ever be so) the Jews are not disheartened nor are they even cognizant of their plight, you might with a good conscience despair of them. For it is impossible that God should let his people (if they were that) wait so long without consolation and prophecy." [25]

"Or if such an event fails to come about, then let them head for Jerusalem, build temples, set up priesthoods, principalities, Moses with his laws, and in other words themselves become Jews again and take the land into their possession. For when this happens, they will see us come quickly on their heels and likewise become Jews. But if not, then it is entirely ludicrous that they should want to persuade us into accepting their degenerate laws, which are surely by now after fifteen hundred years of decay no longer laws at all. And should we believe what they themselves do not and cannot believe, as long as they do not have Jerusalem and the land of Israel?" [26]

Luther is saying that the return of the Jewish people to Jerusalem and the land of Israel would demonstrate the falsity of the Christian faith — "they will see us come quickly on their heels and likewise become Jews." Actually, it only demonstrates the falsity of Luther's interpretation of all the scriptures that promise the restoration of the Jewish people. According to his own words, a faith based on the appropriation by the Church of these scriptures would have to be abandoned with the return of the Jews to Jerusalem and the land of Israel.

Luther says more along this line in his comments on Gen.12:3 in his *Works*. He sums up the situation of the Jews somewhat strangely: "In short, they have no hope for salvation except to invent some idea about God's mercy and goodness." [27] Do Jews need "to invent some idea about God's mercy and goodness"? Isn't God merciful and good? Does anyone have any hope for salvation outside the reality of God's mercy and goodness?

"As concerning the gospel, they are enemies for your sakes (11:28). The word 'enemies' must here be taken in a passive sense; that is, they deserve to be hated. God hates them, and so they are hated by the Apostles and all who are of God. This is shown by the opposite term 'beloved.' They are hated and at the same time beloved. They are hated 'concerning the gospel...for your sakes.' That is to say; As you are loved for receiving the Gospel, so they are hated for rejecting the Gospel. Nevertheless, the lump is beloved 'for the fathers' sakes, as touching the election.' This means that some of them because of their election until this very hour are being accepted. They are beloved for the Fathers' sakes, because they too are friends." [28]

Luther doesn't actually quote the rest of v.28 which says, "but from the standpoint of God's choice they are beloved for the sake of the fathers." The "they" in both parts of the sentence refers to the same group of people, i.e. God still loves those Jews who do not believe because of His love for their fathers.

Luther's treatment of the text is unbelievable. "The opposite term beloved [shows that] God hates them, and so they are hated by the Apostles and all who are of God." Paul says that God loves them, and Luther says the meaning of that is that God hates them. For Luther, the meaning is not only that God hates them, but that Paul, who was willing to be damned forever for their salvation, also hates them. Not only, according to Luther, do God and Paul hate them, but so do the other "Apostles and all who are of God." According to Luther, someone who does not hate the unbelieving Jews is not of God.

What Luther writes is not interpretation. These are not comments on what Paul wrote. They are comments in spite of what Paul wrote. They are comments in defiance of what Paul wrote.

Luther teaches that, "They are hated 'concerning the gospel...for your sakes.' That is to say; As you are loved for receiving the Gospel, so they are hated for rejecting the Gospel." Paul does not say "They are hated." He says that they are enemies of the gospel for the sake of the Gentiles — "through their offense, salvation has come to the Gentiles." Luther maintains that they are hated, and then transfers God's love for them to the Church — "as you are loved."

God has plenty of love for the Church. God is love. No one is diminished by God's love for someone else. God's love is infinite. Why try to steal it? Why try to withhold it?

Luther continues, "Nevertheless, the lump is beloved 'for the fathers' sakes, as touching the election.' This means that some of them because of their election until this very hour are being accepted. They are beloved for the Fathers' sakes, because they too are friends." Here Luther succeeds in doing what he was unable to do in his comments on v.16 and vv.26-27.

He makes the lump represent the believing remnant, instead of all Israel. But even his own prior comments are sufficient in reply. "We must bear in mind that his statement extends to the whole lump of the Jewish people. Even if some among them are cast away, nevertheless, the lump must be honored because of the elect."

Jesus had commanded His disciples, "Love your enemies, and pray for those who persecute you." (Mt.5:44) He said the second greatest commandment, like the greatest, is "You shall love your neighbor as yourself." (Mt.19:39) He had already responded to one who wanted to justify himself in not loving his neighbor. (Lk.10:25-37) Paul repeats the commandment in Rom.13:8-10.

Yet Luther wrote what he wrote. The thoughts and the hatred were not original with Luther. Nor was the system of "interpretation" which he embraced to justify his attitudes. But in this way, Luther became the theologian of the Holocaust. He created a theology which placed the destruction of the Jews in a favorable light.

Some have said that Luther only became anti-Semitic in his later years because of the Jewish refusal to receive his message. That is not tenable. His *Commentary on Romans* was written before he had even nailed his Ninety-Five Theses to the Wittenberg church door.

Luther continues, "*The gifts and calling of God are without repentance* (11:29). This is an excellent statement. God's counsel (*of election and salvation*) is altered by no man's merit or demerit. God never regrets his gift and calling, which He has promised, because the elect are unworthy, and you (the proud, self-righteous Jews) are worthy in your own eyes. He does not change His mind. Hence they (the elect) will surely be converted and come to the truth of faith — (salvation without works)." [29]

Paul is talking about why "all Israel will be saved" and why unbelieving Jews "are beloved for the sake of the fathers; for the gifts and the calling of God are irrevocable." He is **explaining** why "all Israel will be saved."

Luther again says the opposite of what Paul is saying. Luther takes God's gifts and calling away from all Israel and bestows them on the elect. He changes the promise of future restoration into a curse of judgment.

Paul, after talking about **why** "all Israel will be saved," proceeds to talk about **how** "all Israel will be saved." He tells the Gentile believers, "For just as you once were disobedient to God but now have been shown mercy because of their disobedience, so these also now have been disobedient, in order that because of the mercy shown to you they also may now be shown mercy." (Rom.11:30-31)

Luther ignores the verses. He has already eliminated the salvation of all Israel, so what is the point of discussing God's means for bringing it about?

CHAPTER 15

"*And again he saith, Rejoice ye Gentiles, with his people* (15:10). This call goes forth from Jerusalem, that is, from the Lord's people to others, namely, to the heathen who are not (*members of*) Jerusalem. Therefore the Apostle adds 'Gentiles,' and he explains the term 'Jerusalem' with 'his people.' " [30]

It seems that Luther is here recognizing what he previously denied, that the Jews are God's people. He commented on 11:3, "The Jews arrogantly assumed that they were God's people, simply because the heathen were not His people." He does not, however, explicitly state that, and his comments are too brief to know for sure.

"*It hath pleased them of Macedonia and Achaia to make a certain contribution for the poor saints which are at Jerusalem* (15:26). With admirable propriety the Apostle moves the Christians at Rome to make a contribution. For what other reason should he have mentioned this matter to them? But he wants to incite them that they, induced by the example of the others rather than by a demand, do of their own free will, and without any coercion, what there is to do. (*The Apostle means to say*): I demand nothing of you, but I will gratefully accept what you willingly contribute. This obligation and ministry of love was enjoined upon St. Paul before the other Apostles. We read of this in Galatians 2:9,10: 'They gave to me and Barnabas the right hands of fellowship....Only they would that we should remember the poor.'

"*It hath pleased them verily* (15:27). 'It hath pleased them verily' means that (*they gave*) willingly and with joy." [31]

Luther understands Paul's purpose in mentioning the giving of the Macedonians and Achaians. Paul wants the Romans to give also. He does not command them to give, but seeks to 'induce them by the example of others.'

But Paul is talking about giving for a particular purpose, because of a particular reason. He says that the Gentile believers have shared in the Jewish spiritual things, and are therefore indebted to minister to them in material things. He is offering them another inducement. They are indebted to give.

Luther does not comment on this part of Paul's appeal. He was unwilling to recognize a debt to the Jewish people, and he was unwilling to seek their good. Paul's point is thrown away because it will not fit into Luther's theology.

Calvin comments on Rom.15:27, "Paul shows us the value of the Gospel by declaring that they were indebted not only to its ministers, but to the whole Jewish nation, from which these ministers come. We should note the verb λειτουργησαι, to minister. It means to perform the duty appointed by the state, and undertake the burdens of one's calling." [32]

For Paul, the Gentile believers giving materially for the Jews was critical to making the offering of the Gentiles acceptable to God. "Macedonia and Achaia were pleased to make a certain contribution [κοινωνιαν]..." They were pleased to participate. They were pleased to demonstrate that they were in fellowship with the Jewish believers. Their giving demonstrated that they also had a common share in the commonwealth of Israel.

The Macedonian believers in their giving had entreated and begged for "the grace [χαριν] and the fellowship [κοινωνιαν] of the service [διακονιας] which was for the saints..." (2Co.8:4) Without grace, fellowship, ministry, and service, what is there?

FOOTNOTES

1. *Commentary on Romans*, Martin Luther, Translated by J. Theodore Mueller, Kregel Publications, Grand Rapids, MI, 1976, Pp.162-163
2. ibid., P.29
3. ibid., Pp.29-30
4. ibid., P.48
5. ibid., Pp.49-50
6. ibid., Pp.51-52
7. ibid., P.136
8. ibid., Pp.136-137
9. ibid., Pp.145-146
10. *Commentary on Galatians*, Martin Luther, Translated by Erasmus Middletown, Kregel Publications, Grand Rapids, MI, 1976, P.223
11. *Commentary on Romans*, op.cit., P.63
12. ibid., Pp.149-150
13. ibid., Pp.155-156
14. ibid., P.159
15. ibid.
16. ibid., P.160
17. ibid.
18. "That Jesus Christ Was Born a Jew," Weimarer Ausgabe [WA] 11:315.19-21, Quoted in *The Roots of Anti-Semitism in the Age of Renaissance and Reformation*, Heiko Oberman, Fortress Press, Phila., 1983, P.93
19. "That Jesus Christ Was Born a Jew," WA 11:315,19-21, Quoted in *Luther's Last Battles: A Study of the Politics and Polemics, 1531-1546*, Mark Edwards Jr., Cornell U. Press, Ithaca, 1983, P.121
20. WA 51:196,16f.; cf.ibid. 53:530,25-28; 31f, Quoted in *The Roots of Anti-Semitism in the Age of Renaissance and Reformation*, Oberman, P.113
21. *Commentary on Romans*, Pp.160-161
22. ibid., P.162
23. *City of God*, Augustine, Bk.20, Ch.29, P.957
24. *The Roots of Anti-Semitism in the Age of Renaissance and Reformation*, Oberman, P.49
25. WA 50:336, 1-6 in ibid., P.64
26. WA 50:323, 36-324, 8 in ibid., P.64
27. *Luther's Works, Vol.2, Genesis*, edited by Jaroslav Pelikan, Concordia Publishing House, St. Louis, 1960, P.263
28. *Commentary on Romans*, Pp.162-163
29. ibid., P.163
30. ibid., P.213
31. ibid., P.219
32. *Calvin's Commentaries, The Epistles of Paul the Apostle to the Romans and to the Thessalonians*, op.cit., P.316

42

AT THE SAME TIME

The Reformation opened men's eyes to the Scriptures. Its entire thrust was to turn away from the traditions of men which had nullified the Word of God, and to examine the Word itself. Changes in belief and practice were bound to take place.

Neither Calvin nor Luther, for different reasons, were able to break free from the traditional teachings concerning the Jews. Yet at the same time, there were others who began to see that the Bible actually taught something quite different from what the Church, and Calvin and Luther taught. Even in Wittenberg with Luther, and even in Geneva with Calvin, there were those who started to embrace the Biblical teaching.

The story of those around Luther is particularly interesting. One of those who continually confronted Luther over his anti-Semitic views was Andreas Osiander. "When this conflict came to a head, shortly before Osiander's death, Matthias Flacius, leader of the orthodox Lutherans, presented as evidence of Osiander's 'unreliability' the fact that 'eight years ago' (1543) he had written a letter to Luther which sharply criticized Luther's writings on the Jews.

"This letter has not been preserved. Nevertheless it fits Osiander's profile exactly — to have 'withstood' Luther 'to his face' (Gal.2:11) and to have censured the Wittenberg reformer for the harshness of his pronouncements on the Jews." [1]

"Osiander was, however, no isolated Nuremberger deviator from the Wittenberg party line. There is reason to presume that Melanchthon, Reuchlin's great-nephew, was just as unhappy over the harsh writings on the Jews of the late Luther, as were some of the leading city reformers. Melanchthon sought to avoid a scandal when he suppressed the evidence for Osiander's having sent the erudite Jewish scholar from Venice, Elias Levita, a written statement of apology for Luther's splenetic tirades.

"More illuminating still was the stance of Justas Jonas (1493-1555). Luther's lifelong colleague and best man at his wedding, Jonas was entrusted with a unique charge: through the translation into Latin of Luther's German writings on the Jews, Luther's ideas would gain European diffusion. Jonas' autonomous viewpoint has probably gone unnoticed due to the simple fact that he lavished such praise and commendation on Luther's vision that we assume the Latin represents a faithful reproduction of Luther's position on the Jews. But Jonas ventures increasingly, and at critical junctures, to graft his own ideas onto the Luther text, ultimately adducing personal conclusions that approach those reached by modern exegetical practice...

"Jonas underscores the common features in the destinies of Jews and Christians, both of whom have been led astray — the Jews by Talmudic hairsplitting, and the Christians by scholastic subtleties...

"Here [in Luther's writing against the Sabbatarians], he introduced his own notions so emphatically that the resultant text distorts Luther's position, which has in fact hardened, presaging the vitriolics to come. Jonas does his utmost to offset Luther's exasperated disenchantment with the mission to the Jews and in the process manages to draw an entirely novel and positive picture of them...The uncovering of the gospel 'in our day' has opened our eyes to the fact that never have greater 'doctors of theology' existed than among the people of Israel in those times. Reformation readings of the gospel lead to the realization that we Christians are in fact guests in the house of Abraham. Previously impious Gentiles, we are latecomers to the promise of God. Jonas is following Paul (Rom.11:17) when he understands Christians to be the Gentiles grafted onto the 'tree of Israel,' united in one body with the Jews together under the single head of Jesus Christ.

"The reception of the Gentiles into the bosom of Abraham and the subsequent fusion of the two peoples into one body, all made possible through Christ — this is the unprecedented, if un-Lutheran, attitude toward the Jews that Jonas put forward." [2]

Views which were "un-Lutheran" and "un-Calvinist," but thoroughly Biblical, began to emerge from the Reformation. To some extent these views were "anti-Lutheran" and "anti-Calvinist." That is not surprising, for neither the Bible nor history offer support for a belief in human infallibility. Calvin and Luther were wrong. In the next section, we will see how some of these views emerged into **"The Puritan Hope."**

FOOTNOTE

1. *The Roots of Anti-Semitism in the Age of Renaissance and Reformation*, Oberman, P.10
2. ibid., Pp.47-49

43

THE PURITAN HOPE

Iain Murray has written *The Puritan Hope: Revival and the Interpretation of Prophecy*. Some portions that directly concern us are extracted, by permission, below. Murray's thesis is that 1) the way we interpret unfulfilled prophecy affects the way we evangelize, or fail to evangelize, the world; and 2) the Puritan belief in the future salvation of all Israel was a stimulus for both national revival and missionary outreach into all the world.

In this respect — the belief and the fruit it produced — the Puritans differed from both Calvin and Luther. The Puritans were not sure whether or not the children of Israel would be regathered to the land of Israel, but they were sure that the children of Israel would be regathered to the God of Israel. They expected this restoration to bring great blessing to all the earth, but they did not believe in a Millennial reign of the Lord.

The work that Murray has done in support of his two-fold thesis documents the recovery of an important aspect of the Biblical faith. That recovery began in the Reformation. It is approaching its fulfillment today. The following selections from *The Puritan Hope* do not need much comment.

Samuel Rutherford expressed the depth and the thrust of that recaptured faith. "In a letter written on April 22, 1635, [he said],...'O to see the sight, next to Christ's Coming in the clouds, the most joyful! Our elder brethren the Jews and Christ fall upon one another's necks and kiss each other! They have been long asunder; they will be kind to one another when they meet. O day! O longed-for and lovely day-dawn! **O sweet Jesus**, let me see that sight which will be as life from the dead, **thee and thy ancient people in mutual embraces.**'

"Twenty-six years later, when Rutherford lay dying at St. Andrews, in 1661, he spoke with the same anticipation....'[Christ] shall reign a victorious conquering King to the ends of the earth. O that there were nations, kindreds, tongues, and all the people of Christ's habitable world, encompassing his throne with cries and tears for the spirit of supplication to be poured down upon the inhabitants of Judah for that effect.' " [1]

In the beginning, the Reformers had generally retained the amillennial view of Augustine and Eusebius. "Luther, for example, regarded himself as living at the very close of history, with the Advent and Judgment immediately at hand. Others, on the outer fringe of orthodox Protestantism, 'drew out of its grave' (as a Puritan later complained against them) the belief common among some of the early Fathers, that Christ would appear and reign with his saints a thousand years in Jerusalem before the Judgment." [2]

"Neither Luther nor Calvin saw a future general conversion of the Jews promised in Scripture; some of their contemporaries, however, notably Martin Bucer and Peter Martyr, who taught at Cambridge and Oxford respectively in the reign of Edward VI, did understand the Bible to teach a future calling of the Jews. In this view they were followed by Theodore Beza, Calvin's successor at Geneva. As early as 1560, four years before Calvin's death, the English and Scots refugee Protestant leaders who produced the Geneva Bible, express this belief in their marginal notes on Romans chapter 11, verses 15 and 26. On the latter verse they comment, 'He sheweth that the time shall come that the whole nation of the Jews, though not every one particularly, shall be joined to the church of Christ.' " [3]

"The first volume in English to expound this conviction at some length was the translation of Peter Martyr's *Commentary upon Romans*, published in London in 1568. The probability is strong that Martyr's careful exposition of the eleventh chapter prepared the way for a general adoption amongst the English Puritans of a belief in the future conversion of the Jews. Closely linked as English Puritanism was to John Calvin, it was the view contained in Martyr's commentary which was received by the rising generation of students at Cambridge.

"William Perkins had entered the same college [Christ's College, Cambridge], a man whom we noted earlier as doing so much to influence the thinking of many who were to preach all over England. Perkins speaks plainly of a future conversion of the Jews: 'The Lord saith, *All the nations shall be blessed in Abraham*: Hence I gather that **the nation of the Jews shall be called, and converted to the participation of this blessing: when, and how, God knows: but that it shall be done before the end of the world we know.**'...The same truth was opened by the succession of Puritan leaders at Cambridge who followed Perkins, including Richard Sibbes and Thomas Goodwin. In his famous book, *The Bruised Reed*, ... Sibbes writes:...'The faithful Jews rejoiced to think of the calling of the Gentiles; and why **should not we joy to think of the calling of the Jews**?'

"From the first quarter of the seventeenth century, belief in a future conversion of the Jews became commonplace among the English Puritans. In the late 1630's, and in the national upheavals of the 1640's — the period of the Civil Wars — the subject not infrequently was mentioned by Puritan leaders." [4]

"As a ground for hopefulness in regard to the prospects of Christ's kingdom it was introduced in sermons before Parliament or on other public occasions by William Strong, William Bridge, George Gillespie and Robert Baillie, to name but a few. The fact that the two last-named were commissioners from the General Assembly of the Church of Scotland at the Westminster Assembly, which was convened by the English Parliament in 1643, is indicative of the agreement on this point between English and Scottish divines. Some of the rich doctrinal formularies which that Assembly produced, bear the same witness. *The Larger Catechism*, after the question, 'What do we pray for in the second petition of the Lord's Prayer?' (Thy Kingdom come), answers: 'We pray that the kingdom of sin and Satan may be destroyed, the gospel propagated throughout the world, the Jews called... *The Directory for the Public Worship of God* (section on Public Prayer before Sermon) stipulates in similar language that prayer be made 'for the conversion of the Jews.'

"This same belief concerning the future of the Jews is to be found very widely in seventeenth-century Puritan literature. It appears in the works of such well-known Puritans as John Owen, Thomas Manton and John Flavel... It is also handled in a rich array of commentaries, both folios and quartos - David Dickson on the Psalms, George Hutcheson on the Minor Prophets, Jeremiah Burroughs on Hosea, William Greenhill on Ezekiel, Elnathan Parr on Romans and James Durham on Revelation: a list which could be greatly extended.

"Occasionally the subject became the main theme of a volume. Perhaps the first in order among these was *The Calling of the Jews*, published in 1621 by William Gouge, the eminent Puritan minister of Blackfriars, London; the author was a barrister, Sir Henry Finch. A slender work, *Some Discourses upon the Point of the Conversion of the Jews*, by Moses Wall, appeared in 1650, and nineteen years later Increase Mather, the New England divine of Boston, issued his work, *The Mystery of Israel's Salvation Explained and Applied*. **'That there shall be a general conversion of the Tribes of Israel is a truth which in some measure hath been known and believed in all ages of the Church of God, since the Apostles' days.**...Only in these late days, these things have obtained credit much more universally than heretofore.' So **Mather** wrote in 1669." [5]

" [Thomas Brightman, 1607,]...gives considerable attention to the future prospects of the Jews...The Jews' calling, he believed, would be part of a new and brighter era of history, and not the end.

"In the earliest and most popular Puritan exposition of Romans, the *Plain Exposition* of **Elnathan Parr**, published in 1620, ...[Parr wrote] 'The casting off of the Jews, was our Calling; but the Calling of the Jews shall not be our casting off, but our greater enriching in grace, and that two ways: First, in regard of the company of believers, when the thousands of Israel shall come in, which shall doubtless cause many Gentiles which now lie in ignorance, error and doubt, to receive the Gospel and join with them. The world shall then be a golden world, rich in golden men, saith Ambrose. Secondly, in respect of the graces, which shall then in more abundance be rained down upon the Church.' " [6]

"'Pray for the calling of the Jewes, which shall bring so much good to the world: As the sisters sent to Christ in the behalf of their brother Lazarus; so let us Gentiles importune the Lord for our brethren the Jewes.' (1633)" [7]

"In 1627, seven years after Parr's commentary appeared, further impetus was given to the expectation of world-wide blessing connected with the calling of the Jews, by the appearance of a Latin work by John Henry Alsted, *The Beloved City*." [8]

"**Christopher Love**, in his sermons on Christ's Glorious Appearing, preached at Lawrence Jury, London, in the **1640's**, says: 'When the Lord shall bring in the Jews with an eminent and general conversion, then you may conclude the day is not far off; for so all the interpreters say, that **the Jews' conversion, and Christ's coming to judgment, will not be far distant.**' " [9]

"There are several reasons why the future of the Jews was a subject of importance in the minds of so many Christians in the seventeenth century. For one thing they considered that a concern for the welfare of that scattered nation is a necessary part of Christian piety. Of the Jews, concerning the flesh, Christ came; to them first was the gospel preached, and from them was it received by the Gentiles: 'Which should teach us', writes **Edward Elton**, 'not to hate the Jews (as many do) only because they are Jews, which name is among many so odious that they think they cannot call a man worse than to call him a Jew; but, beloved, this ought not to be so, for **we are bound to love and honour the Jews, as being the ancient people of God, to wish them well, and to be earnest in prayer to God for their conversion.**' [1653]

"We shall later note how this awareness of duty towards the Jews did enter into the day-to-day living of many Christians in the seventeenth century. And yet their interest in Israel was always set in a wider context than the particular future of that nation; it was Israel's future *within* the kingdom of Christ and the relation between their incoming and the advancement of Christ's glory that was uppermost in their thinking. The future of the Jews had decisive significance for them because they believed that, though little is clearly revealed of the future purposes of God in history, enough has been given us in Scripture to warrant the expectation that with the calling of the Jews there will come far-reaching blessing for the world. Puritan England and Covenanting Scotland knew much of spiritual blessing and it was the prayerful longing for wider blessing, not a mere interest in unfulfilled prophecy, which led them to give such place to Israel." [10]

" 'I know not any Scripture containing a more pregnant and illustrious testimony and demonstration of the Israelites' future vocation,' says [Increase] Mather, 'it being a main scope of the Apostle in this chapter [Rom.11] to make known this Mystery unto the Gentiles.' Similarly the

eminent Scottish divine, James Durham, writes: 'Whatever may be doubted
of their restoring to their land, yet they shall be brought to a visible Church-
state. Not only in particular persons here and there in congregations; but
that multitudes, yea, the whole body of them shall be brought, in a common
way with the Gentiles, to profess Christ, which cannot be denied, as Romans
11 is clear and that will be enough to satisfy us.' [1680] In the eighteenth
century **Jonathan Edwards** was a spokesman for the same conviction when
he wrote, '**Nothing is more certainly foretold than this national conversion
of the Jews in Romans 11.**' " [11]

"[John Brown of Wamphray, Scotland, gives the following exposition
which] may be taken as typical of the whole school to which he
belonged...On verse 15, he said: '...*If the casting away of them*, that is, if the
slinging away of the Jews, and casting them out of the church, *be the
reconciling of the world*, that is, be the occcasion whereby the gospel should
be preached to the Gentile world, that thereby they might be reconciled
unto God, *what shall the receiving of them be, but life from the dead*: Will there
not be joyful days thro' the world, and among the Gentiles, when they
shall be received into favour again? Will it not be like the resurrection from
the dead, when Jew and Gentile shall both enjoy the same felicity and
happiness? Seeing out of the dead state of the Jews, when cast without
doors, God brought life to the Gentiles, will he not much more do so out of
their enlivened estate? **will it not be to the Gentiles as the resurrection
from the dead.**' [1666]

"In the verses which follow there are three further reasons why the Jews'
conversion is to be expected: because of the holiness of the first-fruits and
the root, v 16; because of the power of God, 'God is able to graft them in
again,' v 23; and because of the grace of God manifested to the Gentiles, v
24, who would in turn be the means of salvation to the Jews, 'that through
your mercy they also may obtain mercy,' v.31. **Matthew Henry** illustrates
the last reason thus, 'If the putting out of their candle was the lighting of
yours by that power of God who brings good out of evil, **much more shall
the continued light of your candle, when God's time is come, be a means
of lighting theirs again.**' [1848]" [12]

"...In 1652, for example, eighteen of the most eminent Puritan divines,
including men of presbyterial convictions as William Gouge, Edmund
Calamy and Simeon Ashe, and Independents as John Owen and Thomas
Goodwin, wrote in support of missionary labours then being undertaken
in New England and affirmed their belief that: 'the Scripture speaks of a
double conversion of the Gentiles, the first before the conversion of the Jewes,
they being *Branches wilde by nature* grafted into the *True Olive Tree* instead
of the *naturall Branches* which are broken off. This fulness of the *Gentiles*
shall come in before the conversion of the *Jewes*, and till then blindness

hath happened unto Israel, Rom.11:25. The second, after the conversion of the Jewes...' " [13]

"**Robert Leighton** of Newbattle, Scotland in January, **1642** [preached that]....'Christ came of the Jews, and came first to them....**Undoubtedly, that people of the Jews shall once more be commanded to *arise* and *shine*, and their return shall be *the riches of the Gentiles*** (Rom.11.12), and that shall be a more glorious time than ever the Church of God did yet behold. Nor is there any inconvenience if we think that the high expressions of this prophecy have some spiritual reference to that time, since the great doctor of the Gentiles applies some words of the former chapter to that purpose, Rom.11.26. **They forget a main point of the Church's glory, who pray not daily for the conversion of the Jews.'** " [14]

"We have already noted the place which the future of Jew and Gentile occupied in the directions for prayer in such representative church documents as *The Larger Catechism* and *The Directory for Public Worship*. A number of years before these were drawn up, the call to prayer for the conversion of the Jews and for the success of the gospel through the world was already a feature of Puritan congregations." [15]

"**John Owen, preaching before the House of Commons in 1649, speaks of 'the bringing home of his ancient people to be one fold with the fulness of the Gentiles...in answer to millions of prayers put up at the throne of grace, for this very glory, in all generations.'** At the same period, days of prayer and humiliation were kept in Scotland, one particular object being 'That the promised conversion of his ancient people of the Jews may be hastened.'

"**Cotton Mather**, the New England Puritan leader, notes in his diary: '**This Day, from the Dust, where I lay prostrate before the Lord, I lifted up my Cries...for the conversion of the *Jewish Nation*, and for my own** having the Happiness, at some time or other, to baptise a *Jew* that should by my Ministry be brought home unto the Lord.' " [16]

[The prayers and heartcry of Cotton Mather were not in vain. R. Judah Monis was a Professor of Hebrew at Harvard University. He wrote the first Hebrew lexicon printed in the New World. In Boston on May 1, **1722**, he followed the Lord in baptism. On that occasion, he delivered an extensive response to "Nine Principal Arguments the Modern Jewish Rabbins do make to prove, the MESSIAH is yet to Come." His discourse was later published with a preface by **Increase Mather**, which Mather delivered on that occasion. Some of Increase Mather's comments are appropriate to our purposes here:

"...**There will a time come when there shall be a General Conversion of the Jewish Nation.** There have been some of that Nation brought home to Christ, who have proved Blessings to the World. In special Emanuel Tremelius was such an one, whose dying Words were, *Vivat Christus, et* *pereat Barrabas*. Let Christ Live, and let Barrabas Die. There were two *Jews*, *viz. John Alexander* and *Theodore John* who joyned themselves to the German Lutheran Congregation in the City of *London*. A Learned Man, *viz. Dr. Kidder* gives an account of *Two Hundred Jews* lately Converted in the City of *Frankford*. The Blessed Day is coming when all *Israel* shall be Saved, as I have Evinced in a Discourse on that Subject, written in the Year 1667, and also in my Answer to the Reverend *Mr. Baxter*, and *Dr. Lightfoot*, printed *Anno* 1695. And the Providence of GOD seems to Intimate this. The Miraculous manner of GOD's preserving the *Jewish Nation* is an invincible Proof hereof; for it is an unpresidented and incomprehensible thing, that GOD should for *Two Thousand Years* preserve this People, dispersed among other Nations, without being confounded with them in their Religions and Customs, as is usual among all dispersed People; this clearly Demonstrates that GOD has preserved them for some great Design, which what can it be but their Conversion?

"...There is no cause to fear that *Mr. Monis* will Renounce his Christianity, since he did embrace it Voluntarily and Gradually, and with much Consideration, and from Scriptures in the Old Testament.

"GOD Grant that he (who is the first *Jew* that ever I knew Converted in *New England*) may prove a Blessing unto many, and especially to some of his own Nation: Which is the Prayer and hearty Desire of Increase Mather, Boston, May 1st. 1722." [17]]

"The faithful witness of **Thomas Boston** in the unsympathetic General Assembly of the Church of Scotland has already been mentioned....Thus in one sermon, **preached in 1716, on 'Encouragement to Pray for the Conversion of the Jews,'** we find the pastor of Ettrick expounding this head of doctrine: '**There is a day coming in which there shall be a national conversion of the Jews or Israelites.** The now blinded and rejected Jews shall at length be converted into the faith of Christ, and join themselves to the Christian Church.'

"The application of this doctrine included the following words:

"'**Have you any love to, or concern for the Church, for the work of reformation, the reformation of our country, the reformation of the world? Any longing desire for the revival of that work now at a stand; for a flourishing state of the church, that is now under a decay? then pray for the conversion of the Jews.**

" '**Are you longing for a revival to the churches, now lying like dry bones, would you fain have the Spirit of life enter into them? Then pray for the Jews. "For if the casting away of them be the reconciling of the world; what shall the receiving of them be, but life from the dead." That will be a lively time, a time of a great outpouring of the Spirit, that will carry reformation to a greater height than yet has been...' "** [18]

"John Albert Bengel...wrote in 1740, 'though it is too early for the *general* conversion of Jews and Gentiles, it appears a sin of omission on the part of Protestant churches, that they have not begun long ago to send missions to both. I, at least, cannot help thinking, that endeavours of this kind would have been far more noble, than the hitherto excessive painstaking of Protestants to settle every subtle question in polemical divinity, or rather, to gain themselves only credit and celebrity in controversy.'

"In [1750, in] a moving plea to others to join in prayer, [James] Robe says:

" 'Methinks, I hear the nation of the Jews (for such is the cry of their case) crying aloud to you from their dispersion... There are many promises and predictions that we shall be grafted in again....**Pray therefore, and wrestle with God, that he may, according to his promise,** *"pour forth upon us the Spirit of grace and supplication, that we may look upon him whom we have pierced, and mourn." ' "* [19]

"By this whole evangelical school, ...the conversion of the Jews was also awaited with keen anticipation. Their interest, as we have seen, was worldwide, and it was indeed for that very reason that their desire for the recall of Israel was quickened, believing as they did that it would gloriously advance the gospel among the Gentiles. 'Though we do not know the time in which this conversion of Israel will come to pass,' writes [Jonathan] Edwards, 'yet thus much we may determine by Scripture, that it will be before the glory of the Gentile part of the church shall be fully accomplished, because it is said that their coming in shall be life from the dead to the Gentiles' (Rom.11.12,15) So [William] Carey and [Henry] Martyn, in India, tempted to weariness, thought thankfully of the promise of the Jews' ingathering. So also Andrew Fuller thought it worthwhile at home to write his *Expository Remarks Relative to the Conversion of the Jews,* even though his primary duties concerned the Mission to India. We read also of **Charles Simeon**, who gave much of his attention to the extension of Christ's kingdom, that the conversion of the Jews was perhaps the warmest interest of his life. Once at a missionary meeting Simeon had seemed so carried away with the future of the Jews that a friend passed him a slip of paper with the question, 'Six millions of Jews and six hundred millions of Gentiles — which is the most important?' Simeon at once scribbled back, '**If the conversion of the six is to be life from the dead to the six hundred, what then?**' " [20]

"...belief in the general conversion of the Jews was prominent in the missionary thinking of Scotland a century ago..." [21] "As this doctrinal outlook was so predominant, it is not surprising that the old conviction that Israel's future is bound up with the evangelization of the earth exerted a powerful influence in Scottish missionary thinking. With the new missionary societies of the early nineteenth century came auxiliaries with a special concern for the Jews. At one such auxiliary at Dundee in 1811,

Walter Tait, a minister of Tealing, summarized the traditional belief in a sermon in which he gave three reasons why Christians should have a particular regard for the Jews:

" '1. Because their salvation must be peculiarly honouring to God.

" '2. Because taking a peculiar interest in the salvation of the Jews is only making a proper return for the spiritual advantages we enjoy by them.

" '3. Because their final restoration must have a favourable aspect on the conversion of the whole Gentile world.'

"This same belief was to be expounded and preached upon with energy and fervour for many years to come. It is to be found in the influential commentaries of Robert Haldane and Thomas Chalmers on *The Epistle to the Romans*. Sometimes whole volumes were given to it, as in Archibald Mason's *Sixteen Discourses from Romans* 11.25-27, published in 1825, and in the work, *The Conversion of the Jews*, 1839, containing the lectures of Glasgow ministers upon the subject.

"By the latter date the attention of the whole country had been directed to Israel by the deputation of four Church of Scotland ministers appointed to visit Palestine in 1839 as Mission of Inquiry into the state of the Jews. Among the four was **R. M. M'Cheyne** who, on his return to Dundee, **preached on 'To the Jew first.'** Converted Israel, he declared, 'Will give life to the dead world...Just as we have found, among the parched hills of Judah, that the evening dew, coming silently down, gave life to every plant, making the grass to spring and the flowers to put forth their sweetest fragrance, so shall converted Israel be when they come as dew upon a dead, dry world. "The remnant of Jacob shall be in the midst of many people as a dew from the Lord, as the showers upon the grass, that tarrieth not for man, nor waiteth for the sons of men" (Micah 5.7).' [22]

"A visit of M'Cheyne's to Ulster in 1840 to plead the interests of the Jews 'was blessed to awaken a deep interest.' The following year the Irish General Assembly unanimously resolved to establish work among the Jews, which they did in Syria in 1844 and Germany in 1845, believing that 'missionary enterprise is one of the means to bring about the restoration of Israel, in accordance with the Scriptures.' " [23]

"One practical result of the Mission of Inquiry was the establishment of a work among the Jews at Budapest with John Duncan and four others appointed as the Church of Scotland's first missionaries to the Jews. The work was abundantly blessed..." [24] "'Our hands now became so full of work that frequently we had not time so much as to eat bread; from early morning till late at night we were occupied in guiding, counselling and instructing those who were inquiring earnestly what they must do to be saved...For a time the whole Jewish community was deeply moved, wondering whereunto these things would grow.' " [25]

"Through the following twenty-eight years until his death in 1870, 'Rabbi'

Duncan continued his work at New College and on several occasions thrilled the General Assembly of the Free Church as he pleaded the necessity of maintaining hope in the future conversion of Israel by the outpouring of the Spirit.

"At the same period **the Scottish missionaries to the Gentiles in India also remembered Israel's place in the unfulfilled promises of Scripture.** The three outstanding Free Church missionaries in Madras, John Anderson, John Braidwood and Robert Johnston, would meet with converts and other Christians on the first Monday of the month, 'to plead for the world's conversion.' At one of these meetings **Robert Johnston** addressed the little gathering on *The Conversion of the Jews; and Its Bearing on the Conversion of the Gentiles.* His address was published posthumously in Edinburgh in 1853. In a Preface, Braidwood writes, 'We could not but express our conviction that the circulation of it was fitted to edify the body of Christ generally; while it would prove to all how strongly the missionaries to the Gentiles sympathize in efforts for the conversion of the Jews.' And he closes his Preface with these considerations 'to stir up our hearts to faith and prayer for Israel':

" '1. *The national restoration of the Jews, and its blessed effects on the world.* For what have they been preserved, but for some wondrous end? If their lapse is the world's wealth, and their loss the wealth of the Gentiles, **how much more shall their replenishment be [than] all this**? Rom.11.12.

" '2. *The Jews are the whole world's benefactors.* Through Jewish hands and eyes God has sent his lively oracles of truth to us. They penned, and they preserved the Bible.

" '3. *Our Redeemer — the God-man — who has all power in heaven and earth, is their kinsman.* "He took on Him the seed of Abraham."

" '4. *Viewed nationally, the Jews are the most miserable of all nations.* The Messiah wept over Jerusalem, their capital, before the curse fell on it: ought not we to weep over the accumulated progressive woe springing from the curse, and drinking up the nation's spirit for eighteen centuries?

" '5. *Their covenant prospects are bright beyond all conception.* On the grand day of their realization, will anyone of us all regret that we pitied Israel apostate and outcast?'

"Johnston's address closed with a quotation from Samuel Rutherford, and there can be no doubt that in mid-nineteenth-century Scottish missions the beliefs of two centuries earlier had come to their fullest practical expression." [26]

"...Though most of [Alexander] Somerville's life had been given to the Gentiles, it was of Israel's six and a half millions, and of the day when the Lord would turn again the captivity of Zion, that he spoke to the Free Church Assembly in 1887. Two years later, as the invited guest of the General Assembly of the Church of Scotland, he spoke for the last time upon the same theme with words of earnest warning: '**Let the Churches of the Gentiles beware,** at this late hour of the world's history, not perhaps of resisting the re-entrance of the Jews into their own privilege, but of yielding to unbelief in the promises of God, and of betraying apathy on the subject of Israel's conversion. **By such neglect we shall commit a perilous mistake and incur the displeasure of the Lord.**' " [27]

"It is well known how openly Spurgeon owned his debt to the literature of the Puritans and how, because of his attachment to their theology at a time when it was again being put aside, he was dubbed 'the last of the Puritans'. In his thought on prophecy, **Spurgeon** certainly continued several of the emphases prominent in the Puritan outlook, particularly belief in the national conversion of the Jews and in the future conversion of the world. In the first volume of his Sermons, for the year 1855, he says, '**I think we do not attach sufficient importance to the restoration of the Jews. We do not think enough of it. But certainly, if there is anything promised in the Bible it is this**' (p.214). He did not place the conversion of the Jews at the consummation of history but rather at the beginning of a period of general revival: '**The day shall yet come when the Jews, who were the first apostles to the Gentiles, the first missionaries to us who were afar off, shall be gathered in again. Until that shall be, the fulness of the church's glory can never come. Matchless benefits to the world are bound up with the restoration of Israel; their gathering in shall be as life from the dead.**' (Vol.17, Pp.703-704)

"On this point Spurgeon spoke with certainty throughout his thirty-eight years' ministry in London." [28]

FOOTNOTES

"In 1971, the Banner of Truth Trust published THE PURITAN HOPE; REVIVAL AND THE INTERPRETATION OF PROPHECY by Iain H. Murray. This book remains in print, 301 pp, and is available from the publishers at 3 Murrayfield Road, Edinburgh, UK, or P.O. Box 621, Carlisle, PA."

1. Iain H. Murray, *The Puritan Hope*, P.98
2. ibid., P.40
3. ibid., P.41
4. ibid., P.42
5. ibid., Pp.44-5
6. ibid., Pp.45-7
7. ibid., P.277, Note 25
8. ibid., P.47
9. ibid., P.272, Note 28
10. ibid., Pp.59-60
11. ibid., P.61
12. ibid., Pp.66-8
13. ibid., P.72
14. ibid., P.75

15. ibid., P.99
16. ibid., Pp.100-101
17. *"The Truth, Being a DISCOURSE Which the Author Delivered at his BAPTISM*, R. Judah Monis, Printed by S. KNEELAND, for D. HENCHMAN, at the Corner Shop on the South-side of the Town-House, Boston, 1722, Pp.ii-iii"
18. Murray, *The Puritan Hope*, P.113
19. ibid., P.132
20. ibid., Pp.154-155
21. ibid., P.173
22. ibid., Pp.175-176
23. ibid., P.283, Note 36
24. ibid., P.176
25. ibid., Pp.283-284, Note 37
26. ibid., Pp.176-177
27. ibid., Pp.177-178
28. ibid., P.256

SECTION C:
CONTEMPORARY THEOLOGIES

44

THESE THINGS HAPPENED AS EXAMPLES

"For I do not want you to be unaware, brethren, that our fathers were all under the cloud, and all passed through the sea; and all were baptized into Moses in the cloud and in the sea; and all ate the same spiritual food; and all drank the same spiritual drink, for they were drinking from a spiritual rock which followed them; and the rock was Messiah.

"Nevertheless, with most of them God was not well pleased; for they were laid low in the wilderness. Now these things happened as examples for us, that we should not crave evil things, as they also craved. And do not be idolaters, as some of them were; as it is written, 'The people sat down to eat and drink, and stood up to play.' Nor let us act immorally, as some of them did and twenty-three thousand fell in one day. Nor let us try the Lord, as some of them did, and were destroyed by the serpents. Nor grumble, as some of them did, and were destroyed by the destroyer.

"Now these things happened to them as an example, and they were written for our instruction, upon whom the ends of the ages have come. Therefore let him who thinks he stands take heed lest he fall." (1Co.10:1-12)

God redeemed Israel out of Egypt. He baptized them in the cloud and in the sea. He fed them with spiritual food. He gave them spiritual drink from Messiah. "Nevertheless, with most of them God was not well pleased."

It was not just a few with whom God was not well pleased. It was most of them. God had warned them, but they did not listen. This is important for believers to understand, because it was "written for our instruction."

Paul warns the Church, "we should not crave evil things...do not be idolaters...Nor let us act immorally...Nor let us try the Lord...Nor grumble..." He warns the Church, "let him who thinks he stands take heed lest he fall."

Israel did not heed the warning, and the Church has not heeded the warning either. It is a grave mistake for Gentile Christians to say, "How could those Jews...?" It shows a failure to understand the nature of man, all men. It shows a failure to understand the necessity of the cross.

The Church has craved evil things. The Church has been filled with idolaters. The Church has acted immorally. The Church has tried the Lord. The Church has grumbled.

Every sin which Israel committed, the Church has also committed. The Church has not omitted a single sin. Not every member of the Church has committed every sin, but then neither did every member of Israel. No one, whether part of Israel, or part of the Church, could or can be saved by his works. Luther, for example, could never be saved by his works. Only by

God's mercy and grace, which He extends to the humble, can anyone, or could anyone, be forgiven and saved.

Every charge and warning that Jesus brought against the Jewish religious rulers applies equally as well to the historic religious rulers of the traditional Church. Every charge and warning that Jesus brought applies equally as well to the religious rulers of the Church today. Not to all, for it did not apply to all the Jewish leaders then either, but to "most of them."

Before proceeding to our examination of contemporary theologies, it will be worthwhile to list some of these common, human sins which the Church and the Jews share in common. These, by God's grace, are not true of all in the Church, and nor of all the Jews. The reality of sin does not diminish God's love for the sinner. It shows how great God's love is.

1. Words without deeds. John the Baptist warned the religious men of his time, "bring forth fruit in keeping with your repentance; and do not suppose that you can say to yourselves, 'We have Abraham for our father'; for I say to you, that God is able from these stones to raise up children to Abraham. And the axe is already laid at the root of the trees; every tree therefore that does not bear good fruit is cut down, and thrown into the fire." (Mt.3:8-10)

It will not do any Jews any good to say, "We are the children of Abraham." They must live a life that proves their repentance. Or else they will, like branches, be cut down and thrown into the fire.

It will not do any Gentiles any good to say, "We are the children of Abraham." They must live a life that proves their repentance. Or else they will, like branches, be cut down and thrown into the fire.

2. Self-serving shepherds, prophets, and sheep. The Lord said, "Woe to the shepherds who are destroying and scattering the sheep of My pasture!...behold, I am about to attend to you for the evil of your deeds." (Jer.23:3)

"You eat the fat and clothe yourselves with the wool, you slaughter the fat sheep without feeding the flock. Those who are sickly you have not strengthened, the diseased you have not healed, the broken you have not bound up, the scattered you have not brought back, nor have you sought for the lost; but with force and with severity you have dominated them. And they were scattered for lack of a shepherd, and they became food for every beast of the field and were scattered. My flock wandered through all the mountains and on every high hill, and my flock was scattered over all the surface of the earth; and there was no one to seek for them." (Ezek.34:3-6)

"And as for you, My flock, thus says the Lord God, 'Behold, I will judge between one sheep and another, between the rams and the male goats. Is it too slight a thing for you that you should feed in the good pasture, that you must tread down with your feet the rest of your pastures? Or that you should drink of the clear waters, that you must foul the rest with your feet?'

" 'And as for My flock, they must eat what you tread down with your feet, and they must drink what you foul with your feet!...Behold, I, even I, will judge between the fat sheep and the lean sheep. Because you push with side and with shoulder, and thrust at all the weak with your horns, until you have scattered them abroad, therefore, I will deliver My flock, and they will no longer be a prey; and I will judge between one sheep and another.' " (Ezek.34:17-22)

"Thus says the Lord God, 'Woe to the foolish prophets who are following their own spirit and have seen nothing.' " (Ezek.13:3)

God's word is just as true today as it ever was.

3. Greed and lust for power. "And Jesus entered the temple and cast out all those who were buying and selling in the temple, and overturned the tables of the money-changers and the seats of those who were selling doves. And He said to them, 'It is written, *"My house shall be called a house of prayer"*; but you are making it a robbers' den.' " (Mt.21:12-13)

Jesus was speaking to the respected religious leaders of their day. They served themselves and not God. Because they did not want to lose their wealth, position, or power, they crucified the Lord of glory. Their counterparts today would do the same.

4. Vain worship. "*...in vain do they worship Me, teaching as their doctrines the precepts of men.* Neglecting the commandment of God, you hold to the tradition of men.' He was also saying to them, 'You nicely set aside the commandment of God in order to keep your tradition...thus invalidating the word of God by your tradition which you have handed down...' " (Mk.7:7-9,13)

When the tradition of men demands the neglect of the commandment of God, the tradition of men must be rejected. The Constantinian Church, with the anti-Judaic traditions which it has handed down, has neglected its responsibilities to the Jewish people. The traditions must be rejected.

5. Ceremonialism and legalism. "Woe to you, scribes and Pharisees, hypocrites! for you clean the outside of the cup and of the dish, but inside they are full of robbery and self-indulgence. You blind Pharisee, first clean the inside of the cup and of the dish, so that the outside of it may become clean also.

"Woe to you, scribes and Pharisees, hypocrites! For you are like whitewashed tombs which on the outside appear beautiful, but inside they are full of dead men's bones and all uncleanness. Even so you too outwardly appear righteous to men, but inwardly you are full of hypocrisy and lawlessness." (Mt.23:25-28)

"For My people have committed two evils; They have forsaken Me, the fountain of living waters to hew for themselves cisterns, broken cisterns, that can hold no water." (Jer.2:13)

God gives men living waters, the waters of life. Men then build cisterns, religious systems, to keep the living waters they have received. Then when they are thirsty, they go to the cisterns rather than to the fountain of living waters, the Lord Himself.

In time, the cisterns break and the living waters seep out. Men continue to go to the cisterns, but there are no living waters there anymore. All that remains is an empty form, devoid of life.

That is the way it was, and that is the way it is. The Church needs to return to the fountain and forget about the theological cisterns. It needs to escape a teaching and a history "which on the outside appear beautiful, but inside they are full of dead men's bones and all uncleanness."

6. Beautiful monuments. "And as He was going out of the temple, one of His disciples said to Him, 'Teacher, behold what wonderful stones and what wonderful buildings!' And Jesus said to him, 'Do you see these great buildings? Not one stone shall be left upon another which will not be torn down.' " (Mk.13:1-2)

Constantine built beautiful buildings and defiled the Church. The Church needs to be beautiful, not its buildings. That will make an impression on men.

7. Neglect of justice and mercy. "Woe to you, scribes and Pharisees, hypocrites! For you tithe mint and dill and cummin, and have neglected the weightier provisions of the law: justice and mercy and faithfulness; but these are the things you should have done without neglecting the others. You blind guides, who strain out a gnat and swallow a camel!" (Mt.23:23-24)

The Church has emphasized and quarreled over the littlest things. It needs to show its love and its faith by its works.

8. Blind pride. "Woe to you, scribes and Pharisees, hypocrites! For you build the tombs of the prophets and adorn the monuments of the righteous, and say, 'If we had been living in the days of our fathers, we would not have been partners with them in shedding the blood of the prophets.' Consequently you bear witness against yourselves, that you are sons of those who murdered the prophets.

"Fill up then the measure of the guilt of your fathers. You serpents, you brood of vipers, how shall you escape the sentence of hell?" (Mt.23:29-33)

It is not our goodness that brought us to the Lord, but His grace. It is not our strength and wisdom that keeps us faithful, but His grace. Those who think they are better than "the Jews" are fatally deluding themselves. "There is none righteous, not even one." (Ps.14:1; Rom.3:10)

"And Jesus said to them, 'You will all fall away, because it is written, "I will strike down the shepherd, and the sheep shall be scattered." '...But Peter said to Him, 'Even though all may fall away, yet I will not.' And Jesus said to him, 'Truly I say to you, that you yourself this very night, before a cock crows twice, shall three times deny Me.' But Peter kept saying insistently, 'Even if I have to die with You, I will not deny You!' And they all were saying the same thing, too." (Mk.14:27-28,30-31)

Trusting in our own goodness, strength, or wisdom is a serious mistake.

9. Seeking the praise of men. Jesus said, "How can you believe, when you receive glory from one another, and you do not seek the glory that is from the one and only God?" (Jn.5:44) "But they do all their deeds to be noticed by men; for they broaden their phylacteries, and lengthen the tassels of their garments. And they love the place of honor at banquets, and the chief seats in the synagogues, and respectful greetings in the market places, and being called by men, Rabbi...But the greatest among you shall be your servant. And whoever exalts himself shall be humbled; and whoever humbles himself shall be exalted." (Mt.23:5-7,11-12)

10. Gentilizers. "I am amazed that you are so quickly deserting Him who called you by the grace of Messiah, for a different gospel; which is really not another; only there are some who are disturbing you, and want to distort the gospel of Messiah. But even though we, or an angel from heaven, should preach to you a gospel contrary to that which we have preached to you, let him be accursed. As we have said before, so I say again now, if any man is preaching to you a gospel contrary to that which you received, let him be accursed." (Gal.1:6-9)

The Judaizers of the first century, in opposition to the revealed mystery of Messiah, sought to make the Gentiles become Jews. They sought to limit the gospel to a Jewish framework. They preached a different gospel.

Gentilizers, in opposition to the revealed mystery of Messiah, seek to make the Jews become Gentiles. They seek to remove the gospel from its Jewish framework. They are preaching a different gospel.

11. Triumphalism. "From that time Jesus the Messiah began to show His disciples that He must go to Jerusalem, and suffer many things from the elders and chief priests and scribes, and be killed, and be raised up on the third day. And Peter took Him aside and began to rebuke Him, saying, 'God forbid it, Lord! This shall never happen to You.' But He turned and said to Peter, 'Get behind Me, Satan! You are a stumbling-block to Me; for you are not setting your mind on the things of God, but of man.' Then Jesus said to His disciples, 'If any one wishes to come after Me, let him deny himself, and take up his cross, and follow Me. For whoever wishes to save his life shall lose it; but whoever loses his life for My sake shall find it.' " (Mt.16:21-25)

"Then the mother of the sons of Zebedee came to Him with her sons, bowing down, and making a request of Him. And He said to her, 'What do you wish?' She said to Him, 'Command that in Your kingdom these two sons of mine may sit, one on Your right and one on Your left.' But Jesus answered and said, 'You do not know what you are asking for. Are you able to drink the cup that I am about to drink?' They said to Him, 'We are able.' And Jesus said to them, 'My cup you shall drink; but to sit on My right and on My left, this is not Mine to give, but it is for those for whom it has been prepared by My Father.' " (Mt.20:20-23)

Jesus gave the Church the sword of the Spirit. Constantine gave it the sword of the State. Ever since Constantine, the Church has been trying to overcome the world with the wrong sword. We overcome this world in the same way that Jesus did. Our victory is on the resurrection side of the cross.

Jesus told John to tell the church in Pergamum, "...you hold fast My name, and did not deny My faith, ...but I have a few things against you, because you have there some who hold the teaching of Balaam, who kept teaching Balak to put a stumbling block before the sons of Israel, to eat things sacrificed to idols, and to commit acts of immorality...Repent therefore; or else I am coming to you quickly, and I will make war against them with the sword of My mouth." (Rev.2:13,14,16)

Balaam taught Balak "to put a stumbling block before the sons of Israel." Some in the church at Pergamum who held to the teaching of Balaam were doing likewise. Jesus told them, "Repent...or else..."

From the first verse of the first book of the New Covenant Scriptures (Mt.1:1) to the last chapter of the last book (Rev.22:16), Jesus is identified as the King of the Jews. In heaven, it is as the Lion of Judah, i.e. the King of the Jews, that He is said to prevail and overcome for the salvation of all who will believe in Him. (Rev.5:5)

It is not good to put a stumbling block before the Jewish people. The greatest obstacle to the salvation of the Jewish people is the Church designed by men. The greatest means of bringing salvation to the Jewish people is the Church designed by God.

Paul warned Gentile believers not to be arrogant towards the Jewish people, nor ignorant of God's faithfulness to them. Yet it is this very arrogance and ignorance that generally characterizes the Church's traditional theology and behavior.

The thrust and effect of much of traditional Church theology, as well as that of rabbinic theology, is to keep the Jewish people and the Church separate from one another. That makes it impossible for both the Church and Israel to fulfill their Divine callings.

45

THE PROBLEM WITH INTERPRETING
THE SCRIPTURES BACKWARD

Much, if not most, of the traditional Church approach to the Scriptures is backwards. Theologians begin in the New Covenant Scriptures, form an understanding of its teachings, and then go backwards to impose this interpretation on Tanakh. Since that is often an impossible task, such theologians find it easier to ignore Tanakh or relegate it to insignificance.

Historically, logically, and Biblically this approach is incorrrect. Because of it, traditional Church doctrine is sometimes formed into the exact opposite of what the Scriptures actually do teach. It is not the right way to approach God's Word. God began in the beginning.

Interpreting the Bible backwards produces a message, a teaching, that is backwards. Beginning at the end obscures the beginning, trivializes all of history that does not fit into a triumphalist march, and severs the end from its context. It invites, it almost insures, that one will read into the text what one thinks it should say, rather than read out of the text what it actually does say.

Equally devastating is the fact that this approach provides absolutely no basis for demonstrating the authenticity of the New Covenant Scriptures or the Messiahship of Jesus. It simply assumes both. That, however, is not faith, but ignorance, and is inconsistent with the New Covenant Scriptures themselves.

How do we know that the New Covenant Scriptures really are what they claim to be? How do we know that Jesus is the Messiah? How should we know?

There are many religions that have their own holy books which claim to be the authentic revelation of God, even the culmination of and the key to understanding all that came before. How can we know whether such a claim is true or false?

Is the Koran what it claims to be? Is the Book of Mormon? What about the many other books which make the same claim of divine inspiration and authority? Each book, each religion, claims to be true, no matter what its teaching. Judged only by itself, each is true, even as all the ways of a man are right in his own eyes.

It is pointless to discuss what is true and what is false if we do not agree on the standard by which such judgments should be made. It is pointless to discuss the implications of what God has said when we do not agree on the proper way to understand what He has said.

A particular religion's belief in some teaching does not make the teaching true, not even if the religion is "Christianity." Nor does a particular religion's rejection of some teaching make that teaching necessarily false. To those who already accept that religion's authenticity and authority, such acceptance and rejection are indeed authoritative, but that begs the primary question: What is the basis for the claim of authority? and, is the claim substantiated?

How could anyone in the first century, or today for that matter, know whether the teachings in the gospels, in the letters, and in Relevation are true or false? Put yourself in the first century when the teaching of Jesus and His disciples first went forth. "The religious authorities say so" or "The religious authorities say 'No' " is not a sufficient answer.

Each of us is responsible before God for judging whether these teachings are true or false. If we want to know and want to do what is pleasing to God, how can we know if these teachings are from God or not? How can we know if Jesus is the Messiah or not? There are many people going around claiming to be the Messiah. There are many people going around with a new revelation. How do we know which claim, if any, is true?

Any claim to authenticity must be based on what is already acknowledged to be true. The claim to New Covenant or Messianic authenticity must be based on what we already know is from God. That is why we are told throughout the "New Testament" that Jesus — who He is, what He said, what He did, etc. — is a fulfillment of what was promised in the Law, the Prophets, and the Writings.

The New Covenant Scriptures base their claim to authenticity upon Tanakh. Matthew 1 begins with a genealogy. Though unimportant in all the creeds of the Church, that genealogy qualifies Jesus to be considered as possibly being the Messiah. Without that genealogy, He could not be the Messiah.

We are told repeatedly throughout the gospels that, "This was done that it might be fulfilled..." in order to demonstrate that Jesus is the promised Messiah. As Revelation 19:10 says, "the testimony of Jesus is the spirit of prophecy." If Jesus, or any other Messianic claimant, does not fulfill the prophetic Messianic promises, then he is not the Messiah and people should not believe in him. Anyone who rejects Tanakh — the prior, authoritative revelation of God — has no Biblical basis for determining who is and who is not the Messiah.

In John 5:45-47, Jesus tells those around Him that their failure to believe in Him is due to their failure to believe the writings of Moses. "If you believe Moses you would believe me for he wrote of me. But if you do not believe his writings how will you believe my words." Anyone who rejects what Moses wrote will have no basis for believing what Jesus said.

The Law of Moses leads us to Jesus. It is our tutor for that purpose. It defines Messiah. It did for the disciples. "Philip found Nathanael and told him, 'We have found the one Moses wrote about in the Law, and about whom the prophets also wrote — Jesus of Nazareth, the son of Joseph.' " (John 1:45)

The foundation of Jesus' teaching is Tanakh. After Jesus had risen from the dead, He taught his disciples so that they would understand correctly and accurately. He taught them what they later wrote down, they lived by, and taught to succeeding generations of disciples. "And beginning with Moses and all the prophets, he explained to them the things concerning himself in all the scriptures." (Luke 24:27)

The Law, the Writings, and the Prophets were the only acknowledged, authentic, written revelation of God. What Jesus taught them had to come out of what God had already taught Israel, what God had already revealed. It could not contradict it in any way. It had to agree fully with Tanakh, or the disciples were commanded by God to reject it. (e.g. Dt. 12:32-13:18)

In the same chapter, Luke 24:44 and 45, Jesus said to His disciples, "These are my words which I spoke to you while I was still with you that all things which are written about me in the law of Moses and the prophets and the Psalms must be fulfilled." He affirmed that all the things written in Tanakh must be fulfilled, and "then he opened their mind to understand the Scriptures."

All of His teaching, its source and foundation, is Tanakh. Jesus wanted His disciples to know who He is and what they should proclaim, so he taught them from Tanakh.

The source and foundation of all of Paul's teaching was also Tanakh. If Paul was going to be faithful to Jesus and what Jesus taught, it had to be so. "For what I received I passed on to you as of first importance: that Messiah died for our sins according to the Scriptures, that he was buried, that he was raised on the third day according to the Scriptures." (1Cor. 15:3-4)

When Paul was on trial for his life, he said, "Neither in the Temple, nor in the synagogue, nor in the city did they find me carrying on a discussion with anyone or causing a riot nor can they prove to you the charges which they now accuse me, but this I admit to you that according to the way which they call a sect, I do serve the God of our fathers believing everything that is in accordance with the law and that is written in the prophets." (Acts 24:12-14)

Everything I believe, Paul said, is in accordance with the law and what is written in the prophets. If it doesn't agree with the Law and the Prophets, I don't believe it. In Acts 26:6, still on trial for his life, Paul said, "Now I am standing trial for the hope of the promise made by God to our fathers." That was why he was on trial. Not for some completely new teaching that had just appeared, but because of the promise of God to Abraham, Issac, and Jacob.

In that same chapter of Acts, verse 22, Paul said, "And so having obtained help from God, I stand to this day testifying both to small and great, stating nothing but what the prophets and Moses said was going to take place."

Paul was saying, I don't have any other message than what is in Moses and the prophets. I don't have any other source for my teaching. As he wrote to the believers in Corinth, "Do I say this merely from a human point of view? Doesn't the Law say the same thing?" (1Cor. 9:8)

We believe that the Spirit of God gave Paul understanding that others hadn't had, but it was still an understanding of what God had already said. On trial for his life, Paul said I'm not afraid to die but I want you to know where my guilt lies. I am not guilty of doing what they have accused me of doing. [The accusations were false, even as those against Jesus had been.] I am guilty of believing the promises of God to Israel.

As we read in the last chapter of Acts, verse 23, Paul calls the Jews of Rome to himself because he wants to communicate to them exactly what he has been saying, what his message is, what the promise of the hope is, the promise that God made to the Fathers of Israel. "And when they had set a day for him, they came to him at his lodging in large numbers, and he was explaining to them by solemnly testifying to the kingdom of God and trying to persuade them concerning Jesus from both the law of Moses and from the prophets from morning until evening."

Paul's message comes from the Law and the Prophets. He spoke from the Law and the Prophets to convince people, to demonstrate that Jesus is the prophesied Messiah. He tried to convince them in Rome, and everywhere else, that the kingdom of God that he proclaimed is what had already been written, already promised, in the acknowledged, authentic revelation of God — Tanakh. He said, I don't have any other source. Of course, the Holy Spirit taught him, but the Holy Spirit taught him from Tanakh. Spiritually, logically, it could not be any other way.

How could a first-century Jew know? How could anyone know whether what Paul was proclaiming was true or not? In Thessalonica, "As his custom was, Paul went into the synagogue, and on three Sabbath days he reasoned with them from the Scriptures, explaining and proving that the Christ had to suffer and rise from the dead. 'This Jesus I am proclaiming to you is the Christ,' he said." (Acts 17:2-3) Paul based his case for the Messiahship of Jesus upon Tanakh.

In Acts 17:11, God commends the Jews in the synagogue in Berea: "Now these were more noble minded than those in Thessalonica for they received the word with great eagerness, examining the scriptures daily to see if these things were so." Paul preached to them, and they examined the Scriptures to see whether what he was saying was true or not. God commends them for checking Paul's teaching against Tanakh.

If the teaching did not agree with the Scriptures, then it was not true. If it did not agree with Tanakh, then this Jesus was not the Messiah, and they were commanded by God to reject him and the teaching that Paul brought. The Lord warned Israel to judge spiritual messages by looking "To the law and to the testimony! If they do not speak according to this word, the light has not dawned on them." (Is. 8:20)

God commends them for judging Paul's teaching by Tanakh: "These were more noble-minded...because they searched the scriptures." They searched the only scriptures there were — the law, the writings, and the prophets. They searched them daily to see if this new teaching was true or not. God commends them for that, because God requires that, for there are many deceivers gone out in the world, many who proclaim they are Messiah, many who proclaim they have a new revelation.

That was the only way they could tell whether or not the teaching was true. If it agreed with Tanakh, they should accept it. If it disagreed with Tanakh, God required that they reject it.

What was the result of their testing Paul's teaching by the standard of Tanakh? "Many of them therefore believed, along with a number of prominent Greek women and men." (Acts 17:12)

How do we test a teaching? We test it according to what we know is the authentic revelation of God. Historically, it couldn't be any other way. Logically, it could not be any other way. The acknowledged Word of God could not be judged — accepted or rejected — by some later revelation. It was the new revelation that had to be judged. If the new revelation did not agree with what was known to be from God, then the new revelation had to be rejected.

Biblically it cannot be any other way. This is the way Tanakh presents it. This is the way Jesus presented it. This is the way Paul presented it. It is the way all the New Covenant writers present it. To establish a point, they refer to what has already been established and accepted.

Paul told Timothy, "From childhood you have known the holy Scriptures, which are able to give you the wisdom that leads to salvation through faith which is in Messiah Jesus. All scripture is breathed of God and is profitable for teaching, reproof, for correction, for training in righteousness that the man of God may be adequate, equipped for every good work." (2Tim. 3:15-17)

What Scripture was Paul talking about? The Scriptures which Timothy had known from childhood. The gospels and letters had not been written when Timothy was a child.

Timothy had known Tanakh — the Law, the Writings, and the Prophets. These are the Scriptures which Paul says are able to give the wisdom that leads to salvation through faith in Messiah. It is these Scriptures that Paul considered necessary to train people in the knowledge and service of God. He had already said of himself that he believed and taught everything that agreed with Moses and the prophets.

It is a tautology, but one which needs to be stated: Those who do not believe as Jesus and Paul believed have a faith that is different from that of Jesus and Paul.

46

THE VIEWS OF CONTEMPORARY THEOLOGIES

Contemporary theologies are those that are currently being taught in Bible colleges, seminaries, and Sunday schools. They form the skeletal structure for the sermons preached from the pulpit and in the electronic media. They do the same for the commentaries and theological works being produced in print.

Contemporary theologies are built upon an anti-Judaic foundation. In varying degrees, they are built upon the assumptions, teachings, and errors of Origen, Eusebius, Augustine, Aquinas, Calvin, and Luther. Those errors have already been discussed in previous chapters. Here we will be looking at some of the theological fruit of those errors.

In terms of the relationship of Israel and the Church, there are only three major types of systematic theology, with many shades, variations, and combinations. This is an examination of these theologies only in terms of their view of that relationship. For comparative purposes, and not for detailed identification, these theologies can be characterized as follows:

1) The **"New Israel"** view maintains that natural Israel, the physical seed of Abraham, failed and was cast away; and that the Church is a new, spiritual Israel—the spiritual seed of Abraham through Jesus—which replaces the old. The apparently physical promises to physical Israel are spiritually fulfilled to spiritual Israel. Consequently, this is generally an amillennial position, since the Millennium implies a physical reign of Messiah upon the earth, from Jerusalem, over all the nations. The "postmillennial" position is similar in this regard.

2) The **"Covenant"** view maintains that Israel and the Church are one and the same throughout history, i.e. the faithful among mankind. There is a "Covenant of Grace," or "Covenant of Redemption," which is partially revealed in all the individual covenants which it embraces. From the Fall of Man in the Garden of Eden to the final consummation of all history, God has dealt with man through this Covenant of Grace. Since its birth, the Church is the only covenant people, since all covenants, prophecies, and promises are fulfilled in the gospel. Individual Jews can be grafted into the Church, but all the Jews as a people or a nation have neither significance nor purpose in the ongoing plan of God.

3) The **"Dispensational"** view maintains that Israel and the Church have separate and distinct identities, promises, and destinies; and that Israel as a people, or nation, has been set aside by God during the "Church Age." After the Church Age, God will again deal with national Israel, and restore the kingdom of David in the Millennium.

Each theology develops and follows these major themes concerning the relationship of Israel and the Church. These major themes, in turn, affect much more. For example, a particular theology's method of interpretation affects all of its doctrines. The method of interpretation, however, is affected by, reinforced by, or even formed by the view held of the relationship between Israel and the Church. The influence is reciprocal. The view of that relationship influences the method of interpretation, which, in turn, then influences the view of that relationship.

We cannot examine every writer's theological variations and combinations. Nor can we examine their every use of Scripture. We do not need to. It is sufficient to examine the major themes, the reasoned use of Scripture by which these themes are reached and supported, and the errors in that reasoning and usage. Since these theologies are built upon the views of theologians of the past, we have already accomplished much of this examination in the preceding sections.

None of the contemporary theologies accurately portrays the relationship of Israel and the Church. This is because they have begun with the Church, and then projected backwards, and forwards. They have looked from within the Church out to Israel, and then asked, "Now how do the Jews fit into all of this?" This has produced a distorted view of reality.

The contemporary theologies, as we will now see, fail to properly take into account three primary realities. Where they appear in the examination of each theology, these primary realities will be signified by one, two, or three asterisks.

* (1) The New Covenant is made with the house of Judah and the house of Israel, not with the Church. It is not a covenant made with all men, but all men may be grafted into it.

** (2) There is now, as there has been since God created Israel, a faithful Jewish remnant.

*** (3) The Church is composed of believers called out of the Gentiles to be joined to the faithful remnant in Israel. It is Israel's fruit. There is a distinction between Israel and the Church, but not a separation. There is a union without a loss of identity.

This is the mystery of Messiah. It was for this that the Apostle Paul was willing to be beaten. It was for this that he was willing to be imprisoned. It was for this that Paul asked prayer that he might boldly proclaim it.

The proclamation of the mystery of Messiah is very important, "in order that the manifold wisdom of God might now be made known through the church to the rulers and the authorities in the heavenly places, in accordance with the purpose of the ages which He carried out in Messiah Jesus our Lord." (Eph.3:10-11)

It shows the wisdom of God in all its facets and diversity. In the eternal purpose of God for the ages, the Church is to proclaim this mystery so that all spiritual powers and principalities know it.

Each of these contemporary theologies denies the reality of the mystery of Messiah. Each of these theologies proclaims that there is no such mystery. Each, therefore, keeps the Church from making the mystery of Messiah known to the rulers and authorities in the heavenly places. Each, therefore, keeps the Church from fulfilling the purpose of the ages which God carried out in Messiah Jesus our Lord.

47

"NEW ISRAEL" THEOLOGY

The "New Israel" view maintains that:

1. Natural Israel, the physical seed of Abraham, failed and was cast away.

2. The Church is a new, spiritual Israel — the spiritual seed of Abraham through Jesus — which replaces the old.

3. The apparent physical promises to physical Israel are spiritually fulfilled to spiritual Israel. Consequently, this is an amillennial [i.e. no Millennium] view which "spiritualizes" or ignores the prophecies of a Millennial reign of Messiah upon the earth from Jerusalem, over all the nations.

This view can be represented by the two circles in **Diagram 6.** "Israel 1/ The Jews" has been crossed out and replaced by "Israel 2/The Church." In this view, if any Jews believe in Jesus, they cease to be Jews.

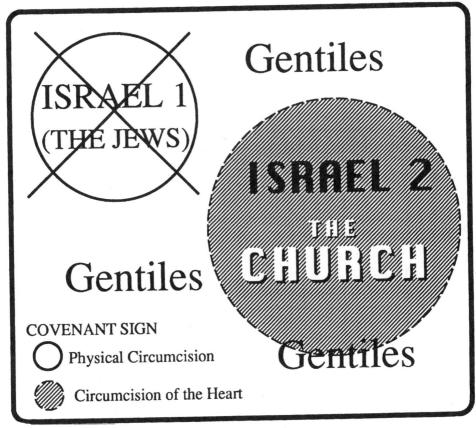

Diagram 6

While it is true that Israel failed, it is not true that therefore the Church, the spiritual seed of Abraham, has replaced Israel, the natural seed of Abraham. The New Israel view is in error because:

* 1. God made the New Covenant with the house of Judah and the house of Israel — the same Israel and Judah which failed. The New Covenant is "not like the Covenant which I made with their fathers...which they broke." (Jer.31:32) The Church does not have its own covenant with God. The Bible does not mention any covenant that God has made with the Church.

2. The failure of the Jews, which followed the failure of the Gentiles, is an integral, essential part of the gospel. Most Jews failed to believe in Jesus when He came. Like all unbelievers, they were blinded by the god of this world. (2Co.4:4) But, in addition to that blindness, "God gave them a spirit of slumber, eyes to see not and ears to hear not, down to this very day." (Rom.11:8) God gave them a spirit of slumber so that they could not awake or understand. God blinded them so that they could not see. He shut their ears so that they could not hear.

God insured that all Israel would not believe, so that salvation might come to the Gentiles through those Jews who did believe. Those in Israel who did not believe were enemies of the gospel for the sake of the Gentiles. It is "because of their disobedience" that God showed mercy to the Gentiles. It is "because of their disobedience" that God still shows mercy to Gentiles, for the scripture says that this is true "down to this very day." Though **many Jews do believe, and any can, all will not believe until God has rescued the full remnant of the Gentiles and brought them into the commonwealth of Israel.**

Every believer was once an enemy of God, "reconciled to God through the death of His Son." (Rom.5:10) "And although you were formerly alienated and enemies in mind, engaged in evil deeds, yet He has now reconciled you in His fleshly body through death, in order to present you before him holy and blameless and beyond reproach." (Col.1:21-22) "For it is on account of these [evil] things that the wrath of God will come, and in them you also once walked, when you were living in them." (Col.3:6-7)

And after having believed, we are still in continual need of the grace of God. "If we say that we have no sin, we are deceiving ourselves, and the truth is not in us. If we confess our sins, He is faithful and righteous to forgive us our sins and to cleanse us from all unrighteousness. If we say that we have not sinned, we make Him a liar, and His word is not in us." (1Jn.1:8-10)

If God were to eternally accept or reject us according to our own faithfulness or righteousness, we would all be lost. "If Thou, Lord, were to mark iniquities, O Lord, who could stand? But there is forgiveness with Thee, that Thou may be feared." (Ps.130:3-4) Whatever we may accomplish, it is by His grace. "For it is God who is at work in you, both to will and to work for his good pleasure." (Phil.2:13) Failure does not disqualify us from receiving the grace of God. It merely shows that the grace of God is necessary.

** 3. There is now a faithful Jewish remnant, as there has been since God created Israel. Since the birth of the Church, this faithful remnant is part of Israel AND part of the Church. Paul writes, "Now the promises were spoken to Abraham and to his seed. He does not say, 'and to seeds,' as referring to many, but rather to one, 'And to your seed,' that is, Messiah." (Gal.3:16) Paul is here, as throughout Galatians, re-emphasizing the distinction between the different "seeds" of Abraham. Isaac and Ishmael were both the seed of Abraham, but they were different seeds. The promises were not made to both seeds, but only to one. "...through Isaac your seed shall be named. And of the son of the maid [Hagar, whose son was Ishmael] I will make a nation also, because he is your seed." (Gen.21:12,13)

When God changed Abram's name to Abraham, He promised him, "And I will establish My covenant between Me and you and **your seed** after you throughout **their generations** for an everlasting covenant, to be God to you and to **your seed** after you. And I will give to you and to your seed after you, the land of your sojournings, all the land of Canaan, for an everlasting possession; and I will be **their God**." (Gen.17:7-8) The word for "seed" is singular, but "their generations" and "their God" are plural possessives. It is one "seed" that contains many individuals and many generations.

When God promises, by a covenant and by an oath, to give the land of Israel to the people of Israel forever, He says, "To you [singular] I will give the land of Canaan as the portion of your [plural] inheritance." (Ps.105:11) The singular refers to the one nation, Israel. The plural refers to the many individuals in Israel who will receive that inheritance.

Jacob and Esau were both the seed of Isaac, but they were different seeds. The promises were not made to both seeds, but only to one, to Jacob. "The Lord appeared to [Isaac]...and said, 'I am the God of your father Abraham; Do not fear, for I am with you. I will bless you, and multiply your seed, for the sake of My servant Abraham.' " (Gen.26:24) The Lord promised Isaac, as He had promised Abraham, one seed that would be multiplied.

The Lord appeared to Jacob and said, "I am the Lord, the God of your father Abraham and the God of Isaac; the land on which you lie, I will give it to you; and to your seed. Your seed shall also be like the dust of the earth, and you shall spread out to the west and to the east and to the north and to the south; and in you and in your seed shall all the families of the earth be blessed." (Gen.28:14) Jacob was the promised seed of Isaac and Abraham, just as Isaac was also the promised seed of Abraham; one chosen, promised seed that would be multiplied as the dust of the earth.

The distinction here is that the one seed of Abraham is only physically his seed, like Ishmael and Esau, whereas the other seed is both physically and spiritually his seed. Those who are the physical AND spiritual, i.e. "faithful," seed of Abraham are the called, promised children of Abraham. It is these who inherit the promises, in Messiah.

Most Jews did not believe in Jesus, "But it is not as though the word of God has failed. For they are not all Israel who are descended from Israel; neither are they all children because they are Abraham's seed, but: 'through Isaac your seed will be named.' That is, it is not the children of the flesh who are children of God, but the children of the promise are regarded as seed."(Rom.9:6-8)

Paul is not saying here that none of those descended from Israel are Israel. Nor is he saying that some who are not descended from Israel are Israel. He is simply saying, "they are not all Israel who are descended from Israel." Some are. Some are not.

God called Abraham when he was only one. Yet Levi, before his own grandfather Isaac was born, was "in" his great-grandfather Abraham (Heb.7:9). All the faithful seed of Abraham, including Jesus, were "in" Abraham when God made the promises. The promises spoken to Abraham and his seed were ultimately promises to Jesus the Messiah, the One in whom, by whom, and for whom all things exist. Isaac and Jacob, and all the faithful of Israel are "in" Messiah, as are all believers, "just as He chose us in Him before the foundation of the world, that we should be holy and blameless before Him." (Eph.1:4)

Eliezer of Damascus had the faith of his master Abraham, but was not physically descended from him. Eliezer was spiritually descended from Abraham, but not physically. God promised Abraham that "one shall come forth from your own inward parts, he shall be your heir." (Gen.15:4) Eliezer, therefore, did not qualify on his own to be Abraham's heir. Isaac, who was **the spiritual AND natural seed of Abraham**, did. The faithful seed of Abraham that is found in Messiah is his heir, bears his name and receives the promises made to him.

Gentile believers, like Eliezer of Damascus, are "in" Messiah because of their faith in Him. Because Messiah is "in" Abraham, Gentile believers are also included in Abraham's faithful seed. To be part of the body of Messiah is to be included in the promises that Messiah inherits.

*** **4. The Church is composed of believers called out of the Gentiles to be joined to the faithful remnant in Israel.** Israel and the Church are not the same. This is made clear in Ephesians 2 and Romans 11.

The Church is made up of "us, whom He also called, not from among Jews only, but also from among Gentiles." (Rom.9:24) "And again he says, 'Rejoice, O Gentiles, with His people.' " (Rom.15:10 citing Dt.32:43) The Scripture does not say, "Rejoice, O Gentiles, **instead** of His people," but rather "**with His people.**" Specific local congregations may be composed of Jews or Gentiles only (cf. Rom.16:4), but the Church as a whole is not.

5. God's promise to Abraham (including the promise of the land of Israel) was repeated to and inherited by Isaac, Jacob, and their faithful descendants. The faithful remnant in Israel was not cast off, nor were they dispossessed of their inheritance. Believing Gentiles were brought into the commonwealth of Israel to be fellow-heirs, not sole heirs. We are told, "For they are not all Israel who are descended from Israel." (Rom.9:6b) Some who are physically descended from Israel are truly "the Israel of God." Some are not.

6. The Law did not replace God's promise to Abraham, but was given to guide Israel to Messiah and His righteousness. "The Law, which came four hundred and thirty years later, does not invalidate a covenant previously ratified by God, so as to nullify the promise." (Gal.3:17) Israel's failure to keep the Law does not invalidate God's promise to Abraham, which Isaac, Jacob/Israel, and the children of Israel inherited. Likewise, neither does the New Covenant, which came 2000 years after Abraham, invalidate God's covenant promise to Abraham and the seed called by his name.

The New Covenant supercedes the Old Covenant, the Covenant of the Law, to bring about the fulfillment of God's covenant with Abraham. It does not alter or replace God's covenant with Abraham. It was given to facilitate the fulfillment of that promise.

God promised a painful list of tragedies that would come upon Israel "if you do not obey Me and do not carry out all these commandments, if, instead, you reject My statutes, and if your soul abhors My ordinances so as not to carry out all My commandments, and so break My covenant." (Lev.26:14-15) Then He reaffirmed His covenant with Abraham to be God to him and his seed.

"If they confess their iniquity and the iniquity of their forefathers,...or if their uncircumcised heart becomes humbled so that they then make amends for their iniquity, then I will remember **My covenant with Jacob, and I will remember also My covenant with Isaac, and My covenant with Abraham** as well, and I will remember the land...I will not reject them as to destroy them, breaking My covenant with them; for I am the Lord their God. But I will remember for them the covenant with their ancestors, whom I brought out of the land of Egypt in the sight of the nations, that I might be their God. I am the Lord." (Lev.26:40-42,44-45)

In unfaithfulness, Israel could not enjoy what belonged to her, but the repentance of Israel causes God to remember and fulfill His promise. "For," concerning Israel, "the gifts and the calling of God are irrevocable." (Rom.11:29) (That applies to the land of Israel as well, for God promises, "I will remember the land.")

7. The New Covenant Scriptures clearly state that God has not cast off that Israel which failed. "For I also am an Israelite, of the [physical] seed of Abraham, of the tribe of Benjamin." (Rom.11:1) I.e., 'I am living physical proof that God has not cast off Israel.' Paul, like Moses, Samuel, and Daniel before him, identified himself with Israel, that failure of a people. For Paul, being an Israelite is something different than being a part of the Church. God has always preserved a faithful Jewish remnant until "the fulness of the Gentiles has come in; and thus all Israel will be saved." (Rom.11:25-26) Paul is part of that remnant.

In **Diagram 6**, in which circle does the Apostle Paul belong? He identifies himself with his unbelieving Jewish brethren who are represented by "Israel 1/The Jews." He also identifies himself as being part of the Church.

8. There is no mention in the Bible of the Church being a new Israel or a spiritual Israel. The word "Israel" appears 73 times in the New Covenant Scriptures. "Israelite(s)" appears 4 times. There is not a single instance where the New Covenant Scriptures equate "Israel" with the Church, but there are many instances where "Israel" is used in contrast to the Gentiles, and many instances where "Israel" is explicitly equated with the Jewish people.

What then would be the rule of interpretation, and the justification for it, by which we could distinguish when "Israel" means "the Jews" and when "Israel" means "the Church"? Is there a point in time when the meaning can be said to have changed? When? The word "Israel" is used continually throughout the Bible. Must one first determine what fits the assumed doctrine in order to know whether "Israel" means "the Jews" or "the "Church"? That would mean that it is the doctrine that interprets the Scriptures, rather than the Scriptures that produce the doctrine.

In what respects is the Church supposed to be the new Israel, replacing the Jews? In what specific ways does the Church not replace the Jews as Israel? What are the Scriptures that tell us this?

The general rule of interpretation that seems to be used in this theology is simply this: If the scripture says or promises something good for "Israel," then "Israel" is the Church. If it says or promises something bad, then "Israel" is the Jews. Apparently, the Church is only the new Israel when there is a blessing to be claimed. That is not a good rule of interpretation.

The Lord often promises good things to the "Israel" that He calls to repentance. Also, we know that the Lord has some harsh things to say to the Church. In scriptures that are explicitly directed to the Church, such as the epistles and the second and third chapters of Revelation, the Lord does not limit Himself to saying or promising only good things. There is much rebuke and correction.

By what rule of interpretation, and by what change in the nature of God, would the "new Israel" be exempt from the judgments of God decreed for "old Israel's" unfaithfulness? If God cast off and dispossessed the Jews for their sins, will He not do the same with the Church? The sins of the Church in the last two thousand years are certainly no less than the sins of Israel in the previous two thousand years. Nor are they less than the sins of Israel since then.

If Israel was cast off and replaced for those sins, despite the promises of God, will not God do the same in response to the unfaithfulness of the Church? If not, then why not? Certainly it cannot be argued, "But we are the children of Abraham." "...For I say to you that God is able from these stones to raise up children to Abraham." (Mt.3:9) Being the children of Abraham is not sufficient to guarantee the inheritance.

9. The destruction of Jerusalem and the second Temple in 70 A.D., at the end of "the Great Revolt," was not the Great Tribulation. There are many reasons why it was not, but the starkest concerns the description that Jesus gave of the Great Tribulation: "For then there will be a great tribulation, such as has not occurred since the beginning of the world until now, nor ever shall." (Mt.24:21)

It may be questioned whether or not it is possible, or wise, to measure and compare tragedies. But if one chooses a measure — whether suffering, devastation, death, or long-lasting consequences — the destruction of Jerusalem in 70 A.D. was exceeded by other events in Jewish history. Both the Holocaust and the Bar Kokhba Rebellion of 132-135 A.D. were greater tragedies than the Great Revolt.

What was the context of what Jesus said? The disciples had pointed out the Temple buildings to Him. "And He answered and said to them, 'Do you not see all these things? Truly I say to you, not one stone here shall be left upon another, which will not be torn down.' And as He was sitting on the Mount of Olives, the disciples came to Him privately, saying, 'Tell us, [1] when will these things be, and [2] what will be the sign of Your coming, and [3] of the end of the age?' " (Mt.24:2-3)

Jesus then answered their three questions, telling them when the Temple would be destroyed, what the sign of His coming would be, and what the sign of the end of the age would be. Some of the things He said were about the destruction of the Temple in 70 A.D. Some were not.

However one understands or divides His comments, it cannot be denied that Jesus said **something** about His return and the sign of His coming. Certainly that did not happen in 70 A.D. There are many other aspects of the answer that Jesus gave that cannot be related to the destruction of the Temple in 70 A.D. If these events have not already taken place in the past, then they will assuredly take place in the future. Let's look at some of them in Mt. 24:14-31.

v.14 "And this gospel of the kingdom shall be preached in the whole world for a witness to all the nations, and then the end shall come." Did that happen before 70 A.D.?

v.15 "Therefore when you see the abomination of desolation which was spoken of through Daniel the prophet, standing in the holy place (let the reader understand)..." Whoever reads this portion of Scripture is to understand what Daniel the prophet said about the abomination of desolation. What did Daniel say?

"Now while I was speaking and praying, and confessing my sin and the sin of my people Israel, and presenting my supplication before the Lord my God in behalf of the holy mountain of my God, while I was still speaking in prayer, then the man Gabriel... gave me instruction and talked with me, and said, 'O Daniel, I have now come forth to give you insight with understanding... so give heed to the message and gain understanding of the vision.

" 'Seventy weeks have been decreed for your people and your holy city, to finish the transgression, to make an end of sin, to make atonement for iniquity, to bring in everlasting righteousness, to seal up vision and prophet, and to anoint the most holy.

" 'So you are to know and discern that from the issuing of a decree to restore and rebuild Jerusalem until Messiah the Prince there will be seven weeks and sixty-two weeks; it will be built again, with plaza and moat, even in times of distress.

" 'Then after the sixty-two weeks Messiah will be cut off and have nothing, and the people of the prince who is to come will destroy the city and the sanctuary. And its end will come with a flood; even to the end there will be war; desolations are determined.

" 'And he will make a covenant with the many for one week, but in the middle of the week he will put a stop to sacrifice and grain offering; and on the wing of abominations will come one who makes desolate, even until a complete destruction, one that is decreed, is poured out on the one who makes desolate.' " (Dan.9:24-27)

Gabriel told Daniel, these seventy weeks "have been decreed for your people and your holy city." So the seventy weeks all refer to the Jewish people and Jerusalem. By the end of the seventy weeks, God will have accomplished certain things for the Jewish people and Jerusalem.

These "Seventy weeks have been decreed for your people and your holy city, to finish the transgression, to make an end [לחתם] of sin, to make atonement for iniquity, to bring in everlasting righteousness, to seal [לחתם] up vision and prophet, and to anoint the most holy [קדש קדשים]." When the seventy weeks are completed, the transgression and the sin of Jerusalem and the Jewish people will be no more. Atonement will have been made for their iniquity. Throughout Daniel's prayer, he has been confessing to the Lord that same transgression, sin, and iniquity. The message that Gabriel brings is in response to Daniel's prayer.

When the seventy weeks are completed, everlasting righteousness will

be brought into Jerusalem and the Jewish people [להביא צדק עלמים]. This
also is in response to Daniel's prayer. "The righteousness [הצדקה] belongs
to Thee, O Lord, but to us open shame, as it is this day — to the men of
Judah, the inhabitants of Jerusalem, and all Israel..." (v.7) "Thus He has
confirmed His words which he had spoken against us and against our rulers
who ruled us, to bring on us great calamity [להביא עלינו רעה גדלה]..." (v.12)

"Therefore, the Lord has kept the calamity in store and brought it on us;
for the Lord our God is righteous [צדיק] with respect to all His deeds which
He has done, but we have not obeyed His voice." (v.14) "O my God, incline
Thine ear and hear! Open Thine eyes and see our desolations and the city
which is called by Thy name; for we are not presenting our supplications
before Thee on account of our righteousness [צדקתינו] , but on account of
Thy great compassion." (v.18)

The Lord told Jeremiah of the time when He would bring that everlasting
righteousness to the Jewish people; a time which would be after the final
destruction of Babylon: "'In those days and at that time,' declares the Lord,
'search will be made of the iniquity of Israel, but there will be none; and for
the sins of Judah, but they will not be found; for I shall pardon those whom
I leave as a remnant.' " (Jer.50:20)

When the seventy weeks are completed, God will give no more vision or
prophet for the Jewish people and Jerusalem. The Lord told Zechariah of
that time, which follows the national repentance of Israel (Zech.12:10-13:1):
"And it will come about that if anyone still prophesies, then his father and
mother who gave birth to him will say to him, 'You shall not live, for you
have spoken falsely in the name of the Lord'; and his father and mother
who gave birth to him will pierce him through when he prophesies. Also it
will come about in that day that the prophets will each be ashamed of his
vision when he prophesies..." (Zech.13:3,4)

When the seventy weeks are completed, God will have anointed that
which is most holy [קדש קדשים]. The term in Dan.9:24 that is usually translated
"the most holy" [קדש קדשים] is a Biblical designation for the portion [חלק,
e.g. Lev.6:17] of certain sacrifices that belongs to the High Priest and his
heirs. (cf. Lev.2:3,10; 6:17,25; 7:1,6; 10:12,17; 21:22)

On one occasion the Lord described the physical blemishes which would
make a descendant of Aaron unqualified to bring an offering into the veil
to the Lord. Though such a man would not be able to fulfill the priestly
role, he still is entitled to eat of the priests' portion, including the most holy
things [קדשי הקדשים] (Lev.21:22).

The phrase is once used to describe the altar after its time of sanctification.
The Lord told Moses, "You shall make atonement seven days for the altar,
and shall sanctify it; and the altar shall become most holy [קדש קדשים],
everything touching the altar becomes holy." (Ex.29:37) Here also, it is the
sacrifices that are being considered.

It is a different term than that used for the Holy of Holies [קדֶשׁ הקדשׁים] (cf. Ex.26:33-34; 1Kings 8:6; 2Chr.5:7). It is also a different term than that used to describe the Lord, "the holy One of Israel"[קדוֹשׁ ישׂראל] (e.g. 2Kings 19:22; Is.47:4; 54:5; Ezek.39:7).

The Lord is the High Priest of Israel. In Dan.9:24, the most holy refers, like everything else, to Jerusalem and the Jewish people. "For the Lord's portion [חלק] is His people; Jacob is the allotment of His inheritance." (Dt.32:9) "For neither Israel nor Judah has been forsaken by his God, the Lord of hosts, although their land is full of guilt before the Holy One of Israel." (Jer.51:5)

After sixty-nine (seven plus sixty-two) weeks, Messiah is cut off, i.e. put to death, and the people of the prince who is to come destroy the city and the sanctuary [הקדֶשׁ], i.e. Jerusalem and the Temple. These three things happen after the sixty-ninth week, but before the seventieth. Note also that it is the people of the prince who is to come that destroy the city and the sanctuary, not the prince himself.

At some time of unspecified length after the death of Messiah and the destruction of Jerusalem and the Temple, he, i.e. the prince who is to come, makes a firm covenant with the many for one week. This one week is the seventieth of the weeks that Gabriel tells Daniel "have been decreed for your people and your holy city." The making, or strengthening [הגביר], of the covenant by the prince, when he has come, marks the beginning of the seventieth week.

Each of these weeks is understood to be composed of seven years rather than seven days. That was historically the case concerning the sixty-nine weeks from the decree to restore and rebuild Jerusalem until Messiah the Prince. Two verses after this section, Daniel says, "In those days, I, Daniel, had been mourning for three weeks of days [שׁלשׁה שׁבעים ימים]." (Dan.10:2) He uses this unusual phrase to contrast the three weeks of days with the seventy weeks of years that have just been discussed.

Each week is a comparable length of time. If one week is seven years, then all the weeks are seven years. If one week is two thousand years, then all the weeks are two thousand years. There is no justification for "interpreting" sixty-nine of the weeks to be seven years in length and one of the weeks to be two thousand or more years in length.

The seventieth week begins after the death of Messiah and the destruction of Jerusalem. It begins with the establishing, or strengthening, of a covenant by the prince whose people earlier destroyed the city and the sanctuary.

"...in the middle of the week, he will put a stop to sacrifice and grain offering..." In order for him to put a stop to sacrifice and grain offering, they must be taking place. In order for sacrifice and grain offering to be taking place, the sanctuary, i.e. the Temple, must be in existence. So before the prince whose people destroyed the city and the sanctuary can put a stop to sacrifice and grain offering, the Temple must be rebuilt from its previous destruction after the death of Messiah.

There are those who maintain that the prince who is to come, the one who makes this covenant, is the same as "Messiah the prince." They say that Messiah's death makes the covenant and causes the sacrifice and grain offering to cease to have any purpose. There are some obvious problems with this view.

According to Daniel: (1) Messiah has been put to death before the seventieth week, but the seventieth week begins when the prince who is to come makes his covenant. (2) The people of the prince who is to come destroy Jerusalem and the Temple. The Romans are the people who destroyed Jerusalem and the Temple. The Bible never calls the Romans the people of Messiah. Throughout Daniel 9, Israel is called the people of God. This is the thrust of Daniel's prayer.

(3) The prince who is to come establishes a seven year covenant. Messiah never made a seven year covenant. The New Covenant does not expire after seven years. It does not expire when "a complete desolation, one that is decreed, is poured out on the one who makes desolate," i.e. the end of the seventieth week. It is an eternal covenant.

(4) The sacrifice and grain offerings are caused to cease in the middle of the seventieth week. If Messiah's death causes them to cease, then what covenant is it that was made three and a half years (half a week) before His death? What is the significance of the three and a half years which would then follow His death?

(5) The city and sanctuary are destroyed before the seventieth week begins. That happened in 70 A.D. How can Messiah's death, about 30 A.D., take place in the middle of the seventieth week, which begins after the city and the sanctuary are destroyed? How can Messiah's death take place in the middle of the seventieth week, when we are told that it takes place before the seventieth week begins? Gabriel explicitly explains that he is telling Daniel things that will happen in a specific chronological order.

(6) If Messiah is "the prince who is to come," then to whom is Gabriel referring when he says, "and on the wing of abominations will come one who makes desolate"? Some say that this is Messiah the prince because He said to Jerusalem, "Behold your house is left to you desolate; and I say to you, you shall not see Me until the time comes when you say, 'Blessed is He who comes in the name of the Lord!' " (Lk.13:35) The problem with believing that Messiah is the one who makes desolate is that Gabriel continues, "and on the wing of abominations will come one who makes desolate, even until a complete destruction, one that is decreed, is poured out on the one who makes desolate." Is there decreed a complete destruction on Messiah the prince after the desolation of Jerusalem?

In Mt.24:15, Jesus said that Daniel the prophet spoke of "the abomination of desolations." What in the text of Dan.9:27 does that refer to? In this scenario, it can only be the Messiah who commits "the abomination of desolations." The best that can be said of such an "interpretation" is that it is impossible.

There is no way to reconcile this kind of "interpretation" with either the text, the context, or the historical reality. This cannot be said to have happened in 70 A.D., or before, or since. On the other hand, there is no problem with understanding the words in their normal meaning.

The establishment of the seven-year covenant begins the seventieth week. This is sometime after the people of the prince who is to come have destroyed the city and the sanctuary. It is in the middle of this seventieth week that the prince who is to come puts a stop to sacrifice and grain offering in the rebuilt Temple. It is then that "the abomination of desolation which was spoken of through Daniel the prophet, ...[stands] in the holy place." It is a prophesied event that has not yet taken place.

Additionally, no matter to what lengths one goes to ignore the text and context, and no matter to what lengths one goes to allegorize verse 24 - "to finish the transgression, to make an end of sin, to make atonement for iniquity, to bring in everlasting righteousness, to seal up vision and prophecy, and to anoint the most holy" — a great difficulty remains. Someone who believes in the New Covenant Scriptures cannot say that vision and prophecy were sealed up in 70 A.D. If they were sealed up then, they would not go forth after that. The Book of Revelation, written after 70 A.D., contains vision and prophecy. It also refers to future prophets. (Rev.11:3)

Let's go back to Matthew 24, v.21: "For then there will be a great tribulation, such as has not occurred since the beginning of the world until now, nor ever shall." As previously mentioned, the destruction of Jerusalem in 70 A.D. was not the greatest tribulation the Jewish people have ever gone through.

v.22: "And unless those days had been cut short, no flesh would have been saved; but for the sake of the elect those days shall be cut short." In what way were those days cut short in 70 A.D.? There is no record of that happening. The siege was lengthy, and multitudes died of starvation.

If the days were somehow cut short in a way that remains unrecorded, how would that have affected "the elect" in Israel? Eusebius says that, "The whole body, however, of the church at Jerusalem, having been commanded by a divine revelation, given to men of approved piety there before the war, removed from the city, and dwelt at a certain town beyond the Jordan, called Pella." [1] So according to Eusebius, "the elect" were not even in Jerusalem at the time of its final siege and destruction. Their lives were not endangered, and, there was no reason to shorten the days for them.

What was the danger to "the elect" in other parts of Israel? Though there had been fighting earlier in Judea and Galilee, that was no longer the case as the siege of Jerusalem continued. There was no reason to shorten the days for them.

What was the danger to "the elect" in other parts of the world, like Antioch or Ephesus? There was none. There was no reason to shorten the days for them.

v.29: "But immediately after the tribulation of those days the sun will be darkened, and the moon will not give its light, and the stars will fall from the sky, and the powers of the heavens will be shaken." Did that happen?

v.30: "And then the sign of the Son of Man will appear in the sky, and then all the tribes of the earth will mourn, and they will see the Son of Man coming on the clouds of the sky with power and great glory." Did that happen?

v.31: "And He will send forth His angels with a great trumpet and they will gather together His elect from the four winds, from one end of the sky to the other." Did that happen?

vv.32-34: "Now learn the parable from the fig tree: when its branch has already become tender, and puts forth its leaves, you know that summer is near; even so you too, when you see all these things, recognize that He [or it] is near, right at the door. Truly I say to you, this generation will not pass away until all these things take place."

When we see that the branch of the fig tree is tender and has put forth its leaves, we know that summer is near. When we see that the branch of the fig tree is not tender, and has not put forth its leaves, we know that summer is not yet near. In the same way, when we see all these things happen, we will know that "He," the Lord, or "it," the end of the age, is right at the door.

The disciples had asked Jesus, "what will be the sign of Your coming, and of the end of the age?" He was answering their questions. The generation that sees these things will not pass away until all these things take place. Through at least the end of the second century the Church held that the canonical meaning of the fig tree was the blossoming of Israel at the end of the age. This point has already been covered in the chapter on "The Historical Development of Anti-Judaic Theology."

Jesus told of many signs by which the end of the age, and the great tribulation that accompanies it, could be known. Many of these signs were clearly not fulfilled in the destruction of the Temple in 70 A.D. Since these events did not take place in the past, we can expect them in the future.

10. Paul's allegory in Galatians 4:21-31 does not teach the replacement of national Israel by the Church. This point was covered in the chapter on "The Allegory of Galatians 4:21-31."

11. Jesus did not teach that the kingdom of God would be taken away

from Israel, but rather that it would be taken away from Israel's rulers. This point was covered in the chapter on "The Restoration of the Kingdom."

12. The claim that the Jews are the earthly seed of Abraham and the Church is his heavenly seed is not supported by the Bible. There are a few scriptures that compare the children of Abraham, Isaac, and Jacob to the stars of the heavens, the sands by the sea, or the dust of the earth. Reviewing all these scriptures will make it clear what God actually intends the comparison to signify.

When Abraham questioned whether he would ever have a natural descendant to be his heir, the Lord told him, "'one who shall come forth from your own inward parts, he shall be your heir.' And He took him outside and said, 'Now look toward the heavens, and **count the stars**, if you are able to count them.' And He said to him, 'So shall your seed be.' " (Gen.15:4-5) In this instance, God pointed to the stars to indicate to Abraham how numerous the people descended from him would be.

Later, after the offering of Isaac, the Lord told Abraham, "because you have done this thing, and have not withheld your son, your only son, indeed I will greatly bless you, and **I will greatly multiply your seed as the stars of the heavens, and as the sand which is on the seashore**; and your seed shall possess the gate of his enemies. And in your seed all the nations of the earth shall be blessed, because you have obeyed My voice." (Gen.22:17-18) No distinction is made here between two different seeds of Abraham, one that is earthly and one that is heavenly. The Lord is again promising to Abraham a great multitude — as the stars of the heavens and as the sand of the sea — which will be descended from him.

After Abraham had died, the Lord appeared to Isaac and promised him, **"I will multiply your seed as the stars of heaven, and will give your seed all these lands**; and by your seed all the nations of the earth shall be blessed; because Abraham obeyed Me and kept My charge, My commandments, My statutes and My laws." (Gen.26:4-5) Here again, the Lord is speaking of multitude.

The Lord then appeared to Jacob when he was fleeing from Esau, and said, "I am the Lord, the God of your father Abraham and the God of Isaac; **the land on which you lie, I will give it to you and to your seed. Your seed shall also be like the dust of the earth**, and you shall break through to the west and to the east and to the north and to the south; and in you and in your seed shall all the families of the earth be blessed." (Gen.28:14) In this instance, the Lord does not specify exactly in what way the seed of Jacob will be like the dust of the earth—whether in multitude or in some other way—but Jacob breaks through the defenses of those who surround him because his seed is as the dust of the earth. The language is the same as in Job1:10, where the multitude of Job's cattle has broken through and filled the land. It is through Jacob's seed, multiplied as the dust of the earth, that all the families of the earth are blessed.

When Moses was on Mt. Sinai with God, and the children of Israel were worshipping the golden calf, the Lord told Moses, " '...let Me alone...that I may destroy them...' Then Moses entreated the Lord his God, and said, '...Remember Abraham, Isaac, and Israel, Thy servants to whom Thou didst swear by Thyself, and didst say to them, *I will multiply your seed as the stars of the heavens, and all this land of which I have spoken I will give to your seed, and they shall inherit it forever.*' So the Lord changed His mind about the harm which He said He would do to His people." (Ex.32:9-14)

In this instance, Moses understood God's promise to Abraham, Isaac, and Jacob — the promise of a seed multiplied as the stars of the heavens — to refer to their physical descendants. Apparently, the Lord understood it the same way, since He accepted the intercession of Moses for them.

And when Moses spoke to the next generation of the children of Israel in the wilderness, he said, "**The Lord your God has multiplied you, and behold, you are this day as the stars of heaven for multitude. May the Lord, the God of your fathers, increase you a thousand-fold more than you are, and bless you, just as He has promised you.**" (Dt.1:10-11) He reminded them, "Your fathers went down to Egypt seventy persons in all, and now the Lord your God has made you **as numerous as the stars of heaven.**" (Dt.10:22) When he warned them of the consequences of disobedience to the Lord, he said, "Then you shall be left few in number, whereas you were **as the stars of heaven for multitude**, because you did not obey the Lord your God." (Dt.28:62)

King David commanded that a census be taken of the sons of Israel. "But David did not count those twenty years of age and under, because the Lord had said **He would multiply Israel as the stars of the heaven.**" (1Ch.27:23) David understood the promise and comparison of the Lord to refer to the number of the physical descendants of Abraham, Isaac, and Jacob.

After God brought destruction and exile upon the children of Israel for their disobedience, the Lord brought back a remnant of the captive ones of Zion. Then the Levites and the priests prayed, reviewing God's dealings with Israel, "...And Thou didst make their sons **numerous as the stars of heaven, and Thou didst bring them into the land which Thou hadst told their fathers to enter and possess...**" (Neh.9:23) "The stars of the heaven" are used to indicate number, nothing more.

By faith, a barren Sarah received power to conceive Isaac, in fulfillment of God's promise. "Therefore, also, there was born of one man, and him as good as dead in these things, **as many descendants as the stars of heaven in number, and innumerable as the sand which is by the seashore.**"(Heb.11:12) The New Covenant Scriptures specifically interpret the comparison as relating to the birth of Isaac and the number of his descendants.

In **every** case, the Bible explains the promise to Abraham that his seed would be as the stars of the heavens as referring to the numerical multitude of his descendants through Isaac and Jacob. It is never interpreted as referring to the difference between Israel and the Church. The comparisons of their seed to the sand of the sea and the dust of the earth also refer to the promised numerical multitude of that seed, not to its nature or destiny.

13. The claim that all the promises of God to Israel were fulfilled long ago, making the present state of Israel irrelevant to the plan of God, is not supported by the Bible. Several scriptures are used to support this claim. For example:

"So the Lord gave Israel all the land which He had sworn to give to their fathers, and they possessed it and lived in it...Not one of the good promises which the Lord had made to the house of Israel failed; all came to pass." (Josh.21:43,45)

"Now behold, today I am going the way of all the earth and you know in all your hearts and in all your souls that not one word of all the good words which the Lord your God spoke concerning you has failed; all have been fulfilled for you, not one of them has failed!" (Josh.23:14)

The first step in understanding these scriptures is to read them in context. The first five chapters of the book of Joshua record Israel's crossing of the Jordan River and preparation for the conquest of Canaan. Chapters 6 through 11 record the different battles. Chapter 12 enumerates "the kings of the land whom the sons of Israel defeated and whose land they possessed...in all, thirty-one kings." (Josh.12:1-24) Chapters 13 through 21 concern the allotment of the land to the different tribes of Israel. Chapter 22 concerns the two and a half tribes which received their inheritance on the other side of the Jordan. Chapters 23 and 24 relate Joshua's final words to Israel.

Chapter 11 ends, "So Joshua took the whole land, according to all that the Lord had spoken to Moses, and Joshua gave it for an inheritance to Israel according to their divisions by their tribes. Thus the land had rest from war." (Josh.11:23) Chapter 12 lists the battles which had already been fought and won, but chapter 13 begins, "Now Joshua was old and advanced in years when the Lord said to him, 'You are old and advanced in years, and very much of the land remains to be possessed. This is the land that remains... I will drive them [i.e., the inhabitants of the unpossessed land] out from before the sons of Israel; only allot it to Israel for an inheritance as I have commanded you. Now therefore, apportion this land for an inheritance to the nine tribes, and the half-tribe of Manasseh." (Josh.13:1-6)

During the rest of the book of Joshua, only one more battle is recorded. It is mentioned in 19:47-48, but described in the eighteenth chapter of the book of Judges. The first chapter of Judges begins, "Now it came about after the death of Joshua that the sons of Israel inquired of the Lord, saying, 'Who shall go up first for us against the Canaanites, to fight against them?' And the Lord said, 'Judah shall go up; behold, I have given the land into his hand.'...And Judah went up, and the Lord gave the Canaanites and the Perizzites into their hands..." (Judg.1:1-2,4)

The rest of the chapter relates the further efforts of the different tribes, "But the sons of Benjamin did not drive out the Jebusites who lived in Jerusalem... But Manasseh did not take possession of Beth-shean and its villages, or Taanach and its villages, or the inhabitants of Dor and its villages, or the inhabitants of Ibleam and its villages, or the inhabitants of Megiddo and its villages; so the Canaanites persisted in living in that land...Neither did Ephraim drive out the Canaanites who were living in Gezer... Zebulun did not drive out the inhabitants of Kitron, or... Asher did not drive out the inhabitants of Acco, or... Naphtali did not drive out the inhabitants of Beth-shemesh, or... Then the Amorites pressed the sons of Dan into the hill country, for they did not allow them to come down to the valley..." (Judg.1)

Joshua apportioned the whole land to the tribes, before his death, even though it was not yet all in their possession. "And there remained among the sons of Israel seven tribes who had not divided their inheritance. So Joshua said to the sons of Israel, 'How long will you put off entering to take possession of the land which the Lord, the God of your fathers, has given you?' " (Josh.18:2-3) In his final words to Israel, he said, "See, I have apportioned to you these nations which remain as an inheritance for your tribes, with all the nations which I have cut off, from the Jordan even to the Great Sea toward the setting of the sun. And the Lord your God, He shall thrust them out from before you and drive them from before you; and you shall possess their land, just as the Lord your God promised you." (Josh.23:5-6)

The possession of some of the land, including Jerusalem, was still in the future. In fact, Joshua warned Israel, "For if you ever go back and cling to the rest of these goyim, these which remain among you, and intermarry with them, so that you associate with them and they with you, know with certainty that the Lord your God will not continue to drive these goyim out from before you; but they shall be a snare and a trap to you, and a whip on your sides and thorns in your eyes, until you perish from off this good land which the Lord your God has given you." (Josh.23:12-13)

THEN, immediately after saying that, Joshua said, "Now behold, today I am going the way of all the earth, and you know in all your hearts and in all your souls that not one word of all the good words which the Lord your God spoke concerning you has failed; all have been fulfilled for you, not one of them has failed." (Josh.23:14) Joshua was stressing the faithfulness of God. The Lord had faithfully done, and would continue to do, everything that He had promised.

Moses had similarly warned Israel, only in much greater detail, of exile and of dispersion among the Gentiles. The exile was to be to Babylon; the dispersion was to be to the ends of earth. But Moses spoke of God's faithful promise of restoration to an unfaithful people. "So it shall be when all of these things have come upon you, the blessing and the curse which I have set before you, and you call them to mind in all nations where the Lord your God has banished you, and you return to the Lord your God and obey Him with all your heart and soul according to all that I command you today, you and your sons, then the Lord your God will restore you from captivity, and have compassion on you, and will gather you again from all the peoples where the Lord your God has scattered you. If your outcasts are at the ends of the earth, from there the Lord your God will gather you, and from there He will bring you back. And the Lord your God will bring you into the land which your fathers possessed, and you shall possess it; and He will prosper you and multiply you more than your fathers." (Dt.30:1-5)

Joshua's statement that all the good promises of the Lord to Israel had been fulfilled must be understood in its context. Joshua was not including the promise of restoration after exile and dispersion, nor any of the many other promises that were yet future—those concerning various laws, sacrifices, the Temple, the king, the circumcision of the heart, the prophet like unto Moses, the New Covenant and the gospel through which all the nations of the earth would be blessed, etc. His statement did not mean that all the land from the Red Sea to the Euphrates (cf. Gen.15:18; Ex.23:31) was physically in the hands of the children of Israel, but rather that, in God's appropriate order and time, He had done everything that He had promised.

Nor was the empire of Solomon a fulfillment of God's promise to Abraham, Isaac, Jacob, and all Israel concerning the land. "Now Solomon ruled over all the kingdoms from the River to the land of the Philistines and to the border of Egypt; they brought tribute and served Solomon all the days of his life. (1K.4:21) Solomon ruled over these different kingdoms, but he did not possess their land. Nor did the children of Israel.

14. The promise by the God of Israel of the land of Israel to the children of Israel did not expire. Neither the Law nor the New Covenant cancel God's promise to Abraham. Part of the original promise to Abraham and his descendants concerning the land of Canaan was that it would be theirs "for an everlasting possession." (Gen.17:8) When they were disobedient, they would be driven off the land, but it would still be their everlasting possession. Both possession and time seem to be different with God than they are with man.

Paul speaks of himself "as sorrowful yet always rejoicing, as poor yet making many rich, as having nothing yet possessing all things." (2Co.6:10) He speaks of "the Holy Spirit of promise, who is given as a pledge of our inheritance, with a view to the redemption of God's own possession, to the praise of His glory." (Eph.1:14) Sometimes, possessions are not in the hands of their owner and he must await a future redemption.

"By faith [Abraham] lived as an alien in the land of promise, as in a foreign land, dwelling in tents with Isaac and Jacob, fellow heirs of the same promise." (Heb.11:9) It was their land, but it wasn't yet in their possession. Obadiah prophesied of the future destruction of Edom for gloating over the destruction of Jerusalem: "For the day of the Lord draws near on all the nations. As you have done, it will be done to you. Your dealings will return on your own head...But on Mount Zion there will be those who escape, and it will be holy. And the house of Jacob will possess their possessions." (Obad.15,17)

Because of the sins of Judah, God had sent judgment and removed them from the land. The land was still one of their possessions, but they no longer possessed it. While that judgment was still in progress, God warned those who sought to take Israel's possessions for themselves. "Thus says the Lord **concerning all My wicked neighbors who strike at the inheritance with which I have endowed My people Israel**, 'Behold I am about to uproot them from their land and will uproot the house of Judah from among them.' " (Jer.12:14)

During the Babylonian captivity, the Lord told Ezekiel the specific physical geography by which the land of Israel would one day be divided among the tribes of Israel. (Ezek.47&48) It was a different division than that given by Joshua. The land has not yet been allotted as the Lord described to Ezekiel, but one day it will be. That will be in a day when Jerusalem is called, "The Lord is there." (Ezek.48:35)

An example of the way an eternal God speaks of events in time is the way the New Covenant Scriptures speak of salvation: believers have been saved, are being saved, and will be saved. "For in hope **we have been saved**, but hope that is seen is not hope; for why does one also hope for what he sees?" (Rom.8:24) "For the word of the cross is to those who are perishing foolishness, but **to us who are being saved** it is the power of God." (1Co.1:18) "Much more then, having now been justified by His blood, **we shall be saved** from the wrath of God through Him. For if while we were enemies, we were reconciled to God through the death of His Son, much more, having been reconciled, **we shall be saved** by His life." (Rom.5:10)

There are numerous other examples in both Tanakh and the New Covenant Scriptures where the Lord speaks of what is future as though it were taking place in the present or had taken place in the past. For example, John, the forerunner of the Lord, was born, "And his father Zacharias was filled with the Holy Spirit, and prophesied, saying: 'Blessed be the Lord God of Israel, for He has visited us and accomplished redemption for His people, and has raised up a horn of salvation for us in the house of David

His Servant.' " (Lk.1:67-69) Jesus had not yet been born, but the Holy Spirit spoke of the redemption of Israel as having been accomplished.

The claim that the Hebrew for "forever" or "everlasting" really means "to the end of the age" is only partly true. In some cases it does mean that, but that is not all that it means. The English word "always" provides a helpful parallel. It means "every time," but it also means "as long as," and "forever."

There are actually several different Hebrew expressions used to signify "forever." Most of them use the word "olam [עלם]" by itself or with a prefix or suffix. Examples are "me-olam" [מעלם from olam], "le-olam" [לעלם to olam], and "olamim" [עלמים the plural of olam]. Looking at the use of such words in context is very helpful in understanding the meaning that they are given in the Bible.

"Olam" is used quite often. Here are some examples of how it is used in terms of the children of Israel and the land. God promised Abraham, "And I will give to you and to your descendants after you, the land of your sojournings, all the land of Canaan, for an **everlasting** possession; and I will be their God." (Gen.17:8) "Then Jacob said to Joseph, 'God Almighty appeared to me at Luz in the land of Canaan and blessed me, and He said to me, *"Behold, I will make you fruitful and numerous, and I will make you a company of peoples, and will give this land to your descendants after you for an everlasting possession."* ' " (Gen.48:3,4)

"He has remembered His covenant forever [le-olam], the word which He commanded to a thousand generations, the covenant which He made with Abraham, and His oath to Isaac. Then He confirmed it to Jacob for a statute, to Israel as an **everlasting** covenant, saying, 'To you I will give the land of Canaan as the portion of your inheritance.' " (Ps.105:8-11)

The word is used to describe God's relationship with Israel. For example, "The Lord appeared to him from afar, saying, 'I have loved you with an **everlasting** love; Therefore I have drawn you with lovingkindness.' " (Jer.31:3) "And I will make an **everlasting** covenant with them that I will not turn away from them, to do them good; and I will put the fear of Me in their hearts so that they will not turn away from Me." (Jer.32:40)

It is also used to describe the length of time that God is God (Gen.21:33), that He is King (Jer.10:10) and His reign endures (Ps.66:7); how enduring are His arms (Dt.33:27), His righteousness (Ps.119:142), His salvation (Is.45:17), His lovingkindness (Is.54:8), His light (Is.60:19,20); and how long the righteous will live and the wicked will be abhorred (Dan.12:2).

"Me-olam" is used to describe when the personification of wisdom was established. "The Lord possessed me at the beginning of His way, before His works of old. From **everlasting** I was established, from the beginning, from the earliest times of the earth." (Prov.8:23)

When David sought to build a house for the Lord, the Lord, in return, promised to build David a house. (2Sam.7) The phrase "ad olam [עד עלם]" appears several times in this chapter. The Lord told David, "When your days are complete and you lie down with your fathers, I will raise up your descendant after you who will come forth from you, and I will establish his kingdom. He shall build a house for My name, and I will establish the throne of his kingdom **forever**. I will be a father to him and he will be a son to Me... And your house and your kingdom shall endure before Me **forever**; your throne shall be established **forever**." (vv.12-14,16) This section is generally understood to be speaking immediately of Solomon, but also to be speaking prophetically of Jesus, the greater Son of David. It is explicitly applied to Jesus in Hebrews 1:5.

David responds to the promise of the Lord by praying. "For Thou hast established for Thyself Thy people Israel as Thine own people forever, and Thou, O Lord, hast become their God. Now therefore, O Lord God, the word that Thou hast spoken concerning Thy servant and his house, confirm it **forever**, and do as Thou hast spoken, that Thy name may be magnified **forever**, by saying, 'The Lord of hosts is God over Israel'; and may the house of Thy servant David be established before Thee." (vv.24-26)

The same phrase, "ad olam," is also used in Psalm 9:7: "But the Lord abides **forever**; He has established His throne for judgment." In these cases, "ad olam" is used to signify how long the throne of the Son of David will be established; how long Israel is established as the people of the Lord; and how long the name of the Lord is to be magnified and the Lord will abide or sit as king.

"Le-olam" is used often in the Bible. Moses used it, for example, in interceding with God when Israel built the golden calf. "Remember Abraham, Isaac, and Israel, Thy servants to whom Thou didst swear by Thyself, and didst say to them, 'I will multiply your descendants as the stars of the heavens, and all this land of which I have spoken I will give to your descendants, and they shall inherit it **forever**.' So the Lord changed His mind about the harm which He said He would do to His people." (Ex.32:13)

It is also the word that is used to describe how long the mercy of the Lord endureth (1Ch.16:34), the truth of the Lord lasts (Ps.117:2), His word stands firm, His righteous judgments abide (Ps.119:89,160), His counsel stands (Ps.33:11), and His name lasts (Ps.135:13); how long the Lord will reign (Ps.146:10), His glory (Ps.104:31) and the Lord Himself shall endure (Ps.9:7).

It is also used to explain how long Jesus is a priest according to the order of Melchizedek. (Ps.110:4) In Hebrews 7:3, Melchizedek is described as "...having neither beginning of days nor end of life, but made like the Son of God, he abides a priest **perpetually**." The same Greek phrase that is translated in this verse as "perpetually"[εις το διηνεκες], also appears in Hebrews 10:12-14, referring to Psalm 110: "But He [Jesus], having offered one sacrifice for sins **for all time**, sat down at the right hand of God, waiting from that time onward until His enemies be made a footstool for His feet. For by one offering He has perfected **for all time** those who are sanctified."

Forever, le-olam [לְעֹלָם], the land of Israel belongs to the people whom God did not destroy in the wilderness. Forever, le-olam [לְעֹלָם, εις το διηνεκες], Jesus is a priest according to the order of Melchizedek. Forever, [εις το διηνεκες], the sacrifice of Jesus atones for sins. Forever [εις το διηνεκες], those who are sanctified are perfected by that sacrifice.

It is incorrect to say that these words and phrases only mean "to the end of the age." That is not the way that the Lord uses them in the Bible.

15. It is Biblically incorrect to speak of the land of Israel as "Palestine." There are seven places in the Bible where the Hebrew word "p'leshet" [פְּלֶשֶׁת] is used; Ex.15:14, Ps.60:8, Ps.87:4, Ps.108:9, Is.14:29 & 31, and Joel 3:4. Sometimes it is translated as "Palestine," other times it is translated as "Philistia." Regardless of which English word is used, the reference is to the land of the Philistines. Essentially, the references speak of God's judgments on the Philistines.

"Palestine" is not a Biblical synonym for the land of Israel. It is simply a designation for a small coastal strip in Canaan, from south of Jaffa to south of Gaza. (cf. Jer.47:1-7; Ezek.25:15-17; Am.1:6-8; Zeph.2:4-7) The name "Palestine" was applied by the Romans to Judea after they had crushed the Bar Kokhba Rebellion. It was intended as a punishment signifying that the Jews would never again live there.

Some 18 centuries later, in the greatest miracle of all that time, the Roman decree was nullified when a language, a people, and a land were brought forth from the dead. The house of Jacob began to again possess their possessions. God demonstrated that His power, His faithfulness, and His Word are greater than the weapons and the decrees of men.

Even as Isaiah had prophesied, "Then it will happen on that day that the Lord will again recover the second time with His hand the remnant of His people, who will remain, from Assyria, Egypt, Pathros, Cush, Elam, Shinar, Hamath, and from the islands of the sea. And He will lift up a standard for the nations, and will assemble the banished ones of Israel, and will gather the dispersed of Judah from the four corners of the earth." (Is.11:11-12)

The return of a remnant from Babylonian captivity was the first return. In it, the dispersed of Judah were not regathered "from the four corners of the earth." The second regathering has taken place in this century. It is not yet complete, but it is evident to all.

Biblically, the land was called Canaan, the land of the Canaanites. God destroyed the Canaanites because of their iniquity, and gave the land to Israel, the people He created, for an inheritance forever. Though it is the common usage of many, God never calls the land of Israel "Palestine."

It is interesting that almost none of the Bibles that have maps have maps of Israel. They have maps of "Canaan" and maps of "The Holy Land," but they do not have maps of "Israel." They have maps of "The divided kingdoms of Judea and Israel," but no maps of "Israel." They have maps of the "Land of the Twelve Tribes," and maps of "The Empire of David," and "The Empire of Solomon," but they do not have maps of "Israel."

They have maps of "Palestine in the time of the Maccabees" and "Palestine in the Time of Christ." That is absurd. There was no "Palestine" in the time of the Maccabees or in the time of Christ. "Palestine" did not come into existence as a designation for the land of Israel until the second century. It is like publishing a map entitled "The British Empire in the time of Christ," or "Downtown San Francisco in the time of the Maccabees."

Such designations show, whether intentionally or not, an anti-Biblical, anti-Judaic bias. So do the maps labelled, "Palestine Today." The geographical annihilation of Israel stands in open hostility to the Word of God. It is an evasion and denial of an important Biblical truth. That is why those who willingly partake of this aspect of Hadrian's and Luther's theology are so against the existence of the state of Israel. It shows the falsity of their doctrine.

Even through the first part of the twentieth century, their modern heirs affirmed Luther's oath that if Israel ever became a nation again, the gospel would be proved false. Philip Mauro, for example, wrote in the late 1920's, "Here then is a two-fold and a conclusive test of the Divine authorship of the prophetic Scriptures. For if, in the course of these 'times of the Gentiles,' either the city [Jerusalem] or the people [the Jews] had passed out of existence, **or if the city had come into Jewish hands again** or the Jewish people as a whole had changed their characteristic attitude towards Christ and His gospel, **the prophecies would have been falsified and the entire New Testament discredited.**" [2]

According to Luther, Mauro, and others who were of the same persuasion, if Jerusalem or the land of Israel ever came into Jewish hands again, it would prove that the Bible was not given by God. That is why, in this century, they opposed the re-establishment of the State of Israel. They opposed it even as many Jews were seeking to flee the Nazis who claimed to be "Christianizing" Europe. They opposed it even as millions of Jews were dying in the Holocaust.

The Bible, obviously, has not been discredited or proven false by the re-establishment of the State of Israel. It has been proven true. What is discredited, of course, is such false teaching.

Since the re-establishment of the State of Israel, those who hold this view are no longer able to swear by Luther's oath. "But those vine-growers said to one another, 'This is the heir; come, let us kill him, and the inheritance will be ours!' " (Mk.12:7) Having the "old Israel" raised from the dead makes the "new Israel" very uneasy about the position it has carved out for itself. That is why those who hold this position hope that Israel will be destroyed.

That is why they embrace "Palestine," but reject Israel. They call for an end to "the Israeli occupation of Palestine." To use God's designation of the land as "Israel" would make the call far less appealing. After all, how many people could be stirred up about ending "the Israeli occupation of Israel"?

Those who want to use the "Palestine" of the Roman, Turkish, and British Empires should be consistent. "Palestine" is the Emperor Hadrian's terminology. They should also then use his terminology for Jerusalem, "Aelia Capitolina," named after himself and the Roman god Jupiter. As for the new Jerusalem, what gate would they go in?

Most of the Bible speaks about the land of Israel. A theology that cannot admit the past, present, and future existence of Israel is not a Biblical theology. Those who believe that God has cast off Israel are in a precarious position. Jesus said, "...let it be done to you as you have believed." (Mt.8:13)

Those who want to follow and glorify the Lord would do better to use His designation for the land of "Israel." As far as God is concerned, there is no question about to whom the land belongs. It is His land, and He gave it to the Jewish people for an everlasting possession.

He has given other lands to other peoples. "And He made from one every nation of mankind to live on all the face of the earth, having determined their appointed times, and the boundaries of their habitations." (Acts 17:26) It is God who determines what land belongs to what people. The God of Israel has spoken very clearly about the land of Israel.

FOOTNOTES

1. *The Ecclesiastical History of Eusebius Pamphilus,* translated by Christian Frederick Cruse, Baker Book House, Grand Rapids, MI, 1989, Bk.3, Ch.5, P.86
2. *The Gospel of The Kingdom with An Examination of Modern Dispensationalism,* Philip Mauro, Grace Abounding Ministries, Inc., Sterling, VA., 1988, P.202.

48

"COVENANT" THEOLOGY

The "Covenant" view, built largely upon Calvin, maintains that:

1. Israel and the Church are one and the same throughout history, i.e. the faithful among mankind.

2. There is a "Covenant of Grace" which is partially revealed in all the individual covenants, which it in turn embraces. From the Fall of Man in the Garden of Eden to the final consummation of all history, God has dealt with man through this Covenant.

3. Since its birth, the Church is the only covenant people, since all covenants, prophecies, and promises are fulfilled in the gospel. Individual Jews can be grafted into the Church, but all the Jews as a people or a nation have neither significance nor purpose in the ongoing plan of God.

Diagram 7 represents Covenant Theology. There is one circle that is both Israel and the Church.

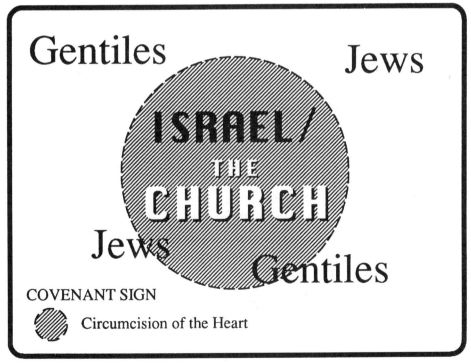

Diagram 7

The Covenant view states correctly that throughout the ages God has kept for Himself a faithful remnant. Those in the remnant today are the children, and brethren, of those in the past. It is correct in recognizing the continuity of God's dealings with man. It is in error, however, because:

1. The Bible does not mention any 'super-covenant' that embraces all other covenants which God has made. This theology depends upon the existence of an all-encompassing "Covenant of Grace," "Covenant of Redemption," "Covenant of Creation," or "Covenant of Conferment" that is not instituted, described, or even mentioned in the pages of the Bible. The New Covenant is a covenant of grace, but this 'super-covenant' is said to be a different covenant.

Knowing what a Biblical covenant is will help us to see how this theology is built upon an assumption that is false. A Biblical covenant is not simply a general understanding or a customary way of relating. It is a specific agreement — a binding contract. In Calvin's French, it is *une alliance*, an alliance. It is an alliance, a contract, an agreement; but it is more than that.

Knowing what the covenants of men are is very helpful in understanding God's covenants, but God is not a man. The covenants of men may reflect, but they do not determine, the covenants of God. Men may use what God has made as their model, but God never uses what men have made as His model.

The Bible tells us that God's covenants have at least two characteristics that some covenants of men share: [1] Validation of the covenant through blood and death; and [2] Specific obligations for those who carry out the covenant.

"For where a covenant is, it is necessary for the death of the one who made it to come in. For a covenant is valid only when over the dead, for it is never in force while the one who made it lives. Therefore even the first covenant was not inaugurated without blood." (Heb.9:16-18)

Those who live can change their minds. The death of someone who makes a covenant means that the covenant expresses his fixed purpose which will not change. That death enforces the conditions of the covenant on those who are to carry them out. There is then no appeal or negotiation possible.

An animal put to death as a substitute signifies the same fixed purpose as though the one who makes the covenant were himself put to death. It is as though the one who makes the covenant were saying, "May I be put to death as this animal has been before I change my covenant." That death is necessary for the covenant to have any force. The power of the life and the power of the death show the strength of the covenant commitment.

When Elijah was about to be taken up into heaven, he "said to Elisha, 'Stay here please, for the Lord has sent me as far as Bethel.' But Elisha said, 'As the Lord lives and as you yourself live, I will not leave you.' " (2K.2:2)

Elisha was saying that only the death of God or the death of Elijah would cause him to be separated from Elijah.

Years before, Elijah had slaughtered Jezebel's prophets of Baal on Mt. Carmel. "Now Ahab told Jezebel all that Elijah had done, and how he had killed all the prophets with the sword. Then Jezebel sent a messenger to Elijah, saying, 'So may the gods do to me and even more, if I do not make your life as the life of one of them by tomorrow about this time.' " (1K.19:1-20) Jezebel put herself under an oath unto death — an oath which she could not keep.

The one who makes a covenant with the blood of a substituted animal is putting himself under an oath that nothing but death will keep him from keeping and enforcing the covenant. When the living God cuts a covenant, shedding life-blood, He is swearing by Himself —" 'As I live,' says the Lord,..."—that He will not break that covenant. He is saying that His purpose is fixed and will never change. He is the great "I AM!"

Even as God, the One making the covenant, puts Himself under oath to death if He should break the covenant, so He also requires the same commitment from those with whom He makes a covenant. Those who break His covenant are guilty unto death.

The death of Jesus applied in different ways to two covenants. First, He took on Himself the guilt of those who had transgressed and broken God's Covenant of the Law. They were guilty unto death, and He freely volunteered to be put to death in their place. His death satisfied the penalty for breaking the Covenant of the Law.

"And for this reason He [Jesus] is the mediator of a new covenant, in order that since **a death has taken place for the redemption of the transgressions that were committed under the first covenant,** those who have been called may receive the promise of the eternal inheritance." (Heb.9:15)

Second, His death inaugurates the New Covenant. It testifies that this covenant will be upheld with all the power of the eternal life of God. Not even death will cut short the living God's faithfulness to and through this covenant. Jesus appeared to John on Patmos and said, "Do not be afraid; I am the first and the last, and the living One; and I was dead, and behold, I am alive forevermore, and I have the keys of death and of Hades." (Rev.1:17b-18)

Death gives a covenant its force. Each Biblical covenant must be validated in blood. The Bible tells us that.

There are some critical questions which must therefore be asked of "Covenant theology." The questions are easy, and the answers are not difficult, but they cannot be fit into this theology. They demonstrate that a 'super-covenant' does not exist, and would be without purpose.

Into what specific covenant with God has the Church entered? Is it the

New Covenant or is it some other? If it is another, then where is that covenant recorded? What are its terms, so that the Church may know its obligations?

If it is another covenant, then what sacrifice validated that covenant? Is salvation available through this other covenant? If salvation is available through some 'super-covenant,' then why is the New Covenant necessary?

Does the New Covenant offer anything that this other covenant does not? Does this other covenant offer anything that the New Covenant does not?

The New Covenant Scriptures declare that the Church has been grafted into the "New" Covenant promised in Jer.31. It is Israel's New Covenant. The faithful in Israel accepted it, proclaimed it to the rest of Israel and to the Gentiles, and invited them to enter in, too.

Though it was prophetically prefigured in many ways, God specifically instituted it through the blood of Jesus, the King of the Jews. A type is intended to point to, but is not the same as the reality. As Jesus said, "This cup which is poured out for you is the new covenant in My blood." (Lk.22:20, cf. Heb.7-10) It is specifically this New Covenant, whose terms are stated in Jer.31:31-34, that brings salvation.

The advocates of "covenant theology" justify the human invention of a 'super-covenant' on the grounds that God did something similar in combining other covenants. There are two problems with such a claim. The first is that God is sovereign, but man is not. Man is obligated to abide by the declarations of God, but God is not bound to abide by the declarations of men.

The one who is sovereign may issue decrees that are binding on his subjects. Those who do not have the sovereignty do not have any authority to issue decrees that are binding on their lord. Nor do they have the power to enforce any such decree.

God established one covenant with Noah, and another with Abraham. That is His Divine prerogative. He did not grant to men any authority to change or combine those covenants. Man is not authorized to obligate God to a covenant which He has not made. God is not brought into covenant by the will of man. Man is brought into covenant by the will of God.

The second problem with the claim that man can combine God's covenants into a 'super-covenant' is that God never did do something similar. The first "example" cited in support of this view concerns the promise of the land of Canaan to Abraham, Isaac and Jacob. Let's look at the scriptures given in support of this position.

Only the verses in italic are actually cited as support, but the rest is added here to provide their context. It is also added here because many of the proponents of this theology maintain that God's promise to the Jewish people of the land of Canaan is no longer valid. The very texts which are used to show that God combined covenants, do not show that He did, but they do show that He has given the land of Canaan to the Jewish people with a covenant oath and promise.

"He has remembered His covenant forever, the word which He commanded to a thousand generations, *the covenant which He made with Abraham, and His oath to Isaac. Then He confirmed it to Jacob for a statute, to Israel as an everlasting covenant*, saying 'To you I will give the land of Canaan as the portion of your inheritance.' " (Ps.105:8-11)

"Now Hazael king of Syria had oppressed Israel all the days of Jehoahaz. *But the Lord was gracious to them and had compassion on them and turned to them because of His covenant with Abraham, Isaac, and Jacob, and would not destroy them or cast them from His presence until now.*" (2 K.13:22-23)

"O seed of Israel His servant, sons of Jacob, His chosen ones! He is the Lord our God; His judgments are in all the earth. Remember His covenant forever, the word which He commanded to a thousand generations, *the covenant which He made with Abraham, and His oath to Isaac. He also confirmed it to Jacob for a statute, to Israel as an everlasting covenant*, saying, 'To you I will give the land of Canaan, as the portion of your inheritance.' " (1Chr.16:13-18)

The question here is, 'Do these verses demonstrate that God treats three or four different covenants - one with Abraham, a different one with Isaac, and a different one with Jacob and all Israel - as though they are one?' The answer seems to be a very simple, 'No.'

God gave Abraham and his seed the right to the land of Canaan by a covenant. (Gen.15:7-21) God gave an oath to Isaac that he and his seed were the heirs of that covenant with Abraham. (Gen.26:1-5) Ishmael was not.

Then God confirmed to Jacob that he and his seed were the heirs of that covenant. (Gen.28:13) Esau was not. Then He told Israel that the land was theirs to possess. (Dt.1:8) God is not combining three or four covenants into one, but merely affirming who it is that is included in the covenant made with Abraham and his seed.

The second "example" offered in support of this view concerns the covenant made by God with Israel at Mt. Horeb (Sinai), when they came out of Egypt, and the covenant God made with Israel in the land of Moab, before they entered the land of Canaan. Are these two different covenants which, along with the later renewals, are treated as one, i.e. the Covenant of the Law?

The later renewals are simply renewals, commitments to observe the covenant previously established. Is the covenant made at Moab more than that? In Deuteronomy we are told, "These are the words of the covenant which the Lord commanded Moses to make with the sons of Israel in the land of Moab, besides the covenant which He had made with them at Horeb." (Dt.29:1)

The book of Deuteronomy begins with a reiteration (chapters 1-10) of what had happened to Israel since God brought them out of Egypt. It also includes the reiteration of some of the previously given commands. The additional material in the covenant made in Moab is the necessary instructions and warnings for that generation which was about to enter and live in the land that God promised to their fathers. It is supplementary instruction for future generations that is quite clearly meant to be combined with the initial covenant.

God, as the sovereign covenant maker, certainly had that right, which Israel recognized and accepted. That is not at all the same as placing radically different covenants that were made with different individuals and groups of people under the umbrella of one 'super-covenant' invented by man.

* 2. When God speaks of making a new covenant with "the house of Judah and the house of Israel," He is not speaking of making a covenant only with the faithful elect, but rather with all Judah and Israel, including those who were unfaithful.

The purpose of saying that the covenant is made only with the elect is to take the covenant away from the Jews and give it to the Church. This procedure follows Calvin. The argument goes like this: "The New Covenant is made with the elect in Israel. The elect are the Church. The Church is the elect. The Church is Israel. The New Covenant is made with the Church."

But God explicitly says, speaking of the Old Covenant of the Law, "My covenant which they broke." Only those who have entered into a covenant can break it. It cannot be broken by those with whom it was never made. All Israel entered into the Covenant of the Law, and subsequently failed to keep it. Even as all the goyim would have failed to keep it, had it been made with them.

Those who have entered into a covenant and have failed to keep it can be judged for that failure. The Bible presents the destruction and exile of the kingdoms of Israel and Judah as just such a judgment by God. As that judgment proceeded towards its climax, the fall of Jerusalem, God gave the promise of a new covenant to those who were being judged for breaking the old — the house of Judah and the house of Israel.

If the covenant of the Law had been made only with the faithful, there would have been no grounds on which to judge, or even to distinguish, the unfaithful. There would have been no need to promise a new covenant.

The New Covenant is made by God between Himself and the same people who broke the Old Covenant. It is Israel's unfaithfulness that demonstrates God's abundant grace in establishing the New Covenant.

Peter preached the gospel to unbelieving Jews. He exhorted them to repent, believe, and fulfill their calling. "It is you who are the sons of the prophets, and **of the covenant** which God made with your fathers, saying to Abraham, 'And in your seed all the families of the earth shall be blessed.' " (Acts 3:25)

Paul said, "Messiah has become a servant to the circumcision [i.e. the

Jews] on behalf of the truth of God to confirm the promises given to the fathers." (Rom.15:8) God promised, and God keeps His promises.

The breaking of the Old Covenant by Israel demonstrates the need for a New Covenant. Israel, God's covenant people, lacked the ability to satisfy the righteous requirements of God's Law, "by which a man may live if he does them." (Lev.18:5) They did not, and could not, so God instituted the New Covenant. "For if a law had been given which was able to impart life, then righteousness would indeed have been from law." (Gal.3:21)

If "Israel" only meant the faithful, then why did God blind the eyes of most Jews so that they would not believe in Jesus? (Rom.11:7-11) There would have been no need for God to do that. To the contrary, Paul explains that it is "through their unbelief that salvation has come to you," the Gentiles. That is because, as Paul points out, it is to Israel, including unbelieving Israel, that the covenants belong. (cf.Rom.9:4) Jesus did not come for the faithful, but to call sinners to repent. (cf. Lk.5:32)

When God presented the Covenant of the Law to Israel, all Israel accepted it. "Moses came and called the elders of the people, and set before them all these words which the Lord had commanded him. And **all the people answered** together and said, **'All that the Lord has spoken we will do!'**..." (Ex.19:7-8)

"Then Moses came and recounted to the people all the words of the Lord and all the ordinances; and all the people answered with one voice, and said, **'All the words which the Lord has spoken we will do!'**...Then he took the Book of the Covenant and read it in the hearing of the people; and **they said, 'All that the Lord has spoken we will do, and we will be obedient!'** " (Ex.24:3,7)

All Israel did not respond that way to the New Covenant when it was presented. That is why it is through the fall of "the rest" of Israel, other than the faithful remnant, that salvation has come to the Gentiles. That does not alter the divine reality that the New Covenant is made with Israel, and belongs to the Jewish people.

In the Song of Moses, God declares, "Indeed, I lift up My hand to heaven, and say, as I live forever...I will render vengeance on My adversaries, and I will repay those who hate Me...Rejoice, O Gentiles, with His people; for He will avenge the blood of His servants, and will render vengeance on His adversaries, and will atone for His land and His people." (Dt.32:40-43; cf. Rev.15:1-4)

God promised to provide atonement for Israel's sins. He invited the Gentiles to rejoice over that with His people Israel. It is possible only through the New Covenant.

3. The New Covenant is not just a continuation or rephrasing of the Old, or of any other covenant. Continuity is not the only characteristic of God's relationship with man. There are differences and discontinuity as well.

The New Covenant is "New," "not like the covenant which I made with their fathers...which they broke." The New Covenant had not yet been cut in the days of Jeremiah. It was still future. That is why God said, "**the days are coming when I will cut** a new covenant with the house of Israel and the house of Judah..." The New Covenant supercedes the covenant which is "Old," the covenant which God had previously cut with the house of Israel.

Though both covenants are made with the same unfaithful people, the two covenants are radically different. Their terms, or conditions, are not the same. Nor is the outcome of man's effort to attain salvation by satisfying those terms.

"Now that no one is justified by the Law before God is evident; for, 'The righteous shall live by faith.' However, the Law is not of faith; on the contrary, 'He who practices them shall live by them.' Messiah redeemed us from the curse of the Law, having become a curse for us..." (Gal.3:11-13) The Law is not of faith, but the New Covenant is.

No one could find salvation through the Covenant of the Law, because no one could fulfill its requirements. "For if that first covenant had been faultless, there would have been no occasion sought for a second." (Heb.8:7)

"And this commandment, which was to result in life, proved to result in death for me. For sin, taking opportunity through the commandment, deceived me, and through it killed me. So then, the Law is holy, and the commandment is holy and righteous and good....For we know that the Law is spiritual; but I am of flesh, sold into bondage to sin...For what the Law could not do, weak as it was through the flesh, God did: sending His own Son in the likeness of sinful flesh and as an offering for sin, He condemned sin in the flesh." (Rom.7:10-12,14; 8:3)

Paul emphasizes the tremendous difference between seeking salvation through the Old Covenant as opposed to the New. "...our adequacy is from God, who also made us adequate as servants of a new covenant, not of the letter, but of the Spirit; for the letter kills, but the Spirit gives life. But if the ministry of death, in letters engraved on stones, came with glory, so that the sons of Israel could not look intently at the face of Moses because of the glory of his face, fading as it was, how shall the ministry of the spirit fail to be even more with glory?" (2Co.3:5-8) He calls the Covenant of the Law given through Moses "the ministry of death," as opposed to the New Covenant given in Jesus, which is "the ministry of the spirit."

There is a tremendous difference between seeking to serve God under the Old Covenant as opposed to seeking to serve Him under the New. "Or do you not know, brethren (for I am speaking to those who know the Law), ...now we have been released from the Law, having died to that by which we were bound, so that we serve in newness of the Spirit and not in oldness of the letter." (Rom.7:1,6)

The contention that the New Covenant is the same covenant made with a different people is totally contrary to the text. The text says the opposite. The text says that the New Covenant is **a different covenant** made with **the same people**. It is NEW, and it is **better**. (2Co.3:6; Heb.7:22; 8:6)

**4. When Paul says, "I ALSO am an Israelite," he is identifying himself with his unfaithful, physical brethren. That identification is not the same as his identification with the Church. Paul is pointing to his own relationship with God as proof of the fact that God has not cast off unfaithful Israel. For indeed, Paul himself was once part of unfaithful Israel.

"But as for Israel He [God] says, 'All the day long I have stretched out my hands to a disobedient and obstinate people.' I say then, God has not rejected His people has He? May it never be! For I too am an Israelite, seed of Abraham, of the tribe of Benjamin. God has not rejected His people whom He foreknew. Or do you not know what the Scripture says in the passage about Elijah, how he pleads with God against Israel?" (Rom.10:21-11:2)

"Israel" in this first verse is physically identified, including the disobedient and obstinate. "Israel" in this third verse is also physically identified, including the disobedient and the obstinate, i.e. the un-faithful, un-believers.

Paul's identification of himself, in the middle verse, as an Israelite is also an obvious physical identification with an "Israel" that includes the disobedient and obstinate. To substantiate his claim that he is an Israelite, Paul points out that he is "of the seed of Abraham, of the tribe of Benjamin." (Rom.11:1) He is referring to his physical descent. For Paul, being "of the tribe of Benjamin" proves that he is an Israelite.

This physically identified "Israel" is still called "His people." Within "His people," God has kept for Himself a faithful remnant.

The fact that the faithful in Israel are a "remnant of Israel" indicates that there is much more of Israel that is not faithful. Paul makes this quite clear. Otherwise, there could not be a remnant. Had "Israel" signified only the faithful, God's continual call to Israel throughout the Bible would not have been to repentance, but to perseverance.

Paul said, "I could pray that I myself were anathema, separated from Messiah for the sake of my brethren, **my kinsmen according to the flesh, who are Israelites**, to whom belongs the adoption as sons and the glory and the covenants and the giving of the Law and the service and the promises, whose are the fathers, and from whom is the Messiah according to the flesh, who is over all God blessed forever. Amen." (Rom.9:3-5)

It is clear that he is talking about physical, natural Israel. It is impossible to understand his words differently. It is for his unbelieving Jewish brethren that Paul is willing to be anathema. It is from them that Messiah came. It is to them that the adoption, glory, and covenants, etc. belong. It is they who are Israelites.

Had "Israel" signified the faithful only, there would have been no need for, and no sense to, Paul's "unceasing grief and continual sorrow," nor to his willingness to be accursed for their salvation. Paul is echoing the sacrificial love and words of Moses: "Alas, this people has sinned a great sin, and they have made a god of gold for themselves. But now, if Thou wilt, forgive their sin — and if not, please blot me out from Thy book which Thou has written!" (Ex.32:31,32)

It is worth noting that Jesus said, "Greater love than this has no man, that he lay down his life for his friends." (Jn.15:13) Paul and Moses were manifesting greater love than that. They were willing to lay down not their lives, but their souls for eternity, for those who counted themselves their enemies. Man does not have love like that. Only God does.

We do not know of anyone other than Moses and Paul who prayed like that, nor do we know anyone else who has known and served God as they did. Abraham was willing to give his only son, but God did not allow it. Instead, God Himself gave His only begotten Son. Paul and Moses were willing to be accursed for the salvation of Israel, but God did not allow it. Instead, Jesus willingly was separated, put to death as "King of the Jews," and accursed, for His people. His Spirit moved Paul and Moses to be willing to do the same for the honor and glory of God - because God is a Father to Israel.

*** 5. The composition of the people who are brought into the New Covenant is markedly different from the people who were brought into the Old Covenant at Sinai. Only Israel and proselytes (and the few "strangers in the camp") entered into the Covenant of the Law. Although initially only Jews and proselytes entered into the New Covenant, God also made it possible for Gentiles, remaining as Gentiles, to be included in the New Covenant. Prior to that, Gentiles were "aliens to the covenants of promise."

The first Church council at Jerusalem, composed of Jews, investigated the question of whether or not Gentiles needed to be circumcised (i.e., had to become Jews) in order to be saved. There was great debate.

The fact that uncircumcised Gentiles could receive the Holy Spirit and be saved was perceived as very unusual. It was radically different from the way that God had dealt with them before. This point has been covered in the chapter on "The Debate in Jerusalem."

The New Covenant Scriptures say that it is contrary to nature, and to natural understanding, that Gentiles, no matter how faithful they are, can be included in what belongs to Israel. "For if you [Gentiles] were cut off from what is by nature a wild olive tree, and were grafted contrary to nature into a cultivated olive tree, how much more shall these who are the natural branches be grafted into their own olive tree." (Rom.11:24)

Jews, even those who do not yet believe, are called "the natural branches."

When they believe, they are grafted back into their own olive tree. Gentiles, even those who do believe, are considered "wild branches." When they believe, they are grafted into Israel's olive tree.

Such terminology would have no meaning if "Israel" meant all who believe, whether Jewish or Gentile. What would the unbelieving Jewish branches have been broken off from? Why would it be unnatural for Gentiles to be grafted in?

In forming the Church, God did something that was contrary to nature. Jews and Gentiles, **for the first time**, were made one in the same body, the body of Messiah. God made [ποιησας Eph.2:14] the two into one. He had not done that before. He did it, "that in Himself He might create [κτιση] the two into one new man, thus making [ποιων] peace; and might reconcile them both in one body to God through the cross, by it having put to death the enmity." [literal, Eph.2:15-16]

In this act of creation, God sovereignly brought into existence something which had not previously existed. God created one new man. In that new creation, contrary to traditional Jewish understanding, Gentiles do not need to become Jews. In that new creation, contrary to traditional Church understanding, Jews do not need to become Gentiles.

Under the Covenant of the Law, Jews were commanded to be separate from the Gentiles. "...I have set you apart from the peoples to be Mine." (Lev.20:26) "You only have Me among all the families of the earth; therefore I will punish you for all your iniquities." (Am.3:2) For that reason, the failure to be separate from the Gentiles was a basis for God's judgment on the physical descendants of Abraham, Isaac, and Jacob.

In the New Covenant, the physical descendants of Abraham, Isaac, and Jacob are commanded to receive the believing Gentiles as equal brothers and sisters. In this new existence, believing Jews and Gentiles are reminded to be, "diligent to preserve the unity of the Spirit in the bond of peace. There is one body and one Spirit, just as also you were called in one hope of your calling; one Lord, one faith, one baptism, one God and Father of all who is over all and through all and in all." (Eph.4:3-6) This was discussed in the chapter on "The Mystery of Messiah."

This new creation, this new relationship, is something "which in other generations was not made known to the sons of men, as it has now been revealed..." It was not previously revealed, and it did not previously exist. It is revealed and it comes into existence through the New Covenant.

6. The salvation in Jesus that is presented in the New Covenant Scriptures is not ; neric, but Jewish — Jewish in the sense of what God created the Jewish people to be.

When unfaithful Jews — like Saul of Tarsus, Sosthenes of Corinth, Peter, Jacob, John, etc. — believe, they are not grafted into the Church, but into "their own olive tree" [τη ιδια ελαια]. Jews are not saved "out" of Israel, but "in" Israel. This is the point of Paul's metaphor in Romans 11:11-29.

Jews are saved as Jews through Israel's New Covenant. They are saved in fulfillment of what God promised to Israel through "all the prophets." They are saved to be a light to the Gentiles.

Gentile believers who follow that light are brought into the commonwealth and polity of Israel, to share what "belongs" to Israel — the hope and the calling. As Paul explained, "...my brethren, my kinsmen according to the flesh, who are Israelites, to whom belongs the adoption as sons and the glory and the covenants and the giving of the Law and the service and the promises, whose are the fathers, and from whom is the Messiah according to the flesh, who is over all, God blessed forever. Amen." (Rom.9:3-5) All of these essentials can be found within the Jewish olive tree.

Jesus felt that the Samaritan woman had to know, "Salvation is of the Jews." She had to know it to worship God in Spirit and in Truth. The God of Israel wants all the world to know Him through His covenant relationship with Israel.

"A covenant-relation between God and men is an absolutely unique fact in [the] history of religions; this was not only the case in the O[ld].T[estament]. times, as Vriezen pointed out, but also in the Hellenistic-Roman world. This holds good for the New Covenant a *fortiori*. If something like a καινη διαθηκη [new covenant] was preached it could only be understood on its O[ld] T[estament] basis, but was something unheard of before by the Gentiles."[1]

The nature of God is revealed in His relationship with the Jewish people. The nature of the New Covenant is revealed in God's relationship with the Jewish people. Neither He nor the salvation that He offers can be properly understood without regard to that relationship. To alter or to ignore that relationship is to transgress against God and His covenant.

A gospel that is de-Judaized is not the same gospel that Jesus and the Apostles preached. They preached "as it is written...that it might be fulfilled...according to the Scriptures." A gospel that is de-Judaized is not a Biblical gospel. It is a different gospel.

7. The Church is the fruit of God's calling of Israel. Because of the faithful Jewish remnant, the Gentiles heard the gospel. This remnant included Paul, Barnabas, Silas, Philip, Apollos, Priscilla, and Aquila, as well as, of course, Peter, Jacob, John, and the rest of the apostles and early disciples. These were the ones who brought the gospel to the Gentiles.

They were evangelizing the goyim in partial fulfillment of Israel's calling. They were evangelizing the goyim in partial fulfillment of the Great Commission. As Paul challenged the unbelieving Jews in Antioch of Pisidia, "Behold, we are turning to the Gentiles. For thus the Lord has commanded us, 'I have placed you as a light for the Gentiles, that you should bring salvation to the end of the earth.' " (Acts 13:46-47, from Is.49:6) In other words, "We know, and will do, what being Jewish is all about." Paul challenges them with the acknowledged mission of Israel - to be a light to the nations.

8. **Jews live in various countries throughout the world, but, Biblically, the children of Israel have a specific geographic, socio-cultural, and political identity. Though the Church exists in different countries and cultures, it has no political or geographic identity, and is transcultural. This is another important example of difference and discontinuity in God's dealings with man.**

Though the Church should have an impact on the different civil governments, it is not a political institution, and is not entrusted by God with the coercive powers of a state. It is given certain authority by God to judge and discipline its own members. (cf. 1Co.5:12-13) The supreme penalty that the Church can inflict is excommunication. The supreme penalty that the State can inflict is execution.

Between these two penalties, there is a great difference both in nature and degree. That great difference comes from the different identifying characteristics of Israel and the Church. The Church that seeks to eliminate that difference is building on a Constantinian foundation, not a Biblical one.

As a state, the nation of Israel is entrusted by God with the same coercive power as any other state. Contrary to the history of the Church since the Council of Nicea, God did not entrust those coercive powers to the Church.

9. **Jesus did not disavow the restoration of the kingdom to Israel, He confirmed it.** This is discussed in the chapter on "The Restoration of the Kingdom."

10. **The Church meets Jesus in the air, but Jesus returns to earth for Israel.** This is discussed in the chapter on "All Israel shall be saved."

11. **When Paul says, "All Israel shall be saved," he is referring to the Jewish people, not the Church.** This point is partially discussed in the chapters on "All Israel shall be saved," and "Chapter 11 of Luther's *Commentary on Romans*." Both "Covenant" theology and "New Israel" theology are built upon the assumption that in this verse "Israel" means the Church, or "the saved Jews and Gentiles of all the ages," or "the elect remnant of the Jews." Whatever "Israel" means here, the advocates of this theology maintain, it cannot refer to the Jewish people.

Both these theologies are **dependent** upon that assumption, which is only an assumption, and not an interpretation. For if there is a future salvation for the Jewish people as a people, then the Church cannot be "Israel." If the Jews are "Israel," then both these theologies fall apart at the very beginning.

That is indeed what happens, for it is more than difficult to fit that assumption into the text and context of Rom.11. It is absolutely impossible. It cannot be done. The only possible interpretation of "Israel" in Rom.11:25-26 is that it means the Jewish people.

That will become evident as we look at the text. That is why the advocates of these theologies must completely ignore both the text and the context. They cannot make it say what they have assumed, and what they have built their theologies upon.

Paul expressly states in Rom.11:13 that he is at this point speaking to Gentile Christians. He makes it clear that these Gentile Christians had become, or who were in danger of becoming, arrogant towards the (unbelieving) Jews. Apparently these Gentile Christians in Rome were asserting that God had cast off the Jews and replaced them with the Church.

That is why Paul begins this section by saying, "I say then, God has not rejected His people has He? May it never be! For I too am an Israelite, of the seed of Abraham, of the tribe of Benjamin." (Rom.11:1)

Paul certainly knew that the Gentiles who believed were also the seed of Abraham. He was the one to whom God had revealed that mystery. He told the Gentile believers in Galatia, "And if you belong to Messiah, then you are Abraham's seed, heirs according to the promise." (Gal.3:29)

So if Paul had meant to indicate that the salvation of some from the Gentiles proved that God had not cast off "Israel," he would simply have said so to the Gentiles in the church at Rome. But instead of pointing to believing Gentiles as proof of God's faithfulness to "Israel," Paul points to himself. The demonstration of God's faithfulness to the "Israel" to which Paul is referring is his own physical, tribal ancestry — "of the tribe of Benjamin."

We have already seen, in Point 4 of this section, that in Rom.10:19-11:2, that when Paul says "Israel," he means the Jewish people. He does not mean the Church. Nor does he mean "the elect remnant of the Jews." As we follow the text, it becomes both obvious and undeniable that Paul's meaning remains the same throughout the chapter.

"God has not rejected His people whom He foreknew, Or do you not know what the Scripture says in the passage about Elijah, how he pleads with God against Israel? 'Lord, they have killed Thy prophets, they have torn down Thine altars, and I alone am left, and they are seeking my life.' But what is the divine response to him? 'I have kept for Myself seven thousand men who have not bowed the knee to Baal.' " (Rom.11:2-4)

Is Paul saying that Elijah was pleading with God against the Church? No. Was Elijah pleading with God against "the saved Jews and Gentiles of all ages," or against "the elect remnant of Jews"? No. Such interpretations cannot be fit into these scriptures. "The elect remnant of the Jews" is obviously "the seven thousand men who have not bowed the knee to Baal." When Paul says "Israel" here, he can only be speaking about the Jewish people.

Paul was comparing the situation in his own day to that in the days of Elijah. Elijah had thought that only he in all Israel was left faithful to God.

Elijah was wrong. God had kept a faithful remnant among Elijah's physical brethren for Himself.

"In the same way [Ουτως] then, there has also come to be at the present time a remnant [λειμμα] according to God's gracious choice [εκλογην χαριτος]." (v.5) It was by God's grace that there was a chosen, physical, faithful remnant of Israel in Elijah's day. In the same way, it is by God's grace that there is "at the present time" a chosen, physical, faithful remnant of Israel according to election [λειμμα κατ εκλογην].

Paul goes on to say, "That which Israel is seeking for, it has not obtained, but those who were chosen [εκλογη] obtained it, and the rest were hardened." (Rom.11:7) He mentions three groups — "Israel," "the election," and "the rest." Here, as throughout, when Paul says "Israel," he does not mean only the faithful, for he is talking about those who did not obtain what they were seeking for.

By "the election," does Paul then mean 'the saved Jews, Gentiles, and generic people of all ages?' Such an interpretation is clearly contrary to, and cannot be reconciled with, the preceding and following context. The context makes it clear that he is talking about the remnant preserved by God's grace.

Paul is part of that elect remnant. He has already spoken of himself as an Israelite in terms of his physical descent. To make "the elect" here mean "the saved of all ages" is to make Paul's point about being an Israelite meaningless. For Paul, it is not meaningless, it is a demonstration of the faithfulness, wisdom and intention of God.

"What then? That which Israel is seeking for, it has not obtained, but those who were chosen obtained it, and the rest were hardened; just as it is written, 'God gave them a spirit of stupor, eyes to see not and ears to hear not, down to this very day.' " (vv.7-8) Here also, there is only one possible meaning. "Israel" means "the Jewish people."

Paul is distinguishing two groups within Israel, "the election" and "the rest." For in context, Paul is contrasting this same elect remnant [εκλογη] in Israel "at the present time" with the rest of Israel who, as in the days of Elijah, do not believe. "Israel," i.e. "all Israel," has **NOT** obtained salvation. Only "those who were chosen" [i.e., the remnant by grace] obtained it, and the rest [of Israel] were hardened.

Paul continues to speak of the rest of Israel, the "some of the branches" who were broken off because of their unbelief. (vv.8-17) He says that when the rest of Israel, other than the remnant, does believe, it will be even greater riches for the Gentiles (v.12), and will, in fact, be life from the dead for the world (v.15).

Next he warns the Gentile believers, to whom God has sent him, not to boast against "these who according to nature" belong to, and can be grafted back into "their own olive tree." (vv.18-24) "These" are "the rest [who] were hardened."

That brings us to v.25 where Paul begins to explain how it is, and how long it will be, that the rest of Israel are hardened. "I do not want you, brethren, to be ignorant of this mystery, lest you be wise in your own estimation that a partial hardening has happened to Israel until the fulness of the Gentiles has come in; and thus all Israel shall be saved..." (Rom.11:25-26)

Does Paul mean that a partial hardening has come to the Church? to the saved Jews and Gentiles of all ages? to the elect remnant of the Jews? Will this partial hardening of the Church or of the saved Jews and Gentiles of all ages or of the elect remnant of the Jews be removed when the fulness of the Gentiles comes in? Such an "understanding" has no meaning.

Paul did not intend "Israel" here to mean "the saved Jews and Gentiles of all ages," or "the elect remnant of Jews." For then, even if the previous context and meaning are ignored, Paul would only have been saying that "those who shall be saved shall be saved." While that is true, it is a meaningless tautology. Such a statement would not reveal a mystery. Nor would it make any difference whether or not Gentile Christians were ignorant of it.

Paul was not willing to be accursed for a tautology, or for a mystery that goes without saying. He was willing to be accursed for his unsaved Jewish brethren. He was not needlessly exhorting Gentile Christians to join with him "if somehow I might move to jealousy my fellow-countrymen [literally, "my flesh"] and save some of them." (Rom.11:14) He was revealing the desire of his Holy Spirit-filled heart.

It is clear that in these verses, "Israel" means "the Jewish people," but let's continue with what Paul has to say. He is not finished yet. Would any other meaning for "Israel" make sense in what Paul goes on to say?

"[v.25] For I do not want you, brethren, to be uninformed of this mystery, lest you be wise in your own estimation, that a partial hardening has happened to Israel until the fulness of the Gentiles has come in; [v.26] and thus all Israel will be saved; just as it is written, 'The Deliverer will come from Zion, He will remove ungodliness from Jacob. [v.27] And this is My covenant with them, when I take away their sins.' [v.28] From the standpoint of the gospel they are enemies for your sake, but from the standpoint of God's choice they are beloved for the sake of the fathers; [v.29] for the gifts and the calling of God are irrevocable. [v.30] For just as you once were disobedient to God but now have been shown mercy because of their disobedience, [v.31] so these also now have been disobedient, in order that because of the mercy shown to you they also may now be shown mercy. [v.32] For God has shut up all in disobedience that He might show mercy to all."

In v.25, "Israel" must mean "the Jewish people," because it is to them that a partial hardening has happened. It is that partial hardening of the Jewish people that allows the fulness of the Gentiles to come in. This verse is related to v.7, "and the rest [of Israel] were hardened."

What then does "Israel" mean in v.26? First of all, Paul says that the salvation of all Israel is future — "all Israel **will be saved**." It is also in the future that "the Deliverer **will come** from Zion." The time that "He **will remove ungodliness** from Jacob" is likewise in the future. The time of these future occurrences follows the time when "the fulness of the Gentiles has come in."

If "Israel" in v.26 means "the Church" — and there is assuredly a sense in which the salvation of the Church is future — then what is the future ungodliness that the Deliverer removes from Jacob? Is Paul saying 'The Church is ungodly now, but Jesus will remove that ungodliness sometime in the future'? Certainly there will be ungodliness in the Church until Jesus returns, but is Paul saying (v.27) that it is in the future that God takes away the sins of the Church?

Such a view raises numerous unanswerable questions. What would be (v.25) the partial hardening that has happened to the Church? What is the fulness of the Gentiles? Does "Gentiles" really mean the saved Jews and Gentiles of all ages? Or are there non-Gentiles that will be brought into the Church?

Into what does this fulness of the Gentiles come? What is the **mystery** concerning these things that Gentile believers should know lest they be wise in their own estimation?

If "Israel" in v.26 means the "Church," then is Paul saying (v.28) that the Church is presently an enemy of the gospel for the sake of Gentile believers, but beloved of God for the sake of Abraham, Isaac, and Jacob? Is Paul saying (vv.28-29) that though the Church is currently an enemy of the gospel, because of God's choice and His previous gifts and calling, the Church will one day be saved? What are these gifts and calling?

Is Paul saying (v.30) that Gentile believers have been shown mercy through the disobedience of the Church? Is he saying that (v.31) the Church has been disobedient so that Gentile believers can be the means of showing mercy to the Church? Such an "interpretation" makes no sense at all. It has no meaning. The entire passage becomes incomprehensible if "Israel" in v.26 means "the Church."

Paul is still specifically speaking to Gentile believers. What is he really saying? If "Israel" in v.26 means what it does in the rest of the context, i.e. "the Jewish people," then the passage is easy to understand: Though God has always kept a remnant of Israel faithful to Himself, one day all Israel will repent and believe.

This is the only way that vv.11-15 can be understood. The current failure of all Israel to believe has become "riches for the Gentiles." "Through their transgression salvation has come to the Gentiles." "How much more will their fulness be?" (vv.11-12) The rejection of most of Israel has brought "the reconciliation of the world." "What will the receiving of them be but life from the dead?" (v.15)

First, there was a remnant of Israel, to whom God added the called out Gentiles. One day the fulness [πληρωμα] of the Gentiles (v.25) will come in. That will be followed by the fulness [πληρωμα] of Israel.

Following this exhortation, Paul reveals a **mystery**. It had been hard for some of the faithful Jewish remnant to believe the revealed **mystery** that Gentiles could also be fellow-heirs and fellow-members of the body, and fellow-partakers of the gospel. (cf. Eph.3:4-11) It was hard for them to believe, but it was "in accordance with the eternal purpose which He [God] carried out in Messiah Jesus our Lord." (Eph.3:11) Literally, it was "according to the purpose of the ages."

In the same way, it was, and still is, hard for some Gentile Christians to accept God's revealed **mystery** concerning the Jews: The major part of Israel has been hardened to the gospel for the sake of the Gentiles. This hardening of a part of Israel will remain until the full measure of Gentiles who will be saved has come in. Then, in just the same way as the fulness of the Gentiles comes in, the fulness of Israel, which will be life from the dead for the world (vv.12-15), will come in. "Thus [ουτως, i.e. in the same way] all Israel shall be saved." (vv.25-26) This is also according to God's purpose of the ages.

"So [ουτος] also these now were disobedient, in order that because of the mercy shown to you they also may now be shown mercy."(v.31) In the same way that the Gentile believers were brought from disobedience to mercy, so will the rest of Israel that has been hardened be brought from disobedience to mercy.

Even as the elect Jews brought the gospel to the Gentiles, so the elect Gentiles are to bring the gospel to the Jews. For Paul, "Israel" clearly means his brethren according to the flesh, i.e. "the Jews." God will bring the gospel full circle. The first will be last.

When Paul says, "And in this way, all Israel shall be saved," he is not uttering a meaningless tautology. He is speaking instead of a future chronological event — the national repentance and restoration of Israel. It takes place after the fulness of the Gentiles has come in. "A partial hardening has happened to Israel until the fulness of the Gentiles has come in."

Before Jesus ascended, the disciples asked Him, "Lord, is it at this time You are restoring the kingdom to Israel?" (Acts 1:6) As Jesus ascended, two men in white clothing said to them, "Men of Galilee, why do you stand looking into the sky? This [ουτος] Jesus, who has been taken up from you into heaven, will so [ουτως, in the same way] come in the manner you beheld Him going into the heaven." (Acts 1:11) Some things God does differently than He has ever done before, some things He does in the same way.

Paul was echoing the word of the Lord to Israel through the prophets. As He said through Ezekiel, "'**As I live,' declares the Lord God**, 'surely with a mighty hand and with an outstretched arm and with wrath poured out, I shall be king over you. And I shall bring you out from the peoples and gather you from the lands where you are scattered, with a mighty hand and with an outstretched arm and with wrath poured out; and I shall bring you into the wilderness of the peoples, and there I shall enter into judgment with you face to face.

"'**As I entered into judgment with your fathers in the wilderness of the land of Egypt, so I will enter into judgment with you,**' declares the Lord God. 'And I shall make you pass under the rod, and **I shall bring you into the bond of the covenant**; and I shall purge from you the rebels and those who transgress against Me; I shall bring them out of the land where they sojourn, but they will not enter the land of Israel. Thus you will know that I am the Lord....

"'For on My holy mountain, on the high mountain of Israel,' declares the Lord God, 'there the whole house of Israel, all of them, will serve Me in the land; there I shall accept them, and there I shall seek your contributions and the choicest of your gifts, with all your holy things.' " (Ezek.20:33-38,40)

"The burden of the word of the Lord concerning Israel" had been revealed to Zechariah: "And it will come about in that day that I will set about to destroy all the nations that come against Jerusalem. And I will pour out on the house of David and on the inhabitants of Jerusalem the Spirit of grace and of supplication, so that they will look on Me whom they have pierced; and they will mourn for Him, as one mourns for an only son, and they will weep bitterly over Him, like the bitter weeping over a first-born. In that day there will be great mourning in Jerusalem, like the mourning of Hadadrimmon in the plain of Megiddo. And the land will mourn, every family by itself; the family of the house of David by itself, and their wives by themselves; the family of the house of Nathan by itself, and their wives by themselves; the family of the house of Levi by itself, and their wives by themselves; the family of the Shimeites by itself, and their wives by themselves; all the families that remain, every family by itself, and their wives by themselves."

"In that day a fountain will be opened for the house of David and for the inhabitants of Jerusalem, for sin and for impurity...And one will say to him, 'What are these wounds between your hands?' Then He will say, 'Those with which I was wounded in the house of those who love me.' " (Zech.12:9-13:1,6)

That is the description of a specific, profound, chronological event - the repentance and salvation of all Israel. It is following this that the Lord Himself descends, and His feet stand on the Mount of Olives, to do battle for Israel. Paul has revealed **a mystery so great** that it causes him to exclaim, **"Oh the depth of the riches both of the wisdom and knowledge of God!** How unsearchable are His judgments and unfathomable His ways!" (Rom.11:33)

This is the fulfillment of what God promised to do for the house of Israel and the house of Judah in the New Covenant. "For they shall all know Me, from the least of them to the greatest of them." It is to this that Paul is referring when he says, "and thus all Israel will be saved."

When Absalom rebelled against his father, King David, most of Israel followed Absalom. Only a remnant was faithful to David. When Absalom's rebellion was finally destroyed, David sent to the elders of Judah, saying, "'You are my brothers; you are my bone and my flesh. Why then should you be the last to bring back the king?' ...Thus he turned the hearts of all the men of Judah as one man, so that they sent word to the king, saying, 'Return, you and all your servants.' The king then returned..." (2Sam.19:12,14-15)

So it will be with the Son of David. As Jesus mourned over Jerusalem, He said to the city of the great King and her children, "Behold, your house is left to you desolate; and I say to you, you shall not see Me until the time comes when you say 'Blessed is He who comes in the name of the Lord!' " When the Jewish people invite the King to return, He and all His servants will do so.

In His last message in the Bible, Jesus says, "Behold I am coming quickly, and My reward is with Me, to render to every man according to what he has done....I, Jesus, have sent My angel to testify to you these things for the churches. I am the root and the offspring of David, the bright morning star." (Rev.22:12,16) The appearance in heaven of the morning star signals the end of the night. The root and the offspring of David is the King of the Jews.

Faithful Jews cannot be excluded from membership in physical Israel. Paul and all faithful Jews are faithful within the physical people of Israel.

FOOTNOTE

1. W.C. van Unnik in "Η καινη διαθηκη — A Problem in the Early History of the Canon," Studia Patristica, Vol.IV, 1961, P.221

49

"DISPENSATIONAL" THEOLOGY

The "Dispensational" view maintains that:

1. Israel and the Church have separate and distinct identities, promises, and destinies.

2. Israel as a people, or nation, has been set aside by God during the "Church Age." After the "Church Age," God will again deal with national Israel, and restore the kingdom of David in the Millennium.

3. Jews who believe in Jesus during the "Church Age" become part of the Church and can no longer receive the promises to national Israel.

This view is represented by **Diagram 8**. The two circles, "Israel" and "The Church," are separate and distinct.

The Dispensational view is correct in recognizing that the New Covenant promise must be understood as referring to Israel. It is correct in recognizing

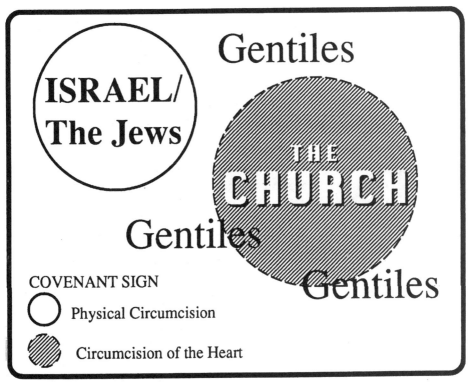

Diagram 8

that Israel and the Church are not the same, but in error in stating that they are separate and distinct. It is correct in saying that the fulness of Israel will come in the future, but in error in saying that God is therefore not dealing with and through Israel now. It is incorrect in stating that Jews who believe in Jesus are disinherited from the promises to Israel.

*1. Israel and the Church are not separate entities. They are integrally related. If they were separate, then what covenant relationship would the Church have with God, since the New Covenant is made with the house of Israel and the house of Judah?

There are four dispensational answers to this question. None of them is correct. All of them seek to avoid the joining together of those who were far off with those who were near. They avoid the literal meaning of the text.

"The first premillennial theory...presents the new covenant with Israel and the church as being essentially one covenant, based on the sacrifice of Christ, but having a twofold application. It is applied to the church in this age, that is, to all who believe in Christ. It will have a future application in a literal millennium after the return of Christ when the promises given to Israel will be fulfilled...

"Another form of premillennial interpretation is that which distinguishes the new covenant with Israel from the new covenant with the church. In other words, it finds two new covenants. The new covenant with Israel is new in contrast to the Mosaic covenant of the Old Testament. The new covenant for the church is new in contrast to the Adamic or old covenant for the church as a whole. Both new covenants are based on the sacrifice of Christ, but the promises belonging to the church and to Israel are sharply distinguished...

"A third theory is suggested which limits the term new covenant to a covenant with Israel to be fulfilled in the millennium. In other words, the only new covenant is the one belonging to Israel and the only fulfillment is future. The church in the present age has a covenant or system of promises through the death of Christ, but it is not specifically a new covenant." [1]

To these three, a fourth theory can be added that is similar to Covenant Theology. It holds that God introduced through Jesus a "covenant of grace" which is different from the New Covenant promised in Jer.31.

This "covenant of grace" does not offer anything that is not provided in Israel's New Covenant. It has the same sacrifice and same provisions, except for those that concern the land of Israel. It is not mentioned in the Bible. This view was sufficiently discussed in the opening remarks on Covenant Theology.

At His last earthly Passover seder, Jesus invited the Apostles to partake of the New Covenant in His blood (Lk.22:20, cf. Heb.7-10). They did, and later brought others into that same covenant. That covenant was the New Covenant, made with the house of Judah and the house of Israel (Jer.31:31-

34). It is Israel's New Covenant that God specifically instituted through the blood of Jesus, the King of the Jews.

The first dispensational "theory" claims that the New Covenant does not apply to Israel now. Jesus did not see it that way. Neither did the Apostles. Neither did the Jews who were filled with the Holy Spirit on Pentecost. Neither did the Jews who were involved in the debate about whether or not uncircumcised Gentiles should be received into the Church or not. Neither did all the Jews throughout the Diaspora who believed.

The second dispensational "theory" claims that there are two New Covenants, one for Israel and one for the Church. That's not what Jesus or any of His Jewish apostles preached. They were men of Israel as well as members of the Church.

If there were some other covenant through which the Church had its relationship with God, then it would be promised somewhere in the Bible, and its conditions would be stated. There is no such covenant promised, or even mentioned. What would be its conditions? Who proclaimed it, and who entered into it?

The New Covenant Scriptures, however, speak of the Church as having been brought into Israel's prophesied New Covenant. There is nothing in the Biblical text to support the view that the new covenant is "new" not in terms of the Covenant of the Law, but in "contrast to the Adamic or old covenant for the church as a whole." This is a complete fabrication.

In the first place, the Adamic covenant was not made with "the church as a whole." There is no Biblical support for such a claim. Did the Church break the Adamic covenant when God brought the Church out of Egypt? This theory deprives almost all the words of the New Covenant of any meaning.

The New Covenant is "new" in terms of the Old Covenant, the Covenant of the Law. The New Covenant Scriptures that speak to the Church about the Law — like Galatians, Ephesians, and Romans — would be irrelevant if that were not the case.

Additionally, Paul affirms that when Jesus brought this covenant to Israel, He also mercifully opened the door to the Gentiles. "For I say that Messiah has become a servant to the circumcision on behalf of the truth of God to confirm the promises given to the fathers, and for the Gentiles to glorify God for His mercy..." (Rom.15:8-9) This is demonstrated throughout the Book of Acts.

Jesus was born, ministered, died, and rose in fulfillment of prophecy made to Israel. The outpouring of the Holy Spirit is partial fulfillment of Joel's prophecy to Israel (Acts 2:16-21; Joel 2:28-32), and the evangelism of the Gentiles is partial fulfillment of God's call to Israel through Isaiah. Continually, the New Covenant Scriptures declare that what Jesus did, and what was done to Him, was in fulfillment of God's promises to Israel.

The third theory claims that, "The church in the present age has a covenant or system of promises through the death of Christ, but it is not specifically a new covenant." The first question that arises is when did the present age begin? Did it begin at the death of Christ? at Pentecost? 70 A.D.? 325 A.D.? Biblically, a covenant is cut through the sacrifice that is made, through the blood that is shed.

In a Jewish context, at Passover with His Jewish Apostles, Jesus said that He was presenting the New Covenant in His blood. He did not mention any other covenant that He was instituting. He presented Himself as the Passover lamb, the fulfillment of what God had set before Israel for 1500 years.

Were the Apostles part of the Church? Were the Jewish believers at Pentecost part of the Church? What about the tens of thousands of Jewish believers in Jerusalem? Yes, they were.

Did any of them mention a different "covenant or system of promises" other than the New Covenant with Israel which Jesus presented? No, they didn't. They presented faith in Jesus as part of the covenant relationship which God established with Israel.

Peter said to his fellow-Jews, "It is you who are the sons...of the covenant which **God covenanted with your fathers**, saying to Abraham, 'And in your seed all the families of the earth shall be blessed.' " (Acts 3:25) Paul said that this covenant with Abraham was a proclamation of the gospel. (Gal.3:8) Jews are therefore sons of the gospel, which is presented in Israel's New Covenant.

Paul said that to his fellow-Jews belonged "the adoption as sons and the glory and **the covenants** and the giving of the Law and the service and **the promises**, whose are **the fathers**..." (Rom.9:4) Jesus came to the Jewish people to fulfill the Law (Mt.5:17), and "to confirm the promises to the fathers" (Rom.15:8). If Jesus did not bring Israel's New Covenant, then He did not fulfill the Law — e.g. "Circumcise then your heart, and stiffen no more." (Dt.10:16) If Jesus did not bring Israel's New Covenant, then He did not confirm the promises to the fathers.

Do Jews who believe in Jesus cease to be Jews? Paul did not think so. He called himself a Jew. He called Peter a Jew. No one else thought so either. The question for the early Church was, **"How can non-Jews follow Jesus without becoming Jews first?"** The Jewish believers were astounded that "God has granted **to the Gentiles ALSO** the repentance that leads to life."

This dispensational theory makes Jewish faith in Jesus, "in this present age," the annihilation of Israel. If Jews do what God requires of them, then they are no longer Jews. To the contrary, it is not faith that diminishes Israel, but unbelief. Faith in Jesus does not disinherit Jews from the promises made to Israel. To the contrary, it is the only way to receive the promises.

What is the faithful remnant? They are Jews who are, by God's grace, faithful to God's calling of Israel. The unfaithfulness of most Jews does not nullify the faithfulness of God. (Rom.3:3) Then how much more does the faithfulness of the Jewish remnant not nullify the faithfulness of God.

Why are Jews natural branches of the olive tree? and Gentiles wild branches? What do the Jewish root and Israel's own olive tree have to do with the Church? Isn't the Church a partaker of the rich root of Israel's olive tree? Why else did blindness in part come to Israel for the sake of the Gentiles?

To what were Gentile believers alien before? Of what are they now fellow-citizens? The commonwealth of Israel. That is how they are brought near to the believing Jews to be made fellow-members of the body, fellow-heirs, and fellow-partakers of the promises. How could this be if the Church has nothing to do with Israel?

Why did the early Church believe the gospel is to the Jew first, if the gospel is not part of the covenant promise to Israel? Why do the New Covenant Scriptures talk about Israel, the Law, and the New Covenant, if the Church has its relationship with God through some other "covenant or system of promises"?

Why was Paul willing to be damned forever for the salvation of Israel? Isn't New Covenant faith in Jesus the only saving faith there is? Did Paul just not understand that God didn't have anything for Israel for another two thousand years or so?

Why should Jews repent and believe in Jesus if He didn't bring the New Covenant? Wouldn't all Israel still be under the Law? Is there one way of salvation for Jews and another way for Gentiles?

If the gospel is not for Israel now, then how and why did Jesus and the early Church preach the gospel from the Law, the Writings, and the Prophets? What is the point of the Epistle to the Hebrews? Why does it quote Jer.31:31-34 and contrast Israel's Old Covenant — the Law, the priesthood, the sacrifices, etc. — with Israel's New Covenant?

What is this vague, undefined, unmentioned "covenant or system of promises" that the church has in the present age? Where is it talked about?

These dispensational theories are not Biblical. Israel's New Covenant has already been brought by Jesus Himself. It was ratified in His own blood. His Jewish disciples entered into it.

Until all Israel responds as at Sinai in accepting what God offered, Gentiles also can enter into Israel's New Covenant relationship with God. The Church has been brought to God through Israel's New Covenant.

*2. The New Covenant Scriptures present the gospel as a continuation of God's dealings with Israel. The early Church preached the gospel from Tanakh, not from the New Covenant Scriptures. In fact, they did not even have the New Covenant Scriptures. They were not yet written, because the early Church was still living it.

They could not have preached the gospel from the prophecies and promises made to Israel if the identities and destinies of Israel and the Church were separate and distinct. They viewed the Church as part of God's continuing work in and through Israel. The history of Israel includes the birth of the Church.

Paul speaks of some of the events that happened to Israel in and following the Exodus. He tells New Covenant believers, "Now these things happened to them as an example, and they were written for our instruction, upon whom the ends of the ages have come." (1Co.10:11) The Church is not an interruption of God's plan, but a planned continuation. What God said to Israel, and what happened to Israel, is also for the instruction of the Church.

After His resurrection, Jesus appeared to two disciples who were walking from Jerusalem to Emmaus. "And He said to them, 'O foolish men and slow of heart to believe in all that the prophets have spoken! Was it not necessary for the Messiah to suffer these things and to enter into His glory?' And beginning with Moses and with all the prophets, He explained to them the things concerning Himself in all the Scriptures." (Lk.24:25-27) From the Law and the prophets, Jesus taught these disciples "the things concerning Himself," that they needed to know.

Jesus healed a man by the pool of Bethesda on the Sabbath. Consequently, there were those Jews who accused Jesus of breaking the Sabbath that God had given to Israel through Moses. (Ex.31:13) Jesus, however, saw the issue differently. He said, "Do not think that I will accuse you before the Father; the one who accuses you is Moses, in whom you have set your hope. For if you believed Moses, you would believe Me; for he wrote of Me. But if you do not believe his writings, how will you believe My words?" (Jn.5:45-47)

The point Jesus was making was that faith in the Law of Moses would lead to faith in the One who fulfilled the Law of Moses. For Jesus had said, "Do not think that I came to abolish the Law or the Prophets; I did not come to abolish, but to fulfill." (Mt.5:17) And as Paul later pointed out, "Therefore the Law has become our tutor to lead us to Messiah, that we may be justified by faith." (Gal.3:24)

The Law is intended to lead all Jews to Messiah. Faith in Messiah makes Jews part of the Church, but it does not make them less Jewish. It makes them wholly Jewish.

Paul and the rest of the early Church proclaimed the New Covenant that was promised in Tanakh. They proclaimed the fulfillment, in Jesus the Messiah, of what God had promised to Israel. They called Jews to follow Jesus, the King of Israel, who fulfilled the Covenant of the Law.

They issued a prophetic call to reconciliation. "Repent!" — that is, "Come back to the Lord" — "and believe" what the whole history of Israel, the Levitical feasts and sacrifices, and the Law, the Writings, and the Prophets teach. This is nothing alien to Israel, it is something natural. It is the ultimate purpose for the creation of Israel.

Paul came to Thessalonica, "where there was a synagogue of the Jews. And according to Paul's custom, he went to them, and for three Sabbaths reasoned with them from the Scriptures, explaining and giving evidence that the Messiah had to suffer and rise again from the dead, and saying, 'This Jesus whom I am proclaiming to you is the Messiah.' " (Acts 17:1-3)

He preached to Jews in the synagogue that Jesus is the Messiah whom God promised to Israel. "From the offspring of this man [David] according to promise God has brought to Israel a Savior, Jesus...And we preach to you the good news of the promise made to the fathers, that God has fulfilled this promise to us their children in that He raised up Jesus, as it is also written in the second Psalm, 'Thou art My Son; today I have begotten Thee.' " (Acts 13:23,32-33) The message that the Church is to proclaim is "the good news of the promise made to the fathers."

When Paul was making his defense before Festus and Agrippa, he said, "And now I am standing trial for the hope of the promise made by God to our fathers; the promise to which our twelve tribes hope to attain, as they earnestly serve God night and day. And for this hope, O King, I am being accused by Jews. Why is it considered incredible among you people if God does raise the dead?" (Acts 26:6-8)

All the twelve tribes of Israel hope to attain to the resurrection of the dead. Every Jew must find the fulfillment of that hope through the resurrection of Jesus. The way to the fulfillment of the promise "made by God to our fathers" is the New Covenant in the blood of Jesus. There is a clear continuity in God's dealings with Israel.

The very same message that God had proclaimed to Israel was the message that Paul proclaimed to all the Gentiles. It is the same gospel. It is the only means of salvation for any man, whether Jew or Gentile.

The only "dispensational" break in the preaching of the early believers was the recognition that the gospel is "also to the Greek." That in itself was presented as a fulfillment of the calling of Israel, not as a turning away from Israel. The Great Commission itself makes such break impossible.

Jesus told His faithful Jewish disciples, "Go therefore and **make disciples of all the Gentiles**, baptizing them in the name of the Father and the Son and the Holy Spirit, **teaching them to observe all that I commanded you;** and lo, I am with you always, even to the end of the age." (Mt.28:19-20) The disciples were commissioned and commanded to teach the Gentiles to observe **ALL** that Jesus had commanded them.

Jesus did not commission them to start from scratch. He commanded them to continue what He had been doing.

Paul reminded the church of "...my brethren, my kinsmen according to the flesh, who are Israelites, to whom belongs the adoption as sons and the glory and the covenants and the giving of the Law and the service and the promises, whose are the fathers, and from whom is the Messiah according to the flesh, who is over all, God blessed forever. Amen." (Rom.9:3-5) Put simply, these are Jewish things.

Yet, in the same letter, Paul writes of how Gentile believers have become partakers of these Jewish things. Chapter 11 explains that the Gentile believers are grafted in to Israel's olive tree. Elsewhere in this same letter, Paul specifically mentions some of these Jewish things in their relationship to the Church — the adoption as sons (8:15,19,23), the glory (8:18-21),the Law (7:7-14), the service (6:11-22; 12:1),the promises (1:1-2), and the fathers (4:11; 11:16). It is clear that the Church, justified in the Messiah, partakes of some of what belongs to Israel.

Jesus said to the Samaritan woman, "Salvation is of the Jews." For Jesus, salvation did not become un-Jewish when He presented it to the Samaritans. It remained part of God's dealings with the Jewish people. Gentiles do not need to be saved through the Jews, but they do need to be saved through what God has given to the Jews.

Paul said, "And the Scriptures, foreseeing that God would justify the Gentiles by faith, preached the gospel beforehand to Abraham, saying, 'All the goyim shall be blessed in you.' " (Gal.3:8) God preached the gospel to Abraham. "For this reason it is by faith, that it might be in accordance with grace, in order that the promise may be certain to all the descendants, not only to those who are of the Law, but also to those who are of the faith of Abraham, who is the father of us all." (Rom.4:16)

There is continuity between the promise and the fulfillment. There is continuity between the Law, the tutor that leads to Messiah, and the New Covenant, the means of being joined to Him.

God preached the same gospel to Isaac. (Gen.26:4) He preached the same gospel to Jacob. (Gen.28:14) He preached the same gospel through David. (Rom.4:6-8) He preached the same gospel throughout Tanakh. There is continuity in God's message to and through Israel. There is such continuity that Jesus and the early Church preached the gospel from Tanakh.

Paul's analogy of the olive tree teaches the continuity of God's work in Israel. The tree grew from the root. The branches grew from the tree. The faithful branches produced good fruit. There is continuity from root to tree to branches to fruit.

The listing of the heroes of the faith in Heb.11 teaches the continuity of God's work in Israel. They lived by faith. They looked to Messiah. They had the same faith, though less explicit. Jesus said, "Your father Abraham rejoiced to see My day; and he saw it, and was glad." (Jn.8:56)

Paul declares the continuing faithful remnant that God has kept for Himself, but he points to the climax of the salvation of all Israel. All Israel will be saved because "the gifts and calling of God are irrevocable."

(Rom.11:29) What He has been doing He will continue to do. One day it will be completed.

**3. Paul states unequivocally, "I ALSO am an Israelite." He is part of Israel AND he is part of the Church. In the middle of the first century, there were tens of thousands of other Jews in Jerusalem alone who also believed in Jesus as the promised Messiah and bringer of the New Covenant.

Paul never recognized in his preaching, his writing, or his life a setting aside of Israel. He, and the other Jewish believers, understood Jesus and the New Covenant to be the fulfillment of what God had promised to the Jewish people. Believing in Jesus did not make him, or them, no longer Jewish.

To the contrary, he explicitly said the opposite. He told the Gentile believers in Rome, "I am an Israelite." He said to Peter, "We are Jews." He wrote to the church in Corinth about some false apostles, "Are they Hebrew? So am I. Are they Israelites? So am I. Are they descendants of Abraham? So am I." (2Co.11:22)

The Jewish believers were not turning away from the God of their fathers. They were turning to Him. They were doing what God wanted all Israel to do. They were faithful Israelites, part of the remnant.

Some of Israel was in the Church, and some of the Church was in Israel. Jewish believers were not taken out of the Commonwealth of Israel. Gentile believers were grafted in. Jewish believers did not lose their inheritance by believing in Jesus. They secured it. The unfaithfulness of the rest of Israel did not nullify the faithfulness of God. The Jewish believers were the faithful remnant within Israel that God kept for Himself. (Rom.11:1-5)

In which of the two circles in Diagram 8 should Paul and the faithful Jewish remnant be placed? They belong in both. To paraphrase what Paul said, 'If God set aside the Jewish people, then why am I here?'

**4. God did not set aside Israel. If God set aside Israel, then He did it in a very strange way. He started with the greatest revival in Jewish history. He then used Jewish believers to spark an unprecedented move to repentance and faith among the Gentiles. He then used Jewish believers to give the New Covenant Scriptures to the world.

If God had set aside Israel, why did the apostles continue to minister in Jerusalem and Judea? Why did the early Church continue to bring the gospel to Jews throughout Israel and in the Diaspora? Why did they preach that Jews should believe the gospel? Were they being disobedient to God in doing so, or did they just not understand God's plan and purpose?

These Jewish believers were carrying out God's calling for Israel, and calling other Jews to do the same. They did not think that what they believed put them outside of Israel, or outside of God's dealings with Israel. Nor did Paul. Their faith was what being Jewish was all about. **"In the same**

way then, there has also come to be **at the present time** a remnant according to God's choice of grace." (Rom.11:5)

"**At the present time** [καιρω] there is a remnant..." - in this time, in this season, the ongoing reality of the Jewish remnant is a proof that God has not set aside Israel. What time or season was Paul writing in? the "Church Age"? In whatever time or season the Epistle to the Romans belongs, God has not set aside Israel.

If God had set aside Israel, how would the Gentiles have heard? They heard through the Jewish remnant that believed. If God set aside Israel, how could Gentile believers become fellow-heirs, fellow-partakers, fellow-members, and fellow-citizens with their Jewish brethren? Paul was not telling the Gentile believers in Ephesus that they were brought into fellowship only with Jews in the past or with Jews in the future. He was speaking about a visible, present reality.

If God set aside Israel, then how did the sons of Israel give the New Covenant Scriptures to the world? Nowhere in them does God say that He has set aside Israel. His message is one of reconciliation that is possible "**today** if you hear His voice."

These Jews who were faithful to God did not lose their Jewish identity by believing in the King of the Jews. They accepted and fulfilled what God created the Jewish people to be. Even so today, there are Jews who believe because God has graciously called forth a remnant for Himself. Individual Jews who believe are not grafted into the Church, but grafted into what is naturally their own olive tree.

The question that confronted the early Church was (Acts 15), 'Can Gentiles enter into Israel's New Covenant without first entering into her Old Covenant, the Covenant of the Law?' "And all the believers from among the circumcision who had come with Peter were amazed, because the gift of the Holy Spirit had also been poured out upon the Gentiles also...'Well then, God has granted to the Gentiles **also** the repentance that leads to life.' " (Acts 10:45; 11:18) Peter did not say that God has granted only to the Gentiles the repentance that leads to life. He said "**also.**"

If God had set aside Israel, how would the Church have come into existence? It was Jews who made up the original Church, just as it was Jews who brought the gospel to the Gentiles.

It is true that there is a gap between the 69th and 70th of the weeks that Gabriel told Daniel had been decreed for his people. But during that gap, Messiah is crucified and raised from the dead. The Holy Spirit is poured out on believing Jews at Pentecost. Jewish believers evangelize the world. The Temple is destroyed, and the prophesied Diaspora among the Gentiles, with all its tragedy, takes place. The restoration to the land and the re-birth of the State of Israel signify the beginning of the time of the end.

Following that, more Jews come to believe in Jesus than at any time since the second century. The Exodus from the land of the north and from all the countries of the earth is set in motion, etc. In what way did God set Israel aside during this time period?

God did not set aside the Jews during this age. It is some in the Church who have set aside the Jews during this age. The Jewish people have only been separated from the gospel by the refusal of the Church to bring the Biblical gospel to them. "How shall they believe unless someone tell them?"

The history of Israel from the first century to today, including tragedy and restoration, was prophesied throughout the Bible. It is God at work, "declaring the end from the beginning and from ancient times things which have not been done, saying, 'My purpose will be established, and I will accomplish all My good pleasure.' " (Is.46:10)

Paul does not say in Rom.11 that all Israel was cut off. He says that those individual Jews who did not believe were cut off, and individual Gentiles were grafted into their place. He does not say that in the future Gentiles as a whole will be cut off. He says that those individual Gentiles who do not believe will be cut off. Paul is very careful to use the singular in the verses (vv.17,18,19,20,21,22,24) where he is exhorting the individual Gentile believer, and the plural where he is addressing Gentiles as a whole. (vv.13,25,28,30,31)

***5. The Church is the combination of the faithful remnant in Israel joined to those called out of the Gentiles**. Israel and the Church are differentiated, but not separated. "For He Himself is our peace, who made both groups into **one** and broke down the barrier of the dividing wall, by abolishing in His flesh the enmity, the Law of commandments in ordinances, that in Himself He might make the two into one new man, thus establishing peace, and might reconcile them both in **one** body to God through the cross, by it having put to death the enmity." (Eph.2:14-16)

God's Law demanded that Jews separate themselves from the Gentiles. (See the chapter on "The Beginning of the Gentiles.") God is the One who erected the wall of separation. To rebelliously seek to breach that wall was to invite death and the wrath of God.

Jesus satisfied the claims of the Law, so that the barrier between Jews and Gentiles would be removed for those who enter into His death. God intends to make one new man from the reconciliation of Jew and Gentile. That was God's purpose in the cross.

In the plan of God for believing Jews and Gentiles, "There is **one** body and **one** Spirit, just as also you were called in **one** hope of your calling; **one** Lord, **one** faith, **one** immersion, **one** God and Father of all who is over all and through all and in all." (Eph.4:4-6) God does not offer one way of salvation for Israel and another for the Church. **Believing Jews and believing Gentiles share the same hope**.

As Peter reminded the Jewish believers in Jerusalem, "But we believe that **we are saved** through the grace of the Lord Jesus, **in the same way as they also are."** (Acts 15:11) To paraphrase Peter, 'We Jews are saved through the grace of the Lord Jesus in just the same way that the Gentiles are.'

Paul had publicly rebuked Peter for acting differently: "We are Jews by nature, and not sinners from among the Gentiles; nevertheless knowing that a man is not justified by the works of the Law but through faith in Messiah Jesus, even we have believed in Messiah Jesus, that we may be justified by faith in Messiah, and not by the works of the Law; since by the works of the Law shall no flesh be justified." (Gal.2:15-16) To paraphrase Paul, 'We Jews who believe are justified in the same way as the Gentiles who believe.'

When Cornelius and his Gentile household believed and received the gift of the Holy Spirit, Peter said, "Surely no one can refuse the water for these to be baptized who have received the Holy Spirit **just as we** [Jews] did, can he?" (Acts 10:47) When Peter was questioned by other Jewish believers about what he had done, he defended himself by saying, "'If God therefore gave to them **the same gift** as He gave to us also after believing in the Lord Jesus the Messiah, who was I that I could stand in God's way?' And when they heard this, they quieted down, and glorified God, saying, 'Well then, God has granted to the Gentiles also the repentance that leads to life.' " (Acts 11:17-19)

The Gentile believers had received the same gift. They showed the same faith. By God's grace, they also turned from the sin that leads to death in a repentance that leads to life. (This has been covered at length in the chapter on "The Debate in Jerusalem.")

They heard and believed the same message. They received the same Spirit and cleansing. They are saved in the same way. In Peter's day, that needed to be said of the Gentiles. Today, it needs to be said of the Jews.

The Biblically defined nature of the Church is Jew and Gentile made one in Messiah. The Church is not Gentile. It is Jew and Gentile together created into one new man. If the Jews are set aside, then what is the Church?

John tells us that Jesus died for Israel, "And **not for the nation only, but that He might also gather together into one the children of God** who are scattered abroad." (Jn.11:52) The Great Shepherd's stated intention and purpose is to make the two, Jews and Gentiles, into one flock. That has not been fully accomplished yet, but when this age is finished, God's intention and purpose will have been fulfilled.

The Church is to proclaim this mystery of the gospel now. Jesus made the two into one. There is power in the proclamation of the mystery of the gospel. It will have its effect on "the rulers and the authorities in the heavenlies." (Eph.3:10)

6. Gentile Christians, along with faithful Israel, are supposed to bring the gospel to unbelieving Israel in the so-called "Church Age." Jesus said, "Do **you** not **say**, 'There are yet four months, and then comes the harvest'? **Behold, I say** to you, lift up your eyes, and look on the fields, that they are white for harvest." (Jn.4:34-35)

Jesus had been speaking with a non-Jew, the Samaritan woman. His disciples didn't understand what He was doing. They didn't recognize that the Samaritans were like a field ready to be harvested. In the contemporary understanding, that might perhaps be the case sometime in the future, at the end of the age, but not now.

Jesus did not tell them that the harvest among the Gentiles was something that God would do, sometime in the future without their involvement. He did not tell them not to be concerned about it. They already knew that God would someday reach the Gentiles. Jesus was telling them, "This is the day that the Lord has made." He said, "**I sent you to reap...**" (Jn.4:38)

Jesus was not denying the sovereignty of God, but He was rejecting the view of those who might say there was no point in bringing the gospel to the Samaritans until later. He was rejecting the view of those who would say, 'God will do it in His time, but it doesn't concern me.' "Behold, I **say to you**" — you are to work this field.

"Already he who reaps is receiving wages, and is gathering fruit for life eternal; that he who sows and he who reaps may rejoice together. For in this case the saying is true, 'One sows, and another reaps.' " (Jn.4:36-37) There is a harvest to be had. You should have a part in it.

Jesus rejected the view of those who would say there is no point in laboring in that field. Today He still rejects that view. No one should say that it isn't time for the harvest of Israel. It is time, "**Today** if you will hear His voice." "**Today** is the day of salvation."

Jesus told His Jewish apostles, "You shall receive power when the Holy Spirit has come upon you; and you shall be My witnesses both in Jerusalem, and in all Judea and Samaria, and even to the remotest part of the earth." (Acts 1:8) Jesus was not telling the apostles to begin in their hometown and work progressively outward. That may be a good strategy, but it was not what Jesus was saying.

The Apostles were not from Jerusalem. They were not from Judea. They were not even from Samaria. They were from Galilee, beyond Samaria.

They were not at home in Jerusalem. When Jesus was arrested, Peter secretly followed after Him. "Now Peter was sitting outside in the courtyard, and a certain servant-girl came to him and said, 'You too were with Jesus the Galilean.' But he denied it before them all, saying, 'I do not know what you are talking about.' And when he had gone out to the gateway, another servant-girl saw him and said to those who were there, 'This man was with Jesus of Nazareth.' And again he denied it with an oath, 'I do not know the man.' And a little later the bystanders came up and said to Peter, 'Surely you too are one of them; for **the way you talk gives you away.'** " (Mt.26:69-73)

Every time Peter opened his mouth in Jerusalem, the people there knew that he was a Galilean. The same was true for the others. Nor could they hide that they were "uneducated and untrained men." (Acts 4:13) Yet they faithfully obeyed the Lord's command to stay in Jerusalem and preach the gospel there. In His order, they brought the gospel to all Israel.

Paul said, "I am a debtor both to Greeks and to barbarians, both to the wise and to the foolish. Thus for my part, I am eager to preach the gospel to you also who are in Rome. For I am not ashamed of the gospel, for it is the power of God for salvation to every one who believes, to the Jew first and also to the Greek." (Rom.1:14-16)

Why was Paul a debtor to the Gentile Greeks and barbarians? He hadn't received anything from them. It was an obligation that God had placed upon him. "For if I preach the gospel, I have nothing to boast of, for I am under compulsion; for woe is me if I do not preach the gospel." (1Co.9:16) Paul owed everything to Jesus, and Jesus called him to preach to the Gentiles.

In the same way, Gentile Christians owe everything to Jesus, and are indebted to preach the gospel to unbelieving Jews. It is an obligation that God has placed upon them. Gentile Christians are to provoke Israel to jealousy (Rom.11:11), and are to be the means by which unbelieving Israel is shown mercy.

In the plan of God, that purpose cannot be relegated to the past by saying, 'They heard in the first century.' Jews living today in Chicago, or Mexico City, or Hong Kong did not hear the gospel when it was preached in Ephesus nineteen hundred years ago. God's purpose and plan have not changed. Nor has the reciprocal responsibility of Gentile believers.

Paul states simply that the gospel is the power of God. He states simply that the gospel is to the Jew first. For the Apostle Paul, that never became a description of the past, but always a very present truth of God. For the whole early Church, as well, that never became a description of the past. It was always a prescription for the present. It is never changed or denied in the New Covenant Scriptures. (This is covered fully in the chapter, "The Gospel Is.")

Jesus said "Go into all the world and preach the gospel to all creation." (Mk.16:15) **The fact that the gospel was once preached in Syria, Greece, and Italy does not mean that there is no longer any obligation to preach the gospel in these nations.**

Jewish believers cannot say, 'The gospel has already been preached also to the Gentiles, so we will not bring it to them anymore.' **The Great Commission is always in the present tense.**

"How then shall they call upon Him in whom they have not believed?

And how shall they believe in Him whom they have not heard? And how shall they hear without a preacher?" (Rom.10:14) Who is supposed to tell them?

The obligation to bring the gospel to the Jewish people cannot be escaped by relegating it to the past. Nor can it be escaped by postponing God's purpose to the future, saying, 'God will do it in His time.' Of course God will do it in His time. He will do everything in His time, but the question is how will He do it? And when is His time?

"And working together with Him, **we also urge you not to receive the grace of God in vain**; — for He says, 'At the acceptable time I listened to you, and on the day of salvation I helped you'; behold, now is 'the acceptable time,' **behold, now is 'the day of salvation.'** " (2Co.6:1-2) "I listened to you...I helped you...we also urge you not to receive the grace of God in vain."

Will Jews believe in Jesus without ever hearing the gospel? No, they won't. If they must first hear the gospel, then who is to tell them? Paul writes to Gentile Christians, "So these also now have been disobedient, in order that because of the mercy shown to you they also may now be shown mercy." (Rom.11:31) Some very important words here are, "**now...you...**"— 'You are to tell them.'

7. **Though the complete establishment of the kingdom of God is still future, the New Covenant Scriptures do not teach that the kingdom was "postponed" when all Israel did not believe.** This is discussed in the chapters on "The Restoration of the Kingdom," and "They Will Reign Upon the Earth."

The reign of Jesus over all the earth from Jerusalem is still future, but He reigns now as Lord and King in the lives of all those Jews and Gentiles who have believed in Him. In that respect, the kingdom of God is present now. God did not postpone anything. Nothing happened that interfered with His plan.

God actively blinded those in Israel who did not believe. He did that because it was His eternal plan and purpose for Jesus to suffer and die for the sins of mankind. Seven hundred years earlier, Isaiah had explicitly prophesied that rejection, suffering, and death.

If all Israel had accepted Jesus as king, events would certainly have been quite different, but God never planned that. As the early church in Jerusalem prayed, "For truly in this city there were gathered together against Your holy Servant Jesus, whom You did anoint, both Herod and Pontius Pilate, along with the Gentiles and the peoples of Israel, **to do whatever Your hand and Your purpose predestined to occur.**" (Acts 4:27-28) Peter preached that Jesus was "delivered up **by the predetermined plan and foreknowledge of God**..." (Acts 2:23) That was God's predetermined plan. He did not postpone the kingdom.

Jesus went to the Father to receive His kingdom. He has not yet returned to forcibly establish it over all the earth, but He has already ascended His throne. Yet, having received His kingdom, He has been told by the Father, "Sit at My right hand, until I make Thine enemies a footstool for Thy feet." (Ps.110:1; Mt.22:41-45)

Until that day, His work on earth continues. He commissioned His Jewish ambassadors to "Go and make disciples of all the goyim, ...teaching them to observe all that I commanded you; and lo, I am with you always, even to the end of the age." From that day to this, and to the end of the age, His work continues without postponement. It continues towards the final goal of the fulness of the Gentiles brought in and the salvation of all Israel.

8. The Church is not all there is to Messiah's kingdom, but it is a part of His kingdom. The Church is Israel's fruit through her King. It has grown on her olive tree.

Every believer will sit down with Jesus in His kingdom. When a Gentile centurion showed great faith, Jesus said to the Jews around Him, "And I say to you, that many shall come from east and west, and recline at table with Abraham, and Isaac, and Jacob, in the kingdom of heaven; but the sons of the kingdom shall be cast out into the outer darkness; in that place there shall be weeping and gnashing of teeth." (Mt.8:11-12) Gentile believers are brought into the same kingdom that faithful Jews are.

When Jesus returns, He will sit on the throne of David, the king of Israel, in Jerusalem, but all believers will be part of that kingdom. When Peter asked Jesus, "'Behold, we have left everything and followed You; what then will there be for us?' And Jesus said to them, 'Truly I say to you, that you who have followed Me, in the regeneration when the Son of Man will sit on the throne of His glory, you also shall sit upon twelve thrones, judging the twelve tribes of Israel.' " (Mt.19:27-28)

Peter and the other individual Jews who have believed are not simply grafted into the Church, with their identity submerged or annulled. As the faithful remnant in Israel — the demonstration that God is faithful to Israel — they will have a part in the kingdom that is restored to Israel. Gentile believers will be just as much a part of Israel's kingdom. They are the fruit of God's faithfulness to Israel.

Jesus warned those Jews who did not yet believe in Him, "There will be weeping and gnashing of teeth there when you see Abraham and Isaac and Jacob and all the prophets in the kingdom of God, and yourselves being cast out. And they will come from east and west, and from north and south, and will recline at table in the kingdom of God." (Lk.13:28-29) The Gentiles who believe in Him will be in the same kingdom as Abraham, Isaac, and Jacob.

Before He ascended, Jesus appeared to the apostles, "speaking of the things concerning the kingdom of God." (Acts 1:3) That was the message they were to proclaim. They proclaimed the kingdom of God to Jew and Gentile alike. Faith in Jesus is the way to enter that kingdom.

"And Philip went down to the city of Samaria and began proclaiming Messiah to them...when they believed Philip preaching the good news about the kingdom of God and the name of Jesus the Messiah, they were being baptized, men and women alike." (Acts 8:5,12)

Paul came to Ephesus, "And he entered the synagogue and continued speaking out boldly for three months, reasoning and persuading them about the kingdom of God." (Acts 19:8) Paul was persuading the Jews in the synagogue that Jesus is the King of Israel who will establish God's kingdom. That is what he always sought to do.

Paul invited the Jews of Rome to come and listen to what he had to say. "And when they had set a day for him they came to him at his lodging in large numbers; and he was explaining to them by solemnly testifying about the kingdom of God, and trying to persuade them concerning Jesus, from both the Law of Moses and from the Prophets, from morning until evening. And some were being persuaded by the things spoken but others would not believe." (Acts 28:23)

The Law of Moses and the Prophets speak about the establishment of God's kingdom on the earth. Paul preached the same to the Gentiles. As he told the Jews in Rome, "Let it be known to you therefore, that this salvation of God has been sent to the Gentiles; they will also listen." (Acts 28:28)

Those Jews who believe receive the salvation of God. They inherit the kingdom promised to Israel. Those Gentiles who believe receive this same salvation of God, and are fellow-heirs of the same kingdom.

9. The Biblical word translated "dispensation" does not refer to a period of time. In "Dispensational" Theology, "a dispensation is a period of time during which man is tested in respect to his obedience to some specific revelation of the will of God." [2] That is not what it means in the Bible.

The word translated "dispensation" [οικο–νομια] means the "law of a house." It refers to the management of the affairs of a household. It is also translated "stewardship." (Lk.16:2,3,4) The one who has a "stewardship" entrusted to him is "a steward" [οικο–νομος]. (Lk.12:42; 16:1,3,8; 1Co.4:1,2; Titus 1:7; 1Pet.4:10) "And the steward [οικο–νομος] said to himself, 'What shall I do, since my master is taking the stewardship [οικο–νομια] away from me? I am not strong enough to dig; I am ashamed to beg.' " (Lk.16:3)

Paul writes, "For if I preach the gospel, I have nothing to boast of, for I am under compulsion; for woe is me if I do not preach the gospel. For if I do this voluntarily, I have a reward; but if against my will, I have a stewardship [οικο–νομιαν] entrusted to me." (1Co.9:17; cf. Eph.3:2; Col.1:25)

The division of time into different "dispensations" is essential for

"Dispensational Theology." The concept of "the Church Age" originates from these divisions. The belief that Israel has been set aside during the Church Age comes from these divisions. This concept of dispensations does not come from the Bible.

FOOTNOTES

1. John Walvoord, "The New Covenant with Israel," *Bibliotheca Sacra*, Dallas, 1946, Pp.17-18
2. C.I. Scofield, *The New Scofield Study System*, Oxford U. Press, NY, 1967, P.3

50

"DUAL COVENANT" THEOLOGY

"Dual Covenant" theology is not a systematic theology that seeks to cover every aspect of divine revelation. It is a teaching that is primarily concerned with God's relationship with the Jewish people. It has arisen in response to, and in opposition to, the Church's historical "teaching of contempt" towards the Jewish people.

Constantine and Eusebius canonized that "teaching of contempt," making it the predominant teaching of the Church from that time to the Reformation. Luther initially rebuked it, and later embraced it. This "teaching of contempt" still characterizes the theology of many today.

The main tenet of "Dual Covenant" theology is that Jews are saved through God's covenant with Abraham, and consequently do not need the gospel. They can be saved without Jesus.

In some respects this is a strangely extended form of Dispensational Theology, placing the salvation of Israel outside the Church. (**Diagram 8** also represents this view.) In some respects, it is a strangely extended form of Covenant Theology, declaring the New Covenant unnecessary for salvation.

Although the "Dual Covenant" approach is not a comprehensive theology, its errors are comprehensive. They are broad and deep. This view is contradicted by most of the Bible. In brief, it is in error because:

*1. The New Covenant Scriptures teach that the gospel is THE means of fulfilling the promise to Abraham. (cf. Lk.1:73; Gal.3:6-9; Rom.4:13) Consequently, Jews must believe the gospel to inherit the promise to Abraham.

Ishmael was Abraham's son, but he was not his heir. Esau was Isaac's son, but he too was not Abraham's heir. Ishmael and Esau were physically descended from Abraham, but they were not heirs of the promise. More than physical descent is required to inherit the promise.

Ishmael and Esau were also physically circumcised. More than physical circumcision is required to inherit the promise. God exhorted the children of Israel to circumcise their hearts. He warned that He would punish those with uncircumcised hearts. (Jer.9:25-26)

Abraham left everything behind to obey and follow God. His children must do the same. The direction of a person's heart shows whether or not he or she is truly a child of Abraham.

Jesus told a Jewish crowd in Jerusalem, "If you are Abraham's children, do the deeds of Abraham...If God were your Father, you would love Me;

for I proceeded forth and have come from God, for I have not come on My own initiative, but He sent Me." (Jn.8:39,42) He also said, "Your father Abraham rejoiced to see My day; and he saw it, and was glad." (Jn.8:56) Abraham looked to Jesus to bring the fulfillment of God's promise to him.

John the baptist went prior to Jesus and said, "Do not suppose that you can say to yourselves, 'We have Abraham for our father;' for I say to you, that God is able from these stones to raise up children to Abraham. And the axe is already laid at the root of the trees; every tree therefore that does not bear good fruit is cut down, and thrown into the fire." (Mt.3:9,10) Children of Abraham must produce what the Lord defines as good fruit.

2. God's covenant with Abraham does not mention either the forgiveness of sin or salvation. It contains no promise or provision of atonement. Since everyone sins, everyone needs atonement. If there were atonement and salvation available through God's covenant with Abraham, Jesus would not have instituted the New Covenant in His blood with His Jewish disciples.

Jesus is God's means of atonement for all the world, including the Jewish people. Jesus spoke almost exclusively to Jews, for He was sent only to the lost sheep of the house of Israel, to seek and to save that which was lost. He said to the Jews around Him, "I said therefore to you, that you shall die in your sins; for unless you believe that I am He, you shall die in your sins." (Jn.8:24)

3. The Bible teaches that Jesus is the only way by which anyone can be saved. Jesus told His Jewish disciples, "I am the way, the truth, and the life; no one comes to the Father, but through Me." (Jn.14:6) "And there is salvation in no one else; for there is no other name under heaven that has been given among men, by which we must be saved." (Acts 4:12)

Jesus said, "I am the bread of life. Your fathers ate the manna in the wilderness, and they died. This is the bread which comes down out of heaven, so that one may eat of it and not die." (Jn.6:48-50) Eternal life comes through Jesus alone.

He said, "I am the light of the world...For everyone who does evil hates the light, and does not come to the light, lest his deeds should be exposed. But he who practices the truth comes to the light, that his deeds may be manifested as having been wrought in God." (Jn.9:5; 3:20-21)

John, His forerunner, said to Israel, "He who believes in the Son has eternal life; but he who does not obey the Son shall not see life, but the wrath of God abides on him." (Jn.3:36) "Jesus said to them, 'I am the bread of life...Truly, truly, I say to you, unless you eat the flesh of the Son of Man and drink His blood, you have no life in yourselves.' " (Jn.6:35,53)

"Then they said therefore to Him, 'What shall we do, that we may work the works of God?' Jesus answered and said to them, 'This is the work of God, that you believe in Him whom He has sent.' " (Jn.6:28,29) "He who rejects Me, and does not receive My sayings, has one who judges him; the word I spoke is what will judge him at the last day." (Jn.12:48)

Jesus said to Israel, "You search the Scriptures, because you think that in them you have eternal life; and it is these that bear witness of Me...Do not think that I will accuse you before the Father; the one who accuses you is Moses, in whom you have set your hope. For if you believed Moses, you would believe Me; for he wrote of Me." (Jn.5:39,45-46)

Moses taught Israel, " 'Cursed is he who does not confirm the words of this law by doing them.' And all the people shall say, 'Amen.' " (Dt.27:26) "For whoever keeps the whole law and yet stumbles in one point, he has become guilty of all." (Jacob 2:10)

Paul wrote, "I do not nullify the grace of God; for if righteousness comes through the Law, then Messiah died needlessly." (Gal.2:21) If righteousness comes through any other way, then Messiah died needlessly. If Jews and Gentile proselytes can be made righteous through the promise to Abraham, then there is no need for Messiah to die for anyone.

4. God sent His Son to Israel, because Israel needed Him. If the Jewish people did not need Jesus, God would not have sent Him to them. As Peter preached in Jerusalem, "It is you who are the sons of the prophets, and of the covenant which God made with your fathers, saying to Abraham, 'And in your seed all the families of the earth shall be blessed.' For you first, God raised up His Servant, and sent Him to bless you by turning every one of you from your wicked ways." (Acts 3:25-26)

*5. God promised to make a new covenant with the house of Israel and the house of Judah. He did that because of His love for, and faithfulness to, Israel. He said that those who entered into this new covenant would receive forgiveness of sin, circumcision of the heart, and the Spirit of God. (Jer.31:31-34; Ezek.36:22-30) This is the only covenant that can bring these things. The crucifixion of Jesus is the sacrifice by which this new covenant is sealed.

The New Covenant Scriptures teach that faith in Jesus is necessary for all Jews. Jews are the natural branches of the cultivated olive tree, but they are cut off from "their own olive tree" because of unbelief. (Rom.11:20) If they believe in the King of the Jews, then they are grafted back in. (Rom.11:23)

6. All the history of Israel points to Jesus. The New Covenant Scriptures specifically mention the sacrifice of Isaac, the Passover lamb, the brass serpent, the Tabernacle, etc. as being representations of what God would do through His Son. Moses and all the prophets wrote about Jesus. "Therefore the Law has become our tutor to lead us to Messiah, that we may be justified by faith." (Gal.3:24)

Isaiah, like the other prophets, prophesied to Israel about Jesus, "Surely our griefs He Himself bore, and our sorrows He carried; Yet we ourselves esteemed Him stricken, smitten of God, and afflicted. But He was pierced through for our transgressions, He was crushed for our iniquities; the chastening for our well-being fell upon Him, and by His scourging we are healed.

"All of us like sheep have gone astray, each of us has turned to his own way; but the Lord has caused the iniquity of us all to fall on Him...He was cut off out of the land of the living, for the transgression of my people to whom the stroke was due..." (Is.53:4-6,8)

Because "the iniquity of us all...fall[s] on Him," we can be forgiven. The Lamb of God is God's **only** provision for eternal forgiveness.

7. The early Church, which was Jewish, believed in Jesus and proclaimed that all Israel needed to repent and believe in Him. (e.g. Acts 2:37-40) The first century witnessed one of the greatest revivals in four thousand years of Jewish history. Even though most of Israel did not believe, great multitudes of Jews did become disciples of Jesus. Jewish apostles and evangelists carried the message of salvation through faith in Jesus the Messiah into all the world. They issued a call to repentance to the lost sheep of the house of Israel, both those in the land and those in the Diaspora among the Gentiles.

God then commanded these Jewish believers to proclaim that same message to the Gentiles, too. This was in accordance with His purpose and plan in calling Abraham and creating the Jewish people. The Jewish apostles, faithful to God's calling of Israel, wrote, or communicated, all the writings of the New Covenant, giving it to the world.

Did these Jews need to believe in Jesus or not? They believed that if they did not believe in Jesus, they would be cast out of the kingdom, and die in their sins. Were they wrong?

Were they wrong to tell other Jews that they too needed to believe in Jesus to be saved from God's coming judgment? If God's promise to Abraham was not sufficient for the salvation of first-century Jews, then it is not sufficient today. His promise to Abraham has not changed.

Did the Jewish disciples of Jesus deceive the Gentiles into believing that Jesus is the only way of salvation? The question that confronted the early church was not, 'Do Jews need to believe in Jesus?' The entire nature of their faith affirmed that all Israel needed to repent and believe in Him.

The question that confronted the early church was, 'Do Gentiles need to become Jewish first in order to follow Messiah?' The gospel was obviously for the Jews. Was it also for the Gentiles? They knew of no other means of atonement for anyone.

8. The love of God is manifested in the gospel. (1Jn.4:9-10) To withhold the gospel from the Jewish people is to withhold God's love from them. In one very important respect then, the result of this "Dual Covenant" theology is exactly the same as the "teaching of contempt" which it seeks to replace.

It keeps the gospel from the Jewish people, and it keeps the Jewish people away from the gospel.

That makes it impossible for the Jewish people to fulfill their irreplaceable, God-ordained role in the harvest of the earth. God has declared that He will not revoke the special gifts and calling which He has entrusted to Israel. According to the unchangeable purpose of God, Israel will fulfill her calling through the gospel. The calling of being Jewish cannot be fulfilled outside of Jesus the Messiah.

Likewise, the Church cannot fulfill its calling without bringing the gospel to the lost sheep of the house of Israel. It is the responsibility and mission of the Church to bring the gospel to those who do not yet believe, especially to the people whom God used to bring salvation to the world. "For just as you [Gentile believers] once were disobedient to God but now have been shown mercy through their disobedience, so these [those Jews who do not yet believe] also now have been disobedient, in order that through the mercy shown to you they also may now be shown mercy." (Rom.11:30-31)

Jesus was willingly crucified and accursed so that Jewish people could believe in Him and find forgiveness and eternal life. That was the love of God. Peter and John suffered beatings and death that they might obey God in bringing the gospel to the Jews. That, also, was God's love.

Paul was willing to be damned for eternity if it would bring the Jewish people to Jesus. Was he misguided by the Holy Spirit, not knowing that Jews could be saved through the Abrahamic covenant? Moses also was willing to be damned to bring forgiveness to Israel. Was he also misguided?

Paul and Moses received that kind of love from the Holy Spirit of the One who gave His life, became accursed, and went to hell to atone for the sins of Israel and of all the world. Moses and Paul knew the Lord quite well. They served Him as no one else ever has. For them, therefore, no price was too great to pay to bring Israel, God's first born son, back to Him.

We can say that this is love, for "By this the love of God was manifested in us, that God has sent His only begotten Son into the world so that we might live through Him. In this is love, not that we loved God, but that He loved us and sent His Son to be the propitiation for our sins." (1Jn.4:9-10) What can we say about a teaching that attempts to deny the gospel to the very people that brought it to the world? to the very people whom God created for the gospel, and for bringing it to the world?

The issue involved in "Dual Covenant" theology is very basic. Do Jews need to believe in Jesus? If they do not, then those who do believe in Jesus do not need to bring the gospel to them. Then also, Jesus and the early Church were quite deceived into thinking that everyone needs to believe in Him. Then also, they spread their deception throughout the world. If the people to whom Jesus said, "Unless you believe that I am He, you shall die in your sins" do not need to believe in Jesus, then no one does.

On the other hand, if Jesus is the Messiah promised to Israel; if the New Covenant in His atoning blood is what God promised to the house of Israel and the house of Judah; if there is salvation in no other name, not even the name of Abraham; then every Jewish person needs Jesus.

Not only is the salvation of the Jewish people important for their sake, but it is also important for the whole world. Jesus said to Jerusalem, "You shall not see Me again until you say, 'Blessed is He that comes in the Name of the Lord.' " (Mt.23:39) When all Israel believes, Jesus will return.

When all Israel believes, the world itself will be raised from the dead. The great apostle to the Gentiles understood this powerful part of God's plan of redemption for the world. That is why Paul, who told us to follow him as he followed Messiah, was willing to forfeit his own eternal salvation for the salvation of Israel.

In the guise of friendship, "Dual Covenant" theology seeks to withhold the gospel and salvation from the Jewish people. It denies the desire of the King of the Jews for His own people. It ignores the catalytic role that the Jewish people must play in God's plan of redemption for the whole world — God's only plan of redemption for the whole world.

51

THE IMPLICATIONS

What are the implications of this plan of God in the relationship of Israel and the Church? Paul says that they are too deep and unsearchable to fully fathom. (Rom.11:33) The Church should therefore be characterized by humility and gratitude towards the Jewish people rather than by arrogance. The Church should therefore be characterized by knowledge and participation in God's purpose and plan for the Jewish people, rather than by ignorance or apathy.

Gentile believers in particular need to recognize their debt and responsibility to Israel. Gentile believers in particular need to recognize their relationship to the Jewish people. There are some specific practical ways to develop that proper recognition and godly character:

1) Gentile believers should start acting like Ruth, and not like Orpah. Orpah was a loving daughter-in-law, but she ended up staying with her own people. Ruth saw something that Orpah did not see.

What did Ruth see in Naomi? Naomi had left the land of Israel with her husband and two sons because there was a famine in the land. They went to Moab, and Naomi's husband died there. Her two sons married Moabite women, but died soon after that.

In Naomi's words, "the hand of the Lord has gone forth against me." (Ruth 1:13) When Naomi returned to Bethlehem, "the women said, 'Is this Naomi?' And she said to them, 'Do not call me Naomi [נעמי, pleasant]; call me Mara [מרא, bitter], for the Almighty has dealt very bitterly with me. I went out full, but the Lord has brought me back empty. Why do you call me Naomi, since the Lord has witnessed against me and the Almighty has afflicted me?' " (Ruth 1:19-21)

It was obvious that the Lord was against Naomi. Just like it was obvious that the Lord was against Job. Just like it was obvious that the Lord was against Paul when the viper bit him, shortly after he had escaped from a shipwreck. (Acts 28:4) Just like it has been obvious that the Lord is against the Jewish people. Such things are obvious, but they are not true.

Despite what people thought, God was not against Naomi, Job, or Paul. Despite what people think, God is not against the Jewish people. God intends to do something more wonderful for all Israel than what He did for Naomi, Job, or Paul. Though His hand may sometimes be against His first-born son, His heart never is.

Naomi is a type of the Jewish people. She was bereaved, bitter, and angry at God. She had no hope. In that condition, she came back to her own land.

Ruth saw that, but she saw something more. There was something that she had seen in her mother-in-law and in her own husband, that was more precious to her than life itself. She saw something invisible that Orpah could not see.

"But Ruth said, 'Do not urge me to leave you or turn back from following you; for where you go, I will go, and where you lodge, I will lodge. Your people shall be my people, and your God, my God.' " (Ruth 1:16) Ruth said, 'I will be joined to the Jewish people, and I will serve the God of Israel.' She knew that He, and He alone, is the only God. She made that choice before she ever met Boaz.

Ruth made the same choice that Abraham made. She left her family, her people, and her land behind. She lost her life in order to find it. Orpah said good-by to Naomi and then went to reclaim her old life. She found her life in order to lose it.

Naomi's Gentile daughter-in-law, Ruth, was to be the means of her greatest blessing. God planned it that way. Ruth embraced the Jewish people, and God blessed her eternally.

What did Cornelius see? He was a military man, and Rome ruled over Jerusalem. Jerusalem itself, as a city of the first-century world, could not compare to "the glory that was Rome."

Cornelius was assigned to a backward, troublesome, superstitious province and people. At least that was the Roman view. They believed that Rome had better ways, more might, and greater gods.

What did Cornelius see in the Israel that is described in the gospels? He saw everything. He saw the corruption, the legalism, the brutality, and the hypocrisy. But he also saw the invisible hand of God, the only God, upon His people Israel.

Cornelius made a choice which would have made him the laughingstock of all his family, friends, and neighbors back home. He started to pray to the God of Israel, and he started to give his money to help the Jewish people. He made that choice before he ever met Peter.

And the angel said, "Your prayers and alms have ascended as a memorial before God." (Acts 10:4) Cornelius embraced the Jewish people, and God blessed him eternally. "Now faith is...the conviction of things not seen." (Heb.11:1)

Gentiles who are believers need to look at the Jewish people and see the invisible. They need to choose as Ruth and Cornelius did: "Your people will be my people; your God will be my God."

2) Prayer: The Church should pray for the salvation of Israel. We should be able to say, as Samuel did, "Far be it from me that I should sin against the Lord by ceasing to pray for you." (1 Sam.12:23) Those who do not want to sin against the Lord should pray for His son Israel.

They should pray for His son Israel whom Pharaoh enslaved and sought to destroy. We should remember that the Father's "soul is bound up with the lad's soul." Many times the children of Israel turned away from the Lord, and many times He brought them back to Himself. "And the sons of Israel said to the Lord, 'We have sinned, do to us whatever seems good to Thee; only please deliver us this day.' So they put away the foreign gods from among them, and served the Lord; and His soul could bear the misery of Israel no longer." (Judg.10:15-16)

God does not need anyone to remind Him of the sins of Israel. The Devil does it continually, but God knows the sins of Israel quite well, for it is against Him that Israel has sinned. God does, however, search for those who will stand in the gap and intercede for Israel that she might find repentance, and her sins might be forgiven.

As well as any individual men can, Moses and Paul represent the Bible — Tanakh and the New Covenant Scriptures. They humbly and faithfully stood before the Lord and brought God's covenant to the people. Moses and Paul knew the heart of God and wanted what God wanted. They were willing to do anything to restore the Jewish people to their God. They were willing to be eternally damned if it would bring forgiveness and salvation to Israel.

The Lord said, "On your walls, O Jerusalem, I have appointed watchmen; all day and night they will never keep silent. You who remind the Lord, take no rest for yourselves; and give Him no rest until He establishes and makes Jerusalem a praise in the earth." (Is.62:6-7) For God's glory, you should remind Him, day and night without ceasing, of the people and the city which are called by His Name. You will not be disturbing Him, for "Behold, He who keeps Israel will neither slumber nor sleep." (Ps.121:4)

Paul was a natural branch who thought he was serving God by persecuting the Church. Then the grace of God opened his ears, eyes, and heart, bringing him to repentance. God heard Stephen's prayer. (Acts 7:60-8:3; Jn.20:23) We cannot measure the fruit that the life of Paul has brought forth, nor can we comprehend all that our prayers for the Jewish people will do.

After all, when the fulness of the Jews comes in, when all Israel is saved, the world will be transformed. It will be so much greater than what the Church and the world have now that Paul compares this present age to death and that time following all Israel's salvation to life from the dead. After all, Jesus will then reign in justice and righteousness on the throne of David, from Jerusalem, over all the earth.

Jesus will return when Israel says, "Blessed is He who comes in the Name of the Lord!" Jesus is the One who comes in the Name of the Lord. When Jerusalem and her children recognize and rejoice in that, then Jesus will return.

Peter preached to his brethren, the men of Israel, "Repent therefore and return, that your sins may be wiped away, in order that times of refreshing may come from the presence of the Lord; and that He may send Jesus, the Messiah appointed for you, whom heaven must receive until the period of restoration of all things, about which God spoke by the mouth of His holy prophets from ancient time." (Acts 3:19-21) When the men of Israel repent, times of refreshing will come from the presence of the Lord, and He will send Jesus back to earth.

Heaven must receive Jesus until that time. Jesus taught his disciples to pray, "Thy kingdom come." The King was there in their midst, even as the King is in our midst today, but the fulness of His kingdom had not, and has not, yet come. Until it comes, "the whole world lies in the power of the evil one." (1Jn.5:18) The totality of the kingdom of God comes with the repentance and salvation of Israel.

That is why the last war in heaven is fought over Israel. Paul exhorts believers, "Put on the full armor of God, that you may be able to stand firm against the schemes of the devil. For our struggle is not against flesh and blood, but against the rulers, against the powers, against the world-forces of this darkness, against the spiritual forces of wickedness in the heavenly places." (Eph.6:11-12) **That is "our struggle."** "For the weapons of our warfare are mighty through God to the pulling down of strongholds." (2Co.10:4)

As Daniel wrestled in prayer, the victory was won in heaven. "And I heard a loud voice in heaven, saying, 'Now the salvation, and the power, and the kingdom of our God and the authority of His Messiah have come, for the accuser of our brethren has been thrown down, who accuses them before our God day and night.' " (Rev.12:10) **This is also "our struggle."**

God asked Cain, "Where is your brother Abel?" Cain replied, "Am I the watchman and security guard [שֹׁמֵר] for my brother?" Apparently God thinks so, because He said, "On your walls, O Jerusalem, I have appointed watchmen [שֹׁמְרִים]; all day and all night they will never keep silent. You who remind the Lord, take no rest for yourselves; and give Him no rest until He establishes and makes Jerusalem a praise in the earth." (Is.62:6,7) We are being conformed to His image, and "Behold, He that keepeth Israel [שׁוֹמֵר יִשְׂרָאֵל] neither slumbers nor sleeps." (Ps.121:4)

3) Evangelism: The Church, in love, should bring the New Covenant gospel to the lost sheep of the House of Israel. It is the only way they can be saved. The only verse in the Bible which positively declares, "The gospel is," is Romans 1:16. The Apostle to the Gentiles wrote, "For I am not ashamed of the gospel, for it is the power of God for salvation to everyone who believes, to the Jew first and also to the Greek."

As much as the gospel **IS** the power of God for salvation to everyone who believes, it **IS** to the Jew first. This is God's unchanging order for the evangelization of the world, which the early Church followed throughout the Book of Acts. It is a priority that God has established, even as He has established priorities in other matters.

Paul was accountable before God for the fulfillment of his ministry, which was to reach everyone in the world who was not Jewish with the gospel. In obedience, to make his ministry to the Gentiles that much more effective, Paul always went to the Jew first. He was not afraid of confrontation. The confrontation only served to create a greater platform for the proclamation of the gospel. No one has ever reached Gentiles as effectively as Paul did. Bringing the gospel to the Jews was the key that unlocked the nations/Gentiles/goyim.

Paul's evangelism was distinguished by three things: 1. He lived and preached the gospel to the Jew first; 2. Multitudes were saved through his ministry; and 3. There were accompanying signs and wonders.

It is God who confirms His Word with signs and wonders. It is also God who causes multitudes to be saved. In these two things we cannot make ourselves imitators of Paul. We can desire it, we can pray for it, but we cannot make it happen.

We can, however, choose to be imitators of Paul in living and preaching the gospel to the Jew first. Though many wonderful things are happening today, the Church is not gaining ground in reaching the world. Something radically different must take place.

The Lord says, "How lovely on the mountains are the feet of him who brings good news, who announces peace and brings good news of happiness, who announces salvation, and says to Zion, 'Your God reigns!' " (Is.52:7) The Septuagint, the Bible of the early Church, says that these lovely feet belong to those who evangelize [ευαγγελιζομενου and ευαγγελιζομενος] Zion.

After His resurrection, Jesus entrusted His eleven disciples, and through them the entire Church, with the responsibility of the Great Commission. "And Jesus came up and spoke to them, saying, 'All authority has been given to Me in heaven and on earth. Go therefore and make disciples of all the nations...' " (Mt.28:18-20) "And He said to them, 'Go into all the world and preach the gospel to all creation....' " (Mk.16:15-18)

No individual believer can "Go into all the world and preach the gospel to all creation...and make disciples of all the nations." We are limited by time, strength, language, culture, etc. However, the entire body of the Lord is able to accomplish this task entrusted to it.

Some travel all over the world to do it. Others stay in their home town. It is a corporate responsibility that rests on each individual. Each member of the body must do his or her part for the body to accomplish its task.

So it is with the order that God has given for the accomplishment of that task. God's order for the evangelization of the world is "to the Jew first and also to the Greek." This is not simply an order of chronology, but rather one of planned priority. God's order can be rejected or ignored, but it will not change. God has no alternative plan. The Church needs to accept God's priorities as its own.

The ONLY way the whole world will be evangelized is God's way. God's priority IS God's way.

4) Giving: The Church should give so that Israel can be comforted by God. The Jewish believers in the early Church gave all that they could, selling land and houses, for the proclamation of the gospel. All the churches that were established among the Gentiles had benefitted from the selflessness of the Jewish believers. The Apostle Paul took up a collection from the Churches among the Gentiles, saying that "if the Gentiles have shared in their spiritual things, they are indebted to minister to them also in material things."

Faith is visible in actions. (cf. Heb.11:1; Jacob 2:14-26) So is love. (cf. 1Jn.3:18) The faith and love of believers is to be visible and tangible in many ways. Gentile believers are to specifically manifest their faith and love towards the Jewish people in prayer, evangelism, and giving.

God has entrusted something to everyone. Each particular member of the body of Messiah is called to be willing to serve the whole body according to the will of God. Every individual Gentile believer, with whatever he or she has, owes an immeasurable debt to the Jewish people — a debt of salvation — a debt that needs to be paid.

Paul did not tell the Gentile believers how much they owed — other than their souls — but he reminded them that, "He who sows sparingly shall also reap sparingly; and he who sows bountifully shall also reap bountifully." (2Co.9:6)

5) The modern state of Israel: The Church should declare that God, the Maker and Owner of Heaven and Earth, has given the land of Israel to the Jewish people. This is not an endorsement of any government or its policies, but an affirmation that, by a covenant promise and by an oath, God has established the unchangeableness of His purpose in giving the land of Israel to the sons of Jacob. When we affirm that, we affirm the trustworthiness of God, the Bible, and the New Covenant. We point to a modern miracle as great as the exodus from Egypt.

Commitment to a covenant made with the house of Judah and the house of Israel necessarily entails a Biblically defined commitment to Israel and the Jewish people. Jesus made the Jewishness of the gospel a central issue for the Samaritans. He is returning to Jerusalem, Israel, to rule over all the earth from the throne of David. Perhaps He could have chosen another way to do it, but this is the way that He has chosen. We are called to declare it as part of the full counsel of God.

God promised the Jewish people, "To you I will give the land of Canaan as the portion of your inheritance [חבל נחלתכם]." Moses told the congregation of Israel, "When the Most High gave the nations their inheritance, when He separated the sons of man, He set the boundaries of the peoples according to the number of the sons of Israel. For the Lord's portion is His people; Jacob is the allotment of His inheritance [חבל נחלתו]." (Dt.32:8,9)

"For the Lord has chosen Jacob for Himself, Israel for His own possession." (Ps.135:4) The people of Jacob are the Lord's inheritance. The land of Canaan is their inheritance. Surely, those who belong to the Lord will have what belongs to them.

There should not be any question concerning to whom the land belongs. God gave all the nations their inheritance, and set their boundaries according to the number of the sons of Israel. He has the right to do that since, "The earth is the Lord's, and all it contains, the world, and those who dwell in it." (Ps.24:1) "And He made from one every nation of mankind to live on all the face of the earth, having determined their appointed times, and the boundaries of their habitation." (Acts 17:26)

God maintains that He has the Sovereign's right to determine the appointed times and boundaries of every people. More than the Sovereign right, God declares that He has already done it. In setting those boundaries, God uses the Jewish people as a measuring rod for the nations. Even as He promised, "I will bless those that bless thee, and curse those that curse thee."

We have neither the authority nor the power to change or diminish God's Word. We ignore it at our own peril. Likewise, they are not wise who seek to hide what God boldly proclaims. More than any other specific designation, hundreds of times in the Bible, the Lord calls Himself the God of Israel.

6) Judgment: The Church should proclaim to the world every aspect of God's judgment. God is a Father to Israel. He devastated the Egyptian empire to set His people free. He made the children of Israel wait until Pharaoh and his army could catch up to them. Then He destroyed Pharaoh and his army.

The Amalekites attacked the children of Israel as they journeyed in the wilderness after leaving Egypt. God gave Israel the victory against her attackers. "Then the Lord said to Moses, 'Write this in a book as a memorial, and recite it to Joshua, that I will utterly blot out the memory of Amalek from under heaven.' And Moses built an altar, and named it, The Lord is My Banner; and he said, 'The Lord has sworn; the Lord will have war against Amalek from generation to generation.' " (Ex.17:14-16)

"Remember what Amalek did to you along the way when you came out from Egypt, how he met you along the way and attacked among you all the stragglers at your rear when you were faint and weary; and he did not fear God. Therefore it shall come about when the Lord your God has given you rest from all your surrounding enemies, in the land which the Lord your God gives you as an inheritance to possess it, you shall blot out the memory of Amalek from under heaven; you must not forget." (Dt.25:17-19)

God never forgot. So when Saul was Israel's first king, "Then Samuel. said to Saul, 'The Lord sent me to anoint you as king over His people, over Israel; now therefore listen to the words of the Lord. Thus says the Lord of hosts, *"I will punish Amalek for what he did to Israel, how he set himself against him on the way while he was coming up from Egypt. Now go and strike Amalek and utterly destroy all that he has, and do not spare him; but put to death both man and woman, child and infant, ox and sheep, camel and donkey."* ' " (1Sam.15:1-3)

It was Saul's failure to obey the Lord in totally destroying the Amalekites and all that they had that caused the Lord to reject him from being king over Israel. As Samuel told Saul, "And the Lord sent you on a mission, and said, 'Go and utterly destroy the sinners, the Amalekites, and fight against them until they are exterminated... I will not return with you; for you have rejected the word of the Lord, and the Lord has rejected you from being king over Israel.' " (1Sam.15:18,26)

God has promised to bless those who bless the Jewish people and curse those who curse them. (Gen.12:3; 27:29; Num.24:9) Individuals and nations are, and will be, judged according to how they treat the Jews. Jesus spoke of how He would judge the goyim when He returns. (Mt.25) We do not do anyone any favors by hiding the truth.

7) The Age to Come: The Church should understand the context of its future, as well as that of its past. The only entrance into new Jerusalem is through twelve gates which are inscribed with the names of the twelve tribes of Israel. Her foundation stones carry the names of the twelve Jewish apostles of the Lamb.

It is even as the Lord, "the Mighty One of Jacob," had promised: "They will call you the city of the Lord, the Zion of the Holy One of Israel. Whereas you have been forsaken and hated with no one passing through, I will make you an everlasting pride, a joy from generation to generation...Instead of bronze I will bring gold, and instead of iron I will bring silver, and instead of wood, bronze, and instead of stones, iron. And I will make peace your administrators, and righteousness your overseers. Violence will not be heard again in your land, nor devastation or destruction within your borders; but you will call your walls salvation, and your gates praise.

"No longer will you have the sun for light by day, nor for brightness will the moon give you light; but you will have the Lord for an everlasting light, and your God for your glory. Your sun will set no more, neither will your moon wane; for you will have the Lord for an everlasting light, and the days of your mourning will be finished.

"Then all your people will be righteous; they will possess the land forever, the branch of My planting, the work of My hands, that I may be glorified.

The smallest one will become a thousand, and the least one a mighty nation. I, the Lord, will hasten it in its time." (Is.60:14-15,17-22)

Some wonder whether physical distinctions like Jew and Gentile, male and female, will continue to exist in the age to come. The Bible indicates that they will. We will not all be exactly the same. We will be recognizable and distinguishable one from another.

After the resurrection, the Lord, appeared to the disciples and said, "See My hands and My feet, that it is I Myself; touch Me and see, for a spirit does not have flesh and bones as you see that I have." (Lk.24:39) The disciples could see it was the Lord. Thomas could touch the wounds in His side. (Jn.20:27)

It is difficult, if not impossible, for us to understand or even conceptualize what a "spiritual body" is, but we are told that we will have them. (1Co.15:44) There will be visible body differences.

The Lord gave the Apostle John many visions. John recorded of one of them: "After these things I looked, and behold, a great multitude, which no one could count, from every nation [εθνους] and all tribes and peoples and tongues, standing before the throne and before the Lamb, clothed in white robes, and palm branches were in their hands; and they cry out with a loud voice, saying, 'Salvation to our God who sits on the throne, and to the Lamb.' " (Rev.7:10) John could see and hear that these redeemed worshipers in heaven were from different tribes, peoples, nations, and languages.

In his description of new Jerusalem, he says, "And the nations [εθνη, i.e. the Gentiles] shall walk by its light, and the kings of the earth shall bring their glory into it." (Rev.21:24) [The *Textus Receptus* has "the nations of the saved shall walk in its light."] John's description of new Jerusalem also informs us that "On either side of the river was the tree of life, bearing twelve kinds of fruit, yielding its fruit every month; and the leaves of the tree were for the healing of the nations [εθνον]." (Rev.22:2)

Jesus said to the church in Pergamum, "He who has an ear, let him hear what the Spirit says to the churches. To him who overcomes, to him I will give some of the hidden manna and I will give him a white stone, and a new name written on the stone which no one knows but he who receives it." (Rev.2:17) Each overcomer will have a different, distinctive, new name, given by the Lord.

He made us individually to be what we are. We will all be transformed and glorified in the new Jerusalem, but we will not be identical. What we are and what we do here and now will somehow be a part of us when this age is over.

8) The Integrity of the Church: The Church should demonstrate its unique, genuine unity that transcends physical, national, racial, and social

distinctions. "There is not Jew and Gentile, there is not male and female, there is not bondman and free; for you all are one in Messiah." (Gal.3:28)

Believers are not identically the same, but "Messiah is all, and in all." Messiah is the ONE new man, and we are all part of Him. There are many members in the body, with different appearances and functions, but only one body.

"For even as the body is one and yet has many members, and all the members of the body, though they are many, are one body, so also is Messiah." (1Co.12:12) The members of a body are different in appearance, composition, need, and function. The performance of an individual member must be judged in terms of the specific identity of that member and its function in the body.

Every individual has a unique genetic code. Every healthy cell in the body, regardless of its function, contains that same genetic imprint. Even so, every member of the body of the Lord is to bear His unique, unmistakable imprint — "By this all men will know that you are My disciples, if you have love for one another." (Jn.13:35)

When the Church can demonstrate that kind of love and unity, THEN unbelieving Israel will be provoked to jealousy. There are many obstacles to that demonstration, but pride should not be one. Given the glorious future that awaits those who are the Lord's — "things which eye has not seen and ear has not heard, and which have not entered the heart of man, all that God has prepared for those who love Him" (1Co.2:9) — we should walk humbly with God and with each other now. When we no longer boast one against another but seek to serve instead, others will see, will know that we are disciples of Jesus, and will want to be His disciples, too.

For over 1600 years, the Church has denied the very mystery of the gospel which defines its own identity. For over 1600 years, the Church has denied the very mystery of the gospel which proclaims the manifold wisdom of God to the rulers and authorities in the heavenlies. For over 1600 years, the Church has denied the very mystery of the gospel which tells the world that we are disciples of the One crucified as King of the Jews.

This must change. It will change. The Church must reject the way in which Constantine made the Church in his own image. It must embrace the way in which Messiah made it in His own image. Today is the day.

BIBLIOGRAPHY

Scripture Taken From:

1. *New American Standard Bible,* „ 1960, 1962, 1963, 1968, 1971, 1972, 1973, 1975, 1977 by the Lockman Foundation, La Habra, CA. Used by permission.

Scriptures Often Rendered More Literally:

2. Berry, George Ricker, *The Interlinear Literal Translation of The Greek New Testament,* Zondervan Publishing House, Grand Rapids, MI., 1966
3. Green, Jay, general editor and translator, *The Interlinear Hebrew/Greek English Bible,* Vols.1-3, Associated Publishers and Authors, Inc., Lafayette, IN., 1979
4. Vincent, M.R., *Word Studies in the New Testament,* Associated Publishers and Authors, Wilmington, DE., 1972
5. Vine, W.E., *A Comprehensive Dictionary of the Original Greek Words with their Precise Meanings for English Readers,* MacDonald Publishing Co., McLean, VA.
6. Wuest, Kenneth S., *Wuest's Word Studies From the Greek New Testament,* Wm. B. Eerdman, Grand Rapids, MI., 1983

Supplementary Sources:

7. Aquinas, Thomas, *Summa Theologiae, A Concise Translation,* Edited by Timothy McDermott, Christian Classics, Westminster, MD., 1989
8. Arnold, Eberhard, *The Early Christians after the Death of the Apostles,* Plough Press, Farmington, PA., 1972
9. St. Augustine, *Concerning THE CITY OF GOD against the Pagans,* trans. by Henry Bettenson, Penguin Books, London, 1984
10. *The Babylonian Talmud,* edited by Isadore Epstein, The Soncino Press, London, 1938
11. Calvin, John, *Institutes of the Christian Religion,* Vols.1&2, Trans. by Ford Lewis Battles, The Library of Christian Classics, Vol.XXI, Ed. by John T. McNeill, The Westminster Press, Philadelphia, 1960
12. Calvin, John, *Calvin's Commentaries, The Epistles of Paul the Apostle to the Romans and to the Thessalonians,* Translated by Ross Mackenzie, Edited by David W. Torrance & Thomas F. Torrance, Oliver and Boyd, Edinburgh, 1961
13. DeLange, N.R.M., *Origen and the Jews,* Cambridge Univ. Press, Cambridge, 1976
14. Drake, H.A., *In Praise of Constantine, A Historical Study and New Translation of Eusebius' Tricennial Orations,* Univ. of California Press, Berkeley, 1976
15. Dugmore, C.W., "A Note on the Quartodecimans," *Studia Patristica,* Vol.IV, Berlin, 1961, Pp.411-421
16. Edwards, Mark, Jr., *Luther's Last Battles: A Study of the Politics and Polemics, 1531-1546,* Cornell U. Press, Ithaca, 1983
17. *Encyclopedia Judaica Jerusalem,* Vol.15, "Taw," The MacMillan Co., NY, 1971, P.835
18. Eusebius, *The Ecclesiastical History of Eusebius Pamphilus,* translated by Christian Frederick Cruse, Baker Book House, Grand Rapids, MI., 1989
19. Ferguson, E., "The Terminology of Kingdom in the Second Century," *Studia Patristica,* Vol.XVII, Part Two, Edited by Elizabeth A. Livingstone, Pergamon Press, Oxford, 1982, Pp.669-676
20. Frend, W.H.C., "Church and State: Perspective and Problems in the Patristic Era," *Studia Patristica, Vol.XVII, Part Two,* Edited by Elizabeth A. Livingstone, Pergamon Press, Oxford, 1982, Pp.38-54

21. Godet, Frederic Louis, *Commentary on Romans*, Kregel, Grand Rapids, 1977

22. Gustafson, B., "Eusebius' Principles in handling his Sources, as found in his Church History, Books I-VII," *Studia Patristica, Vol.IV*, Berlin, 1961, Pp.429-441

23. Jedin, Hubert, and Dolan, John, editors, *History of the Church, Vol.IV*, Translated by Anselm Biggs, Crossroad Publishing Co., NY, 1986

24. Justin, *The Dialogue with Trypho*, translated by A. Lukyn Williams, S.P.C.K., London, 1930

25. Kesich, V., "Empire-Church Relations and the Third Temptation," *Studia Patristica, Vol.IV*, Berlin, 1961, Pp.465-471

26. Lecky, W.E.H., *History of the Rise and Influence of the Spirit of Rationalism in Europe, Vol.II*, D.Appleton & Co., NY, 1867

27. Lightfoot, J.B. and Harmer, J.R., editors, *The Apostolic Fathers*, Baker Book House, Grand Rapids, MI, 1988

28. Luther, Martin, *Commentary on Galatians*, Translated by Erasmus Middletown, Kregel Publications, Grand Rapids, MI, 1976

29. Luther, Martin, *Commentary on Romans*, Translated by J. Theodore Mueller, Kregel Publications, Grand Rapids, MI, 1976

30. Luther, Martin, *Luther's Works, Vol.2, Genesis*, edited by Jaroslav Pelikan, Concordia Publishing House, St. Louis, 1960

31. McBirnie, William Steuart, *The Search for the Twelve Apostles*, Tyndale House, Wheaton, IL., 1977

32. Mears, Robert, Personal correspondence, 6/15/91

33. *Melito of Sardis, On Pascha and Fragments*, Edited by Stuart George Hall, Oxford Clarendon Press, 1979

34. Monis, R. Judah, *The Truth, Being a DISCOURSE Which the Author Delivered at his BAPTISM*, Printed by S. KNEELAND, for D. HENCHMAN, 1722

35. Murray, Iain H., *The Puritan Hope*, Banner of Truth Trust, Edinburgh, 1971

36. Oberman, Heiko, *The Roots of Anti-Semitism in the Age of Renaissance and Reformation*, Fortress Press, Philadelphia, 1983

37. Origen, *Origen, Homilies on Genesis and Exodus, in The Fathers of the Church, Vol.71*, translated by Ronald E. Heine, Catholic University Press, Washington, D.C., 1982

38. *The Pentateuch and Haftorahs*, ed. by Dr. J.H. Hertz, Soncino Press, London, 1956

39. Schaff, Philip, *History of the Christian Church, Vol.II, Ante-Nicene Christianity*, A.D. 100-325, Charles Scribner's Sons, NY, 1883

40. Scofield, C.I., *The New Scofield Study System*, Oxford U. Press, NY, 1967

41. Shestov, Lev, *Athens and Jerusalem*, Translated by Bernard Martin, Ohio U. Press, Athens, OH, 1966

42. Taylor, R.E., "Attitudes of the Fathers toward Practices of Jewish Christians," *Studia Patristica, Vol.IV*, Berlin, 1961, Pp.504-511

43. van Unnik, W.C., "Η καινη διαθηκη - A Problem in the Early History of the Canon," *Studia Patristica, Vol.IV*, Berlin, 1961, Pp.212-227

44. von Balthasar, Hans Urs, *Origen, Spirit and Fire*, translated by Robert Daly, Catholic University of America Press, Washington, D.C., 1984

45. Walvoord, John, "The New Covenant with Israel," *Bibliotheca Sacra*, Dallas, 1946

Index of Scripture References